To the memory of Pam Hill.

For Kyla, Tom, Jed and Toby – of course!

Social Psychology

Social Psychology

Donald C. Pennington
Dean of the School of Health and Social Sciences, Coventry University

Kate Gillen
Principal Lecturer, School of Health, University of Teesside

and

Pam Hill
Formerly Senior Lecturer in Psychology, School of Health and Social Sciences, Coventry University

A member of the Hodder Headline Group
LONDON
Co-published in the United States of America by
Oxford University Press Inc., New York

First published in Great Britain in 1999
This impression published in 2001 by
Arnold, a member of the Hodder Headline Group,
338 Euston Road, London NW1 3BH

http:/www.arnoldpublishers.com

Co-published in the United States of America by
Oxford University Press Inc.,
198 Madison Avenue, New York, NY 10016

The advice and information in this book are believed to be true and
accurate at the date of going to press, but neither the authors nor the publisher
can accept any legal responsibility for any errors or omissions.

British Library Cataloguing in Publication Data
A catalogue record for this book is available from the British Library

Library of Congress Cataloging-in-Publication Data
A catalog record for this book is available from the Library of Congress

ISBN 0 340 54846 0 (pb)
ISBN 0 340 75953 4 (hb)

3 4 5 6 7 8 9 10

Production Editor: Liz Gooster
Production Controller: Iain McWilliams
Cover design: Terry Griffiths

Typeset in 11 on 13 pt Sabon by
Cambrian Typesetters, Frimley, Surrey
Printed and bound in India by Replika Press Pvt. Ltd., 100% EOU,
Delhi-110 040

What do you think about this book? Or any other Arnold title?
Please send your comments to feedback.arnold@hodder.co.uk

Contents overview

Contents

Preface

This book provides an introduction to social psychology through consideration of theory, concepts and important empirical research. The aim is to provide a simple, clear and readable introduction to the empirical discipline of social psychology. The emphasis is on social psychology as a scientific area of enquiry using numerous techniques of empirical research, including the laboratory experiment. A decision was taken by the authors to present each chapter in a way that makes use of summary diagrams to help the reader remember the central theories, concepts and ideas in social psychology.

The emphasis of the chapter on social development is on childhood: however, adolescence and adulthood have been given adequate consideration. The chapter on pro-social and anti-social behaviour has been written to reflect not only the growing interest by social psychologists in this area, but the high degree of relevance such behaviour has for contemporary society.

A theme that runs through all the chapters of this book, apart from Chapter 1, is an 'application' section. Social psychology has enjoyed application to help society deal with and understand a range of social issues and social problems. Applications in this book range across education, health, organizational behaviour, mental illness, and the legal context. The wide range of areas that social psychology affects evidences the value of theory and research underpinned by a rigorous scientific methodology.

This book is intended to appeal to all sudents of social psychology encountering the discipline for the first time. In particular, it should prove invaluable for those studying for GCE 'A' Level, first year undergraduates studying psychology, and students of social psychology where psychology is not their main area of study. Finally, I hope the interested layperson will also find the book of interest.

This book has taken longer than anticipated, partly due to other demands on the first author's time, but also because of the untimely death of Pam Hill. Pam completed three chapters – Social Cognition I, Non-Verbal Communication and Interpersonal Behaviour, and Social Influence. Pam had made a start on a further chapter, but was unable to complete it.

This book would not have been possible without the support and encouragement of numerous colleagues and friends. In particular I would like to thank Isobel Ford for continual support, encouragement and help when motivation flagged.

Donald Pennington

Acknowledgements

The author and publisher would like to thank the following for their permission to reproduce the following figures. Full citation is given in the bibliography.

Springer-Verlag GmbH & Co., K. G. (Figure 6.4); JohnWiley & Sons Limited (Figure 6.6); Alexandra Milgram (Figure 8.10); Simon & Schuster Inc. (Figure 11.10).

1   Introduction

- Social psychology and everyday life
- The scope of social psychology
- Assumptions about human behaviour
- Historical perspective
- Social psychology as science
- Methods of investigation

- Validity of experiments
- The social psychology of experiments
- Ethics and values in social psychological research
- About this book
- Summary
- Suggestions for further reading

1.1 Social psychology and everyday life

The cover of this book is taken from a painting by L. S. Lowry of people in a park; take a careful look at the cover. You will see numerous people, older and younger, engaged in social interaction. But these people all seem a little 'strange' in one way or another, for example, the man with one leg, or the woman at the bottom left with only one eye open. In the middle towards the right, is what seems like an older woman, with a bent back looking at the ground. Lowry chose to depict people in a social setting in a way that arrests our attention. This picture was chosen as the cover of a social psychology text book for two main reasons: first, the picture reflects a basic principle of social psychology that each person constructs a different social reality. This means that how we perceive, understand and imagine ourselves and other people to be is often different from one person to another. Second, the picture serves to remind us that other people have an important influence on how we think, feel and behave.

How we experience and enjoy life is strongly affected and determined by other people: how we think about ourselves and how others think and react to us are important determinants of both how we feel and behave. Specific social situations also influence our behaviour, for example, behaviour appropriate at a party would be largely inappropriate at an interview or our place of work. Social behaviour, our actions in the presence of one or numerous other people, is governed both by perceptions and social norms. Much of the time we are unaware of these influences. The discipline of social psychology – the scientific study of social behaviour, thought and feelings – offers insight and understanding based upon theory and sound evidence.

In everyday life we depend upon, interact with, influence and are influenced by many people. The presence of others is comforting; brief encounters with strangers are common when, for example, we go shopping. Relationships reveal a wide diversity from acquaintances, workmates, friends through to lovers and marriage partners. Some people we interact with just once and never see again; others become well known to us through work or social activities. A small number of people are very special to us, such as spouses and close friends, who are permanent features of our lives. As a baby and young child our dependence upon others is total; not only do parents or caretakers provide for our physical needs but they also socialise us. As we get older we are able to interact, with confidence and ease, with peers and adults. Inadequate socialisation, as will be seen in Chapter 2, is regarded by many social psychologists as a critical factor explaining anti-social behaviour and low self-esteem in an individual. In later life, as adults, we depend upon people for company (being alone for long periods of time is often a very distressing experience), for information (in the form of, for example, how we are expected to behave in a specific social situation) and for pleasure (simply talking to somebody we are close to is enjoyable in itself and, when worried, may relieve us of a mental burden). This is summarised in Figure 1.1.

Acting appropriately, assessing ourselves and others, knowing when to succumb to the influence of other people and when to attempt to influence others round to our way of thinking, are all common features of everyday life. To function effectively in these ways means we are all social psychologists in a sense. Without intuition, common sense and shared understanding our ability effectively to engage in our social world would be greatly impaired, resulting in socially clumsy, ineffective and inappropriate actions. Social psychology attempts to assess the soundness and validity of these common-sense notions. Sometimes, as we shall see in this book, social psychological research yields surprising results: empirical evidence occasionally overturns what we commonly believe to be the case.

The aims of both the lay-person and professional social psychologist are the same: both are attempting to understand and predict the behaviour of others and ourselves in the diversity of social situations that can and do confront us. Without prediction and understanding, organised society, of any sort, would soon disintegrate and collapse. If we or others behaved unpredictably without control or order, we would find

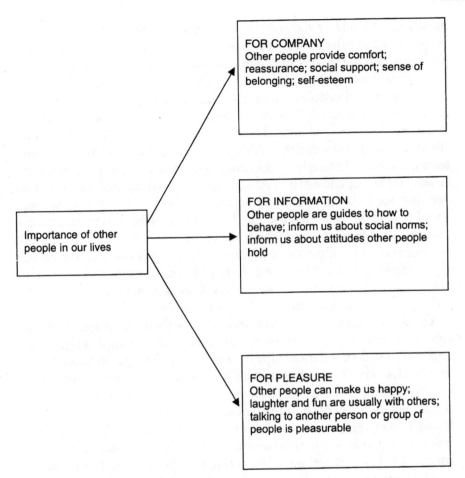

Figure 1.1: Some examples of the importance of other people in our lives

it almost impossible to interact in a sensible way with other people. We often make mistakes by misjudging people and how they will behave; common sense is often a good guide but one which lacks objective, rigorous, empirical support. As a result, our experience of the world is inevitably biased and subjective. The scientific study of social behaviour, thought, and feelings attempts to provide an unbiased and objective means of understanding and predicting human social behaviour. If social psychology can offer greater understanding and prediction it should enable us to achieve greater control over our own lives.

1.2 The scope of social psychology

Gordon Allport (1985), one of the founders of modern social psychology, offers the following definition of social psychology: 'Social psychology is the scientific study of the way in which people's thoughts, feelings and behaviours are influenced by the real or imagined presence of other people.' This definition serves to highlight five aspects of social psychology that you will encounter again and again in the following ten chapters of this book. First, this definition firmly establishes the discipline as one proceeding and progressing by scientific enquiry. More will be said about this in Section 1.5 of this chapter. Here it is sufficient to say that social psychology gains knowledge through empirical enquiry by formulating and testing theories. Throughout this book the results of empirical research, largely from experimental methods, are referred to and described to demonstrate how they offer support or refutation of a theory. Second, social psychology concerns itself with what cannot be directly observed – thoughts and feelings – but which we know affect our social lives in all sorts of ways. Cognitive social psychology is broadly concerned with our social thinking and has become a dominant area of enquiry in the last 20 years. Social thought refers to such constructs as attitudes, values, beliefs, self-esteem, social perception, and personal and social identity.

Third, including how people feel reflects the central role that our emotional lives play in our interactions with other people. Friendships and more intimate relationships have strong affective components, and how we feel about ourselves in relation to self-esteem or self-perception is often critical for our general mental health. Fourth, the focus on behaviour in this definition recognises that this is all that can be directly and objectively observed. We cannot see what people think and feel; it is only a person's actual behaviour that leads us to infer another person's thoughts and feelings. The influential *behaviourist* approach in psychology staunchly adheres to this principle. Fifth, people may influence how we think, feel and behave through our social interaction or by simply thinking or imagining them to be present. For example, before deciding what birthday present to buy a close friend, you will most likely think about what their likes and dislikes are. What you imagine these to be will influence the present you buy.

Representing social psychology as the scientific study of social behaviour, thought and feelings, avoids imposing boundaries on legitimate areas of enquiry. This is necessary since the interests of social psychologists range from detailed enquiries into thought processes (social cognition) through to broader considerations of the individual in a societal context (sociological social psychology). Uniting these widely different perspectives is the attempt to understand how people interact and influence each other.

Perusal of the chapter headings in this book will give you some idea of the scope of social psychology. These chapters do not exhaust the areas of study but, in our view, represent the essential and fundamental areas of enquiry. To do justice adequately to the full range and scope of social psychology would require a volume many times this size. Specialist books, dealing with particular areas or topics can be more profitably read by the student once he or she has a general foundation in social psychology. This book aims to provide a sound and representative account of social psychology.

1.3 Assumptions about human behaviour

In general conversation we often say 'it is in his nature to behave like that' or 'being like that comes naturally to her'. In everyday usage the words 'nature' or 'naturally' are ill-defined and ambiguous. In psychology, however, such a characterisation would be taken to mean the person's behaviour is biological in origin and results from the action of inherited genes.

Two positions are possible, both representing long traditions in psychology and philosophy: first, behaviour and characteristics such as intelligence and personality are entirely a result of *genetic make-up*. Second, behaviour and human characteristics result entirely from our *experience* of the world, from birth onwards. Few, if any, psychologists would now argue solely for a nature or nurture (experience) position; most now agree that human behaviour and characteristics are a result of the *interaction* of these two influences. Controversy still rages, however, often in a bitter and emotional way, over the relative contribution of each in determining a person's intelligence. Apart from the problem of no adequate, agreed-upon definition of intelligence (cynics say IQ is simply the ability to do IQ tests), evidence for one viewpoint or another is less than clear.

In social psychology the contemporary approach claiming biology to be important, by drawing upon Darwin's theory of evolution, is known as *socio-biology* (Wilson, 1975). The claim is a relatively simply one, but difficult to substantiate satisfactorily with respect to human social behaviour: if human beings are solely a product of evolution then many social behaviours will have evolved in a similar way. Parental behaviour, aggression and altruism are claimed by socio-biologists to be a product of evolution rather than environmental experiences. One of the fundamental problems is that human beings inherit their genetic make-up and also a society and culture which are continually evolving. Perhaps with non-human primates and other animals it is easier to see the biological and evolutionary contribution since animal 'societies' do not progress and change in any way comparable to that of humans. In the topics that are dealt with throughout this book the nature/nurture theme will arise many times. Mostly reference will be made to animal studies; however, relevance and applicability to human social behaviour will be provided as appropriate.

The view that social behaviour can be explained in biological and/or evolutionary terms is one that dates back to the beginnings of modern social psychology. McDougall (1908) attempted an explanation of *all* social behaviour in terms of instincts. Two logical flaws caused the demise of this approach: first, the number of instincts could be extended indefinitely so that every social behaviour could have an instinct attached to it. Second, saying people have an instinct to be altruistic, for example, does not explain the causes of altruistic behaviour, but simply renames the behaviour. What is not explained is why people have instincts and how so many instincts could have evolved. The discipline of ethology offers a more sensible and circumscribed approach to the role of instincts in animal – both human and non-human – social behaviour.

1.4 Historical perspective

Social psychology, like other areas of psychology, emerged as an empirical discipline from strong philosophical roots that can be traced back to the ancient Greeks. Much of the philosophical work of Plato and Aristotle concerns itself with speculations about human thought and behaviour. Plato, for example, recognised that when individuals come together as a crowd, they can be transformed into an irrational mob. This was taken up by Gustav Le Bon in 1908, who wrote about the *group mind*, and how individual behaviour is transformed to crowd behaviour. Le Bon's theorising has influenced our understanding of crowd psychology to the present day.

The identification of social psychology as an independent area of enquiry was, perhaps, established through two text books which appeared in 1908 and 1924, together with important, early experiments at the turn of the century. In 1908 William McDougall published a book entitled *Social Psychology*, this was not empirically based but put forward the view that social behaviour was a direct result of *instincts* that we inherit. Such a view has not endured in modern social psychology. Floyd Allport published a text in 1924 which emphasised the importance of experimentation and presented research conducted in such areas as conformity, recognition of emotion in facial expressions, and how individuals perform a task in front of an audience (to become known as social facilitation – see Chapter 10). Many of the themes that Allport considered, together with the use of evidence from empirical research, set the scene for the development of social psychology as a scientific discipline of enquiry.

The first experiments in social psychology can be traced back to Triplett (1898) and Ringelmann (1913). Triplett conducted an experiment to investigate whether the presence of other people enhances or inhibits an individual's performance of a task. For example, Triplett asked schoolchildren to wind fishing line onto reels in the presence and absence of other people. He found that performance was enhanced by the presence of others. This early research represents the first experiments in a major area of inquiry in social psychology called **social facilitation**. Ringelmann (1913) conducted a study in 1880 investigating the amount of effort a person expends on a task either alone or working with others. He found, using tasks such as pulling a rope or pushing a cart, that a person puts in less effort when working with others than when alone. Contemporary research has looked at this in terms of **social loafing**.

The rise of Nazi Germany and the persecution of Jews in the 1930s and early 1940s had a profound impact on the development of social psychology. Many psychologists fled Europe in the 1930s to live in North America and Great Britain. Furthermore, the rise of Nazism and the persecution and slaughter of Jews raised profound questions about human behaviour, which social psychologists investigated. For example, Sherif's (1936) famous summer camp study with teenage boys vividly demonstrated how conflict develops between groups (see Chapter 10). Adorno *et al.* (1950) developed the idea of an *authoritarian personality* in an attempt to understand and explain prejudice and blind obedience to authority. Stanley Milgram's famous experiments investigating obedience to authority were conceived to help understand why so many Germans had blindly obeyed orders which resulted in the Holocaust.

Some of the classic and highly influential experiments in social psychology were conducted in the 1930s, 1940s and 1950s. These laid the foundation and set the scene for modern social psychology. These early pioneers identified key areas of study such as intergroup behaviour, social influence, prejudice and discrimination, individual and group performance which have been the subject of theorising, empirical enquiry and continual debate. As you will see in the chapters that follow, social psychology has adopted an increasingly cognitive perspective, while at the same time wishing to demonstrate application to such areas as health, work behaviour and the legal process.

1.5 Social psychology as science

Earlier it was pointed out that to function effectively with other people and in different social situations we need to be what might be called intuitive social psychologists. Our experiences of others and ourselves in different social situations provide us with knowledge about why people behave as they do, as well as expectations about future social behaviour. Unfortunately, this common-sense or intuitive approach has a major shortcoming: each of us has different experiences of people and social situations, which leads to personal knowledge becoming idiosyncratic. Different people may explain the same behaviour differently, have different expectations and make different predictions about likely future behaviour. Social psychology as science attempts to provide objective and verifiable knowledge about human social behaviour, and hence escapes the dangers of idiosyncratic personal knowledge.

1.5.1 Scientific enquiry

Controversy exists within the philosophy of science over how scientific enquiry proceeds. However, few would disagree that science is characterised by theory, hypothesis and observation. How these are related will be considered below. It is worth noting from the outset that the relationship between these three elements is often a source of dispute.

A theory is a generalisation concerning how we think the world or some part of it is. A theory offers a way of imposing order and sense on the world and does so by offering a set of rules or regulations to explain a number of facts or observations. For example, a theory might be propounded claiming that people who are prejudiced make friends with others who are also prejudiced. Our first question of such a theory would be to ask what supportive evidence exists, then we could decide whether the theory is supported or to be rejected.

Theories operate at a level of abstraction, allowing many hypotheses or empirically testable predictions to be derived. So, for example, we may derive the hypothesis that men who are prejudiced against women will tend to have male friends who are also sexist. Alternatively, we may derive the prediction that people prejudiced towards Jews will have friends who are prejudiced towards Chinese (this is permissible since our theory was very general – too general perhaps !). To test the validity of one or both of these predications we would need, first, to devise some *reliable* measure of the specific type(s) of prejudice, then see if the relationship between prejudiced people and their friends was as we predicted. If so, this would count as evidence supporting our theory, if not evidence against the theory would have been obtained.

Karl Popper, a highly influential philosopher of science, has argued that a scientific theory cannot logically be proved true, but it can be refuted. In fact, Popper claims that in order for a theory to be scientific it must, in principle, be capable of empirical refutation. A theory can never be accepted as true since there is no guarantee, logically, that the future will be the same as the past. We all expect the sun to rise tomorrow, but there is no logical reason why it should. When observations disconfirm a theory it has, logically speaking, been refuted. Few scientists apply such stringent criteria; for a theory to be refuted *numerous* counter-observations are required. Of course, this does pose the problem of knowing how many counter-observations are needed. No hard and fast rules exist, unfortunately. Evidence consistent with a theory offers support for that theory but nothing more; it does not and cannot prove a theory to be true. This may seem surprising since we are usually told science provides objective, true knowledge. However, because of the relationship between theory, hypothesis and observations, science may offer objective knowledge but whether it is true (ultimately) or not is another matter. Perhaps the best that can be claimed for science is it offers a way of discovering what is false, not what is true. Figure 1.2 provides a summary of the scientific process; showing how theory, prediction, empirical investigation and results fit together.

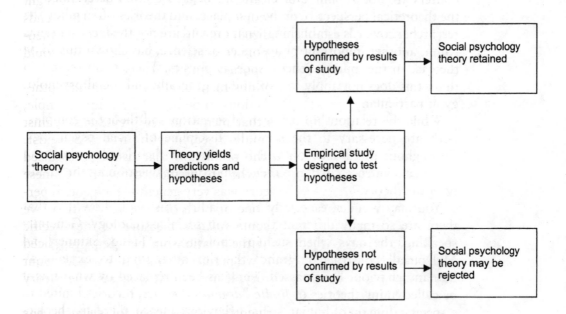

Figure 1.2: The scientific process of theory, hypothesis, empirical enquiry and consequences for the theory

1.5.2 Theory and research in social psychology

Social psychology is an empirical discipline. This not only means, as outlined above, that predictions are tested by empirical enquiry, but also that studies can be *replicated*. Provided the researcher can clearly state the hypothesis, and describe how observations were made and data collected, it is possible for another researcher to conduct a similar study. Replication enables the researcher to have greater confidence in accepting the implications of the data for the theory, as long as replications produce consistent data.

Where do theories come from and how are they constructed in social psychology? Many introductory texts will tell you theories are constructed from observations and facts. The story goes something like this: numerous observations lead to a regularity or number of regularities being noticed, these regularities lead to a theory. Take our previous example: on numerous occasions, suppose people we regard as prejudiced have friends who are also prejudiced. The role of the social psychologist is to determine the extent to which this 'theory' holds. Such an account, simplified as it is, places the derivation of theories from observations and facts, making these observations and facts neutral, objective and free from theory in the first place. Unfortunately matters are not as simple or clear-cut, 'facts' are often determined by the theoretical perspective in the first place, and theories often guide the researcher towards establishing what are and are not the facts. Thomas Kuhn, another important philosopher of science, has shown this to be the case in the 'pure' sciences, such as physics. There is no reason to think this does not apply to psychology generally and social psychology in particular.

While the relationship between observation and theory is complex, both are necessary to the scientific discipline of social psychology. Throughout this book you will find different theories described and empirical evidence cited as either supporting or questioning the validity of the theory.

You may wonder, especially after reading this book, how it is that there are so many different theories in social psychology. Generally speaking, the days when such psychologists as Freud, Skinner and McDougall constructed 'grand' theories attempting to explain all human behaviour have passed. This has been replaced by what might be called 'mini' theories or *limited domain theories*, theories limited to a specific domain of human social behaviour. Hence, there are theories about child development, prejudice, aggression and social influence, to name but a few areas in social psychology. Grand theories present problems of testability and general applicability; limited domain theories are more easily tested but have the drawback of segmenting social behaviour into compartments. Such compartmentalisation is an unrealistic representation of the interlinking and continuity that exist between different social behaviours and our social life in general.

This may seem less than satisfactory to someone encountering social psychology for the first time; however, a parallel may be drawn between this state of affairs and how the sciences of physics and astronomy were in their infancy. Historians of science argue that science progresses by the emergence of new theories which incorporate a number of other more limited theories. Gradually, theories come to explain more, becoming more 'grand' in their scale. Optimists amongst philosophers of psychology argue that the same process is happening in psychology. As social psychology progresses, new theories will emerge which combine numerous earlier theories. Since social psychology as an empirical, scientific discipline is only about 100 years old, it is too early to expect grand theories to have developed.

While some of these issues may be hard to grasp, it is important to keep two points in mind: first, although social psychology may appear fragmented on first encounter, there is coherence. Second, empirical enquiry, especially in the form of experiments, is vital for assessing the validity of a theory.

1.5.3 Alternative approaches

British and European social psychology has established a tradition of asking fundamental questions about the appropriateness and validity of applying a scientific method to the study of human social behaviour. Much of the research reported and discussed in this book is based on the laboratory experiment; *positivism* is a philosophical view based on the assumption that such a method is the only way to produce objective evidence and test a theory. Alternative approaches in social psychology (for example, Harré, 1979; Potter and Wetherell, 1987) have started from the position that social psychology cannot be objective since people are studying and researching themselves. This is quite different, it is argued, from biology or chemistry where objectivity can be attained.

The *ethogenic* approach of Harré (1979) or the *discourse* approach of Potter and Wetherell (1987) both emphasise the importance of studying the person in their social and everyday context. Attempting to study human social behaviour in artificial settings, such as a laboratory, is meaningless and results obtained are of little value, according to these approaches. The research methods employed in the ethogenic or discourse tradition focus much more on the individual through in-depth case studies or analysis of naturalistic accounts given by people in their everyday social life. People's experiences and subjective views are of paramount importance to the understanding of human social behaviour.

More recently Stainton Rogers *et al.* (1995), in offering alternative methods for the study and understanding of social behaviour, claim that objective reality in the human social domain cannot be achieved. Their argument is that objective measurement of social behaviour requires a definition. In providing a definition, 'scientific' social psychology merely substitutes a person's own meanings with those of the psychologist.

One of the major challenges that these alternative approaches have had difficulty in facing is how to turn the findings and methods into practical use, for example, to reduce prejudice, to counter the undesirable effects of stereotypes, and to help groups of people to function more effectively. The scientific and experimental approach in social psychology has endured partly because it has been able to apply findings and theory to help tackle social problems that a society may face. Perhaps the test of these alternative approaches will be whether they too can offer valuable, practical application.

1.6 Methods of investigation

Social psychology employs numerous methods of scientific investigation; these include: laboratory experiments, field research, correlational studies, archival research, case studies, and meta-analysis. It should be noted that none of these methods is better than another. Laboratory experiments offer a high degree of control of variables, but findings are often difficult to generalise to everyday social life. By contrast, field experiments, as their name implies, are conducted in real-life settings and hence have obvious relevance to everyday life. Here, though, the social psychologist has much less control over variables and, as a consequence, can never be as certain as with laboratory experiments that variables found to influence behaviour are indeed the ones that *do* influence behaviour. It may be that an extraneous or uncontrolled variable, not thought of by the social psychologist, is able to explain the observed behaviour.

In what follows we will take a more detailed look at laboratory experiments, field research and correlational studies since most of the research detailed throughout this book uses these three methods. Some consideration will also be given to the other three methods of investigation mentioned above.

1.6.1 The laboratory experiment

The laboratory experiment offers the highest degree of control over variables; however, it is not intended to replicate real-life situations. The primary aim is to establish, as far as possible, the effect upon behaviour of manipulating a certain variable, or number of variables.

Supposing we wished to conduct a laboratory experiment to test the theory that prejudiced people chose prejudiced friends. Many experiments could be devised, but let us consider the following: our theory would lead us to predict that, on first acquaintance, prejudiced people get on better with, and hence like, other people who share the same or similar prejudices on first acquaintance. Specifically, prejudiced people will like and be attracted to similarly prejudiced rather than unprejudiced strangers. The following experiment would test this: 100 people complete a questionnaire designed to measure prejudiced attitudes, the 30 highest and 30 lowest scores are selected. Splitting each group, randomly, into sub-groups of 10 we could arrange for prejudiced people to converse with another prejudiced person for, say, 15 minutes. We could also arrange pairs of people such that unprejudiced people talked to other unprejudiced people, and prejudiced people talked to unprejudiced people. There would be 10 pairs of participants for each type of dyad, as shown in Figure 1.3. The experimenter is manipulating how dyads (groups of two people) are constituted: the variable manipulated by the experimenter is called the *independent* variable.

Some measure or measures of attraction and liking would have to be taken. We could, for example, measure the amount of eye-contact taking place within the differently constituted dyads. Since eye-contact is a good indicator of whether we like somebody or not (see Chapter 6), we would expect higher levels for prejudiced dyads than in the other two types of pairings. Another measure of liking would be to ask participants, on a previously devised questionnaire, how much they enjoyed talking to their partner, would like to talk to the person again, etc. These measures of the variables of liking and attraction are called the *dependent* variables.

Controlled variables are another important class of variables the experimenter must consider. The experimenter may want to control for age, for example, (just use people in a given age-band), sex (all male, all female, or mixed groups of participants), skin colour or any other variable which may seem important. This can be crucial. Suppose we did find higher levels of eye-contact with the prejudiced dyads, we would take this as support for our theory. However, if prejudiced dyads were all females and unprejudiced dyads all males, doubt would be cast

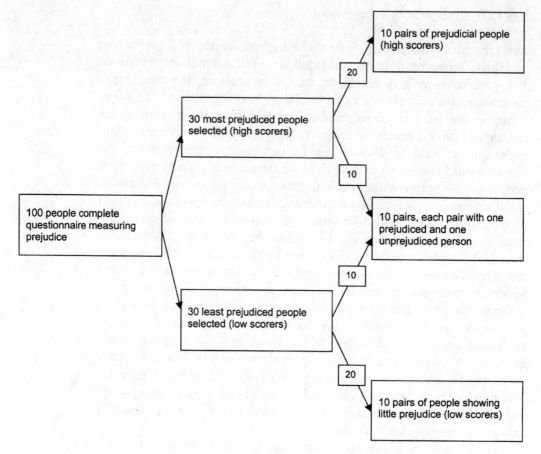

Figure 1.3: Design of experiment showing constitution of the three types of dyads

on our interpretation of the data since research has consistently shown females to engage in more eye-contact than males. With this design of experiment we would have what is known as a *confounding* variable: sex of dyad has been confounded with prejudice of each person in the dyad. It would be impossible to claim that eye-contact was high because participants were prejudiced, it could be because the participants were females.

Laboratory experiments allow cause–effect relationships to be established, but only if the experiment is carefully designed to control for important variables, avoids confounding of the independent with another, uncontrolled, variable and if the dependent variables provide reliable and valid measures. As you can appreciate, laboratory experiments require a great deal of careful planning. Problems of laboratory experiments will be dealt with later in this chapter (see Section 1.8).

1.6.2 Field research

Field research is not conducted in a grassy field but in the field of a real-life social setting, i.e. anywhere where people are going about their normal day-to-day activities. There are three main types of field research: *naturalistic observation*, the *natural experiment* and the *field experiment*. The researcher has little or no control over events with the former two types, with the latter, the field experiment, control over some variables is possible but not as much as in the laboratory experiment. The main advantage of field research is that findings can be generalised to other social situations; the main drawback is lack of control which may bring dangers of confounding variables. Generalisability of findings is achieved at the expense of loss of control and precision.

Naturalistic observation involves going into a social setting and simply observing the behaviours that take place, without attempting or intending to influence the situation or the behaviours in any way. An ethical code must be adhered to, while public social behaviour is there for anybody to see, any naturalistic observation must not intrude or violate the privacy people are entitled to. It is usually necessary for the observer to decide beforehand which behaviours to record and measure. It is impossible to observe and record everything that takes place, even between just two people in conversation – try it some time and you will very quickly realise this! Naturalistic observation is a useful method for pilot studies, generating ideas for further research and understanding how people interact. This method is not very good for testing predictions derived from a theory since the researcher has no control over what takes place.

The *natural experiment* capitalises on real-life social events which offer a test of a theory or hypothesis. The most famous example of this is reported in the book *When Prophecy Fails* by Festinger *et al.* (1956). These researchers heard of a spiritual group, headed by a woman called Mrs Keech, who believed herself to be in contact with aliens from outer space. The group expected the world to end on a particular date. Some of the researchers joined the group, becoming *participant observers*, to discover how the attitudes of the real members changed after the 'doomsday' date had passed and the world had not ended. Festinger predicted, from his theory of cognitive dissonance (see Chapter 3), that members of the group should show greater belief and conviction in Mrs Keech *after* the date on which the world was supposed to end. By becoming members of the group the researchers were able to observe, at first hand, the behaviour and expressed attitudes both before and after the doomsday date. Results were consistent with the predictions of cognitive dissonance theory.

A *field experiment* is like conducting a laboratory experiment but in a real-life social setting. All the planning and preparation of a laboratory experiment is required – manipulation of the independent variable, measures of dependent variables and deciding which variables to control for. In the field experiment the researcher is trying to influence how people behave, testing predictions derived from a theory. For example, a field experiment could be devised to answer the question: are people more willing to take risks when they see somebody else (a model) taking a risk than in the absence of another risk taker? A field experiment could be conducted at a pedestrian crossing at traffic lights, and by counting the numbers of pedestrians crossing when the light (for the pedestrian) is on red. In the *control* condition, researchers could simply observe the number who cross when they are not supposed to. In the experimental condition one of the researchers would act as a 'model' and cross the light at red. A second researcher would count the number of people who also crossed. If repeated many times, at different traffic lights, with the finding that more were found to cross in the presence of a model, we might conclude the data supported the hypothesis.

Field experiments offer the advantage of a real-life setting but have less control over the situation than laboratory experiments. Variables like the weather, number of people in the street, time of day, day of the week, etc., may all influence behaviour and be potential confounding variables. Field experiments are very popular in social psychology, as you will see, but require more careful planning than you might at first think.

Using naturally occurring social events as social psychology experiments often requires the researchers to become participant observers. There is a penalty for this: researchers may, inadvertently or otherwise, influence the attitudes and behaviours of those in the group. Another problem is that it is difficult, if not impossible, to predict when an event suitable for social psychological research is going to take place. Often a researcher will only get very short notice and may be unprepared or less well prepared than he or she would like to be. The main advantages are that naturally occurring events provide social situations which could not practically or ethically be conducted in a laboratory or field experiment.

1.6.3 Correlational studies

Correlational research has two aims: to assess (a) whether two or more variables are related; and (b) the type of relationship existing between the two variables. Consider again our example of prejudiced people having prejudiced friends, this could be investigated using correlational research as follows. To test our theory a questionnaire could be administered, say, to 100 people and the 20 highest scorers selected as our pool of prejudiced people. These 20 people would then be asked to name a friend; the researcher would then administer the same questionnaire to these 20 friends. Support for our theory would be obtained if the 20 friends also scored high on the questionnaire.

A statistical procedure, resulting in a *correlation coefficient* provides a means of assessing this. A correlation coefficient can take on any value between −1.00 and +1.00. A correlation of +1.00 would tell us that a perfect *positive* relationship exists between the two variables. With our example this would mean prejudiced people's scores on the questionnaire are exactly the same as the scores of their friends. Rarely are correlations this high in social psychology; a correlation of +0.75 . would be taken to indicate support for the theory. A correction of −1.00, by contrast, would indicate a perfect *negative* relationship between two variables. This would mean, with our example, that people with high scores on the questionnaire had friends who scored very *low* on the same questionnaire, i.e. were unprejudiced. Perfect negative correlations are also very rare, again a correlation of around −0.75 would be a good indication of such a negative relationship. A correlation coefficient around zero indicates that *no* relationship exists between the two variables. Knowing somebody was prejudiced would not allow us to predict if their friends were or were not prejudiced. A low correlation (around zero) may not, however, mean our theory is incorrect; it could be that the questionnaire we had used was an inappropriate measure or did not measure prejudice adequately.

Correlation research has the advantage of being relatively straightforward and easy to carry out. As long as the people to whom you want to administer the questionnaire can be identified and you have some confidence in the questionnaire itself, little further planning or expenditure of time is required. This type of research does have a major drawback though: *it cannot provide evidence for cause and effect*. The problem is this: suppose we find a high positive correlation between prejudiced people and their friends, this allows us to say prejudiced people have prejudiced friends, but it does not tell us why. Do these people (cause) choose them (effect)? Often it may seem intuitively obvious what is cause and what is effect, but the correlation coefficient can never provide evidence to support our intuitions. Evidence of cause and effect is best achieved through the use of laboratory experiments, since it is clear that the independent variable directly influences the dependent variable (as long, of course, as the experiment is properly designed).

1.6.4 Archival research and case studies

Archival research makes use of official documents, biographies, analysis of articles in newspapers and the television, etc. This type of research is usually conducted to find evidence for an hypothesis or theoretical construct. Perhaps the most famous use of archival records was that undertaken by Janis (1972) when looking at faulty group decision-making. Janis used the term *groupthink* to describe decision-making groups who did not properly consider alternatives and work through the full consequences of a decision (Chapter 11 deals with this more fully). Janis (1972) used various types of archival research to establish that the then President Kennedy was a member of a group which made decisions to invade Cuba with disastrous consequences. Archival research is valuable, but it may be easy for a researcher to look for material to confirm his or her hypothesis rather than look for disconfirming evidence as well. Another shortcoming of this approach is that the researcher can only work with the material that is available. This ranges from extensive and reliable, to skimpy and unreliable.

Case studies are in-depth enquiries or investigations of a person or group of people. They may often be conducted over a relatively long period of time so that *change* in a person can be observed and recorded. Case studies use a range of techniques for collecting data; these include structured, semi-structured and unstructured interviews. Also, standardised questionnaires may be used, or even simple observation of a person or group of people. Case studies are often used in social psychology to generate ideas or hypotheses for more formal research. However, case studies in themselves may be valuable in providing detailed information with a high degree of insight into the person or group of people. Case studies suffer from the danger of subjectivity on the part of the researcher, especially when the social psychologist is seeking confirming evidence for an hypothesis or a theoretical construct. The danger here is that the perceptual processes of the psychologist may be biased by knowledge of what he or she is looking for. This may result in ambiguous material or behaviour being interpreted to confirm the hypothesis. Finally, it is difficult to generalise the findings from a case study more widely to other people or groups.

1.6.5 Meta-analysis

The findings of just one experiment in social psychology are unlikely to be taken as conclusive evidence so that we can generalise to everybody or the appropriate population of people on which the sample in the experiment was based. *Meta-analysis* (Rosenthal, 1991) provides a methodology for combining the results of a number of different, but related, studies to summarise and assess the strength of the evidence. When a number of empirical studies in the same area of social psychology all produce similar results, meta-analysis gives confidence in the findings or the theory for which the results provide supporting evidence. *Replication* is crucial to establishing a high level of confidence in findings or a theory. In published research it is not often that exact replications of other research are undertaken. Replications which represent variations on a theme are more common. It is here that meta-analysis is valuable.

In this section we have considered a range of methods of investigation commonly used in social psychological research. As you can see, no one method is ideal and controversy does exist over whether a scientific approach is the right one for studying and attempting to understand human social behaviour.

1.7 Validity of experiments

Experiments are powerful tools in the process of scientific enquiry, and because of this we need to be sure they can stand up to certain questions asked of them – questions to do with *validity*. There are three types of validity – internal, external and ecological. Social psychology experiments are unlikely to be valid in all these three ways; however, without internal validity an experiment is meaningless (Campbell and Stanley, 1966). These types of validity are summarised in Figure 1.4 and the strengths and weaknesses of each are indicated.

An experiment has *internal validity* if the results (measures of the dependent variables) can be clearly and confidently related to the manipulations of the independent variable. A confounding variable, you will remember, is where both the independent variable and some other variable not controlled by the experimenter are both capable of explaining the results. An experiment with a confounding variable has *low* internal validity. No experiment can be devised to control for all possible variables; randomly assigning participants to different experimental conditions ensures variables such as age, sex, personality, etc., are equally distributed among each of the conditions. This avoids, as far as it is possible, confounding variables.

External validity refers to the generalisability of results from one specific experiment to other experiments, people and measures. The question asked is: 'Can different experiments, using different procedures, participants and measuring instruments, produce results consistent with that

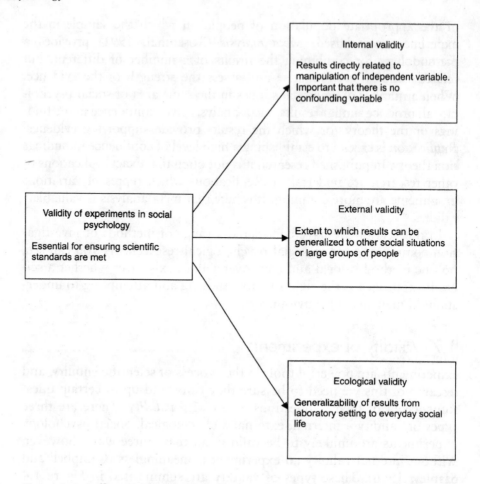

Figure 1.4: Different types of validity that need to be considered when evaluating experiments in social psychology

of the original experiment?' If the answer is yes, an experiment can be said to be externally valid. This type of validity is important since support for a theory from numerous different experiments gives us more confidence in the theory than if support comes from only one experiment. Internal and external validity may stand in opposition to one another: an internally valid experiment is where very high control over external variables is achieved. However, such very high control might make the experiment so unique as to prevent generalisation to other situations.

Ecological validity refers to the generalisability of results from the experimental situation to the 'real' world. Laboratory experiments are conducted in artificial environments where many, if not most, aspects of everyday social life are absent or controlled. A laboratory experiment has ecological validity if the results are relevant and apply to similar situations in everyday life. For example, we will see in Chapter 6 that knowing patterns of non-verbal behaviour occurring between two people in conversation has proved useful for identifying both how people fail socially and how they may be helped to be more socially skilled. Such knowledge has been obtained by analysing video recordings of people interacting in a social psychology laboratory. When reading an experiment described in this book, ask yourself whether it has relevance to you or other people's social lives. If you are able to see ways in which it is relevant it will, in all probability, have good ecological validity.

1.8 The social psychology of experiments

A physicist conducting an experiment does so on inanimate matter, and an interaction between the physicist and the material he or she is working on is not thought to take place. Things are very different in social psychology, since the subject matter is other people and people do interact with the experimenter. In view of this, the social psychology experiment is itself a social situation and one which has attracted much research in attempts to identify sources of error and bias. Three main sources have been identified; demand characteristics, experimenter effects and participant (subject) effects.

Demand characteristics are aspects of any social situation providing tacit or implicit cues concerning the behaviour expected. If you go to a party, for example, you would be expected to socialise with others, not sit in a corner quietly on your own getting drunk! According to Orne (1962) the primary demand characteristic of social psychology experiments is that of being a good participant. This involves co-operating with the experimenter and providing him or her with the results wanted. This may seem innocuous, but it is not when participants try to puzzle out for themselves what the experiment is about and then act in a way to confirm the hypothesis the psychologist is attempting to test. Participants may do this by trying to be helpful to the experimenter. If this happens, the whole point of the experiment and the validity of the data are undermined. For an experiment to produce valid results participants should respond to the specific experimental conditions in a natural and spontaneous way, ignoring or in ignorance of what the experiment is actually about. To avoid demand characteristics as much as possible, the researcher may conduct pilot studies in which post-experimental interviews are given to participants to discover if there are obvious cues being picked up which could be eradicated. In the final analysis there can be no guarantee that an experiment is without demand characteristics.

Experimenter effects occur when results are influenced or distorted, either intentionally or unintentionally, by the characteristics or behaviour of the experimenter (Rosenthal, 1969). These include influences both on the participants taking part in the experiment and on the data. Unintentional errors of observation, recording or computation may be made to provide results consistent with the hypothesis under test. In extreme and rare cases data may be faked, for example, the Cyril Burt scandal (Mackintosh, 1995), where it was shown that Burt made up IQ scores in twin studies in order to support a genetic explanation of intelligence.

Rosenthal (1969) identified three types of experimenter effects: biosocial, psychological and situational. *Biosocial* effects are aspects of the experimenter about which little can be done, for example, age, sex, race and physical appearance. An attractive female experimenter may obtain different responses from participants than an unattractive male experimenter. The way round this is to have a number of experimenters, rather than just one, conducting the research. *Psychological* factors are to do with the general attitude and personality of the experimenter: is the experimenter friendly or cold when giving instructions to participants? Does the experimenter have an introvert or extrovert personality? Again using numerous experimenters goes some way to overcoming this problem; in addition, a prearranged strategy, rehearsed beforehand, on how to interact with the participants should be devised.

The most important and extensively researched is the *situational* factor; this revolves around the issue of knowing the hypothesis the experiment is designed to test. Rosenthal (1969) found a tendency for experimenters to produce results consistent with an hypothesis when this should not happen. Such *experimenter expectancy* effects were demonstrated by Rosenthal and Fode (1963) in a study where students were asked to train rats to run a maze. Half the students were told they had 'maze-bright' rats (would learn a maze quickly) and the other half told they had 'maze-dull' rats (would only learn slowly). In fact, Rosenthal and Fode gave rats of equal capability, neither dull nor bright, to both groups of students. The researchers found students who believed they had maze-bright rats produced results showing better performance than students who believed they had maze-dull rats. To avoid expectancy effects experimenters should be 'blind' to the hypothesis under test, or if this is not possible, a number of experimenters should be used but not told which experimental condition they are running at any one time.

Participant (or subject) effects are many and varied. We have already encountered the problem of the 'helpful participant'; but participants may come along with a negative or hostile attitude attempting to disrupt or act in opposite ways to normal. Perhaps the most widespread effect is that of *evaluation apprehension*. People who know little about scientific psychology or encounter it through participation in an experiment often believe psychologists have immediate and deep insight into one's mind. Not only is this wrong but it may lead the person to behave in ways he or she would not normally. Evaluation apprehension may result in the participant attempting to present him or herself in a good light – as likeable, happy and fully understanding the experimenter's instructions. Often participants are afraid or embarrassed to ask questions when unclear about what they are being asked to do. The experimenter has a duty to make the person both feel at ease and clearly understand what the task requires of him or her.

In summary, the social psychologist must make great efforts to overcome or not fall victim to these social psychological aspects of the experiment. Both awareness and ensuring certain procedures are adhered to will help alleviate the worst of these problems, which challenge the validity of the experiment in social psychology. Figure 1.5 provides a summary of these three effects.

1.9 Ethics and values in social psychological research

> In all their work psychologists shall conduct themselves in a manner that does not bring into disrepute the discipline and profession of psychology. They shall value integrity, impartiality and respect for persons and evidence and shall seek to establish the highest ethical standards in their work. Because of their concern for valid evidence, they shall ensure that research is carried out in keeping with the highest standards of scientific integrity.
>
> (*A Code of Conduct for Psychologists* published by the British Psychological Society, July 1998)

The above extract summarises quite clearly what is expected of psychologists, and taken together with the British Psychological Society's *Ethical Principles for Conducting Research with Human Participants* serves to emphasise the critical importance of ethics and values in psychological research. Throughout this book the word 'participants' is used instead of the more common 'subjects'. This is because the authors

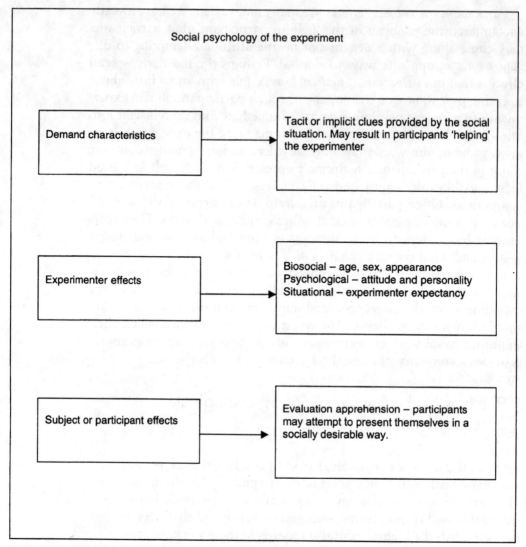

Social psychology of the experiment

| Demand characteristics | → | Tacit or implicit clues provided by the social situation. May result in participants 'helping' the experimenter |

| Experimenter effects | → | Biosocial – age, sex, appearance Psychological – attitude and personality Situational – experimenter expectancy |

| Subject or participant effects | → | Evaluation apprehension – participants may attempt to present themselves in a socially desirable way. |

Figure 1.5: Demand characteristics, experimenter effects and participant (subject) effects as sources of potential bias and error in the social psychology experiment

believe that the dignity and self-determined behaviour of people are better represented by the word 'participants'. The use of the word 'subjects' may imply that people are passive and only respond when requested to.

Some experiments conducted by social psychologists, perhaps already known to you, have caused widespread controversy because some people have regarded them as unethical and claim that they should not have been conducted in the first place. Milgram's (1965) experiments on obedience, where 'teachers' believed that they were giving increasingly dangerous levels of electric shocks to a 'learner' are widely cited in this context. These experiments are described in some detail in Chapter 8; you can make up your own mind. However, the problem is not an easy one to resolve; does the pursuit of knowledge condone the means by which it is achieved? At what point do we say someone is suffering unjustifiable personal harm or mental distress from taking part in an experiment? Most experiments conducted in social psychology do involve deceiving participants in one way or another.

Suppose, for the sake of argument, you wished to find out how people look at each other when in conversation. To measure looking and eye-contact you could place two people in a laboratory equipped with closed-circuit television so you could take a video recording and analyse looking behaviour at a later time. Your dilemma, as the researcher, is this: two people turn up, you take them into the laboratory, sit them down and instruct them to converse with each other for 15 minutes. One participant says, 'What's this all about?' You say you are studying how two people get acquainted, this satisfies the inquirer and the two people then have a conversation. Now consider the other option open to you as the experimenter: the participant also asks, 'What's this all about?', you tell the truth and say it is an investigation concerned with looking behaviour between two people in conversation. Now the participants know what the study is about, but how might this knowledge affect their behaviour? It is bound to make each one conscious of how he or she looks at the other person when in conversation and so make it difficult for them to act normally. Self-consciousness may result in participants avoiding looking at each other altogether, looking at each other all the time or looking in 'abnormal' ways. Ideally, the experimenter wants to observe and measure spontaneous looking behaviour, and telling the truth may seriously threaten this. Given the objectives of the experiment, therefore, it may be necessary to deceive participants so they are not sensitised to the behaviours being observed.

Is there a way in which research could be carried out without the use of deception? Kelman (1967) proposes that people should be asked to role play. Participants would be told about the experiment and asked what they would do in such a situation. The trouble with such an 'as if' approach is that people often behave in ways different from how they say they would behave (see Chapter 3 on the relationship between attitudes and behaviour). Furthermore, people asked to act or think as if they were not in possession of a certain piece of knowledge find it difficult to ignore what they already know (Pennington, 1981). Kelman's suggestion is interesting but, unfortunately, it is difficult to find a real substitute for spontaneous behaviour.

One concern of using deception in social psychological research is that harm may come to the people deceived (Baumrind, 1985). Participants may get upset in the experiment, or may have their self-esteem damaged through knowing, for example, that they might have harmed another person. Sharpe *et al.* (1992) report that participants deceived in an experiment regard this as acceptable if the research has potential value to the good of society and the research is difficult to conduct in another, non-deceptive way. Nevertheless, social psychologists must take great care when using deception in their research.

Informed consent and the option of *withdrawal* from participation in an experiment are essential, especially where deception has been used and participants are feeling uncomfortable and may not want to continue. In addition, a full *debriefing* at the end of the experiment allows the social psychologist to explain what the research is about and why, if employed, deception was essential. When debriefing, the experimenter should ensure that participants leave the laboratory feeling more or less satisfied and in a positive state of mind. If a participant chooses to withdraw from an experiment, the researcher should respect this and, if requested, destroy the data obtained from the participant. Finally, the research should guarantee *confidentiality* to participants in their research. This means that participants should not be identified, unless this was part of the research and agreed by the participant beforehand.

Field studies raise further ethical problems: first, people are not usually asked if they wish, for example, to be observed. The researcher may stage some event in a public place and observe the responses of the passers-by. Second, unwitting participants in a field experiment are not usually debriefed; it is usually accepted that it is best for the people who have been observed to remain ignorant of the fact they have just taken part in an experiment. Field experiments pose more ethical problems for social psychology than do laboratory experiments. At the very least they must conform to the highest ethical standards and not make fools of, or upset, people.

Social psychological research may be unique in the use of deception of people through the scientific method. Some have argued that no matter what the justification, deception should never be used because it betrays the trust between researcher and people researched (Baumrind, 1979). The safeguards detailed above, summarised in Figure 1.6, go some way to protecting participants where deception is regarded as essential to use in the pursuit of knowledge and in trying to help society tackle the social problems that it faces.

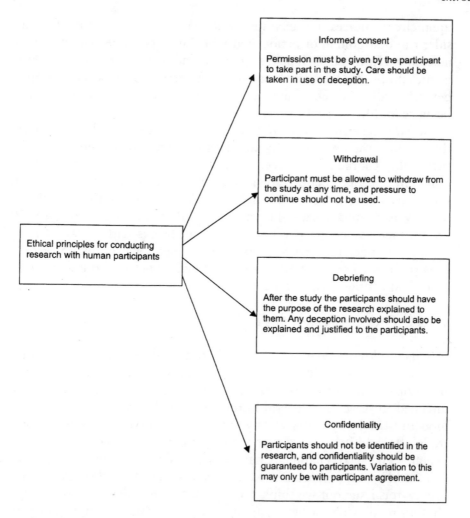

Informed consent

Permission must be given by the participant to take part in the study. Care should be taken in use of deception.

Withdrawal

Participant must be allowed to withdraw from the study at any time, and pressure to continue should not be used.

Ethical principles for conducting research with human participants

Debriefing

After the study the participants should have the purpose of the research explained to them. Any deception involved should also be explained and justified to the participants.

Confidentiality

Participants should not be identified in the research, and confidentiality should be guaranteed to participants. Variation to this may only be with participant agreement.

Figure 1.6: Ethical principles of informed consent, withdrawal, debriefing and confidentiality required of research in social psychology, after BPS principles

1.10 About this book

1.10.1 Themes in social psychology

Two themes recur throughout the chapters that follow: these are spontaneous versus deliberative thought and behaviour; and individual versus social identity. *Spontaneous versus deliberative* thought and behaviour reflects a growing recognition and understanding by social psychologists that people use both strategies at different times depending upon circumstances. For example, when you do not have time to consider the best course of action you will think spontaneously or automatically. However, such a strategy may lead to bias or error in judgement, and procedures which encourage a person to think more deeply before deciding or behaving in a certain way often lead to error or bias being reduced.

Individual versus social identity recognises that people sometimes think about themselves solely in terms of being an individual – here personality characteristics, feelings and thoughts are of central importance. In contrast, people are members of numerous different social groups and have a 'collective' or social identity. This allows people to identify with and accept the values and norms that any one social group, such as being a psychology student, brings with it. Social psychological understanding of social identity has, for example, provided important insights into both understanding and helping to reduce prejudice and conflict (see Chapter 10).

1.10.2 Organisation of this book

In what follows, we have attempted to provide coverage of the key areas in social psychology. To do so, recognition has been given to both traditional and up-to-date theory, concepts and research. This book is intended to serve as a general introduction, with critical evaluation of modern social psychology. Any introductory text makes numerous trade-offs, and it is hoped that the ones made here have been to your benefit. The next chapter, Chapter 2, considers social development from a life-span perspective. Many texts in social psychology do not discuss this issue but we think it important that students of social psychology reading about the discipline, for perhaps the first time, have an understanding of how the individual develops and changes as a social being throughout their life. Chapters 3 to 5 focus more on the individual by considering attitudes and attitude change, and social cognition. The remaining five chapters, Chapters 7 to 10, place emphasis on people in social interactions. The final chapter, Chapter 11, looks at how people in groups perform compared to individual performance.

At the start of each chapter you will find an outline of the contents, and a scan of these will give you a good idea of the areas of social psychology being presented. Towards the end of each chapter is an 'Applications' section which provides you with an example of how theory and research in social psychology have been applied to understanding and changing people's social cognition or behaviour. Applications to education, health, reducing prejudice, and people at work are made. Following this, a summary of the main points of the chapter is given, together with suggestions for further reading. A few comments have been made about these suggestions for further reading to help you decide which might be the most appropriate for you to pursue.

Finally, liberal use has been made of figures in all chapters. These both highlight results of research and provide helpful summaries of key ideas and concepts that are referred to in the text. We hope you find this book valuable and accessible in providing you with an up-to-date introduction to social psychology.

1.11 Summary

- Our enjoyment of life is strongly influenced by other people. Social psychology seeks to establish the validity of our common-sense views of social behaviour.
- Allport (1985) defines social psychology as 'the scientific study of the way in which people's thoughts, feelings and behaviours are influenced by the real or imagined presence of others'.
- The aims of scientific, social psychology are to understand, explain and predict human social behaviour and thought.
- Social psychology emerged as an independent area of scientific enquiry at the beginning of the twentieth century. Early experimentation concerned the effects of the presence of other people on individual performance. Social psychology was strongly influenced by the inhumanity of human behaviour before and during the Second World War.
- Social psychology uses empirical methods of enquiry both to test and construct theories about human social behaviour. Some psychologists question the appropriateness of using scientific methods to help understand and explain social behaviour. These psychologists emphasise the importance of studying people in their everyday social context.
- The main methods of investigation used by social psychology include: laboratory experiments, field research, correlational studies, archival research, case studies and meta-analysis.
- Correlational studies cannot provide proof of cause–effect relationships between variables; laboratory experiments offer a high degree of control, but may be difficult to generalise to real life; field research has high ecological validity but findings may inadvertently be influenced by the researcher.
- Internal, external and ecological validity of experiments can be assessed; without good internal validity an experiment has little value. There may be a trade-off between internal and external validity: the former may be achieved at the expense of the latter.
- Social psychology experiments are themselves a special kind of social situation, as such, they may be affected by demand characteristics, experimenter effects, and participant effects.

- Research in social psychology must conform to high moral and ethical standards. Some studies in social psychology involve deception: psychologists should take great care here and look for alternatives first. Guidelines for research include participants making informed consent; participants being able to withdraw; participants being debriefed at the end of the study; and confidentiality being ensured.
- Two themes that recur in a number of chapters throughout this book are: spontaneous versus deliberative thought; and individual versus social identity.

1.12   Suggestions for further reading

Breakwell, G., Hammond, S. and Fife-Shaw, C. 1995: *Research Methods in Psychology.* London: Sage.

> Good collection of chapters by numerous authors covering the range of methods used in social psychological research – both quantitative and qualitative. Useful chapter on practical and ethical issues that arise when designing research.

British Psychological Society 1998: *Code of Conduct, Ethical Principles and Guidelines.* Leicester: British Psychological Society.

> It is essential that all students of psychology read and adhere to the principles laid down by the BPS.

Coolican, H. 1994: *Research Methods and Statistics in Psychology.* 2nd edition, London: Hodder and Stoughton.

> Good introductory text providing coverage of a wide range of quantitative techniques. Also has useful chapter on designing research and how to write up research reports.

Robson, C. 1993: *Real World Research.* Oxford: Blackwell.

> Written by a social psychologist with interests in ensuring that research is relevant, related to everyday life and valid. Covers field research and qualitative methods well, also helpful on interviewing and questionnaire design.

Jackson, J. M. 1993: *Social Psychology, Past and Present.* Hillsdale, NJ: Erlbaum.

> Interesting consideration of the historical development and theoretical/philosophical formulations of social psychology. The book also highlights the multi-disciplinary aspects of social psychology. Not introductory material, but written in a readable style.

2 Social development

2.1 Introduction

Some years ago, two young children were found living in dreadful conditions. Davis (1949) reports that both these children, Anna and Isabelle, were kept almost totally isolated for the first few years of their lives. Anna was kept tied to a chair in a windowless room, her hands fastened behind her back, as a punishment for being born illegitimate. When she was discovered, it was believed that she was both blind and deaf, though this was not the case. She subsequently learned rudimentary communication skills, and became able to utter short phrases. She also learned to look after herself until her early death at the age of 10. Isabelle was discovered living with her mother, a deaf person who could not speak. She had been raised in the dark and was kept away from any contact with the outside world. Isabelle was at first thought to be deaf and learning disabled, but she surprised researchers by learning to speak and rapidly progressing through several cognitive and social developmental stages, even finishing high school.

We cannot be sure whether Anna and Isabelle were born with very different cognitive capacities, but is interesting that Isabelle made excellent progress on her introduction to the world, especially in language development, and it was she who had the company of another person during her early life. Theories of social development assert that infants need care and attention from another person (usually the mother) in order to achieve psychological health. This chapter examines the nature of the first relationship and its significance for later relationships. This chapter traces social development throughout the lifespan, from infancy through childhood, adolescence, adulthood and old age, and considers the 'psychological work' associated with each life stage.

2.1.1 Development as a lifelong process

An early approach to developmental psychology was to concentrate on a relatively short period of life, usually from birth through adolescence to early adulthood. This approach implied that development was complete by the early stages of adulthood. More contemporary approaches to the study of social development track developmental processes throughout the lifespan, and see development as a lifelong process, enduring from the rapid development of infants right up to old age. Each stage of life has a series of tasks associated with it, which must be satisfactorily completed for optimum psychological functioning. In this chapter the tasks or psychological work associated with each developmental stage will be examined. It has been said that future psychological health depends on the quality of the first relationship, that between the child and its mother, and it is to this topic that we now turn. In this chapter the word 'mother' is used to refer to the child's biological mother or its primary caregiver. Where it is intended to signify only the biological mother, this will be indicated.

2.2 Infancy

The word infant literally means 'without speech'. Of course, babies do not arrive with speech fully developed but they do arrive with enormous potential to communicate with their caregivers. Small babies are social creatures and begin to socialise almost from birth. If a newborn is left with its mother immediately after birth, it will gaze intently at its mother's face, and she will gaze back and gently stroke the child (Klaus and Kennell, 1976). Thus the beginnings of the strong maternal bond are established. The fact that most babies are very attractive (at least to their parents) helps to encourage this relationship, for who could fail to respond to a new baby with its smooth soft skin, large eyes, rounded features and soft vocalisations. It seems that we are biologically programmed to respond to small infants. Social development continues apace during the early months, when infants are particularly interested in the people in their environment. Research has shown that babies prefer to look at human faces, especially those of children (Cohn and Tronick, 1983). They are also efficient at regulating interaction between themselves and their caregivers. Infants have one particular resource at their disposal, crying, which is a sure-fire way of eliciting attention from the caregiver; they also have much more subtle means of communicating in their repertoire. Infants indicate that they want company by gazing at their caregiver and producing pre-vocal sounds, or alternatively attempt to terminate an interaction (sometimes if it has become too intense for them) by turning away from the other person (Tronick, 1989).

2.2.1 Temperament

If you think about the people you know, you will note that some of them are sunny, optimistic people, some are calm and sanguine, others complain a lot and still others seem to make a fuss over every little thing. The same is true of infants, who from the moment of birth display different behavioural tendencies. Some babies tend to lie peacefully in their cribs for long periods of time, while others scream and thrash their limbs about. Some babies approach new objects and people with delight and enthusiasm, others are more timid and withdrawn. The tendency to behave in certain ways makes up an infant's *temperament*. The term temperament refers to the collection of behaviours, including the type and frequency of emotions, the infant presents to others. It refers to the infant's own special style of interacting and is based on the infant's constitutional, biological and genetic make-up (Bernstein *et al.*, 1997).

Thomas, Chess and Birch (1970), whose study reflects the two influences of biology (nature) and the environment (nurture) on social development, carried out the earliest work on temperament. Thomas *et al.* recruited 85 families, who had 141 children between them, to a longitudinal study. The children's developmental progress was followed from birth to age 14 years, and researchers measured nine different behaviours including motor activity, regularity of physical behaviours, response to novel stimuli (including people and objects), and the child's general disposition. They found three main categories of temperament to which the majority of children belonged; these are shown in Table 2.1.

The largest category was for children judged to be easy. *Easy* babies become hungry and tired at regular times, enjoy new situations and are rarely irritable. It was found that easy babies were asleep early in the evening by six months of age, and by the age of 10 years slept for consistent lengths of time each night. However, *difficult* babies were found to have irregular patterns of hunger and wakefulness, display discomfort in new situations and were frequently irritable. Children in

Temperament category	Behaviour measured			
	Motor activity	Regularity	Response to novel stimuli	General mood
Easy	Variable	Regular	Positive approach	Positive
Slow to warm up	Low to moderate	Variable	Initial withdrawal	Slightly negative
Difficult	Variable	Irregular	Withdrawal	Negative

Table 2.1: Temperament categories and behaviours associated with each. From Thomas, Chess and Birch (1970)

this category were found to experience severe homesickness at summer camp at age 10 years. Babies in the intermediate category, '*slow to warm up*' were initially fearful in new situations but gradually relaxed and reacted positively.

Temperament at birth reflects an infant's biological inheritance and generally remains stable. Thomas *et al.*'s study, and later ones (Guerin and Gottfried, 1986), demonstrated that in the main easy infants remain easy and difficult infants stay difficult. However, Thomas *et al.* did find that for some children, temperament differed with age, suggesting an interaction between their biological inheritance (nature) and their environment (nurture). Thomas and Chess (1977) suggest that one powerful environmental influence could be the parent's personal styles. For example, parents who value independence might be more accepting of difficult babies. This study demonstrates both enduring biological influences on social development, as well as the effects of environmental influences on behaviour.

2.2.2 Cultural factors in social development

As noted in the previous section, social development does not take place in a vacuum but is the product of different influences on the growing child. One such influence is the *social context,* that is, the family structure, the values and attitudes of the society and the political and economic structure of the culture the child belongs to. Culture can be defined as the set of values, methods of expression, religious practices and employment, etc. for a social group which shares the same language and environment (Triandis, 1994). Cultural factors play an important role in social development and serve to encourage or discourage certain behaviours, (for example, premarital sexual intercourse). They also help individuals to make sense of and predict the behaviour of other members of their culture.

In most societies the immediate family is the most powerful source of influence on a child's social development. The family provides the first exposure to the cultural values of its particular society for the child, and research has shown that cultural differences can affect a child's social development. Kagan *et al.* (1994) investigated the temperament types of Chinese–American and European–American children. They found that at birth Chinese–American infants displayed a calm, relatively changeless and easily comforted temperament when compared with European–American infants. This may reflect an innate tendency towards the greater self-control generally displayed by Chinese people. Chinese–American parents reinforced their children's behaviour by being less likely to acknowledge and reward infant vocalisations and by keeping their children under strict parental control. This results in Chinese–American children displaying quieter and more passive tendencies than their European–American counterparts.

The child is exposed to other influences beyond the family as it grows up and is able to expand its social sphere. The school years, discussed in Section 2.6, provide a formalised introduction to the rules, values and attitudes held in the child's culture, and the influence of peers and the peer group has been shown to have profound effects on social development. In adolescence, the subject of Section 2.7, social development is to some extent regulated by cultural norms including the political, legal and economic structures of the culture. For example, training for and securing employment involve all of these structures.

2.3 The first relationship

The infant has a tendency to engage in social exchanges with others and can to a certain extent control these exchanges by its non-verbal behaviour. The strongest pattern of social exchanges usually occurs between the mother and her baby, a process known as *attachment*. Attachment can be defined as a strong, enduring, loving and caring bond between two individuals. Attachment also occurs between adults, but the intense first relationship between mother and child has been most often studied. It has been claimed that the quality of the first attachment can influence the type of romantic relationships formed between adults (Feeney and Noller, 1990). In most cultures, the mother is the first person to whom the infant forms an attachment, though later the infant develops attachments to other people in its environment, particularly its father and siblings (Bernstein *et al.*, 1997). For the first few months, infants usually show a preference for their mother over any other person, and try to maximise contact with her by crawling after her, vocalising to attract her attention, cuddling her and showing upset when she leaves the room (Ainsworth, 1973), see Figure 2.1.

2.3.1 Measuring attachment

Social psychologists have devised two main ways of measuring attachment in infants. These are *fear of strangers* (the response shown by the infant when a stranger enters the room when the mother is either present or absent); and *separation anxiety* (the degree of distress shown by the infant to the departure of the mother and the degree of comfort and joy displayed on her return). Researchers assume that there is a strong

Figure 2.1: Infants and their mothers usually develop an enduring, loving relationship, a process known as attachment

attachment between the mother and infant if the child shows discomfort at the approach of a stranger, for example by crying, trying to get close to its mother and seeking comfort from her, *and* if the infant shows considerable distress at her departure and relief and happiness when she returns.

Using these measures, it is possible to map the progress of attachment during the early months of life. Schaffer and Emerson (1964) explored attachment by observing 60 babies and their families, in the family home, during the first 18 months of life. They found, in general, that babies followed a three-stage pattern in attachment: *indiscriminate attachment, specific attachment* and *multiple attachment*. These three stages are shown in Table 2.2.

The indiscriminate phase begins the rather complex process of attachment and during this phase the infant narrows down its social attention to focus specifically on its mother. The infant is innately programmed to respond both to pairs of eyes and to female voices (Argyle, 1995) and since the mother usually undertakes infant feeding, both of these features occur in the infant's environment at feeding time. This ensures that infant and mother have plenty of opportunity for interaction during which time the infant becomes used to being handled, comforted and smiled at by one person. Usually this results in a co-operative, enriching and rewarding bond between the two. The first communicative sounds an infant makes are usually cries. These are pitched at a level that makes them almost impossible for adults, especially female adults, to ignore. Mothers quickly learn to recognise the 'meaning' or emotional intent of these cries. Wolff (1969) has classified cries into three types: *hunger, anger* and *pain*. By giving an appropriate response to these cries (feeding, soothing or relief from discomfort) the

Attachment stage	Approximate age	Typical characteristics
Indiscriminate	Birth to six months	Infant willing to be held by anyone; protests when put down. Smiles at anybody
Specific	Six to twelve months	Infant shows strong preference for mother. Shows fear of strangers and separation anxiety
Multiple	Twelve months onwards	Infant widens range of attachments to include father, siblings and close family

Table 2.2: Three stages of attachment identified by Schaffer & Emerson (1964)

mother strengthens attachment between herself and her child. During the first few weeks after birth the infant adds two other important communicative acts to its repertoire: *looking* and *smiling*. Looking is an important communication skill and is used to gain and direct adult attention. Smiling, too, has enormous communicative capacity. Parents and indeed other observers find infants' first smiles immensely rewarding and are likely both to smile back and to repeat the behaviour that elicited the smile. At first, infants smile at any human face in their environment, and even smile at their toys. Gradually, however, smiling becomes reserved for the mother, indicating a shift from the indiscriminate phase of attachment towards *specific attachment*.

During the specific attachment phase the infant begins to focus more exclusively on its mother for social interaction, and also to show increasing wariness of strangers. This has been investigated empirically by Ainsworth *et al.* (1978) by using what is known as the *strange situation*. Here, mother and infant arrive at an unfamiliar room, where they are left alone to play. After a while a stranger enters the room and attempts to engage the child in play. Following this the mother leaves the room, leaving the infant and stranger alone together. After a brief period, the mother returns to the room. Ainsworth observed the reactions of infants to this situation and classified them into two main attachment types, *secure attachment* and *anxious insecure attachment*.

Infants who are securely attached use their mothers as a secure base from which to explore the unfamiliar surroundings, returning to her periodically for comfort and reassurance. They are wary of strangers and react positively to their mothers following the brief separation, showing joy, happiness and relief on their mothers' return. Karen (1994) estimates that most infants show this attachment style. However, some infants form an anxious insecure attachment. Their responses may either be *avoidant*, *ambivalent* or *disorganised*. Infants with an avoidant attachment style avoid contact with the mother when she approaches or when she returns from the brief separation and appear uninterested in her behaviour. Those with an ambivalent style show distress when their mother leaves but then display anger towards her when she returns, and reject her efforts at restoring contact, often trying to escape from her arms. Infants classified as disorganised display confusing behaviour; for example they may appear to have been soothed by the mother on her return but then begin to cry again. This is summarised in Figure 2.2.

It has been suggested that poor maternal skills such as rejecting, neglecting or abusing the infant lead to the child becoming insecurely attached (Schneider-Rosen *et al.*, 1985). Van den Boom (1994) carried out a study in which she randomly assigned mothers of 'difficult'

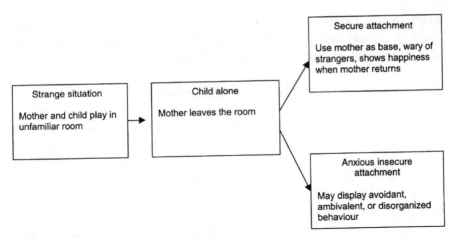

Figure 2.2: Ainsworth *et al.*'s (1978) strange situation showing two types of attachment behaviour by the child

infants either to a no-treatment condition or to a three-month training programme that taught mothers the skills of accurately recognising and responding to their babies' needs. Babies in the treatment group were much more likely to show secure attachment to the mother when observed at a year old. However, concentrating on maternal deficits in sensitivity ignores the important contribution of the other partner in the process of attachment, the infant. Reddy *et al.* (1997) point out that even at six weeks or earlier the infant has an active role in communicative interactions with its mother, making the argument that attachment patterns depend solely on the mother indefensible. Reedy *et al.* believe that studies of the infant's contribution to its own attachment should not be ignored nor treated at the level of gross temperamental differences, but should examine the fine-grained differences in infants' preferences to initiate or terminate communication with their mother.

Multiple attachment begins to be displayed around the age of one year. At this point the child no longer focuses exclusively on its mother for a co-operative and loving relationship, but extends the circle of people to whom it displays attachment to include its father, siblings and other close relatives. Schaffer and Emerson (1964) found that by the age of 18 months most of the infants in their sample had formed multiple attachments to others. Though the child seeks to be close to these people and displays distress and anxiety when separated from them, the intensity of these later attachments does not reach that of the child's attachment to its mother. Much psychological research has focused on examining and observing attachment, particularly the child's response to separation from the mother and reaction to strangers. Why do young children display such distress on separation? One account of this is the *communication theory of attachment* discussed below.

2.3.2 Communication theory of attachment

During the early months infants and their mothers develop a complex, co-operative and mutually rewarding communication system based in part on the non-verbal behaviours of the infant. Smiling and eye-contact form the basis of this communication system, which is often directed by the infant as an active partner. Rutter (1984) observed that by two years of age infants use eye-contact to begin, structure and end an interaction, as well as to receive feedback on their activities. Indeed, this pattern is found in adult conversations too. Gradually the mother and infant develop their own unique pattern of non-verbal communication, from which the infant is able to gather information about its surroundings. When separation occurs, the infant literally has no one near who 'speaks its language', resulting in the distress on separation and the fear of strangers described above. The communication theory of attachment proposes that infants show distress on separation because they no longer have access to a communication style that allows them to receive information about the world. It is interesting to note that separation anxiety begins to recede at about two years of age, coinciding with the onset of language and the ability of the child to communicate with others outside its immediate circle.

2.4 Effects of maternal deprivation

In considering attachment styles, the impact of short absences by the mother has been examined. The first relationship is undeniably important, and after Bowlby's theory of attachment was published, researchers began to investigate the effects both of not forming an attachment relationship or of a subsequent breakdown in this relationship. The outcomes of maternal deprivation for infants are discussed in the following sections.

2.4.1 Effects on animals

The most famous of the animal studies on maternal deprivation was carried out by Harlow (1959). Harlow separated newborn monkeys from their mothers and raised them in cages. Each of the monkeys had access to two artificial 'mothers'. One mother was a wire model and the other was made from wire covered with soft terrycloth. In one of

Harlow's experimental conditions the wire mother was equipped with a feeder nipple through which the infant monkey could get milk; in the second condition the terrycloth mother held the feeder nipple. If attachments form purely because the mother supplies food, then one would expect the infant monkeys to spend their time with the mother equipped with the feeder. In fact, in each condition they preferred to cling to the soft terrycloth mother, enjoying the comfort afforded. They also ran to the terrycloth mother and clung to it when frightened by a mechanical bear, showing that they had formed an attachment to it. The infant monkey's preferences are displayed in Figure 2.3. Further research showed that infant monkeys preferred to spend time with a rocking mother rather than a still one, and a warm mother rather than a cold one. These findings do not support the behaviourist school of thought that holds that attachments are formed purely because the infant is 'rewarded' with food from the mother.

Harlow also carried out studies to investigate the effects of not forming an attachment. He again separated newborn monkeys from their mothers, but this time isolated them from all social contact for one year. The monkeys developed disturbing behaviour patterns. When normally raised active monkeys entered their cage, the socially deprived monkeys huddled in a corner of the cage, rocked constantly and displayed extreme fear. Their later social development was also dramatically affected. Both sexes were unable to mate successfully, the males failing to initiate sexual contact and the females rejecting all mating attempts. When some of the females gave birth after being artificially

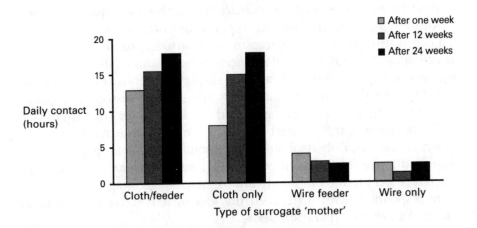

Figure 2.3: Preference of infant monkeys for different types of 'mothers'. Adapted from Harlow (1959)

inseminated, they showed a distinct lack of care towards their off-spring, often killing the babies when they showed distress.

Kaufman and Rosenblum (1969) investigated the effects of breaking an attachment. They took infant monkeys from their mothers at six months of age and reunited the mother infant pairs after four weeks. They found that the infant monkeys greeted the initial separation with great distress, though this distress abated over the four-week period. When the infants were reunited with their mothers they displayed an elevated level of cling-ing behaviour which persisted for the next three months.

Harlow, Kaufman and Rosenblum's research indicates that there is a *critical period* for attachment to develop. Failure to develop an attach-ment results in severe disruption of social functioning, though tempo-rary separation appears to cause no long-term damage.

2.4.2 Effects on children

Psychologists would never rear human infants isolated from all social contact, but there are some extremely sad cases, including those of Anna and Isabelle, where children have been raised without social con-tact. Such children are known as *feral* children because it is suggested that they behave as if they had been raised in the wild. These children may eventually be able to interact successfully with others. Freud and Dann (1951) report the case of six Jewish children who were incarcer-ated together without their parents in a series of concentration camps during the Second World War. The children formed strong attachment bonds towards each other, and did not develop an attachment to an adult until they reached England at the age of three or four. This study shows that attachments can be *plastic*, that is, they can alter over time.

Rutter (1981) claims that four types of disorder result from mater-nal deprivation in humans. These are *acute distress, conduct disorders, affectionless psychopathy* and *intellectual retardation*. These are sum-marised in Figure 2.4. Children often display acute distress on admis-sion to hospital or other formal care setting. Acute distress is charac-terised by intense anxiety and grief and is related to the strength of the attachment bond; the stronger the bond the greater degree of distress shown. However, Robertson and Robertson (1971) found that children displayed much less acute distress if their new environment had what the researchers termed a 'family atmosphere', suggesting that children were responding with distress to the loss of a familiar environment rather than to the separation *per se*.

Conduct disorders, which as the name suggests are disorders charac-terized by inappropriate behaviour, sometimes amounting to delinquency, actually result from dysfunction within the family rather than maternal

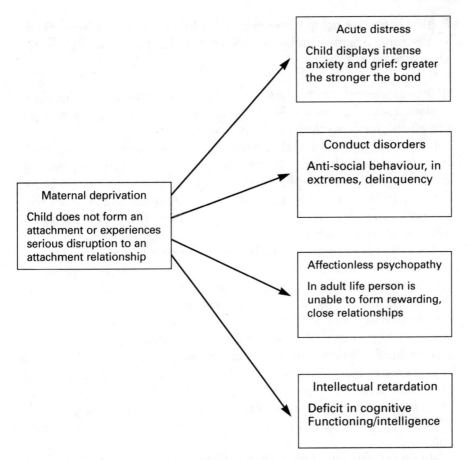

Figure 2.4: Possible consequences of maternal deprivation. After Rutter, M (1981) *Maternal Deprivation Reassessed.* 2nd edn. Harmondsworth: Penguin.

deprivation. Hetherington *et al.* (1979) found that anti-social behaviour increased among children of divorced parents, but after two years the children showed much less evidence of conduct disorder compared to children who lived in an atmosphere of discord within the home.

Affectionless psychopathy is a type of personality disorder characterised by an inability to form useful, rewarding, close social relationships. Rutter (1981) provides a summary of evidence for the claim that the lack of a strong attachment bond in infancy leads to affectionless psychopathy. Claims for this rest on three main premises:

1 that psychiatric problems in adulthood can be traced back to childhood experiences;
2 that children suffering extreme deprivation have a better chance of developing normally the earlier they are found;

3   that the relationship between early childhood and adult functioning is stronger than the relationship between later childhood and adult functioning.

However, research on this topic presents a mixed picture, and firm conclusions about the relationship between the lack of an attachment bond and affectionless psychopathy remain elusive.

It has also been claimed that intellectual retardation is a consequence of maternal deprivation. A number of studies by Tizard and her colleagues (Tizard and Joseph, 1970; Tizard and Rees, 1972; Tizard and Hodges, 1978) have investigated this claim by observing children who had been in residential care for between two and four years. Of the 65 children who took part in her study, 24 were adopted by the age of four and a half, 15 had returned to live with their natural mothers and 26 were still in residential care. All children had at least average intelligence, with the adopted group having the highest IQ scores. In a further study, Tizard investigated the relationship between type of care and the development of language skills. She classified the care environments as highly centrally organized, mixed organisation and highly decentralised. Children in the decentralised units, characterised by a high degree of staff and child autonomy and organised around family groupings, had the highest test scores. These findings indicate that being raised in a caring, stable and intimate environment may be more influential for cognitive and social development than maternal attention.

However, more recently, researchers have argued that the daily separation of infants from their working mothers in day care centres may increase the risk of psychological problems for the child in later life (Karen, 1994). Robertson and Robertson (1971) found that while children protest on first being separated from their mother, their distress turns to apathy as time passes and eventually they seem to lose interest in the missing mother. Day care involves only very short-term separation, and Clarke-Stewart and Fein (1983) found that infants in day care not only form strong attachment bonds with their mothers but also prefer their mothers to the day centre caregivers. Despite this finding further research suggests that fewer babies in day care form secure attachments. Lamb and Sternberg (1990) found that around 36 per cent of infants in day care had an insecure attachment to their mother, compared with 29 per cent of infants who were not in day care, suggesting that day care has a detrimental effect on the attachment process. However, in measuring the strength of the attachment bond, the researchers judged infants to be insecure if being left alone briefly with an unfamiliar person did not unduly worry them. One could argue that this is not an accurate measure of attachment for infants in day care, since they may be more used to new people than infants who stay at home with their mothers.

Though childhood and infancy involve great strides in the process of social development, the process does not end with infancy. The next sections will show that in our relationships with others and in our moral behaviour, social development continues throughout all of our life.

2.5 Erikson's stages of psychosocial development

The first year of life is crucially important for sowing the seeds of later social development, however, further development of skills gained in infancy is necessary for us to meet the demands of our social worlds in childhood, adolescence, adulthood and old age. Erikson (1968) proposes that our social development progresses through a series of *psychosocial stages* with a specific crisis associated with each. Erikson's stages of psychosocial development are outlined in Table 2.3.

Erikson's work was strongly influenced by Freudian theories of psychodynamism, but instead of focusing on the unconscious part of our minds as Freud did, Erikson concentrated on the *ego* and its interaction with the world. His basic premise was that we are shaped by our experiences at each of these stages. Of Erikson's eight psychosocial stages, four refer to childhood, one to adolescence and three to adulthood and old age. At each stage, it is necessary to resolve a *crisis* from which an *attitude* towards the self and others develops. Successful resolution of the crisis associated with each of these stages results in a favourable outcome; an increase in ego strength and the establishment of an enduring positive attitude. Unsuccessful negotiation of these crises results in a negative outcome; a weakening of ego strength and an incomplete resolution of that stage. Therefore, the ways in which people resolve each of Erikson's stages shape their personalities and their social relationships.

The crisis associated with infancy is the conflict between *trust* and *mistrust*, as forming strong feelings of trust during infancy provides the foundation for future successful psychological development. A strong attachment will allow the infant to develop enduring feelings of trust about the world, and the attitude (or ego strength) resulting from successful resolution of this crisis is hope.

The next three of Erikson's psychosocial stages concern the social developmental work of childhood. During childhood the child not only expands the social circle of infancy but also begins to encounter novel situations, which require new strategies and abilities. It is at this point

Stage	Age	Issue associated with stage
1	Birth to 1 year	*Trust versus mistrust* Infant learns to trust that his/her needs will be met (especially by parents) or learns to mistrust the world
2	1–3 years	*Autonomy versus shame* Child learns to use will to make choices; learns self-care or develops uncertainty and doubts own abilities
3	3–5 years	*Initiative versus guilt* Child learns to initiate activities to direct behaviour, acquiring purpose; or develops guilt over desire for independence
4	6 years to puberty	*Industry versus inferiority* Child develops sense of industry in response to demands of home and school; or begins to feel inferior to others
5	Adolescence	*Identity versus identity diffusion* Adolescent develops integrated sense of identity; or suffers from role confusion
6	Early adulthood	*Intimacy versus isolation* Young person able to commit to an intimate relationship; or develops sense of isolation
7	Middle age	*Generality versus stagnation* Adult willing to care for children and others and work for the common good; or becomes self-centred and stagnates
8	Old age	*Integrity versus despair* Older person reflects on meaningfulness of life and accepts own mortality; or despairs over past failures

Table 2.3: Erikson's stages of psychosocial development. At each stage a new psychological crisis must be resolved

that the child tries out its own abilities. The first task is concerned with achieving *autonomy* (vs. *shame*) by learning basic tasks of self- care. Failure to achieve this results in an enduring sense of doubt. Next, the third stage involves the issue of *initiative* versus *guilt*. At this stage children learn to introduce activities and to begin to enjoy a sense of mastery in their own abilities, thereby acquiring purpose in their lives. If children are prevented from exercising initiative at this stage, an attitude of guilt about their wish for independence will persist. It is also at this stage that sex roles begin to form, a topic that will be discussed later in this chapter. The work of the fourth stage, from late childhood leading up to puberty, is characterised by the crisis of *industry* versus *inferiority*. At this stage, the child has to cope with the formalised demands of school and an increasing amount of personal responsibility. Successful completion of this stage results in a sense of industry and an eagerness to learn. However, trying out new things may lead to failure and if the child does not develop a sense of competence at this stage then it will adopt an attitude of inferiority.

Adolescence is generally the time for establishing one's own identity and reflects the growing child's need to see itself as separate from and different to its caregivers. At Erikson's fifth stage, *identity* vs. *identity diffusion*, the adolescent must achieve a coherent self-identity, or set of values and beliefs which marks it out as a unique individual. Failure to do this will result in role confusion and a diffusion of identity. Erikson's final three stages concern the developmental work of adulthood and old age. Stage six concerns the struggle to achieve *intimacy*, by learning to give enough of yourself to another person to facilitate a loving and enduring relationship or series of relationships. The ego strength associated with this stage is love, and if this is not achieved, social isolation will result. In middle age, Erikson identifies the psychological crisis as *generativity* versus *stagnation*. At this stage adults become willing to help others without the expectation of reward. They also become committed to their work and to the common good, and the ego strength associated with this stage is care for others. Unsuccessful negotiation of this stage results in stagnation, with self-centred behaviour and inactivity becoming the norm. The final stage in Erikson's model concerns old age, which may be taken to mean the age at which most people in the West retire from their permanent job. At this stage the crisis is between *integrity* and *despair*. Older adults may reflect on their lives positively and evaluate their experiences as meaningful, accepting death. Alternatively, they may feel bitter and resentful about life goals unfulfilled, past failures or a misspent youth. Integrity or sagacity is the ego strength associated with this life stage, while the negative outcome is despair.

The main thrust of Erikson's argument is that the way we approach and ultimately resolve one psychosocial stage influences the way we approach and resolve the next stage. A positive outcome at any one stage results in an increase in ego strength and sense of self, with positive feelings of self-worth and mastery associated with it. Negative outcomes at any stage not only damage the chances of successful negotiation of the next stage, but, according to Erikson, lead to psychological problems and poorer social functioning in later life.

2.6 Childhood

As we have already noted, the social world of the infant gradually develops during childhood to include siblings, friends and classmates. Dunn (1992) has shown that at the age of one year infants show intense interest in the activities of other children in their environment, and by the age of eighteen months they show knowledge of how to comfort or hurt other children (Bernstein *et al.*, 1997). From this age social skills develop apace. For example, Mueller and Lucas (1975) showed that at the age of two children simply exchange or debate ownership of toys; by the age of three they use toys in co-operative play with other children, and by the age of four they are able to hold conversations about their toys when playing with other children (Parten, 1971). In addition, children develop an understanding of the *social roles* of others during childhood. For example, they may begin by forming the opinion that parents answer the telephone, go shopping and go to work. By the time they reach the age of six or seven they can play 'school' with a clear understanding of the social roles of pupil, teacher, caretaker, etc. (Watson, 1981).

The primary school years are immensely important for social development, since during this time children learn the *social rules* of interacting with others, especially their peers. Relationships with other children develop through learning and playing together, and through working co-operatively or in competition (Hartup, 1983). Friendships begin to develop beyond mere acquaintanceship and are very rewarding to young children, affording a safe place to practise social skills. Those who fail to make friends at school often develop into 'loners' and may experience problems with relationships later in life (Parker and Asher, 1987). The qualitative changes in peer interactions are partly related to the child's level of social skills; very young children simply do not have the ability to from deep relationships with others but develop the necessary skills over time. By the age of around four children can identify facial expressions denoting the basic emotions of anger, fear, happiness and sadness (Camras, 1977), and quickly learn to recognise the facial expression of other emotions. In addition, they learn to empathise with other children and to put themselves in another person's shoes (Gnepp, 1983). Developing social skills like these is at least as important as developing competency in cognitive skills, since the child needs to learn the appropriate way of joining a group of other children, and how to respond to praise or criticism, all of which involve encoding and interpreting another person's behaviour (Dodge and Price, 1994).

2.6.1 Parenting styles

Parental influence does not end with the completion of the intense period of social development in infancy. *Socialisation* is the process by which adults (and other authority figures) deflect a child's uncontrolled impulsive behaviour into behaviour appropriate to and acceptable in their society. Clearly, socialisation has a cultural basis. Some societies, for example Hispanic cultures like those in South and Central America, emphasise the value of working co-operatively for the benefit of the family and the community above individual ambition. In these cultures, adults adopt a more rule-setting role and are unlikely to condone the type of discussion and negotiation which occurs in many European societies (Delgado-Gaitan, 1994). European and American parents tend to adopt one of three parenting styles (Baumrind, 1971). *Authoritarian* parents are strict, punish misdemeanours, and have a set standard of behaviour which the child is expected to attain. They discourage independence, encourage obedience and tend to be cold and aloof in their dealings with their children. *Permissive* parents have very few if any rules of discipline and allow their children complete freedom of behaviour. *Authoritative* parents represent the middle course between these two extremes. These parents are reasonable and consistent in their relationships with their children. They gradually increase the child's level of responsibility in line with the child's competencies and encourage independence. For our purposes, the important question is the effect of these parenting styles on social development. Can you make a guess at the outcomes of the three parenting styles? Baumrind (1971) found that parenting styles showed a consistent relationship to children's social development. She found that the children of authoritarian parents were shy, withdrawn and unfriendly in social situations, and slow to trust others. Those reared by permissive parents were unruly, immature and likely to give up on a task as soon as they encountered difficulty. Children raised by authoritative parents fared best in social development. They were friendly, happy, independent individuals, and Baumrind found that the advantages conferred by authoritative parenting persisted for some years through childhood. The three parenting styles are summarised in Figure 2.5.

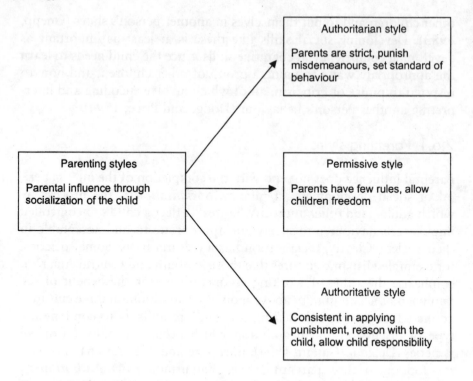

Figure 2.5: The authoritarian, permissive and authoritative parenting styles suggested by Baumrind (1971)

Although Baumrind's findings seem persuasive, they do have some shortcomings. Firstly, her results are based on correlations between the parents' behaviour and that of their offspring. Correlations can only prove a link between two items (in this case between parental and child behaviour) but they cannot show causation (see Chapter 1). Second, unexpected results were also found, for example, a small number of children raised in permissive households were found to display none of the unpleasant behaviours normally associated with this parenting style. A final criticism is the argument that it is not the parenting styles themselves that socialise children in different ways, but rather the way the children themselves perceive and evaluate the care they receive (Dunn and Plomin, 1990).

2.6.2 Development of language

Language has been described as 'one of the greatest intellectual feats' we achieve (Bloomfield, 1933). The psycholinguist Noam Chomsky is famous for his work, stemming from the 1950s until the present day, on the acquisition of language. Chomsky's main thesis is that we are innately programmed for language and that we have a sort of blueprint for language in the brain at birth. This plan enables children to acquire language extremely quickly, so by the age of three or so children are able to communicate very effectively using language. Mostly, language is studied outside social psychology, by psycholinguists who are concerned with the production, comprehension and mental representation of language (Durkin, 1995). However, cast your mind back to the introduction of this chapter and Anna and Isabelle. You will recall that Isabelle, who had some human company during her early childhood, eventually developed adequate language skills while Anna, deprived of such company, did not. This should alert you to the fact that purely cognitive explanations for the development of language cannot tell the whole story. Indeed, it has been suggested (Kaye, 1982) that the feed and pause pattern observed in breastfeeding acts as a rudimentary introduction to the turntaking we utilise for successful conversations. Brown (1973) carried out an observational study of language in three pre-school children, using their spontaneous speech in naturally occurring contexts as her data. She found that language was related to social contexts, especially to the activities of other people in the child's environment. Brown's work was the forerunner for later work on the social aspects of language development, research which has addressed *reciprocity*, the *role of adults* in language acquisition and the *type of linguistic input* a child receives from others.

Reciprocity

Both infant and caregivers attempt and achieve a useful and rewarding communication system utilising the limited means they have at their disposal and at an early stage, turn taking in communication becomes established. Even though the child cannot yet speak, its parent often continues the interaction as though the infant had in fact made a verbal response. This gives the infant numerous opportunities to become familiar with the intricacies of conversational speech and to learn how conversation works.

The role of adults in language acquisition

The type of verbal/non-verbal 'conversation' described above quite quickly becomes an actual verbal/non-verbal conversation as the child acquires its first words. Research has shown that adults support children in this endeavour by developing a shared context, and initiating a conversation about the context (Bruner, 1983; Messer, 1983). They establish a context of shared attention either by monitoring where the child is focusing its attention or by directing the child's attention towards an object. Typically, adults will then talk about what the child is attending to. The routine basis of many parent–child interactions also helps the child to acquire language by providing opportunities to teach the names of things (Bruner, 1983). For example, many books aimed at young children use the format 'That's an x' (Durkin, 1995), where x can be substituted with an appropriate name (e.g. 'That's a dog', 'That's a cat', 'That's a mouse'). According to Durkin, the routine part of this interaction may serve as advance notification to the child that an interesting new word is about to crop up, thereby facilitating expansion of the child's grammar. Akhtar, Dunham and Dunham (1991) have shown that new words are most often introduced when parent and child are sharing the same focus of attention.

Type of linguistic input

Some early theorists believed that children learn to speak simply by imitating the speech of adults around them. This cannot be the case for at least two reasons. First, adults never produce grammatical errors of the type 'the mouses runned away', whereas children often do. Second, much of the adult speech a child hears around them is sloppy; we leave sentences unfinished, change the structure of a sentence midway through and make slips of the tongue. However, if you listen carefully to the speech adults use when they converse with young children, you will notice that this speech is qualitatively different from that used with adults and older children. Typically, adults will speak in a higher pitch than normal, use simpler words and phrases, speak more slowly and use repetition, almost automatically (Garton, 1992; Snow, 1986). Children also modify their speech in a similar way when they speak to others younger than themselves. This type of speech used to be known as 'motherese' but is now more commonly referred to as 'child-directed-speech'. Speaking to young children in this way provides a clearer form of linguistic input than adult-to-adult speech, and introduces simple vocabulary for the child to acquire.

2.6.3 Problems for social aspects of language

If children can communicate effectively without language, then why should they develop language anyway? Perhaps the strongest criticism for the social aspects of language can be levelled at the first aspect we discussed, reciprocity. While it has been argued that the reciprocal turn-taking begun during the attachment phase mimics later turn-taking in conversations, this can only be a broad comparison. For example, some species of birds exhibit reciprocity in their songs, yet do not go on to develop a language (Durkin, 1995).

Although evidence for the role of parental support in language acquisition is more robust, it has been shown that in cultures where such support is not routinely given, children pass through the same developmental stages in acquiring language (Schieffelin, 1990). Evidence for the simpler linguistic input adults provide for children has also been contradicted. For example, Gleitman and Wanner (1982) argued that parental speech is shorter because it has a simpler communicative intent, and serves as interjections, directives or questions. The researchers also argue that child-directed speech is untidy and unlikely to provide the child with an adequate input for developing language. Finally, it has been shown that our pets receive the same type of linguistic input as our children (Hirsh-Pasek and Treiman, 1982), yet they do not develop language!

These criticisms do not, of course, destroy evidence for social aspects in language acquisition. It has never been known for a child to acquire language without interacting with other speakers. However, it has been known for those to have been deprived of such company to fail to develop language (Davis, 1949).

2.6.4 Gender roles

By the age of six or so, children can recognise quite complex networks of social roles, for example those that exist within a school (Watson, 1981). Many of the social roles children learn are linked to gender, that is either males or females predominantly carry them out. For example, in European cultures bricklayers have traditionally been male, and nurses have traditionally been female. Though there have been some challenges to these traditions, it is still the case that our society establishes strong beliefs about gender roles. For example, TV advertising makes extensive use of traditional gender roles (Lovdal, 1989). Gender roles can be described as the patterns of occupation, style of dress and behaviour associated with being male or female.

There are some biological bases for gender roles, since it has been found that males and females show different patterns of brain organisation and function, and different hormonal influences on behaviour (Begley, 1995; Witelson, 1994). In addition, cross-cultural work supports a biological basis for gender roles since in every culture, socialisation processes not withstanding, males are more violent than females. From an early age, boys and girls display different behaviour patterns (Eagly, 1995; Feingold, 1988). Girls have a greater verbal capability than boys. They are less vulnerable to deficits in speech and learning abilities and less likely to suffer from mental retardation. Their spoken and written language exceeds that of boys, and they tend to be more nurturing, empathetic and caring. Boys have a greater spatial ability than girls, and their strengths lie in constructing and manipulating objects, and the mental rotation of complex figures. Boys also tend to be more active and, as noted earlier, more physically aggressive. These different gender roles had great evolutionary value in the distant past when women would be left to care for children while the men hunted for food.

However, it is almost impossible to separate the effects of nature from those of nurture in considering gender roles. Research has demonstrated that from the moment of birth boys and girls are treated differently. Culp *et al.* (1983) had adults interact with infants they were told were boys, though some of them were girls, and infants they were told were girls, though some of them were boys. The researchers found that adults used more active and energetic play with infants they believed to be boys, and were more gentle and spoke more to infants they believed to be girls. Rubin *et al.* (1974) interviewed the first-time parents of 15 baby girls and 15 baby boys just 24 hours after the babies were born. Despite the fact that there was no difference in height and weight amongst the babies, Rubin found that the parents of girls rated their babies as gentler, smaller with softer facial features. Parents of boys rated their babies as stronger, bigger and more co-ordinated. Children are also socialised by their peer group into adopting gender appropriate behaviour. Boys usually display more skill with computer games and other games of this type than girls, but boys initiate and praise each other for skill at these games more than girls do (Law *et al.*, 1993). In short, then, biological differences are exaggerated and encouraged during children's socialisation.

2.7 Adolescence: stormy or sunny?

Adolescence is quite loosely timed. It begins with the onset of puberty, marked by the menarche (beginning of menstruation) in girls, and spermarche (the production of live sperm) in boys. It is, therefore, easy to pinpoint the start of adolescence. It is less easy to say when adolescence ends, and it may be that there are considerable individual differences, both biological and psychological, which decide this. Adolescence has for some time been viewed as a period of psychological upheaval and distress for young people. While adolescence is undoubtedly a period of great change, both physically and in the psychological and emotional experiences of young people, most adolescents enjoy the years between childhood and adulthood (*see* Fig. 2.6). Peterson (1987) reports that

Figure 2.6: Most adolescents enjoy the years between childhood and adulthood

only around 15 per cent of young people suffer serious problems in adolescence. The 'work' of this developmental stage is the creation of a coherent *self-identity* with which to enter the adult world.

2.7.1 Self-esteem in adolescence

During adolescence, young people experience a rapid surge in growth, sometimes adding as much as five inches in height in one year (Bernstein *et al.*, 1997). The development of sexual characteristics accompanies this growth spurt. The physical changes that mark adolescence can lead to challenges to *self-esteem*. Boys in Wesern culture who reach puberty early are likely to be more satisfied, happy and relaxed and are more likely to achieve leadership positions. In contrast, boys who are physically late maturing are more likely to feel rejected and dominated by the peer group (Peterson, 1987). Girls who mature early tend to feel a sense of embarrassment at the emergence of their sexual characteristics, and they are also more at risk from early sexual activity and less close relationships with their parents. Therefore, the reaction of self and others to the emerging adult body shape can affect self-esteem.

In addition, during adolescence young people face further challenges. They become interested in sex, and begin to form sexual relationships with others. They are exposed to cigarettes, alcohol and illegal drugs and need to make choices about their consumption of these substances. The choices they make can define their belonging to other groups of young people, and thus enhance or dilute self-esteem. As any adolescent will tell you, relationships with parents begin to change during adolescence. In part, this reflects the wish of the adolescent to achieve an independent identity for himself/herself, a topic we will turn to in the next section. While serious parent–child conflict can lead to severe difficulties for the adolescent, including leaving the parental home, teenage pregnancy and illegal activities (Montemayor, 1983) most adolescents and their parents cope adequately with conflict in the home (Steinberg, 1989; 1990). Parents who employ the authoritative style of parenting mentioned in Section 2.6.1 generally raise psychologically healthy young people (Baumrind, 1991).

2.7.2 Development of self-identity

Some years ago, it was common practice for British children to leave school at the age of 14 and take up a job, an event that clearly marked the transition from childhood to the world of work and the assumption of adult responsibilities. This transitional period has gradually stretched and in contemporary society it is common for young people to leave school at the age of 17 or 18 and take up some form of training, whether vocational or in higher education. Thus, the stage of assuming adult responsibilities may not loom until the early or even mid-twenties, representing an elongated period of adolescence.

According to Erikson (see Section 2.5), the main task of adolescence is the development of an integrated self-identity. Erikson theorises that the events of adolescence (leaving school, finding a job or securing a university place, forming intimate relationships with others) bring about an *identity crisis* by challenging the young person's concept of self. If the earlier psychosocial tasks have been completed satisfactorily, the young person will have developed a sense of trust, autonomy and initiative, and the identity crisis will be resolved positively. If, however, childhood experiences have resulted in mistrust, guilt and shame, the adolescent will not resolve their identity crisis satisfactorily and will not develop an integrated concept of self. Successful resolution of the identity crisis results in the ego strength of fidelity and the ability to offer commitment not only to other people but also to employment and to political beliefs. Conversely, poor resolution of the identity crisis results in apathy and lack of commitment. Erikson further refines his theory by proposing that there are four stages of identity status, and these are shown in Table 2.4.

Identity achievement represents the optimum identity status, where the identity crisis has been resolved and commitment to others, job and causes is complete. During the *moratorium* phase, the adolescent has not yet settled on an identity and is still experimenting with alternatives; for example, being studious or lazy, gregarious or a 'loner'. At *foreclosure*, an identity crisis has simply never been reached because the young person has never sought to question the beliefs of their parents and her society, and accepts their values without question. A person in *identity diffusion* status not only displays lack of an integrated identity but does not actively look for an identity. The question is, is there any empirical evidence in support of Erikson's claims?

Evidence is broadly supportive. Waterman and Waterman (1971) carried out a longitudinal study of 92 college freshmen, assessing them for changes in identity status and stability in identity status at two stages. They found that for intended occupation, students moved into the moratorium stage after their first year in college, and also showed a decrease in identity diffusion. However, for political and religious beliefs, identity achievement actually decreased and

Identity status	Description of status
Identity achievement	Identity crisis has been successfully negotiated and sense of identity achieved. Person has firm commitment to work, religion, morality, etc.
Moratorium	Identity crisis is ongoing and person is trying out different lifestyles in an attempt to find commitment
Foreclosure	Identity crisis has not been reached. Person shows unconditional acceptance of parental/societal values and identifies unquestioningly with parents
Identity diffusion	Identity status is negative; person shows no commitment to work, religion, morality, etc., and does not attempt to make a commitment. Identity not actively sought

Table 2.4: Erikson's four identity statuses and their description. Adapted from Erikson (1968)

identity diffusion increased. Why should this be? The researchers argued that the results came about because they used engineering students as participants in the study. They reasoned that as engineering is a vocational choice their participants would have had well worked out views about employment, whereas their political and religious beliefs were less developed. It would be interesting to repeat this study with students reading for degrees in the social sciences, which place greater emphasis on political and religious values and are less vocational. In a later study (Waterman, 1982) support was found for the view that young people 'experiment' with different identities, by changing physical characteristics such as hairstyle and clothes, and also personality characteristics such as conforming and non-comforming behaviour.

Stark and Traxler (1974) tested Erikson's claim that late adolescence involves an identity crisis by measuring identity diffusion in students between the ages of 17 and 20 and comparing this with measures of identity diffusion in students between the ages of 20 and 24. According to Erikson's theory, older adolescents should experience less identity diffusion since identity achievement would already have occurred. Table 2.5 records Stark and Traxler's findings.

In the older group, identity diffusion is less than in the 17–20 year old age group, providing support for Erikson. This study also showed that being in a state of identity diffusion is uncomfortable; students in the 17–20 age group showed increased levels of anxiety compared to those in the older age group, though of course this could have been due to other factors.

Waterman (1982) found that by the time adolescents reach the age of 21, around 50 per cent have successfully resolved their identity

Age	Sex	Mean identity diffusion score
17–20	M	28.1
17–20	F	30.6
17–20	M & F	29.0
21–24	M	32.1
21–24	F	34.0
21–24	M & F	33.8

Table 2.5: Identity diffusion scores for males and females across two age groups. Higher scores indicate *less* identity diffusion. Adapted from Stark and Traxler (1974)

crisis and progressed to adulthood sure of themselves and confident in their own abilities. The basic characteristics of such people remain unchanged from childhood, but they develop psychological strength, resilience and confidence and finish adolescence with a clearer idea of who they are (Adams and Jones, 1983; Savin-Williams and Demo, 1984). For the unfortunate few who do not resolve their identity crisis, difficulties lie ahead. A key feature of Erikson's theory is that unsuccessful resolution of one stage of psychosocial development adversely affects completion of the next. Orlofsky *et al.* (1973) tested this by examining the relationship between identity achievement and the sixth stage in Erikson's model, isolation vs. intimacy. They found that participants with identity achievement were more likely to be involved in loving and close relationships with others, while those of identity diffusion status were more likely to be isolated. Therefore, Erikson's model is broadly supported by research findings. However, psychologists are increasingly recognising that social development continues into old age, and perhaps it would be rewarding to test out Erikson's later psychosocial stages in this context.

2.7.3 Development of moral reasoning: Kohlberg's theory of moral development

Developing and arriving at an integrated identity involve thinking, reasoning and forming conclusions about abstract concepts. Piaget (1952) believed that adolescence is marked by a specific cognitive development, the ability to think hypothetically and to imagine a series of outcomes. He termed this the *formal operations* period. At this cognitive stage adolescents are able to think about the world as it is, as it might be given different social and political structures, and how they think it should be. They are able to understand how the past affects the present, and how the present might affect the future.

While Piaget examined adolescents' cognitive skills on scientific experiments, one area where adolescents can use their reasoning skills is in a consideration of morality. Just as Piaget saw cognitive development as proceeding through a series of developmental stages, so Kohlberg saw moral reasoning as a set of stages through which each person must pass. Kohlberg (1976) defined morality as involving justice or fairness; he saw conflicts of morality as essentially dealing with conflicts of interest which could be solved by applying the principles of justice. He proposed that there were three levels of development in moral reasoning, and that at each level there were two stages. These levels are summarised in Table 2.6.

Level	Description of level	Reasoning perspective
Level 1: Pre-conventional Stage 1: Punishment and obedience	The worth of a behaviour depends on whether the outcome is pleasant or unpleasant	Egocentric; does not take into account the views of others
Stage 2: Instrumental Purpose	Uses rules for own good. 'You scratch my back and I'll scratch yours'	Notion of right and wrong depends on own interests
Level 2: Conventional Stage 3: Interpersonal expectations and conformity	Right depends on the expectations of others. Rules obeyed because of need to be seen as a 'good person'	Aware of needs, feelings and interests of others. Able to take another's perspective
Stage 4: Social system and conscience	Right is upholding and maintaining the law. Doing right depends on duty and respect for authority	Adopts perspective of the social system, not other people
Level 3: Post-conventional Stage 5: Social contract and individual rights	Individuals have the right to own point of view and values. Acceptance that rules and laws are for the common good	Considers people independently of social rules and laws. Puts people before society
Stage 6: Universal ethical principles	Moral reasoning is determined by ethical humanitarian principles. Laws valid if they take account of these	Respect for the moral principles of others if they result from rational consideration of moral principles

Table 2.6: Kohlberg's three levels of moral development and stages of moral reasoning. Adapted from Kohlberg (1976)

These levels of moral development, Kohlberg argues, are not linked to a person's chronological age, and some people pass through them at a later age than others. In addition, not everyone reaches the highest level of moral reasoning. Level 1 is usually occupied by children under the age of nine or so and is essentially selfish in nature. Kohlberg referred to this stage as *pre-conventional* as reasoning at this level is not yet based on the conventions or rules prevalent in the child's culture. People at this level are more concerned with avoiding punishment or using rules for their own good. At stage 1, reasoning is based on the idea that good things are pleasurable and bad things are unpleasant. The stage is egocentric, since children do not recognise the needs and rights of others. At stage 2, obeying rules is good only if it is to the advantage of the individual.

At the *conventional* level of moral reasoning, concern for others enters the reasoning process. At stages 3 and 4, occupied in general by those aged 9–19, duty to others, to the family and to the country enters the equation. This represents a huge leap forward in moral reasoning, since the views and wishes of others are now taken into account. At stage 3, reasoning about what is right and wrong is based on gaining the approval of others and morality is based on behaving according to the rules of the society. At stage 4, what is right is the collection of rules, values and laws as it exists in society. Morality concerns upholding these rules. Stage 4 differs from Stage 3 in that instead of what is right simply being what others expect of you, 'right' is seen as both maintaining and adhering to the law and (crucially) recognising that this must happen to avoid moral decline and chaos.

At the highest level of moral reasoning, the *post-conventional* level, moral decisions are based both on personal standards and on universal principles of justice, fairness, equality and respect for human life. At stage 5, individuals see laws etc. as an attempt at reaching long-term security, but accept that such laws can be rejected if they are unfair. At stage 6, the highest and most aspirational of Kohlberg's stages, moral reasoning about right and wrong goes beyond the laws of any particular society to consider respect for human life and the basic rights of others as the key principles which govern morality. In Kohlberg's view only a very few people actually attain stage 6 in the ladder of moral development.

Kohlberg based his theory on the responses of people to various moral dilemmas that he asked them to solve. Perhaps the most famous of these is the 'Heinz dilemma'. In Europe a woman was near to death from a rare form of cancer. There was one drug that the doctors thought might save her, a form of radium that a druggist in the same town had recently discovered. The druggist was charging £2,000, ten times what the drug cost him to make. Heinz went to everybody he knew to borrow the money, but he could only get together about half of what the drug cost. He told the druggist that his wife was dying and asked him to sell it cheaper or let him pay later. But the druggist refused. So Heinz got desperate and broke into the man's store to steal the drug for his wife. Should Heinz have done that? Why? Kohlberg categorised people as belonging to one of the six stages of moral development depending on the conclusions they reached and the reasons they gave. For the Heinz dilemma, the following responses in Table 2.7 would be typical at each stage.

2.7.4 Criticisms of Kohlberg's theory

While Kohlberg's theory of moral development may seem persuasive, it has limitations. A large number of studies show cross-cultural evidence that people do progress sequentially through the stages of moral reasoning Kohlberg has identified (Snarey, 1987). Also, Stages 1 to 4 appear to occur universally, while 5 and 6 are not always reached. However, there are moral judgements made in some cultures that are not accounted for in Kohlberg's theory. For example, people from cultures which have a community-based approach to life, such as Israeli kibbutzim and Taiwan, included the importance of the community in their answers to moral dilemmas. People in India referred to the importance of behaving

Stage	What does 'right' consist of?	Should Heinz steal the drug?
Pre-conventional 1	Avoiding punishment	*No*, because he will be sent to prison
2	Getting a good deal	*Yes*, because his wife will care for him when she recovers
Conventional 3	Securing the approval of other people	*Yes*, because his wife and family will approve
4	Upholding the law and doing one's duty	*Yes*, because he has a duty to look after his wife, and *No*, because he should uphold the law
Post-conventional 5	Respecting laws while recognizing their limits	*Yes*, because the druggist is acting unfairly by charging so much
6	Following universal ethical principles	*Yes*, because the principle of preserving and respecting life is paramount

Table 2.7: Typical responses to the Heinz dilemma at each stage of moral development

in gender and caste appropriate ways, and maintaining personal good-ness in their moral reasoning (Shweder *et al.*, 1994).

As well as culture, gender also determines moral judgements. For example, Gilligan (1982; Gilligan and Wiggins, 1987) found that when asked about moral dilemmas, all of the male participants in her study concentrated on the concept of justice, though only half of the females did. The other half of the females concentrated on caring. Gilligan and colleagues argue that while males may well focus on impersonal con-cepts like justice, this does not hold true for females, who are more like-ly to consider prolonging rewarding relationships and attending to human needs.

2.7.5 Moral behaviour

Kohlberg's theory addresses moral reasoning and not moral behaviour; it tackles how we think about moral issues rather than how we act. It is perfectly possible to have the ability to reason at a particular stage of moral development yet not to do so (Emler *et al.*, 1983). Similarly, it is possible to reason in a moral way and yet not act morally; Krebs (1967) found that the likelihood of being caught exerts at least as strong an influence on behaviour as does moral reasoning. However, there is some evidence of a link between moral reasoning and moral behaviour. Gregg *et al.* (1994) found that among a group of juvenile criminals most saw obeying the law as a way of avoiding incarceration (a Stage 2 belief), while non-criminal juveniles believed obedience to the law prevented social chaos (a Stage 3 belief).

The development of moral reasoning can be accelerated by exposing children and young adults to a stage of moral reasoning higher than their own, perhaps by participating in debates on moral issues. This and finding yourself in a situation which requires more advanced moral reasoning than usual appear to force people to a higher level of moral reasoning (Enright *et al.*, 1983). Having to deal with real situations involving a high degree of emotionality (becoming accidentally preg-nant, being asked to help carry out a burglary or having a friend ask for help to cheat in an exam) also increases the complexity of moral reasoning. Unfortunately research has shown that while we have the capacity for advanced moral reasoning we sometimes fail to use it; Denton and Krebs (1990) found that both moral reasoning and moral behaviour deteriorated when people were out drinking with friends!

2.8 Adulthood

Social development does not end with adolescence, since adults also experience life transitions and change. In this section the path of adult social development will be traced through the three main spans of adulthood; early adulthood (around ages 20 to 40), middle adulthood (around ages 40 to 65) and late adulthood (around age 65 on). It is important to note that in adulthood, changes in social relationships and life circumstances are always unpredictable, since the social development of adults depends on individual experiences such as divorce, returning to education, changing career and remarrying (Schlossberg, 1987).

2.8.1 Early adulthood

The first stages of early adulthood usually coincide with getting a job and beginning a career, at least in Western culture. Young adults also become concerned with finding someone to love (Vaillant, 1977; Whitbourne *et al.*, 1992). In Erikson's theory, early adulthood is concerned with the resolution of the intimacy versus isolation crisis (see Table 2.3). Clearly, intimacy involves sexual relationships with others, but it also includes strong intellectual relationships and close friendship. Conversely, early adulthood coincides with leaving the parental home and all its supports, perhaps leaving the young adult isolated and lonely for a time. According to Levinson *et al.* (1978), young adults may feel insecure, apprehensive and anxious about their future.

Section 2.3 detailed the importance of secure attachment relationships. Researchers have found that patterns of attachment are reflected in adult relationships (Bartholemew and Horowitz, 1991; Horowitz *et al.*, 1993). Those who see intimate relationships in terms of a secure attachment style tend to feel worthy of the affection and love of others, find it easy to become close to others and enjoy relationships characterised by trust and happiness. Those with an ambivalent attachment style may feel under-valued and under-appreciated, and have relationships characterised by obsessive and jealous feelings, undermined by a fear of rejection. Some young adults display an avoidant attachment style in relationships and, while they desire intimacy, fear it at the same time and are wary of commitment.

By the age of 30 or so, most people 'settle down' and organise their priorities in life (Levinson *et al.*, 1978). This period coincides with Erikson's crisis of generativity versus stagnation, and he argued that in order to resolve this crisis successfully people need to produce things that will last beyond their lifetime. The usual means of achieving this is by having children or through career achievements. However, for a large sector of the population it is precisely these two themes, parenthood and career, that cause a certain degree of anguish. Women can often find that they are torn between the costs and benefits of child rearing and having a career outside the home, fearing that they are neglecting either or both job and family.

Producing a family of one's own heralds a major developmental change for young adults. New parents often speak of their new baby as having changed their lives, and indeed the changes are often far-reaching, encompassing personal, social and work-related domains. Unfortunately, ratings of marital satisfaction tend to dip following the arrival of children, and relationship problems can interfere with looking after the children (Belsky and Kelly, 1994). In addition, research has shown that the nature of care given to children is dependent on the mother's attachment style. New mothers who experienced a secure attachment style as infants tend to be responsive and nurturing towards their infants, helping the infants in turn to develop secure attachment to them (Ward and Carlson, 1995).

2.8.2 Middle adulthood

At around the age of 40, people experience a mid-life transition. Those who approach this positively may reappraise their lifestyle and set new goals or change their career completely. For a minority, the mid-life period brings with it a crisis (Levinson *et al.*, 1978). For both sexes the exciting lifestyle and burgeoning sexuality of teenage children, children leaving home, the demands of work or the beginnings of poor health may bring about such a crisis (Bernstein *et al.*, 1997). However, freedom from the demands of caring for children may come as a welcome relief for parents, especially mothers, who can now pursue or further develop interests outside the home (Helson and Moane, 1987). Unfortunately, many people experience the stress of divorce and its negative consequences such as anxiety, depression and loneliness. On a positive note, research has shown that the adverse effects of divorce on families have almost completely disappeared after two or three years (Furstenberg and Cherlin, 1991). For most people the period of middle adulthood is one of settled happiness, achievement and satisfaction.

2.8.3 Late adulthood

The beginning of the period of late adulthood coincides with the usual retirement age in the West. Neugarten *et al.* (1968) found that those who saw retirement as a choice they had made rather than a forced end to employment were most able to adjust to retired life. In social relationships, while older adults have less contact with others, they enjoy interactions more, enjoying more fulfilled and rewarding relationships than in earlier life (Cartensen, 1992). Older adults begin to focus

Figure 2.7: Older adults who see their lives as happy and fulfilled achieve a sense of peace and harmony in old age

inwards on their world (Neugarten, 1977), perhaps as a result of their failing physical capacities which may limit their activities and interactions. However, older people demonstrate levels of life satisfaction and self-esteem which are *at least* equivalent to any earlier period of adulthood (*see* Figure 2.7).

As people grow older they become more aware of their own mortality, and experience the death of relatives and friends of their age. The awareness of death brings about Erikson's final psychological crisis, the resolution of integrity vs. despair. Those who see their lives as meaningful, fulfilled and satisfactory achieve integrity. In contrast, those who fret about wasted opportunities, misspent lives and find no meaning in their lives succumb to despair. Older adults continue to thrive psychologically if they receive plenty of attention, for example by having parties given in their honour, receiving gifts or having pets (Kastenbaum, 1965; Rodin and Langer, 1977). When approaching death, older adults take comfort from their friends and family, from their life achievements and sometimes from their religious faith (Kastenbaum *et al.*, 1989). For the most part, older people come to accept the inevitability of death and to achieve psychological peace at the end of their lives.

2.9 Application: why do adolescents take risks? The effects of peer influence

In Section 2.7 it was noted that most adolescents navigate puberty and young adulthood with few problems. However, adolescence is the time when young people tend to take risks, so much so that risk taking may be considered the norm at this life stage. Recent figures from the United States indicate that 25 per cent of high school adolescents smoke every day, and more than 75 per cent have drunk alcohol, 50 per cent regularly drink alcohol and, even more worryingly, 50 per cent admit to driving after drinking (Ozer, 1998). In Britain many health education programmes have been aimed at reversing the upward trend of smoking and drinking among youth, as well as reducing the number of teenage pregnancies. But why do young people take risks? Lightfoot (1997) discusses two views of adolescent risk taking – *risk taking as trouble* and *risk taking as opportunity*. The first conceptualises youth as reckless, feckless and truculent, indulging in risky behaviour as a means of causing problems for adults. The second conceptualises youth as a romantic hero, taking risks as a consequence of adventures on the path to adulthood. Clearly, both of these are extreme views. A more realistic influence on adolescent risk taking, and perhaps one of the most well documented, is the effect of peer influence.

Substance use and abuse begin in adolescence (Cotterell, 1996) and the peer group is almost universally accepted as the major influence in initiating and maintaining risky health behaviours like this, even when evidence for peer influence has not been systematically measured. Kandel (1978) and Kandel *et al.* (1978) name three types of peer influence: *direct influence*, where others provide a model for and reinforce specific behaviours; *direct influence*, based on shared values of the peer group; and *conditional influence*, where one person affects another's chances of exposure to influence from elsewhere. Most studies of peer influence on health-risk behaviour concentrate on direct influence known as *peer pressure*, where, for example an adolescent is either encouraged or discouraged to smoke, depending on group norms. Brown *et al.* (1986) provide a clear explanation of peer pressure as 'when people your own age encourage you or urge you to do something or to keep from doing something else, no matter if you personally want to or not'.

Smoking and drinking alcohol usually occur in social situations when there is some ambiguity as to how adolescents should behave. In these kinds of situations, the peer group can provide two types of influence to guide behaviour: *informational influence* and *normative influence* (Deutsch and Gerard, 1995). Informational influence provides information about the correct way to behave from others whose opinions are valued. Normative influence involves using information to act in ways which elicit the approval of others. Through these young people learn to conform to the approved behaviours of their group.

A refinement to the notion of conformity outlined above is included in social identity theory. Social identity theory (Abrams and Hogg, 1990b) proposes that while peer pressure to conform shapes adolescent behaviour, behaviour is also affected by the personal motivations of the individual, including self-perception and self-categorisation as a member of a particular group. For example, peer pressure alone is not sufficient for an adolescent to take up smoking, unless it is coupled with the individual's perception of himself or herself as a smoker (or perhaps as a risk taker) and as a member of a group where smoking is an approved activity.

In addition, *positive self-esteem* can be gained by establishing a positive social identity for the group (*the in-group*) in comparison to others (*the out-groups*). By belonging to a group perceived as enjoying a positive social identity, an individual can find and maintain a positive self-image and reputation (Emler and Hopkins, 1990).

In a series of experiments Abrams and Hogg (1990a) showed that adolescent decisions are affected not by peer pressure in its widest sense, but by comparison with others perceived as from the same social group or category who act as reference points for individuals. This explains why health education programmes have only limited success in reducing adolescent health risk taking. Health education programmes and advice or warnings about unhealthy behaviours come from parents, teachers and health educators. These people form the outgroup, and as such their information is largely disregarded. Also, both smoking and drinking are seen as deviant behaviours in adolescence, though not in adulthood. In Chapter 7, the powerful effects of modelling on behaviour are discussed (see in particular Chapter 9, Section 9.3.5); perhaps adults should lead by example!

2.10 Summary

- Contemporary approaches to the study of social development track developmental processes throughout the lifespan, and see development as a lifelong process, enduring from the rapid development of infants right up to old age.
- Future psychological health depends on the quality of the first relationship, that between the child and its mother.
- Small babies are enormously social creatures and begin to socialise almost from birth. Social development continues apace during the early months, when infants are particularly interested in the people in their environment.
- The temperament an infant displays reflects the biological bases of the child's early personality development. Babies have been categorised as having easy, difficult and slow to warm up temperaments.
- Cultural factors play an important role in social development and serve to encourage or discourage certain behaviours. The family provides the first exposure to the cultural values of its particular society for the child.

- The strongest pattern of social exchanges usually occurs between the mother and her baby, a process known as *attachment*. Attachment can be defined as a strong, enduring, loving and caring bond between two individuals. Social psychologists have devised two main ways of measuring attachment in infants: *fear of strangers* and *separation anxiety*. Babies follow a three-stage pattern in attachment: *indiscriminate attachment, specific attachment* and *multiple attachment*.

- Infants fall into two main attachment types, s*ecure attachment* and a*nxious insecure attachment*. The responses of babies who show anxious insecure attachment may either be *avoidant, ambivalent* or *disorganised*. The communication theory of attachment proposes that infants show distress on separation because they no longer have access to a communication style that allows them to receive information about the world.

- Maternal deprivation can have serious consequences for human and animal infants.

- Erikson (1968) proposes that social development progresses through a series of *psychosocial stages*. At each stage, it is necessary to resolve a *crisis* from which an *attitude* towards the self and others develops.

- Social skills develop apace in childhood and children learn about social roles and social rules. *Socialisation* is the process by which adults (and other authority figures) deflect a child's uncontrolled impulsive behaviour into behaviour that is appropriate to and acceptable in their society. Authoritarian, permissive and authoritative parenting styles differentially affect social development in childhood.

- Language is a crucial social skill. Language development is related to social contexts, including *reciprocity*, the *role of adults* in language acquisition and *the type of linguistic input* a child receives from others.

- Many of the social roles children learn about are linked to gender. There are some biological bases for gender roles, but it is almost impossible to separate the effects of nature from those of nurture in considering gender roles.

- Most adolescents enjoy the years between childhood and adulthood as ones of increasing independence, autonomy and self-confidence. The physical changes that mark adolescence can lead to challenges to *self-esteem*.

- The main task of adolescence is the development of an integrated self-identity (Erikson, 1968). *Identity achievement, moratorium, foreclosure* and *identity diffusion* are four possible identity states.

- Kohlberg (1976) defined morality as involving justice or fairness and believed moral reasoning progressed through a series of stages: *pre-conventional, conventional* and *post-conventional*.

- Adulthood provides challenges for social development at early, middle and late stages. The final task of old age is the acceptance of mortality.

2.11 Suggestions for further reading

Durkin, K. 1995: *Developmental Social Psychology: From Infancy to Old Age.* Oxford; Blackwell.

A thorough account of the main topic areas of developmental social psychology.

Maccoby, E. E. 1980: *Social Development.* New York; Harcourt, Brace Jovanovich.

A comprehensive classic dealing with many of the issues discussed in this chapter.

Magen, Z. 1998: *Exploring Adolescent Happiness.* Thousand Oaks, CA: Sage Publications.

A very readable book which takes a positive approach to adolescent experiences.

Reddy, V., Dale, H., Murray, L. and Trevarthen, C. 1997: 'Communication in infancy: mutual regulation of affect and attention'. In Bremner, G., Slater, A. and Butterworth, G. (eds.), *Infant Development: Recent Advances.* Brighton: Psychology Press Erlbaum (UK).

An interesting synthesis of up-to-date research on infant communication.

3 Attitudes, attitude change and behaviour

- The importance of attitudes
- Formation of attitudes
- What are attitudes?
- Measuring attitudes
- Attitude change and persuasion

- Resisting attitude change
- Attitudes and behaviour
- Application: attitudes and health
- Summary
- Suggestions for further reading

3.1 The importance of attitudes

The concept of attitude has been, and remains, central and fundamental to social psychology. Allport (1954), for example, viewed attitudes as 'the most distinctive and indispensable concept in social psychology'. It is not hard to see why. In virtually all aspects of our social life we are continually seeking to discover other people's attitudes, telling others of our views, and trying to change someone else's opinions. In the world of communication and information technology advertising campaigns are often aimed at instilling in us a positive attitude towards a particular product with the hope that this will result in us buying what they have to sell. Other advertising campaigns aim to persuade us to change our behaviour by changing our opinions. Disagreements with others over what may be the appropriate or correct attitude make us aware of their powerful emotional foundations. Attitudes, then, are important to understanding stereotyping, prejudice, voting intentions, consumer behaviour and interpersonal attraction to name but a few major areas in social psychology.

Attitudes are also important simply because people hold a very large number of them towards many objects, other people and themselves. How attitudes come to be formed will be dealt with shortly; suffice to say that our parents, peers, powerful others, media and cultural norms all play an important role in determining the attitudes we hold. Attitudes towards minority groups (racial, ethnic or religious, for example) when strongly held and evaluated negatively provide the foundations of prejudice and discrimination. It is also important to remember that people differ markedly in their attitudes towards the same object or person. Social norms (implicit or explicit 'rules' of behaviour in one's peer group, social class difference, etc.) as well as cultural norms (more general codes of conduct and ethical standards of a society – which may also be either explicit or implicit) are responsible for a certain degree of uniformity, but an individual's direct experience produces a diverse range of attitudes and opinions. For example, early childhood experiences, family values, level of educational attainment and sub-culture ethos all contribute to creating differences among people.

Two reasons for social psychologists directing so much attention to the study of attitudes are: (a) given that the goals of social psychology are to understand, explain and predict behaviour (see Chapter 1), then knowledge of people's attitudes provides crucial insights; (b) attitudes are relatively enduring but also relatively easy to change (when considered in relation to beliefs and values), hence variables and circumstances which cause attitude change and behaviour change through persuasion are important to understand.

It may prove useful to distinguish between beliefs and values. *Beliefs* are what we hold to be true about the world; beliefs vary in how strongly they are held and how important those beliefs are for us. For example, a person believing in the existence of God would regard that belief as important and one which affected many other beliefs the person holds, for example, in marriage and attending church. By contrast, a person may believe, with good reason, that it is important to wear sunglasses while driving in sunshine, but such a belief is not likely to be of central importance to the person and hence it is unlikely to affect many other beliefs. Strongly held beliefs which are of central importance to us are highly resistant to change. This is also true of attitudes, as we shall see later in this chapter (Section 3.6).

Values represent our ethical and moral codes of conduct and are highly influenced by cultural, social and peer group norms. Values influence the way we conduct our life, what we look for in a relationship, how law-abiding we will be, etc. Like beliefs, values are highly resistant to change; when they do change, for example when a person becomes a member of a religious cult, a person's beliefs, attitudes and behaviour may also change dramatically. To make a simplistic summary, beliefs represent what we *think* is true about the world and values represent how we *feel*, morally and ethically about the world in which we live.

3.2 Formation of attitudes

Most social psychologists would agree that attitudes are learned through direct or indirect experience. However, recent research by Waller *et al.* (1990) and Keller *et al.* (1992) has produced evidence to show that genetic factors may also play a role. As with much other research on genetic influences in psychology, research by Waller *et al.* (1990) found that the attitudes of identical twins correlated more highly than the attitudes of non-identical twins. This was found both when identical twins were reared together and reared apart. The attitudes investigated ranged from religious matters to job satisfaction. However, the more generally accepted view is that social learning exerts the strongest influence on the formation of our attitudes.

3.2.1 Learning theory approaches

The social learning of attitudes may come about through classical conditioning. Early studies have shown that when initially neutral words are paired with a stimulus, such as an electric shock, which elicits a strong negative response from a person, the neutral word soon comes to elicit the negative response on its own (Staats *et al.*, 1962). More recently Krosnick *et al.* (1992) have shown that classical conditioning may occur subliminally (i.e. below the level of consciousness of the person). Here pictures of a stranger engaged in routine daily activities were shown to students. Interspersed with these pictures were others designed to produce positive feelings (such as laughing) but for very brief periods of time. Students shown such positive pictures subliminally evaluated the stranger more positively than students not shown subliminal pictures.

Instrumental or operant conditioning, through the use of rewards and punishments, clearly has an important role to play in the formation of attitudes. Modelling also has a strong influence on the formation of attitudes. Modelling is a Social Learning Theory (Bandura, 1973) approach where attitudes are learned through observing the behaviour of significant others and, crucially, how that behaviour is rewarded or punished (i.e. evaluated positively or negatively). When children model their behaviour from their parents, this often results in the child behaving as the parents do rather than how the parents tell the child to behave!

3.2.2 Direct experience

Many of the attitudes we hold are based upon our own direct experience, and attitudes formed as a result of frightening or traumatic experiences are often resistant to change (Oskamp, 1977). The type of social learning discussed above often accounts for formation of attitudes. However, repeated exposure to an attitude object may be sufficient to affect your evaluation and hence form an attitude (Zajonc, 1968). When we first hear a new record we may feel neutral or mildly dislike it, however repeated listening often serves to make us like the record very much (or strongly dislike it!).

Finally, social comparison also contributes to attitude formation; this is where we compare ourselves with another person or group of people and adjust our attitudes as we think appropriate. In a study conducted by Maio *et al.* (1994) participants were led to believe that negative views about a group of people ('Camarians' – a fictitious group) they knew little about came from another group of people (British) the participants respected. Participants expressed negative attitudes towards the 'Camarians' as a result of the social information from the British.

3.3 What are attitudes?

The challenge of providing a clear, valid and useful definition of attitudes is a product of (a) the term 'attitude' being used in extremely diverse and imprecise ways in everyday language; and (b) an attitude being a psychological construct used to refer to certain mental processes of a person. The latter presents a problem for scientific psychology since attitudes may only be inferred from what people say and do. An attitude cannot be directly observed or measured, as many phenomena can in the physical sciences such as chemistry or biology. The term attitude is used to represent and summarise a collection of psychological phenomena: it is a shorthand way of summarising simply that which is complex.

In trying to understand better what attitudes are we will look at two approaches: first, the *functions* that attitudes serve for a person; and, second, a *structural* approach that relates attitudes to other key psychological phenomena. Neither approach, on its own, offers a complete answer to the question of what attitude are, however, taken together they may come close to doing so.

3.3.1 The functional approach

Traditionally, the functional approach (McGuire, 1969; Katz, 1960; Smith *et al.*, 1956) suggests that attitudes promote the well-being of an individual by serving, essentially, four functions. These are the adaptive function, the self-expressive function, the ego-defensive function, and the knowledge function. The basic idea is that attitudes help a person to mediate between the inner demands of the self and the outside world (especially material, social and informational aspects).

The *adaptive* (or *utilitarian*) function concerns the extent to which attitudes enable a person to achieve a desired goal and avoid what is distasteful. Socially, an important process of identification takes place. A person develops similar attitudes to those people he or she likes and seeks out as friends those perceived to have similar attitudes. In short, this function is hedonistic in that it serves the purpose of increasing satisfaction or pleasure and avoiding punishment or pain.

The *self-expressive* function acknowledges a need to tell others about oneself and to know one's own mind, i.e. be conscious of what we feel, believe and value. One aspect of this relates to the discussion of 'identity' in Chapter 2, where Erikson's view that a sense of identity is important for the well-being of a person was discussed, and how emotionally devastating loss or lack of identity can be for people.

The *ego-defensive* function suggests that attitudes can serve to protect people from themselves and other people. Katz (1960) used a psychoanalytic perspective employing the Freudian concept of defence mechanisms. With respect to self-protection, attitudes may serve to maintain self-image, for example, often there are times when we find it painful to think about how we have behaved. Probably most people, at some time, have experienced guilt and remorse upon waking in the morning after being rather the worse for drink at a party the night before where they did or said something over-the-top or embarrassing. Our attitude towards ourselves as, essentially, a sensible, thoughtful and considerate person may help us not to think about the embarrassing episode or dismiss it as unrepresentative of how we normally behave. In short, positive attitudes about ourselves help maintain a positive self-image. With respect to the ego-defensive function and other people, it is often the case that in dealing with threats to our ego (self-image, self-esteem), we project our own conflicts onto other people, as is sometimes the case with prejudice.

The *knowledge-function* concerns how a person organises, structures and processes information about their social world. This function allows us to see the world as a more familiar, predictable and less uncertain place. The knowledge function allows us to simplify our world. This has both advantages and disadvantages, for example, stereotypes of people may lead to prejudice and discrimination (see Chapter 10).

Recent theory and research regards information processing as of central importance to understanding the function of attitudes. In recent reviews of attitudes and attitude change (see Olson and Zanna, 1993;

Tesser and Shaffer, 1990) psychologists now regard attitudes as either serving one central function or multiple functions. The principle of cognitive consistency, first introduced by Heider (1946), is where people strive to maintain consistency between: different attitudes; beliefs, values and attitudes; and attitudes and behaviour. The lack of cognitive consistency may lead to an unpleasant mental state, as with cognitive dissonance (see Section 5.1). The attempt to maintain consistency may affect how information is processed (Frey and Rogner, 1987), for example, holding a strong negative attitude to the Conservative Party may lead us to interpret information about the 'privatisation' policy over the past 15 years negatively. Research on schemata in social psychology (Taylor and Fiske, 1981) indicates that both the encoding and retrieval of information are often guided by a person's desire to maintain cognitive consistency.

The functional approach has implications for changing attitudes: to achieve attitude change two things need to be known: (a) the attitude held; and (b) the function that attitude serves for the person. To effect attitude change the approach should match the function, for example, an attitude serving a knowledge function is most likely to be changed by exposing the person to new information. On the other hand, an attitude serving an ego-defensive function is unlikely to be changed by the presentation of new information, but may be changed by appealing to a person's self-image.

3.3.2 The structural approach

The structural approach regards attitudes as an evaluation, positive or negative, of an attitude object (person or animate). This reflects a traditional *three component model* relating cognitions, affect and behaviour (Katz, 1960). Eagly and Chaiken (1993) define an attitude as 'a psychological tendency that is expressed by evaluating a particular entity with same degree of favour or disfavour'. In this definition the evaluation includes both overt and covert cognitive, affective and behavioural aspects. This is represented in Figure 3.1.

The cognitive component refers to beliefs, opinions and ideas about the attitude object: the affective component refers to the evaluation (good or bad, liking or disliking) of the attitude object and often reflects a person's values (see earlier); the conative component refers to behavioural intentions and/or actual behaviour associated with the attitude object. Newcomb's (1950) definition of an attitude as a 'learned predisposition to respond in a consistently favourable or unfavourable manner with respect to an object' clearly related attitudes to behaviour – which is problematic as we shall see later in section 3.7. Newcomb's

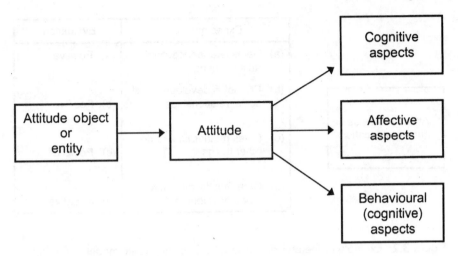

Figure 3.1: Relationship between attitude object, attitude and the three aspects. After Eagly and Chaikan (1993)

definition also assumes attitudes are learned and that people strive to achieve consistency (discussed earlier in this chapter).

The three component model, shown in Figure 3.1, assumes there is a high degree of consistency between beliefs, affect and behaviour. However, people often act in ways opposite to how they think or feel they should; in short, inconsistency is a feature of our lives. Fishbein and Ajzen (1975) proposed a *one-dimensional model* in which the evaluation (positive or negative and from strong to weak) is the key factor. In this model an attitude is simply an evaluation of an attitude object and is determined by the various expectations about the attributes of the attitude object and our evaluation of the attributes. This is represented in Figure 3.2.

From this example, a mother's attitude towards nursery education is a function of various expectancies about the effects and consequences of such education together with an evaluation of each. The example also shows that some expectancies are positively evaluated and one is negatively evaluated. This reflects how an attitude may be a mixture of positive and negative evaluations. In the nursery education example the mother will hold a positive attitude. The shortcomings of this *expectancy value* model of Fishbein and Ajzen (1975) are that it does not take into account the relative importance of each expectancy. For example, the influence on moral development may be an overriding factor resulting in a negative attitude to nursery education. The model also assumes that people carefully think about expectancies and their evaluations when forming an attitude. Sometimes only one expectancy or attribute

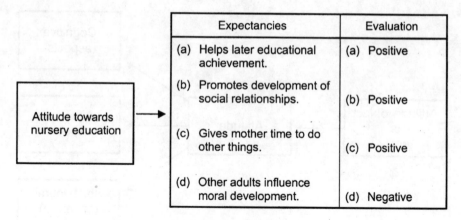

	Expectancies	Evaluation
	(a) Helps later educational achievement.	(a) Positive
	(b) Promotes development of social relationships.	(b) Positive
	(c) Gives mother time to do other things.	(c) Positive
	(d) Other adults influence moral development.	(d) Negative

Attitude towards nursery education →

Figure 3.2: Example of the one-dimensional expectancy-value model of Fishbein and Ajzen (1975) of attitudes

may be important in determining the attitude held (McGuire, 1985) or attitudes are learned without a person thinking a lot (see the previous section on the role of classical and operant conditioning in attitude formation).

The structural approach provides insight into how attitudes, beliefs, intentions and behaviour may be related. However, the assumptions identified in the discussion above often are not truly reflective of what people do, how they think, or how attitudes are formed in the first place.

3.4 Measuring attitudes

Social psychologists have been very inventive in their attempt to measure attitudes; this inventiveness ranges from asking people (through various types of self-report questionnaires), observing people (sometimes as participant observers) to indirect measures (for example, physiological responses).

Three main aims inform this desire to obtain measures: (a) often it is not enough to know that a person feels positively or negatively about an attitude object, an indication of the *strength* with which an attitude is held may also be important; (b) the use of standard, reliable and valid approaches allows different psychologists, who may perhaps research in different countries, to obtain measures that can be compared with each other; and (c) attempts to change attitudes, for example by persuasion, may be assessed through objective measures obtained before and after the attempt to change the attitude is made.

3.4.1 Indirect measures

Scientifically, and ideally, the most objective methods for measuring attitudes would be those which people were either unaware of or unable consciously to affect. Indirect measures, where you do not ask the person about his or her attitude directly, have taken a number of forms: the three most common being physiological, unobtrusive and projective techniques.

Physiological techniques (such as galvanic skin response, heart rate, pupillary dilation) of measuring attitudes assume that the affective (emotional/evaluative) component of attitudes correlates with the activity of the autonomic nervous system (that part of the nervous system thought to be beyond our conscious control). While little evidence exists showing correlation between physiological measures and attitudes, Hess (1965) demonstrated that if a person's pupils dilated (increase in pupil size), a positive attitude was indicated, and if there was pupil constriction (decrease in pupil size), it was indicative of a negative attitude. Generally, though, such an approach has met with only limited success. It is now accepted that most physiological measures are sensitive to other variables but may provide an indication of intensity of feeling but not direction, i.e. whether the attitude held is positive or negative (Cacioppo and Petty, 1981).

Unobtrusive measures rely on the assumption that behaviour is consistent with attitudes. So, for example, a measure of attitude towards religion may be frequency of church attendance. Or, to take another example, the extent to which two people like each other may be reflected in the amount of eye-contact they engage in (the more two people look at each other, the more they like each other). But as will be seen in Section 3.7, behaviour may not always provide a good guide to attitudes.

Projective techniques take advantage of the fact that people often project their own attitudes on to others. Hence asking someone to, for example, fill in the balloons in Figures 3.3 and 3.4 may provide us with knowledge of the person's attitude to authority. Both examples are designed to investigate a person's attitude to authority; from responses given it may be inferred whether a person has a submissive or disrespectful attitude.

There are both advantages and disadvantages associated with indirect techniques of attitude measurement. The advantages are that such techniques are less likely to produce socially desirable responses, the person is unlikely to know what attitude is being measured, an indication of the

Figures 3.3 & 3.4: Examples of indirect, projective techniques for measuring a person's attitude. In figure 3.3 you are required to give an explanation for why you are late. In figure 3.4 you have to give an explanation for smoking. Adapted from Oppenheim (1992)

strength with which the attitude held is obtained, and the attitude is unlikely to be affected by being measured. The disadvantages are that it is difficult to measure an attitude directly (i.e. positive or negative); attitudes are inferred, and such methods are not as reliable as one would desire. In the case of physiological measures there exists conflicting evidence about their validity. Nevertheless, indirect measures often offer an appropriate approach when investigating highly sensitive social topics.

A measurement technique developed by Cacioppo and Tissinary (1990) purports to measure both the direction and intensity with which an attitude is held through measurement of a person's facial muscles. Measurement of facial muscles is made using the facial electromyograph (EMG), which detects minute muscle movements not normally visible to the human eye. A positive attitude is indicated by increased activity of the zygomatic muscles (see Figure 3.5). A negative attitude is indicated by increased activity in the corrugator muscles. Furthermore, it is proposed that the degree of activity of either sets of muscles is an indicator of the strength with which the attitude is held.

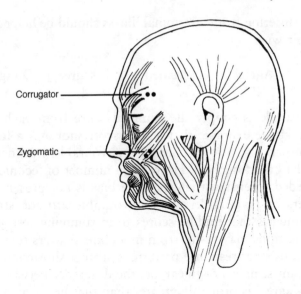

Figure 3.5: Facial muscle movement and attitudes. A positive attitude is associated with increase in the activity of zygomatic muscles; a negative attitude by increase in activity of corrugator muscles. Adapted from Cacioppo and Petty (1981)

3.4.2 Direct measures

Direct measures (rating scales) of attitudes are, perhaps, those best known since they commonly appear in magazines, newspapers, etc. Two approaches will be described: the Likert scale and the Semantic Differential. These are probably the most widely used rating scales in social psychology.

Likert (1932) developed a method of attitude measurement by summating responses to a considerable number of statements representative of the attitude in question, for example, if a social psychologist were interested in attitudes to euthanasia, a list of, say, 30 statements relevant to the topic would be generated. Half these should be favourable and half unfavourable. People would rate each statement on a five-point scale which would be drawn up as follows:

(1) It is the duty of doctors to keep people alive for as long as possible

Strongly Agree	Agree	Undecided	Strongly Disagree	Disagree
1	2	3	4	5

(2) People suffering from a terminal illness should be helped to die if it is their wish

Strongly Agree	Agree	Undecided	Strongly Disagree	Disagree
1	2	3	4	5

A person's attitude is simply the summed score from each question (notice in the above example that a high score indicates a favourable attitude to euthanasia, a low score an unfavourable attitude). This is the basis of the Likert method. However, a number of technical procedures are needed to ensure that response bias is not present, such as equal numbers of favourable and unfavourable attitude statements. One shortcoming is that middle scores from summing responses to a number of questions may result from moderate answers to each question or an inconsistent response pattern. A further shortcoming is that such a five-point scale is not linear, i.e. the difference between 'strongly agree' and 'agree' is probably greater than that between 'agree' and 'undecided'. Nevertheless, the Likert scale remains popular because it is both easy to construct and administer.

The Semantic Differential, developed by Osgood, Suci and Tannenbaum (1957), provides both a measure of attitude strength and further information concerning the significance of the attitude to the individual. The Semantic Differential entails the rating, on seven-point scales, of an attitude object (person or thing) using numerous bipolar adjective scales. For example, below is a number of bipolar adjectives related to attitudes to pornography:

			Pornography					
Good	__	__	__	__	__	__	__	Bad
Clean	__	__	__	__	__	__	__	Dirty
Beautiful	__	__	__	__	__	__	__	Ugly
Strong	__	__	__	__	__	__	__	Weak
Active	__	__	__	__	__	__	__	Passive
Cruel	__	__	__	__	__	__	__	Kind

People would simply be asked to place a tick above one of the dashes corresponding to how they feel about pornography in relation to that particular bipolar adjective. This would then be converted into a rating value rating from +3 through zero to –3.

The Semantic Differential provides three types of information about the attitude object: evaluative, potency and activity information. The *evaluative* dimension (in the above example, good–bad, clean–dirty, beautiful–ugly), measures the favourableness or unfavourableness towards the attitude object. The *potency* dimension (strong–weak, cruel–kind) and the *activity* dimension (active–passive) provide additional information about the significance of the attitude object to the individual whose attitude is being measured.

Generally, the evaluative dimension has been regarded as the most important of the three, as it is the dimension that measures the strength with which a person holds a particular attitude. The main advantage of the Semantic Differential is that the same bipolar adjectives are applied to different attitude objects. The main disadvantage is that these bipolar adjectives may not be applicable or appear relevant to a wide range of different attitude objects.

The expectancy-value approach of Fishbein and Ajzen (1975), discussed earlier, offers a way of measuring attitudes that asks a person: (a) to indicate the extent to which a belief is thought to be true; and (b) to evaluate, from extremely desirable to extremely undesirable, each of the attributes identified in (a). Table 3.1 provides a worked example and shows that the person has a very positive attitude towards the police (because each attribute is evaluated positively with those most positively evaluated thought to be true about the police).

This approach has proved popular in applied settings such as marketing, politics and family planning, since the features (beliefs) about the attitude object are specified. One problem, though, is achieving agreement between different researchers concerning the major features of beliefs.

Such direct methods used to measure attitudes are popular mainly because they are extremely easy to administer and construct, as well as providing reasonably valid and reliable measures. Considering both

	Beliefs	Evaluation
Attributes	On a scale of 0–10 rate the extent to which you believe the attributes to be true about the police	On a scale of –10 to +10 rate your evaluation of each of the attributes
Police are:		
Trustworthy	8	+10
Reliable	6	+8
Intelligent	7	+6
Quick to respond	3	+6

Table 3.1: Measuring a person's attitude towards the police using Fishbein & Ajzen's (1975) expectancy-value scale

direct and indirect measures of attitudes it would be true to say that there is room for improvement and refinement of techniques to make attitude measurement both more reliable and accurate. Part of the problem social psychologists experience in predicting behaviour from attitudes (see Section 3.7) comes from inappropriate or poorly constructed measuring instruments.

3.5 Attitude change and persuasion

In our everyday lives we are exposed to countless attempts to change our attitudes, strengthen existing attitudes and form new attitudes. Politicians, advertisers, friends and authority figures, to name but a few, try to persuade us round to their point of view. Advertisements for brand products, such as soap powders, are as much about maintaining customer loyalty as they are about winning new customers. In what follows we will be investigating different approaches to attitude change and persuasion. As we shall see, there is no simple recipe that guarantees success: in some circumstances people behave rationally, at other times people may make snap judgements. Additionally, an underlying assumption of all attempts at attitude change through persuasion is that behaviour will be affected.

3.5.1 Cognitive consistency and dissonance

The principle of *cognitive consistency* underlies much of what we mean when we talk about thinking and behaving as rational human beings. Essentially the idea is that people strive to maintain consistency between: (a) beliefs, values and attitudes; (b) attitudes, intentions and behaviour; and (c) different attitudes. Organising attitudes, beliefs and behaviour into internally consistent structures both underscores and presumes what we mean by human rationality. It follows, then, that a person placed in an *inconsistent* position will be motivated to reduce or avoid the inconsistency. However, people often find themselves holding two attitudes which are inconsistent and not wanting to change either, or continue to act in ways that conflict with their attitude (for example, thinking smoking is bad for you but continuing to smoke).

Festinger's (1957) theory of *cognitive dissonance* is the most widely researched cognitive consistency theory, and the main reason for this is that it offers a general theory of human social motivation. Dissonance was defined by Festinger (1957) as 'a negative drive state which occurs when an individual holds two cognitions (ideas, beliefs, attitudes) which are psychologically inconsistent'. Basically cognitive dissonance is an uncomfortable (negative) state of tension which a person wishes to change (drive) towards feeling comfortable. Festinger's original view was that any inconsistency would cause tension and hence dissonance. However, Cooper and Fazio (1984), in reviewing two decades of research on dissonance detailed four main conditions necessary for dissonance to occur. To understand dissonance better we will look at Festinger's often quoted example of cigarette smoking.

For a person who smokes cigarettes the fact 'I smoke cigarettes' and the knowledge that cigarette smoking causes lung cancer should produce a state of dissonance (assuming that the person cares about their health and does not wish to die). Cognitive consistency or consonance may be achieved in a number of ways: the person could (a) stop smoking; (b) try to ignore or refute the link between smoking and lung cancer; or (c) trivialise the importance of the discrepancy between attitudes and behaviour. No doubt you can think of other ways in which consistency could be achieved. One reason social psychologists have paid so much attention to cognitive dissonance is that *attitude change* is predicted to occur if there is no change in a person's behaviour to achieve consistency. Before looking at classic research demonstrating the breadth of application of cognitive dissonance we will detail the conditions identified by Cooper and Fazio (1984) as necessary for dissonance to occur.

▩ Conditions for dissonance

The first condition is that the person must be aware that an inconsistency between an attitude and a behaviour has negative consequences. Scher and Cooper (1989) demonstrated that when people see no problems or undesirable consequences arising between an attitude and behaviour, dissonance does not occur. In our smoking example, if a person believed that smoking did not cause lung cancer (or more generally ill-health), dissonance would not arise and change (of attitudes) would not take place. The second condition is that the person must take responsibility for the behaviour – in attributional terms (see Chapter 5) an *internal* attribution is made in which the behaviour is under our control and we choose to engage in it. A smoker freely chooses to smoke, but dissonance may not occur if the smoker regards his or her behaviour as an addiction or as a result of being forced to smoke (i.e. an *external* attribution).

The third condition is that physiological arousal must be felt. Losch and Cacioppo (1990) demonstrated that when people are put in a dissonant situation they show physiological arousal. However, evidence is needed that such physiological arousal is experienced as an unpleasant state. If this were not the case, there would be no motivation to change.

Elliot and Devine (1994) conducted an experiment whereby participants in one condition were asked to write an essay counter (i.e. opposite) to their own attitude – in this case students were asked to write in favour of increased tuition fees. In another condition, participants wrote essays against tuition fee increase. Participants in the counter-attitudinal condition provided significantly higher ratings of unpleasant feelings than participants who wrote essays consistent with their own attitudes.

The fourth condition identified by Cooper and Fazio (1984) is that the person must attribute the dissonance or discomfort felt to the inconsistency between their attitude and behaviour. When a person attributes the physiological arousal to something other than their behaviour (for example, some external factor), dissonance does not occur and no attitude (or behaviour) change results.

Table 3.2 summarises the above and provides, using the general example of smoking, instances which produce and do not produce dissonance. In summary, for dissonance to occur in relation to attitudes and behaviour, a person must be aware of inconsistency, take responsibility for the behaviour, experience negative physiological arousal and attribute that arousal to the inconsistency.

As mentioned earlier, the breadth of application of dissonance theory is the main reason social psychologists have conducted research on Festinger's (1957) original idea for over 40 years. Three areas have

Condition	Dissonance present	Dissonance absent
1. Attitude – behaviour inconsistency seen to have negative consequences	Smoking causes lung cancer	Research has not proved that smoking causes lung cancer
2. Person takes responsibility for their behaviour	It is my choice to smoke	Smoking is an addiction. I can't do anything about it
3. Negative physiological arousal experienced	I feel uncomfortable about the consequences of smoking	Avoid thinking about consequences of smoking
4. Arousal/discomfort attributed to inconsistency	I am concerned about my smoking	I feel discomfort because other people are always hassling me to stop smoking

Table 3.2: Conditions necessary for cognitive dissonance and ways in which dissonance may be avoided. After Cooper and Fazio, 1984

received considerable attention: decision-making, forced compliance behaviour and justification of effort.

Decision-making

Anyone who makes a decision in which the alternatives considered have both positive and negative consequences is predicted to experience 'post-decisional dissonance'. The important point to note is that dissonance is experienced only *after* a decision has been taken; this is because the alternative taken will nearly always embody both positive and negative aspects. The alternatives rejected, by contrast, may have positive features which are absent from the choice made. Cognitive dissonance arises for the decision-maker because the cognitions of having selected an alternative with negative aspects and rejected others with positive aspects means a trade-off has been made. The decision-maker expects and hopes the trade-off will prove worthwhile, but does not really know this at the time. An example will help clarify the points being made here.

Suppose you are trying to decide which car to buy, and, for sake of simplicity, further suppose the choice is between a Rover and a Peugeot. One approach to assist decision-making would be to draw up a checklist of the important features you are looking for in a car and see how the two makes compare. Table 3.3 summarises such an exercise. Assuming these six features are the important ones for you and that they are equally weighted (of equal importance), the make of car with the greatest number of positives, if we implement a simple decision rule, is the one to buy. So you go out and buy the Rover. It is now, having bought the car, that you will experience dissonance: this is because you have made a choice in which there are negative features (expensive, spares hard to get, etc.) and rejected a choice with some positive features (Peugeot is cheap, easy to get spares for, etc.).

Feature	Peugeot	Value	Rover	Value
Price	Relatively cheap	–	Expensive	–
Comfort	Hard and noisy	+	Smooth and quiet	+
Petrol	Not economical	–	Economical	+
Spares	Available and cheap	–	Hard to get and expensive	–
Servicing	Infrequent and cheap	+	Frequent and expensive	–
Reliability	Poor	+	Good	+

Table 3.3: Balance sheet of features considered when buying a car and how Peugeot and Rover compare on these features

One way in which dissonance may be reduced is by *bolstering* the alternative decided on, this means that consonant information will be *selectively* sought to make the choice taken seem even more attractive and the alternative rejected less attractive. Ehrlich *et al.* (1957) found that people who had just bought a new car looked at magazine articles and advertisements which praised their choice of purchase, and, at the same time, ignored or read reports criticising other alternatives considered but rejected.

Brehm (1956) further demonstrated that people downgrade the rejected alternative and upgrade the alternative taken. In this experiment a number of women were shown various household appliances, then asked to rate each appliance in terms of attractiveness.

Subsequently, each woman was given the choice of one of the two appliances she had rated most attractive. The women received the appliance of their choice and were asked to rate the two appliances again. Brehm found, as predicted by dissonance theory, that the appliance chosen was rated as more desirable and the rejected appliance as less desirable than before having made the choice.

Another way of reducing post-decisional dissonance is to trivialise positive aspects of the alternatives rejected (Simon *et al.*, 1995). Individual decision-making operates at many levels in our lives – from deciding what car to buy, through organisational decisions up to international levels in politics – but at all levels the phenomenon of *post-decisional* dissonance applies. Figure 3.6 summarises the decision-making process, and ways of reducing post-decisional dissonance. The point to emerge is that while pre-decisional behaviour may be rational, justification of the decision taken by cognitive bolstering or trivialisation of alternatives not taken (bolstering the chosen alternative and downgrading the merits of the rejected alternative) may not be rational.

Forced compliance behaviour

The less a person is paid for doing something against his or her beliefs or attitudes, the more he or she is likely to change those beliefs or attitudes. Conversely, the more a person is paid to do such a thing, the less he or she has to justify it to him or herself, consequently, the less likely are his or her attitudes to change. This is perhaps one of the more surprising predictions of cognitive dissonance theory. The prediction derives from dissonance theory since a state of dissonance arises for a person when he or she is unable to justify his or her behaviour. Hence, doing something you do not agree with or arguing for a position opposite to your own views or attitudes where there is insufficient justification (external reward of

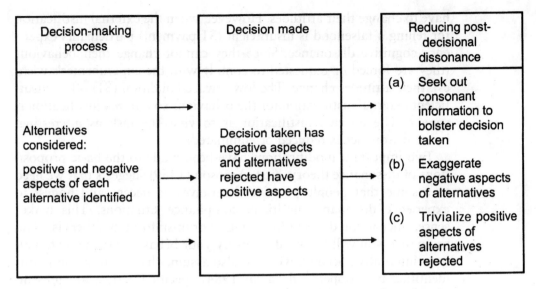

Figure 3.6: Post-decisional dissonance: how it occurs and how it may be reduced

money, for example) causes dissonance. The two cognitions, 'I am of such and such a view' and 'I am acting or arguing against my view' creates dissonance. Dissonance may be reduced by changing one of the cognitions: the person has already done or said something against his or her view so this cannot change (unless he or she distorts the past). In consequence, it is most likely that the person's own views will change to be consonant (or less dissonant) with his or her behaviour. This was first investigated in the classic experiment by Festinger and Carlsmith (1959).

Festinger and Carlsmith (1959) had students perform a very dull and boring task (turning pegs in a peg-board) for one hour. The students were then asked to tell another participant in the study, who was waiting to do the task, that the task was very interesting, worthwhile and good fun to do, i.e. they were asked to misinform the waiting participant. There were two experimental conditions: students asked to lie about the task were paid either $20 or $1 to do so. Festinger and Carlsmith were interested in the students' attitude to the task *after* telling the waiting participants that it was interesting. It was found that participants who were paid $20 rated the task, after performing it, as boring and of little relevance, whilst participants paid $1 rated the task, again after performing it, as interesting, relevant and enjoyable.

Findings from numerous forced-compliance experiments are explained in terms of justification. The claim is that when there is sufficient external justification ($20 in the Festinger and Carlsmith experiment) participants experience little, if any, dissonance and hence don't have to change their attitudes. However, when the external justification for telling a falsehood is insufficient ($1 payment) participants experience cognitive dissonance. Since they cannot change their behaviour (they are forced or requested to comply with the experimenter's wishes), their attitudes change. The low reward condition ($1) offers insufficient external justification for the behaviour so *internal* justification is sought. The internal justification is to view the task as interesting, hence dissonance is reduced or eliminated.

Two important modifications have been made to the basic propositions of dissonance theory. First, Aronson (1969) suggests that we need to assume that people perceive themselves as decent and honest to experience dissonance in forced-compliance situations. This makes sense, since if you do not think lying to or misinforming others is a bad thing then you will not need to justify your behaviour (either externally or internally). Second, we must also assume that the four conditions identified by Cooper and Fazio (1984) specified earlier, are present, only then can we say that post-decisional dissonance is present.

▓ Justifying effort

Before gaining acceptance to clubs, fraternities, groups, gangs, etc., there are often 'initiation rites' to go through. Dissonance theory explains how these 'rites of passage' serve a distinct social psychological function. The prediction is that the more effort a person puts into achieving a goal, the more attractive and worthwhile it is perceived to be when finally achieved. Dissonance theory states that *regardless* of how attractive, desirable, interesting, etc., the goal actually is, it is what a person goes through to achieve it that determines its worth. Why should a person experience dissonance here? If you gain membership to a club or society and have to go through 'hell and high water' to get this, you are likely to be extremely upset if you subsequently discover the club or society to be boring and worthless. Dissonance arises because the cognition 'I have put a lot of time and effort into gaining entry to this club' and 'the club is dull and worthless' are dissonant; people do not normally put a lot of time and effort into something useless. To reduce dissonance the person could leave the club or society he or she has just joined – this is unlikely since the person would have to acknowledge and accept that he or she had wasted time and effort. Festinger and Carlsmith predict the person will perceive the club or society to be interesting and worthwhile; this justifies the expenditure of time and effort.

Aronson and Mills (1959) devised an experiment to test this. They recruited women to join a group discussing the psychology of sex.

However, before the women could join the discussion group they were told they had to go through a screening test (the screening test being the 'initiation'). Participants were randomly allocated to one of three 'screening-test' conditions: (a) 'severe initiation' where the women had to recite aloud, in the presence of a male, obscene words and sexually explicit passages; (b) 'mild initiation', where women recited aloud sexual but not obscene words; (c) 'no initiation' where women were admitted to the discussion group without any screening.

After this the participants in each condition listened to what they thought was a live discussion of the psychology of sex (in fact all participants listened to the same tape recording of a discussion), which was deliberately made to be dull and boring. After listening to this boring discussion the participants were asked how much they liked it, found it interesting and worthwhile, etc. Aronson and Mills found, consistent with the prediction of dissonance theory, that participants who had gone through the 'severe initiation' found the discussion interesting and worthwhile. Participants admitted to the discussion without any initiation thought it dull and boring, while 'mild initiation' participants found the discussion only slightly interesting and worthwhile. Generally, research has found that whatever we put effort into may result in dissonance and hence attitude change (Axsom and Cooper, 1985) and the more effort put in, the more something is liked (Wicklund and Brehm, 1976).

Summary

Cognitive dissonance theory has attracted a great deal of research because of its wide range of application. The dissonance arousing aspects of decision-making, forced-compliance behaviour and justifying effort have all shown that while the desire to achieve harmony or consonance may be rational, the means of achieving it often is not. More recent research has identified the conditions necessary for dissonance to occur and shown that physiological arousal resulting from inconsistency between attitude and behaviour can be measured. Finally, Axsom and Cooper (1985) further demonstrated that attitude change resulting from attempts to reduce dissonance may be long-lasting and persist for a year or more.

3.5.2 Self-perception theory

Bem (1967) pointed out that our actual behaviour often determines what attitude we hold. So to quote one of Bem's examples, 'since I eat brown bread then I must like brown bread'. Applying this logic to the

Festinger and Carlsmith study described above, Bem would say that since the participants are telling the other that the peg-board task is interesting then they find it to be so.

Self-perception theory states that a person *forms* his or her attitudes through self-observation of behaviour, followed by a self-attribution of a consistent attitude. In Bem's approach there is no need, as he says, 'to postulate an aversive motivational drive toward consistency' but it is important to ask how general an explanation of attitude formation and change this approach can offer. In cases where a person does *not* already possess an attitude or set of beliefs towards something, behaviour may be a good guide to attitudes. However, when a person already holds a strong attitude, self-perception theory would seem less applicable.

To understand *attitude formation* self-perception theory may be very useful, but in looking at *attitude change* the approach seems less productive.

3.5.3 Traditional approach to persuasion (Yale studies)

The classic studies of Janis and Hovland (1959) investigated how the three factors of source of the communication, structure of the message and who the message is aimed at may affect attitude change. Most of this research was concerned with how persuasive communications associated with advertising may change or strengthen attitudes. Janis and Hovland proposed that attitude change resulting from source factors occurred because such factors influenced the amount of *attention* paid to the communication; message factors influenced the comprehensibility of the message for the audience; and audience factors resulting in attitude change occurred because of acceptance by the audience of the communication. This, as well as the specific variables studied for each of the factors, is summarised in Figure 3.7.

Hovland *et al.* (1953) have shown that the source (the person making the communication) is more likely to be effective if that person is seen as, for example, trustworthy or an expert in the field. The motives of the source are also important – Walster *et al.* (1966) showed that a person who argued for a position against their own best interest was perceived as more credible (and hence more influential) than a person who argued for a position in their own best interests (resulting in little influence over others). If a murderer asks to be hanged you can believe they are telling the truth!

The message itself in a persuasive communication has been looked at in two main ways: first, fear appeals; second, organisation of message. Are strong or weak fear appeals more effective in changing attitudes? It

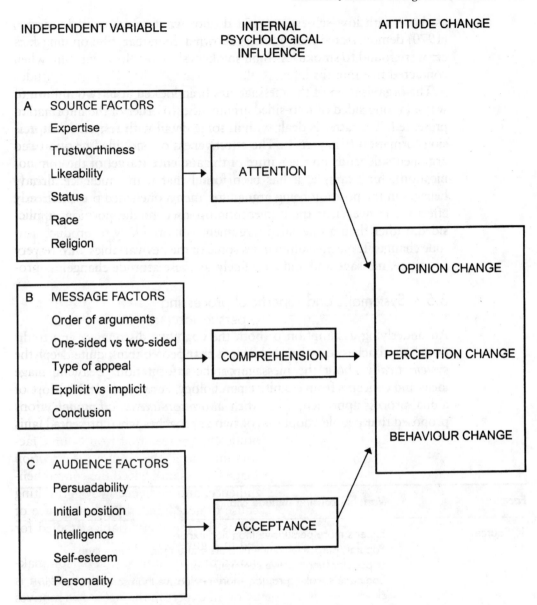

INDEPENDENT VARIABLE   INTERNAL   ATTITUDE CHANGE
PSYCHOLOGICAL
INFLUENCE

A   SOURCE FACTORS
   Expertise
   Trustworthiness
   Likeability
   Status
   Race
   Religion

ATTENTION

B   MESSAGE FACTORS
   Order of arguments
   One-sided vs two-sided
   Type of appeal
   Explicit vs implicit
   Conclusion

COMPREHENSION

C   AUDIENCE FACTORS
   Persuadability
   Initial position
   Intelligence
   Self-esteem
   Personality

ACCEPTANCE

OPINION CHANGE

PERCEPTION CHANGE

BEHAVIOUR CHANGE

Figure 3.7: Diagram showing how different types of persuasive communication (independent variable) have psychological influence which results in attitude change. After Janis and Houland (1959)

depends: for example, people high in self-esteem are more likely to be influenced a long time after the high fear appeal. This has been further refined by Baumeister and Covington (1985) who found that in other circumstances people with high self-esteem are just as easily persuaded as those with low self-esteem, but do not want to admit it! Leventhal (1970) demonstrated that smokers shown a 'high fear' film on lung cancer were found to smoke less than smokers shown a 'low fear' film when contacted five months later.

The organisation of the message has been looked at in two important ways: (a) one-sided or two-sided arguments; (b) order of the information presented. The latter is dealt with in some detail with respect to impression formation (Chapter 4). The effectiveness of one-sided or two-sided arguments depends on the nature of the audience (target of the communication), for example, it has been found that if the audience already believes in the position being argued for, then a one-sided presentation is effective. However, if the audience is opposed to the position, a two-sided, rather than a one-sided, argument is more likely to produce attitude change. Table 3.4 summarises some of the key variables with respect to source, message and audience likely to cause attitude change.

3.5.4 Systematic and superficial processing

An underlying assumption of both the cognitive dissonance and traditional approaches to attitude change is that people think quite deeply or *systematically* about the message or the information. Drawing upon ideas and concepts from cognitive psychology, Petty *et al.* (1994) propose a dual-process approach, called the *elaboration-likelihood model*, which proposed that people adopt one of two approaches when presented with

Factor	Variable causing attitude change
1. Source	Experts more persuasive than non-experts Popular/attractive communicators cause more change than unpopular/unattractive communicators Someone speaking rapidly more persuasive than someone speaking slowly
2. Message	High fear appeals cause more change than low fear appeals Message not intended to persuade more likely to cause change than if seen as intended
3. Audience	People with low self-esteem generally easier to persuade than people with high self-esteem Hostile audiences more persuaded by a two-sided argument rather than one side being presented

Table 3.4: Source, message and audience variables causing attitude change

attitude-relevant information. People may process information given in a persuasive communication either *superficially* or *systematically*. When using superficial processing to deal with information a person will not spend much time analysing the information but respond using rules of thumb (heuristics, see Chapter 4) or more 'automatic' responses. In this case the information will not be elaborated very much. Attitude change resulting from superficial processing is described by Petty and Cacioppo (1986) as taking a *peripheral route*. By contrast, when using systematic processing a person will invest considerable cognitive effort in understanding and analysing the information. Attitude change resulting from systematic processing has taken what has been called a *central route*. Attitude change through the central route will depend on the quality of arguments and information presented. By contrast, attitude change through the peripheral route will depend upon areas that are responded to in a more 'automatic' or less thought out way. Figure 3.8 depicts the details of the elaboration-likelihood model.

What determines whether high elaboration (central route) or low elaboration (peripheral route) of the persuasive communication occurs? Petty and Cacioppo (1990) identified two main factors – a person's motivation and cognitive capacity. If a person is highly motivated, and has the time and ability (cognitive capacity) to process the information, the central route will be used. Where motivation is low and/or cognitive capacity is limited the peripheral route will be used.

A person's *motivation* is affected by concern for accuracy, self-relevance and certain personality factors. When investigating personality factors such as need for cognition Cohen (1957) and Cacioppo *et al.*, (1983) found that people with a high need for cognition are more likely to elaborate information and hence take the central route to attitude change. People who have a concern for accuracy and find information of great personal relevance are also more likely to take the central route to attitude change.

Cognitive capacity is determined by three things: a person's cognitive ability, relevant knowledge possessed and the absence of distractions. Hence, where there is ability, knowledge and no distractions, the central route will be used; conversely, lack of ability, little knowledge and the presence of distractions is most likely to result in the use of the peripheral route.

Research has demonstrated that attitude change which results from the central route is more enduring than change resulting from the peripheral route (Petty and Cacioppo, 1986). Furthermore, behaviour is more consistent with attitudes when the change occurs through the central route. Attitude change resulting from the peripheral route is

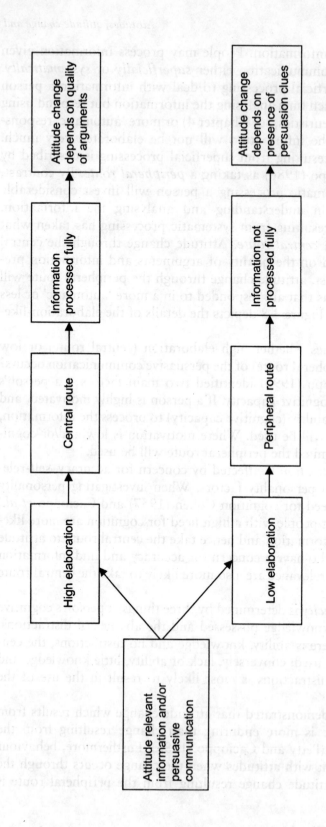

Figure 3.8: The elaboration-likelihood model of attitude change, based on Perry and Cacioppo (1986)

likely to be relatively short term and behaviour less likely to be consistent with attitudes. Figure 3.9 summarises what has been said above.

A variation of the elaboration-likelihood model called the heuristic-systematic model has been proposed by Chaiken *et al.* (1989). The systematic aspect is virtually identical to that described above. Heuristic processing of information represents one type of superficial processing. Heuristics of thinking (see Chapter 4) are simple rules that people use to make rapid decisions or judgements. For example, a simple rule might be 'statements made by experts are to be trusted', hence an expert providing support to a persuasive communication may influence a person to change their attitude. Any thought about the communication itself is not needed since it is 'underwritten' by an expert and experts are trusted. Other heuristics that might be used are feeling good or bad about something where we like what we feel good about (Schwarz and Clore, 1988); or an 'attractiveness heuristic' where we think attractive people are likeable and that we tend to agree with people we like, for example, Chaiken (1979) showed that attractive people can be more persuasive than people not judged to be attractive; Pallak (1983) demonstrated this in an experiment on product advertising. In summary, attitude change and persuasion can come about both through superficial and systematic processing of information. However, the effect is more enduring when the central route (systematic processing) is used. Heuristics are an aspect of the peripheral route (superficial processing) that allow us to make quick judgements.

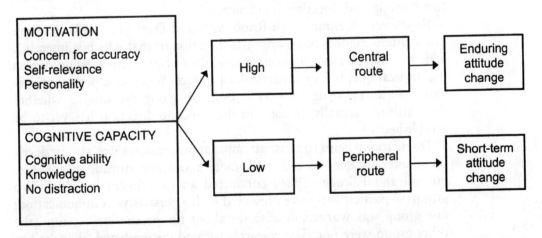

Figure 3.9: Effects of high and low motivation on central and peripheral routes and permanence of attitude change

3.5.5 Cultural differences

Hofstede (1980) reported a social psychological study of over 40 countries. One result of his analysis was to classify countries using just a few dimensions. One dimension was labelled 'individualism-collectivism' which is to do with whether a person's identity is characterised by personal choice and achievements or collective harmony and group belongingness. Hofstede found North Americans to fall into the former category and Asians the latter category. If this is the case, different types of persuasive communications should be effective in each culture. Han and Shavitt (1993) analysed American advertisements and found that on the whole they promoted individualism such as personal success and independence. By contrast, Korean advertisements had strong themes of collective harmony. This research also showed that advertisements promoting individuality were more persuasive to Americans than those promoting family and shared values. The reverse was found with Koreans.

3.6 Resisting attitude change

In our everyday social life we are constantly bombarded by attempts to change our attitudes; this may come from friends, colleagues at work, the media, etc. If we were susceptible to all persuasive communications our attitudes and behaviour would be constantly changing. Strongly held attitudes are resistant to change, and social psychologists have explored three main ways in which we resist attitude change: reactance, forewarning and selective avoidance.

Reactance (Brehm, 1966; Rhodewalt and Davison, 1983) is where our attitude changes in an *opposite* direction to that which is intended. This may happen in situations where a lot of pressure is being put on us, for example, to buy a particular product. Whether a person merely expresses an opposite view as a result of strong pressure or whether their attitude actually changes in the opposite direction has yet to be established.

Forewarning helps to resist attempts at persuasion since we can develop counter-arguments, and think more about our attitude in advance. Hiromi and Fakuda (1986) conducted an experiment in which two groups of participants were presented with a persuasive communication; one group was warned in advance about the persuasion attempt, the other group were not. The researcher found, as predicted, that the latter group showed more attitude change than the former group. This approach of forewarning has been found to be particularly effective in 'inoculating' young children (four to eight year olds) against television advertising (Feschback, 1980).

Selective avoidance is a strategy often used to avoid information that challenges our attitudes; in research on cognitive dissonance the converse is found whereby people seek out information that confirms their attitude or decision (Brehm, 1956). To resist attempts to persuade, people adopt a strategy that results in selected exposure to information. This means that attitudes may be maintained even though objectively there is sufficient good evidence to justify change. Selective avoidance may not, therefore, be a rational approach to dealing with attitude relevant information.

3.7 Attitudes and behaviour

At the beginning of this chapter it was stated that attitudes have a central place in social psychology, and one important reason for this is that attitudes determine behaviour (Allport, 1935). Early research, as we shall see, reported a poor relationship between attitudes and behaviour. However, more recently social psychologists have looked closely at *how* and *when* attitudes influence behaviour. The picture that emerges is more complex than originally thought.

La Piere (1934) conducted what has now come to be regarded as a classic study. La Piere travelled around America with a Chinese student and his wife and recorded how the two Chinese people were treated in numerous hotels and restaurants. On only one occasion were they treated inhospitably. Six months later La Piere sent a letter to all the places he had visited with the Chinese couple and asked the restaurants and hotels if they would accept Chinese clientele. The surprising result was that over 90 per cent of the replies to the letter were negative: Chinese people would not be welcome. Figure 3.10 summarises the findings.

The apparent inconsistency of people saying one thing and doing something different is of major interest to attitude-behaviour research. Why should this discrepancy exist? Many reasons come to mind, for example, inaccurate measurements, not taking account of how strongly a person holds an attitude, or attempting to relate general attitudes to specific behaviour as in the La Piere study (general attitudes to Chinese people against specific attitudes to a Chinese couple accompanied by an American).

Defleur and Westie (1958) attempted to relate specific attitudes to specific behaviours to overcome the problems of the La Piere study. They asked a large number of white people specific questions about blacks and whites in order to gain a measure of prejudice. This allowed

Percentage accepting
Chinese clientele

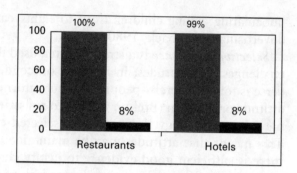

Figure 3.10: Responses to actual visits and letters to owners of hotels and restaurants to serving Chinese people. After La Piere (1934)

them to identify prejudiced and unprejudiced people. Participants in both groups were asked to pose for a photograph with a black person. Prejudiced people were less willing to do this than unprejudiced people. Generally, research has found that a better attitude-behaviour link is found where the level of specificity of attitude and behaviour is the same.

3.7.1 Reasoned action and planned behaviour

Fishbein and Ajzen (1975) suggest that behaviour may be more accurately predicted if we know about a person's intentions with respect to behaving in a particular way. This is the basic idea behind their *theory of reasoned action*. The theory takes into account subjective norms (normative beliefs about appropriate and inappropriate behaviour), attitudes towards the behaviour (determined from expectancies and values described when we looked at attitude measurement – Section 3.4) and behavioural intention to predict behaviour. This is summarised in Figure 3.11.

Using this model Fishbein *et al.* (1980) found a good correlation between voting intentions and how people actually voted in both an American Presidential election and a referendum on nuclear power. One shortcoming of the theory of reasoned action is that it does not take into account whether the behaviour is under the control of a person, i.e. how easy or difficult it would be for a person to behave in a certain way. For example, you may intend to achieve a high mark for an assignment but there may be many factors outside of your control (availability of books, time, etc.) which may prevent this. To take this into account Ajzen (1989) modified the theory to incorporate a person's *perceived behavioural control*. This is called the theory of *planned behaviour*. Perceived behavioural control influences both the behavioural intention and the behaviour itself (as represented in Figure 3.11). Beck and Ajzen (1991) investigated this theory by asking students to indicate ways in which they had been dishonest. The dishonest behaviour ranged from cheating in examinations, or shoplifting to telling lies. Students were also asked to indicate how much control they thought they had over each of these behaviours. It was found that cheating in the future could be better predicted than shoplifting. This may be explained by the finding that students reported greater perceived control over cheating than shoplifting. This indicates that the latter may be more of a spontaneous behaviour, and cheating a more planned behaviour.

Overall, the approach of Fishbein and Ajzen has resulted in a much better understanding of the attitude-behaviour link and how attitudes, mediated through behavioural intentions, influence actual behaviour. However, while this may work quite well when we have time to think and plan what we do, there are many occasions when our behaviour appears to be more *automatic* and not thought about carefully or planned.

3.7.2 Automatic behaviour

Fazio (1989) proposed an approach in which easily accessed attitudes that quickly come to mind, spontaneously almost, have an automatic influence on behaviour. This is most likely to happen with more general, rather than specific, attitudes, for example, if somebody comes up

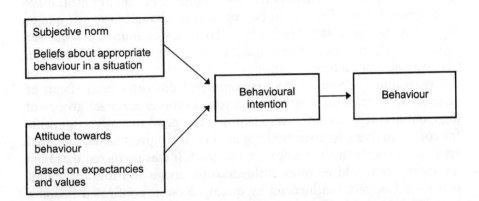

Figure 3.11: Key components in Fishbein & Ajzen's (1975) theory of reasoned action

to you in the street asking you to fill in a questionnaire, your behaviour is most likely to be related to your general attitude towards people requesting your time in public places. Additionally, as stated above, the attitude must be readily *accessible,* and Fazio (1986) proposes that the greater the accessibility of the attitude, the more consistency there will be between attitudes and behaviour. For example, attitudes based on personal experience are likely to be more vividly recalled from memory and hence more accessible. Attitudes that are constantly brought to mind will have greater accessibility as shown in an experiment by Powell and Fazio (1984).

3.7.3 Personality variables

Behaviour may not be consistent with attitudes because some people may simply not behave in ways consistent with what they believe. If this is the case neither methodological or theoretical advances, as described earlier in this chapter, will be of much use. Self-monitoring (Snyder, 1979) offers a way of accounting for poor attitude-behaviour relations by saying that some people *do* behave in consistent ways (low self-monitor) while others *do not* (high self-monitor). The behaviour of the high self-monitor is determined more by the demands of the social situation and behaviour appropriate to that social situation (for example, social norms).

The low self-monitor exhibits a high degree of consistency between attitudes and behaviour since behaving according to one's own beliefs and attitudes is the prime consideration for this personality type. The high self-monitor, by contrast, may seem to others like a different person in different social situations with different people present.

The self-monitoring personality dimension has implications for research on cognitive dissonance, for example, in counter-attitudinal tasks low self-monitors would be expected to change their attitude to be consistent with their behaviour. High self-monitors would not change their attitudes as they would see it as appropriate to behave in that way in that kind of situation.

Snyder and De Bono (1985) demonstrated the differential effects of advertising on high and low self-monitors. In this experiment groups of high and low self-monitors were exposed to one of two advertisements for coffee. In one advertisement the quality of the produce was emphasised, in the other the image was emphasised. It was predicted that high self-monitors would be more influenced by image and low self-monitors would be more influenced by quality. Results confirmed this and found that not only did high self-monitors prefer coffee when advertised by image but they were willing to pay for it!

In summary, early research questioned the link between attitudes and behaviour. More recent theoretical developments have highlighted the importance of knowing a person's behavioural intentions, how much perceived control there is over behaviour and whether there is time to plan a behavioural response or whether circumstances produce a more automatic action. The picture is more complicated than once thought, but social psychologists now understand *how* and *when* attitudes related to behaviour much more fully.

3.8 Application: attitudes and health

Health psychologists are concerned to understand both health and illness from social, psychological, individual and psychophysiological perspectives (Taylor, 1995). In attempts to change people's behaviour to a more healthy lifestyle, health promotion campaigns often attempt to change our attitudes. Social psychologists have contributed greatly in the past ten years or so. For example, Baron and Richardson (1994) have shown that a persuasive communication which induces fear results in people paying more attention to a message than if fear is absent. This should have the consequence of encouraging *systematic processing* of information and a *planned-action* approach to behaving. However, if the fear in a message is made to be personally relevant attitude, change may be resisted through avoidance and defensiveness (Liberman and Chaiken, 1992).

A study investigating the effect of different mass media campaigns aimed at getting people to change behaviours to reduce their risks of cardiovascular disease was conducted by Maccoby *et al.* in 1977, and followed through over ten years later by Perlman (1990). In this study three American towns in the same state were subjected to different campaigns over a two-year period. In one town the campaign was conducted through the mass media – television, radio, leaflets, etc. In the second town the same media campaign was conducted together with workshops available for individuals who were in the higher risk categories. The third town was the control condition and received no media campaign or instructions for higher risk categories. The researchers took measures of (a) change in knowledge about cardiovascular diseases; and (b) behavioural changes in the high risk categories. Greatest behavioural change was found in the town that was given both the media campaign and workshops. Figure 3.12 shows that the greatest increase in knowledge was in the same town.

The media campaign plus workshops was most effective in changing

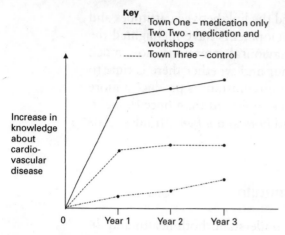

Key
.... Town One – medication only
——— Two Two - medication and workshops
------ Town Three – control

Increase in knowledge about cardio-vascular disease

0   Year 1   Year 2   Year 3

Figure 3.12: Change in knowledge about cardiovascular disease in three towns exposed to different campaigns

attitudes, and maintaining consequent changes in behaviour. This approach is most likely to invoke the systematic or central route to attitude change. In line with claims made in Section 3.5.4 earlier, attitude change has been found to be more enduring and those attitudes to be more consistent with behaviour. The findings of this study seen in the context of systematic processing of information to bring about attitude change may offer health psychologists powerful ways of promoting healthy behaviour in people.

3.9 Summary

- Social psychologists regard attitudes as central and fundamental to understanding social thought and behaviour. Attitudes are important for understanding stereotyping, prejudice and interpersonal attraction.
- Most social psychologists regard learning through direct or indirect experience as the major explanation for the formation of attitudes; some evidence from twin studies offers a genetic explanation for attitude formation.
- Attitudes may be seen to serve both structural and functional purposes for a person. The structural approach relates attitudes to values, beliefs, intentions and behaviour. The functional approach concerns adaptive, knowledge, ego-expressional and self-expressive functions.
- Attitudes may be measured by both direct and indirect means. Indirect measures, such as physiological or projective techniques, are less reliable but not so obtrusive as direct measures such as the Likert and Semantic Differential rating scales.
- The principles of cognitive consistency state that attitudes are related to other attitudes, beliefs and behaviour in a consistent way. Cognitive dissonance occurs under poor conditions and is a general theory of human social motivation.
- The conditions for cognitive dissonance are: person must be aware of inconsistency between attitude and behaviour; the person must take responsibility for the behaviour; physiological arousal must be felt; and, person must attribute discomfort to the attitude – behaviour inconsis-tency.
- Research on cognitive dissonance has focused on the three main areas of decision-making, forced-compliance behaviour and justification of effort.

- The traditional approach to persuasion (Yale studies) investigated the factors of source of communication, structure of message and who the message was aimed at. A range of variables for each of these factors has been found to cause attitude change.
- The elaboration-likelihood model proposes that people may adapt one of two approaches to information: superficial or systematic. Superficial information processing results in low elaboration with the person following a peripheral route. Systematic results in high elaboration causing the person to follow a central route.
- High motivation and/or high cognitive capacity will usually lead to a person following a central (high elaboration) route. Attitude change is more enduring when information is processed through a central route.
- Cultural differences have shown Americans to be more influenced by advertisements emphasising individuality while advertisements emphasising collectivity had greater influence over Asians.
- People may resist persuasive communications and attitude change through reactance, forewarning and selective avoidance.
- Social psychologists have had an enduring interest in how and when attitudes influence behaviour. The classic study of La Piere demonstrated a poor link; however, a general attitude should not be compared with a specific attitude in this context.
- Fishbein and Ajzen's theory of reasoned action takes into account subjective norms, a person's attitude towards the behaviour and behavioural intentions in predicting behaviour from knowledge of a person's attitudes.
- The theory of reasoned action was modified to take account of the perceived control a person has over the behaviour; this is called the theory of planned behaviour.
- Fazio proposed that attitudes which come readily and easily to mind may have an automatic influence on behaviour. This happens for general attitudes and attitudes that are readily accessible.
- The study of attitudes has received extensive application in health psychology. Theory and research here aim to change both attitudes and behaviour to promote a healthy lifestyle.

3.10 Suggestions for further reading

Eagly, A. H. and Chaiken, S. 1993: *The Psychology of Attitudes.* San Diego: Harcourt, Brace, Jovanovich.

Provides a comprehensive, readable and reasonably up-to-date review of theory, research and advances in the general field of attitudes.

Hewstone, M., Stroebe, W. and Stephenson, G. M. (ed.) 1996: *Introduction to Social Psychology.* Oxford: Blackwell Publishers.

Provides two good chapters on attitude structure, measurement and function, and attitude formation and change by leading European researchers. Up-to-date with good critical analysis.

Oppenheim, A. N. 1992: *Questionnaire Design, Interviewing and Attitude Measurement.* 2nd edition. London: Pinter.

Second edition of a classic text expanded to include more on the pros and cons of different approaches to attitude measurement. Good advice for avoiding pitfalls when designing a study to measure attitudes.

Stroebe, W. and Stroebe, M. S. 1995: *Social Psychology and Health.* Buckingham: Open University Press.

Follows on from the application given in this chapter to show a wider range of ways in which theory, concepts and principles in attitudes and attitude change apply to a variety of health aspects.

4 Social cognition I: Perception of self and others

4.1 Introduction

This chapter and Chapter 5 introduce a particular approach in social psychology, known as *social cognition*. Cognition can be defined as the way in which people acquire, process, organise and use knowledge and information. The central components of cognitive psychology are attention, perception, memory, thought and language (Eysenck and Keane, 1995). Social cognition is therefore concerned with these same topics but in a social context – that is, what people attend to, perceive and remember about themselves and other people. It specifically takes into account how different social situations and contexts influence these cognitive processes within people. Social cognition can be defined as the manner in which we interpret, analyse, remember and use information about our social world (Baron and Byrne, 1997). This chapter specifically deals with the basic components of social thought: schemas and prototypes. These can be defined as mental structures or frameworks which allow us to organise large amounts of diverse information in an efficient manner (Fiske and Taylor, 1991). Once schemes and prototypes are formed, they tend to be stable and persistent, exerting a strong influence on how we process new information. The accuracy of our information processing can therefore be questioned, as it is inevitable that we have to take short cuts to deal with potentially large amounts of information.

Chapter 5 is concerned with *attribution theory,* which involves the process by which people attribute causes for their own and others' behaviour. Central to the attribution process is the distinction between causes which are internal to the person (that is, dispositional or due to personality traits), or external to the person and due to the situational or environmental factors. This chapter will begin by analysing the processes and components involved in social perception.

4.2 Social perception

4.2.1 Categorisation

Categorisation is a process basic to perception. It refers to how we identify stimuli, and group them together as members of a particular category, similar to other items in that category, and different from members of another category. Categorisation occurs automatically, with little cognitive effort. For example, it is simple to categorise a book, tree or animal. As soon as items are categorised, order is imposed on what would otherwise be a very complex social world and physical environment. We also put ourselves into categories, for instance, when we complete an application form, we are asked to categorise ourselves in relation to gender, ethnicity, age and marital status. As well as hair colouring or physical build, personality trait, etc., there are an infinite number of categories that we use to make sense of ourselves and other people.

4.2.2 Prototypes

Rosch and Mervis (1975) proposed that some members of a category are more representative than other members and these are called prototypes. This can be demonstrated using the category of 'birds', for instance, sparrows and robins are more representative of birds than penguins because an important distinguishing feature of birds is that they fly. Therefore, members of a category can be on a continuum from typical to atypical with the prototype or most typical best representing the category. Cantor and Mischel (1979) suggest that prototypicality is defined in relation to the number of characteristics that a category member shares with other members and the fewer items that it shares with members of another category, the more prototypical it is deemed to be. Cantor and Mischel goes on to suggest that prototypical people are quicker to process information, hence making it easier to predict their behaviour. An example may help clarify what is meant here. Imagine the attributes you associate with Hell's Angels motor cyclists – these may be:

rides a Harley-Davidson motorcycle, wears leather jacket with denim waistcoat, rejects conventional society, is violent and dangerous. These are what you might call typical qualities of members of this group. Whenever you see someone dressed like a Hell's Angel – or riding a Harley-Davidson, etc. – you will try to 'fit' the person to the social category. The prototype has the key aspects described above, but the particular person you are trying to categorise may only have a sub-set of these qualities. In doing this you will make a judgement of best fit. Figure 4.1 summarises this.

From the example of the individual shown in Figure 4.1 you would probably have difficulty deciding whether to categorise the individual as a Hell's Angel or not. However, if you substitute 'works as motorcycle mechanic' for 'works as teacher' you could probably have no difficulty in the categorisation.

We hold 'mental models' or mental prototypes of many different aspects of people; racial groups, professionals such as lawyers or doctors, homosexuals, psychologists, etc. In a sense a prototype is an 'ideal type' and what each of us does when meeting a specific person is categorise that person according to the salient features which may fit into one or more of the prototypes we hold in our mind. Prototypes are strongly determined by societal, cultural and development factors.

4.2.3 The concept of schema

A concept related to prototypes is that of schema. This can be defined as a *mental framework* containing information relevant to self, other people, specific situations or events. Schemas, or schemata, are established on the basis of previous experience, cultural and social norms or a preconceived understanding. Once schemas are established, they help us to interpret new situations and guide our behaviour. Fiske and

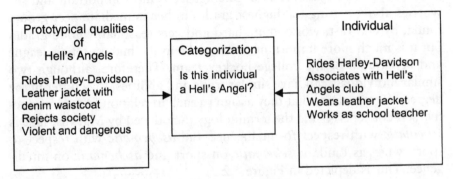

Figure 4.1: Fitting an individual to the prototype of 'Hell's Angel'

Taylor (1991) have identified four main types of schema which all serve similar functions in terms of encoding new information and memory for old information. These four types are: self schemas, person schemas, role schemas and event schemas, which are dealt with below. Schemas also lead us to make inferences, in the absence of other or further information, which can result in erroneous judgements being made about people or events.

4.3 Schema types

Fiske and Taylor (1991) identified four main schema types: self, person, role and event schemas, all of which serve vital functions in our processing of information. Self schemas will be discussed first and in more detail, as they are the starting point of our processing of information about other people and events.

4.3.1 Self schemas

Self schemas can be defined as cognitive generalisations about the self based on past experience. They organise and guide the processing of self-related information (Markus, 1977). Self schemas form the cognitive component of the self-concept and are organised around the specific traits or features which we think of as most central and important to our own self-image.

Schematic traits are those that we use most often when we define who we are. They have the most impact on how we feel about ourselves and for this reason are closely related to our self-esteem. Self-esteem is the affective part of the self and is the value or worth that we place on ourselves. Each individual is likely to have different traits or features which are most central to their self-concepts. For example, two college students Jane and Linda, might both be moderately intelligent and also good at sport. For Jane, level of intelligence is most important and she worries about getting the highest grades in her immediate peer group. Linda, by contrast, works quite hard and gets reasonably good grades but it is much more important to her to be in the highest tennis league and be captain of the college hockey team. Therefore, although two similar individuals can have similar traits and abilities, they differ in the degree of importance that they assign to each in relation to their respective self-concepts. Using the terminology introduced by Markus, Jane is *schematic* with respect to intelligence and *aschematic* with respect to sport, whereas Linda is *schematic* on sport and *aschematic* on intelligence. This is depicted in Figure 4.2.

Markus (1977) believes that we respond differently to incoming

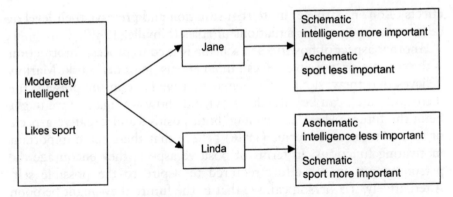

Figure 4.2: Self-schemas and the concepts of schematic and aschematic

information depending on its relevance or irrelevance to our schematic traits. Markus and her colleagues have researched several dimensions of the self in relation to this, with similar results. For example, in one experiment moderately overweight females were classified as either schematic or aschematic with respect to body weight. It was found that schematic respondents processed silhouettes of a fat person quicker than those of a thin or neutral silhouette (Markus *et al.*, 1987).

While any schema information is powerful in processing new information, there is the question of whether each individual has a single self schema that is active in all situations or a number of different self schemas for different areas of their lives. This could be related to the role schema, to be discussed later, as most individuals have a number of roles in their lives. Working mothers, for instance, juggle their time between trying to be efficient and organised in the workplace and caring and nurturing at home. Their schematic and aschematic traits may therefore differ depending on which context they are in.

Linville (1985) suggested that individuals differ in the degree to which their self-concept is organised into sub-structures to accommodate multiple roles. She refers to the dimension of *self-complexity* which relates to the degree to which individuals perceive themselves differently or in much the same way across different situations or roles. Individuals are considered low in self-complexity if they rely on one self schema, or high in self-complexity if they have a number of self schemas relevant to the roles they play. Self-complexity, according to Linville, has important implications to a person's self-esteem. For instance, if a stressful event occurs in one area of a person's life which affects their self-image, if they are low in self-complexity the effects are likely to spill over into other areas of their life. However, having high self-complexity acts as a buffer because the individual can contain the effects of one negative event to that situation and preserve their level of self-esteem across other situations or roles (Linville, 1987).

Another aspect of how the self schema is used to process information is the concept of 'possible selves'. In an extension of her work, Markus believes that the various self schemas that we have in the present, the 'here and now', can be extended to include how we imagine we might be in the future. These can include both positive and negative aspects of self. Markus and Nurius (1986) believe that these serve important motivating functions. In terms of positive aspects they encourage the person to put in the effort required to aspire to the possible self. Alternatively, if a person can see that in the future they might be poor, depressed, homeless, etc., they are motivated to take precautions to avoid these outcomes. Ruvolo and Markus (1992) believe that encouraging the perception of future selves strongly affects performance and motivation in the present. Higgins (1987) suggests there are three other types of self schema, which have implications regarding how an individual feels about themself. They are:

1 Actual self – how we are at present.
2 Ideal self – how we would like to be.
3 Ought self – how we think we should be.

If there is a wide discrepancy between the actual and the ideal self schemas, self-esteem is likely to be low. Discrepancy between the actual and ought self schema is likely to cause anxiety, threat or even fear. Figure 4.3 provides an example of this.

The best way to resolve the discrepancy and consequent effects on self-esteem and feelings of threat if you find yourself in this situation is to work harder for the examinations. You probably knew this all along! These three types of self proposed by Higgins (1987) are reminiscent of Freud's (1932) concepts of ego, reality and superego, where the superego consists of the ego-ideal (ideal self here) and conscience (ought self here).

4.3.2 Person schemas

Person schemas are mental structures which represent knowledge about the traits or goals either of a particular type of person or a known individual (Fiske and Taylor, 1991). For instance, if somebody asks the question, 'What is X or Y like?', you are likely to answer in terms of your person schema and, for example, may use *extrovert* to describe X or Y. The other person, having this knowledge, will be able to anticipate how the X or Y might behave in a future meeting, since it is likely that a schema for an extrovert is held mentally.

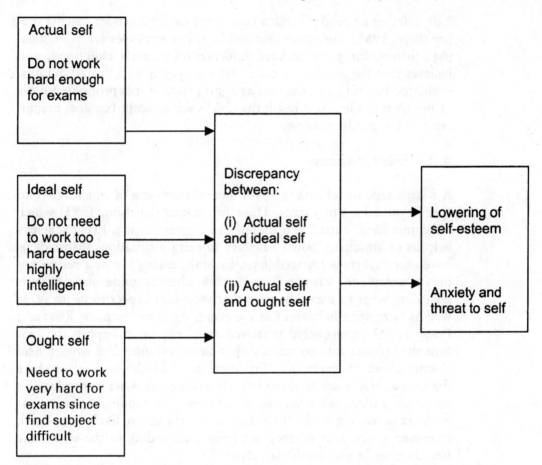

Figure 4.3: Self-esteem and discrepancies between actual self, ideal self and ought self. After Higgins (1987)

4.3.3 Role schemas

Role schemas refer to the knowledge structures people have about norms and expected behaviours of people who hold specific role positions in society. These roles can either be achieved or ascribed. Achieved roles are acquired through effort and training as in occupational roles, whereas the latter refer to those over which we have no control, such as age, gender and ethnicity. Role schemas are often considered as a form of stereotype (Fiske and Taylor, 1991), especially in relation to the ascribed roles of gender and race. Stereotypes are in general a type of schema resulting from the process of categorisation which organises information and knowledge about people from different social categories. The concept of stereotypes will be discussed in more detail later in this chapter.

In relation to gender Sandra Bem developed the gender schema theory (Bem, 1981). She states that gender role stereotypes act as organising schemas for gender-related information in early childhood, and believes that the developing child, often as young as 18 to 20 months, evaluates incoming information as appropriate or inappropriate for his or her own gender. As a result the child's self-concept becomes assimilated to the gender schema.

4.3.4 Event schemas

A fourth type of schema involves mental frameworks which relate to specific situations or events. These are *scripts* (Abelson, 1981) which indicate what is expected to happen in a given setting. Event schemas help us to anticipate how to behave in certain situations. Most of us have event schemas for weddings, funerals, eating out at a restaurant or an 'aeroplane' schema. These event schemas guide our decisions regarding what to wear, the time that we might expect to be away, as well as normative behaviour at the event. An experiment by Rose and Frieze (1993) investigated what teenagers expect to happen the first time they go out with somebody on a date. Both men and women held a script about the event of a 'first date' in which the man calls to take the woman out, worries about his appearance, takes her some place (to eat or see a film), takes her home and kisses her goodnight. As long as both act according to the 'first date script' things are likely to go well. However, if one person does not behave according to the script, the first date might also be the last date!

In this section we have looked at the importance of four types of schema for how we process social and other information about people. Figure 4.4 summarises each of these.

4.4 Schematic processing

Schematic processing requires the three main cognitive processes of attention, encoding, and retrieval, involved in social cognition (Wyer and Srull, 1994) and because of this has an influence upon our social interaction with other people.

4.4.1 Attention

Our social world is a 'buzz' of social stimuli and as it is impossible for an individual to pay attention to everything that is going on, it is necessary to be selective. We are likely to notice some aspects of people and situations more than others, and schemas provide us with the

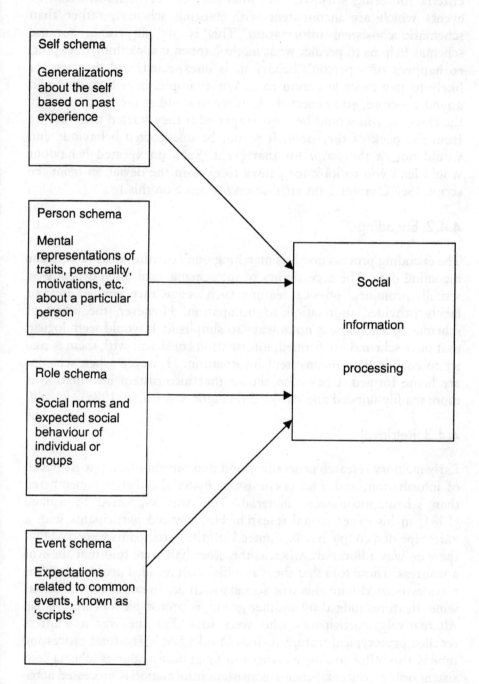

Figure 4.4: Four main schema types. After Fiske and Taylor (1991)

criteria for being selective. We often take notice of information or events which are inconsistent with existing schemas, rather than schematic consistent information. This is not surprising, because schemas help us to predict what might happen if something unexpected happens or a person's behaviour is unexpected, and then we are likely to pay more attention to it. For example, if as a student you attend a lecture, you expect the lecturer to stand at the front and face the class, so you would be most surprised if they started their lecture from the back of the room. It would be unexpected behaviour and would not fit the *script* for that event. Such unexpected behaviour would lead you to look for causes to explain the deviation from the script. (See Chapter 5 on attribution for more on this.)

4.4.2 Encoding

The encoding process involves matching one's existing schema with the incoming data. The accessibility of the schema used often depends on visually prominent physical features such as age, race, gender, dress or labels provided in relation to occupation. However, the effect of schemas on encoding is not always so simplistic. It would seem logical that once schemas are formed, information consistent with them is easier to encode than inconsistent information. However, when schemas are being formed it has been shown that inconsistent information is more readily noticed and encoded (Stangor and Ruble, 1989).

4.4.3 Retrieval

Early memory research generally found that schemas facilitate the recall of information, and schema-consistent material is better remembered than schema-inconsistent material. This was supported by Cohen (1981) in his experimental research. He provided participants with a videotape of a couple having dinner. Half the participants were told that the wife was a librarian, whereas the other half were told that she was a waitress. Those told that she was a librarian recalled prototypical features associated with this role schema such as, 'wears glasses', 'drinks wine' (features judged by another group as prototypical of librarians). Alternatively, participants who were told that she was a waitress recalled prototypical feature such as 'drinks beer'. The total processing time is also influenced by whether incoming information is schema consistent or inconsistent. Schema-consistent information is processed automatically with little effort but schema-inconsistent information receives more in-depth processing (Devine and Ostrom, 1988). It will be seen in the next section that this in-depth processing is not always possible.

4.5 Biases in schematic processing

4.5.1 Cognitive 'short cuts' or heuristics

In our social world we are often subjected to information overload when our ability to process information is exceeded by the amount of information available (Baron and Byrne, 1997). When this happens, we fall back on strategies which reduce cognitive effort and provide a reasonably efficient way of dealing with large amounts of social information. The strategies referred to as 'heuristics' in social psychological terminology are simple 'rules of thumb' which we use to make complex inferences by simplifying and streamlining the amount of information available. However, while heuristics might be considered reasonably efficient, they often lead to error, as we shall see later in this section. The early work on heuristics was conducted by Tversky and Kahneman, in the 1970s and early 1980s, and involved three most commonly used heuristics. These are summarised in Table 4.1.

Heuristic	Field of application	Example
Representativeness	Judgements of the likelihood that current stimuli or events resemble other stimuli or category members	A person described as a chess player, interested in computers, is more likely to be thought of as a scientist than a teacher
Availability	Judgements made on the basis of how easily specific kinds of information can be brought to mind	The more often an event is reported in the media leads us to judge that it is more frequent than it really is
Anchoring and adjustment	Quantitative estimates biased towards starting point	Plous (1989), showed that when people were asked if the odds on nuclear war were more or less than 1 per cent, they gave 11 per cent, whereas when initial odds were more or less than 90 per cent, they gave 26 per cent

Table 4.1: The three most commonly used heuristics (Tversky and Kahneman, 1973)

4.5.2 Representative heuristic

The representative heuristic is where a judgement is made about a person, event or object based on how similar or representative it is thought to be of a category or prototype. Tversky and Kahneman (1973) illustrated this very well in one of their early studies. Participants were told that an imaginary person had been selected from a group of 100 men and they were asked to estimate the probability that he was an engineer. Some participants were told that 30 per cent of the men were engineers, the others were told that 70 per cent of the men were engineers. A control group were given no further information, whereas the two experimental groups were provided with a personal description of the man, which either resembled or did not resemble the common role schema of an engineer. Participants in the control group, who had only received information about frequencies, estimated the likelihood of the man being an engineer on this basis. That is, they thought that he was more likely to be an engineer when the base rate was 70 per cent than when 30 per cent. However, those who were given his personal details tended to overlook the frequency or base rates and operated in terms of representativeness, i.e. if the personal description of the man was representative of an engineer, the person was categorised as such regardless of the base rate information. This tendency to ignore the base rate information is known as the *base rate fallacy*, which can be defined as a tendency to ignore or under-utilise information relating to base rates, i.e. the relative frequency with which events or stimuli actually occur (Baron and Byrne, 1997).

4.5.3 Availability heuristic

When asked to judge the likelihood of an event we are more likely to make our judgement on the availability of relevant information. For instance, you might estimate that the divorce rate is higher than it really is if a large number of friends in your social network have recently separated or divorced (Tversky and Kahneman, 1973). Another example is if you are in the position to buy a new car. You go to a number of garages, collect information regarding reliability, safety, petrol consumption, etc., and finally make a decision regarding what would be the best buy. Having made the decision, you then go to a party in the evening where you meet somebody who graphically describes all the problems that one of their friends has had with the make of car which you have decided to buy. The next day you cancel your order, on the basis of this anecdotal information, in spite of having a great deal of objective data available to you. This is because the anecdotal information is highly salient and from an acquaintance.

Tversky and Kahneman (1982) provided testable evidence for this heuristic. In the English language there are more than twice as many words with 'K' as the third letter in the word as there are with 'K' as the first letter. Irrespective of this, when asked the question about the relative frequency of 'K' most participants respond by saying there are more words beginning with 'K' rather than having 'K' as the third letter. This is because it is easier to think of such words – they are more available from memory. The use of the availability heuristic is likely to cause bias in social perception for a number of reasons. First, it does not control for idiosyncratic exposure, as in the example of buying a car, or unusual samples or instances (Hogg and Vaughan, 1995). Second, the storage and retrieval of information can lead to availability biases. For example, if you are working on a group project you might believe that you have contributed far more than the other group members because examples of your own efforts are more readily available in memory. This is due to you using more cognitive effort, such as attention to, and consideration of your own efforts, as compared with that of others.

A concept closely aligned to the availability heuristic is that of *priming*. This can be defined as a process whereby stimuli that heighten the availability of certain types or categories of information cause them to come more readily to mind. It is acknowledged to be a very strong effect, so much so that following such television programmes as *Crimewatch* viewers are reassured that violent crime is relatively rare, even though after watching the programme it might seem uncomfortably frequent, causing you to go round the house checking doors and windows are locked! The occurrence of a priming effect has been demonstrated by numerous studies, and has even been shown to operate when individuals are unaware of the priming stimuli. Known as automatic priming, it was supported in a study by Erdley and D'Agostino (1989). A group of participants had personality traits, related to honesty, flashed upon the screen so briefly that they were unaware of them. A control group were similarly exposed to neutral words unrelated to this trait. Following this, all participants were asked to read a description of an imaginary person depicted in an ambiguous way. After reading it they were asked to rate the hypothetical person on a number of trait dimensions, some of which were related to honesty. Results showed that those participants briefly exposed to honesty related words, albeit with no conscious awareness of this, rated the person higher on the honesty trait than those participants exposed to neutral words.

The availability heuristic often leads people to misjudge the frequency of events such as causes of death, rate of drug use, etc. Media coverage of 'dramatic deaths' (shooting at a robbery) or programmes on drug use may make such recent events more available and influence our judgements concerning how common they are.

4.5.4 Anchoring and adjustment heuristic

When making inferences most people need an anchor from which to start their decision-making. Hogg and Vaughan (1995) suggest that when making social judgements or inferences about others we use our own self schema. This is a form of social comparison, as we often use one of our own traits, such as intelligence, to make inferences regarding whether others are more or less intelligent than ourselves. Anchors also come from a quantitative estimate, as indicated in Table 4.1. Even though most evidence has come from controlled experiments, this heuristic operates across a number of everyday situations. For instance, Greenberg *et al.* (1986) showed that in a mock jury study participants who were instructed to consider the harshest verdict only made small adjustments and gave a relative harsh verdict. Alternatively, if the jury members were instructed to consider the most lenient verdict first, they used this as an anchor and delivered a relatively lenient verdict. This has important implications for the judicial system, since judges in their summing up often make comments regarding what evidence jury members should consider.

4.5.5 Social stereotypes

A stereotype may be defined as a 'mental representation of a social group and its members' (Stangor and Lange, 1994). The content of a stereotype includes shared beliefs about personal attributes, personality traits, and behaviour of a specific group of people. A stereotype has all the properties of a schema and often the two concepts are used synonymously, especially when applied to a person or a role group. Stereotypes have received considerable attention from social cognitive theorists over the last two decades due to their social consequences, which are often negative and lead to prejudice and discrimination (see Chapter 10). For instance, they are often derogatory when applied to out-groups; this is clearly demonstrated in a study of Northern and Southern European nations (Linssen and Hagendoorn, 1994). Linssen *et al.* supported the suggestion made by Von Ehrenfels (1961) that the reciprocal stereotypes of northern and southern inhabitants of countries tend to be polarised. Northerners are perceived as 'hard working' and 'cool' whereas southerners are viewed as 'easy going' and 'emotional'. Peabody (1985) confirmed this polarisation hypothesis with research on people living in North and South Italy, and North and South Greece. The north–south divide is often discussed in relation to England, but as yet there is no published research to support this.

Stereotyping is the process whereby stereotypes are activated and used in social information processing. Similar to schematic processing, perceptual and memory processes are influenced by stereotyping. Underlying the process of stereotyping is categorisation. Tajfel and Wilkes (1963) demonstrated this in an early judgement experiment. They used eight lines of varying length between 16cm and 22cm long. These lines were presented to some judges with the four shortest being labelled 'A', and the four longest lines labelled 'B'. Other judges had no labels attached to the eight lines. All judges were shown the lines one at a time in random order and were asked to estimate the length of each. Compared to the judgements made by those in the no-label condition, participants in the experimental condition exaggerated the difference in the length between the lines labelled 'A' and those labelled 'B'. To a lesser extent they also tended to estimate the lengths of the lines sharing the same label as being more similar in length than they actually were. This has been termed *the accentuation principle*, which can be defined as a result of categorisation of stimuli where there is an over-estimation of intra-category similarities and an over-estimation of inter-category differences on dimensions believed to be associated with the categorisation. There has been considerable support for the existence of this principle using both physical and social stimuli. Figure 4.5 provides an example of how accentuation might operate in a social context.

This principle can be illustrated when people are asked to judge heights of men and women. On average men are taller than women but the difference is exaggerated when judges are asked to make estimates of individual males and females (Biernat *et al.*, 1991). The effect is further enhanced when the categorisation is of particular importance, value or relevance to the person (Hogg and Vaughan, 1995).

While a classifying label can accentuate both the inter-group effect of difference and the intra-group effect of similarity, there is little support for both effects occurring together. McGarty and Penny (1988), in a review of research carried out between 1963 and 1986, suggest that this is due to the lack of category salience for the subjects. This issue will be further discussed in relation to social identity theory in Chapter 10. The social identity function is often seen as a positive consequence of stereotyping because individuals can enhance their self-esteem and gain support from people categorised as similar to themselves.

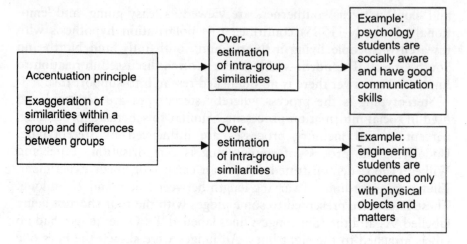

Figure 4.5: The accentuation principle effect on intra-group categorization

The original thinking about stereotypes was that they were construed as faulty, inflexible and inaccurate, pre-dating the concept of 'the cognitive miser'. However, perception without classification of some sort is almost impossible due to stimulus overload and as accentuation occurs as a result of this classification-based perception, stereotyping can be reasonably considered as a normal and inevitable process in social cognition! In general, stereotypes offer a quick and convenient way of processing information with regard to individuals and social groups. The fact that they are often over-generalised beliefs causes us to frequently overlook the detail and diversity of an individual member of the stereotyped group which leads to a mistaken impression being made of that individual. The relationship between the cognitive component and a possible affective component of a stereotype will be discussed in relation to prejudice and discrimination in Chapter 10.

4.5.6 Illusory correlation

A correlation may be defined as the naturally occurring relationship between two variables. For instance, as the weather becomes warmer, people tend to wear less clothes. Alternatively, an illusory correlation is the perception of a relationship between two variables where none exists, or the perception of a stronger relationship than actually exists. This phenomenon was first identified by Chapman in 1967 using objective experimental conditions in which he presented participants with lists of paired words, such as lion – tiger, lion – eggs, bacon – tiger, and bacon – eggs. Participants were then asked to estimate the frequency with which each word was paired with every other word. Although the words were actually paired with each other an equal number of times two biases emerged. First, participants over-estimated the number of times the conspicuous or distinctive words were paired, for example, blossoms – notebook, and second, the pairing of meaningfully associated words, for example bacon – eggs, was also over-estimated. Subsequent experimentation has supported this phenomenon (Hamilton and Gifford, 1976; Trolier and Hamilton, 1986). It appears that if we expect a correlation to exist, we are more likely to notice and recall confirming information. Similarly, if we believe that premonitions which are distinctive correlate with actual events, we recall this joint occurrence. However, we rarely recall the occasions when unusual events do not coincide. For instance, when a friend rings after a considerable length of time, we might consider it to be a coincidence as we were just thinking about them. However, we do not recall all the times that we have thought about the same friend and she has not called.

Both distinctiveness-based and associative meaning-based illusory correlations can account for the development of stereotypical thinking, especially in relation to negative stereotypes. In real life negative events are made distinctive and considered more rare than usual, run-of-the-mill events. Members of a minority group are distinctive and, on the whole, people have less contact with them. So the criteria for distinctive-based illusory correlation are met. Similarly, the associative-based illusory correlation is evident, in that people have preconceptions that negative attributes are associated with members of a minority group.

There has been some support for the distinctiveness-based explanation for illusory correlation, but more recent findings have modified the theory. It seems that information does not have to be distinctive when first experienced, but can become more distinctive over time and as a result produce the illusory correlation (McConnell *et al.*, 1994). This could mean that individuals do not necessarily encode negative information about minority group members when they first meet them, but as a result of new information which links a minority group member with a negative behaviour, it may then produce an illusory correlation. This has implications for media coverage of such trials as O. J. Simpson, which could act as a cue to individuals to link, in this case, an African American with negative information. This is similar to the use of the availability heuristic or the process of priming which are both common in social information processing, and are also likely to cause a degree of bias.

In summary, schematic information processing may often lead to people making biased, erroneous or oversimplistic social judgements. Much of the time, however, schematic processing does an adequate job of helping us deal with the 'buzz' and confusion of a potentially overwhelming amount of information about ourselves, other people, social pressures, societial and cultural norms, etc. Figure 4.6 summarises the five main aspects of schematic processing that we have considered in this section.

4.6 Forming impressions of people

We are constantly forming impressions of other people and, similarly, others are likely to be forming an impression of us. This two-way reciprocal process of impression formation is at the heart of social interactions. Often these impressions are formed on the basis of little or no direct experience with the other person, with the information often coming indirectly from somebody else. Also, non-verbal cues, which include appearance, provide important information. The mutual impressions formed of somebody have important implications, since they tend to be enduring and may affect whether a relationship develops or not. Similarly, in formal situations, such as an interview, the initial impression made on either side could influence a job offer or a job acceptance. However, as we shall see, first impressions can be inaccurate, reflecting faulty information processing, stereotypical thinking

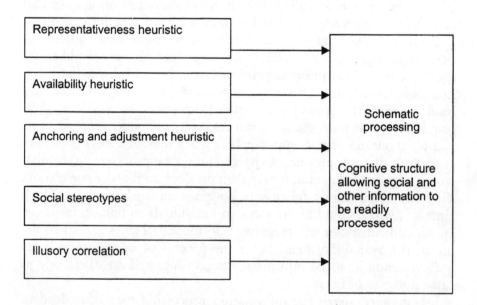

Figure 4.6: Summary of the main aspects of schematic processing used in social cognition

and even prejudice. They are, therefore, as the word implies, only a very rough and highly selective view of what a person is really like.

Impression formation has been the source of much social psychological research over the last 50 years. A number of different approaches have been put forward and in order to understand the sequence and current thinking it would be logical to take an historical perspective. The section will start by outlining the early work of Soloman Asch (1946). His work formed the cornerstone of all subsequent work on impression formation, and it was some years before an alternative view was proposed by Anderson in 1968. Anderson's Cognitive Algebra approach was originally thought to be in direct opposition to the model proposed by Asch, but later work by Fiske and Neuberg (1990) suggested that the two models, rather than being in opposition, are actually complementary to each other. As a result Fiske and Neuberg proposed the continuum model of impression formation. Following the discussion of these models in chronological order, the common basis in impression formation will be identified.

4.6.1 The configural model: Soloman and Asch (1946)

Soloman Asch (1946), from a Gestalt position, argued that the quality of a psychological experience as a whole is more than the sum of its individual components. In order to understand this concept you might use the analogy of a favourite tune, which means far more to you than the collection of individual notes, while an orchestral performance is more than the individual performance of each player.

Initially Asch (1946), developing a configural model, found that when people were asked to form an impression of a hypothetical person on the basis of being given seven personality traits, they were able to do this fairly easily. Not only could they do this but they were able to generate further descriptions of the person using more adjectives and even suggest what sort of job that the person might do. As a result Asch pioneered an experimental method which has been used on countless occasions to investigate impression formation. Basically, a list of adjectives describing a person (*stimulus traits*) are given, then participants are asked to indicate, on the basis of this description, how another set of adjectives (*response traits*) best describe this target person. Asch, investigating *central* and *peripheral* traits, gave participants slightly different lists of adjectives describing an imaginary person. There were four experimental conditions and a control condition. In the control condition participants were given just six stimulus traits and in the experimental conditions seven stimulus traits were given.

The additional stimulus traits were ones which Asch thought to be central. All of these conditions are shown below:

Experimental Group A: intelligent, skilful, industrious, *warm*, determined, practical, cautious

Experimental Group B: intelligent, skilful, industrious, *cold*, determined, practical, cautious.

Experimental Group C: intelligent, skilful, industrious, *polite*, determined, practical, cautious.

Experimental Group D: intelligent, skilful, industrious, *blunt*, determined, practical, cautious.

As you can see, Groups A and B were given additional traits opposite to each other (*warm* or *cold*), as were Groups C and D (*polite* or *blunt*). Participants were then asked whether they thought the target person would also be generous, wise, happy, good-natured, reliable and important. Table 4.2 summarises the results.

Figure 4.8 shows that participants given the adjective trait of 'warm' thought that the person would be 'generous' (91 per cent), 'happy' (90 per cent), and 'good-natured' (94 per cent). By contrast, those given the trait of 'cold' did not think the person would possess such traits. Participants given either the 'polite' or 'blunt' trait made less extreme judgements. This is shown, for example, by the fact that only 58 per cent and 56 per cent thought the stimulus person would be generous and good-natured, respectively (compare this with the percentages for these traits in Groups A and B). Asch argued, on the basis of these results, that warm/cold are central traits while polite/blunt are peripheral. Central traits, Asch suggested, infer the presence of certain other traits and exert a powerful influence over the final impression. On the other hand, peripheral traits, such as polite/blunt, have relatively little impact on the overall impression.

Response Adjective	Control group	Group 'A'	Group 'B'	Group 'C'	Group 'D'
Generous	55	91	8	56	58
Wise	49	65	25	30	50
Happy	71	90	34	75	65
Good-natured	69	94	17	87	56

Table 4.2: Percentage of participants who thought the target person possessed generous, wise, happy, good-natured characteristics. Adapted from Asch (1964)

Subsequent studies have supported the idea of central and peripheral traits both under controlled experimental and naturalistic conditions such as education. For example, Kelley (1950) distributed two versions of a biographical description of a guest lecturer to students who would be meeting him later. One version included the trait 'warm' and the other 'cold'. When the guest speaker arrived and was delivering his teaching session the experimenter recorded how much each student participated in discussion. After the session, when the speaker had left, students were requested to rate the speaker on a 15-trait rating scale. Those who had been given the 'warm' description rated him more positively on traits such as *considerate, informal, sociable, good-natured, humorous* and *humane,* and participated more in the class discussion. A replication of this study was carried out in another educational setting, 38 years later, with similar results (see Widmeyer and Loy, 1988). An additional result in this later study was that the guest lecturer was rated as a more effective lecturer by students given the 'warm' description prior to meeting him. Central traits, therefore, give rise to certain expectancies about what a person will be like, and this then affects how new information about the person is processed. This will be discussed further under the biases inherent in impression formation (see Section 4.7).

Critics of this approach have questioned how a central trait can be determined. From a Gestalt perspective, it would depend on the degree of correlation a trait has with other traits. However, it could depend on context, because in Asch's experiments *warm/cold* was central because the dimension was semantically linked to the *response* dimensions.

4.6.2 The implicit personality theory

Bruner and Taguiri (1954) had previous to this suggested that everybody has their own idea of which personality characteristics go with which and are consistent with other characteristics. The *implicit personality theory,* as this became known, was further developed by Rosenberg *et al.* (1968). Rosenberg *et al.* asked college students to think of a number of people known to them but who were very different to each other. They were then given 60 trait terms and asked to put them in separate piles, each pile representing the description of each of the different known persons. All students had the same 60 traits but each student had thought of different people.

The results of their analysis of the 60 trait terms revealed that (a) there was a shared implicit personality theory and (b) there were two

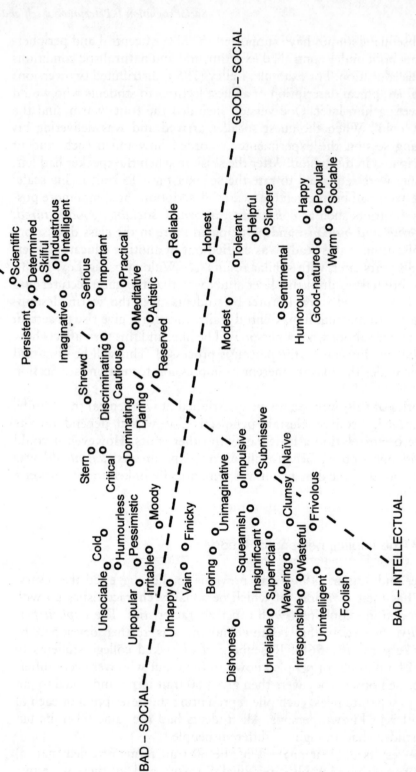

Figure 4.7: Two major trait dimensions of bad–social and bad–intelligent/good–intellectual. Adapted from Rosenberg, Nelson and Vivekānanthan *et al.* (1968)

related but distinct types of good–bad evaluations. One they termed the *intellectual* good–bad dimension, and the other the *social* good–bad dimension. Figure 4.7 shows how different traits are arranged along the two dimensions. As can be seen, this goes some way to explaining the centrality of the *warm-cold* distinction in impression formation that Asch (1946) found, since these two traits are located at either extremes of the social desirability axis.

The early ideas of implicit personality theories preceded the work on schema theory that we looked at in Sections 4.3 and 4.4, but in fact serve the same function as any schema. The theories demonstrate our tendency to be *cognitive misers* (Fiske and Taylor, 1991) when we form impressions of people using very little knowledge of them or having spent a relatively short period of time with them.

Cultural variation has been shown in implicit personality theories (Hoffman *et al.*, 1986). Hoffman *et al.* noted that in western culture we have a shared idea about somebody who has an *artistic* personality: characteristics of creativity, intensity, being temperamental and likely to have an unconventional lifestyle. However, the Chinese for instance, do not have a label for a person with this cluster of characteristics. Similarly, there are shared ideas of personality types held by the Chinese which do not exist in western culture. For instance, a *shi gu* type is a person who is worldly, family oriented, socially skilled but reserved.

In order to test this cultural difference Hoffman *et al.* (1986) wrote stories which described how an artistic person behaved but without using the verbal label. The stories were written in both English and Chinese. The English was given to English-speaking people who spoke no other language and also the Chinese–English bilinguals. The Chinese version was given to another group of Chinese–English bilinguals to read. The participants were then asked to write their impressions of the character described.

Figure 4.8 shows the results. The English speakers were more likely to form an impression of an artistic type and the Chinese speakers formed an impression of the *shi gu* type. The role of language was also demonstrated as the Chinese–English bilinguals who read the English version were also much more likely to form the impression of an *artistic* type.

4.6.3 Halo effect – Cooper (1981)

As shown in Figure 4.7, certain traits seem to go together along both dimensions. For instance, traits that are evaluated as *positive*,

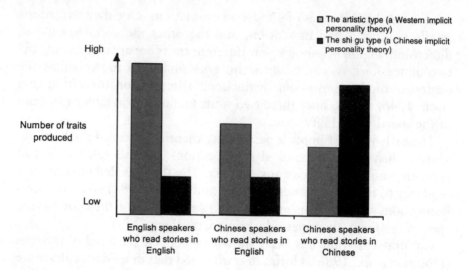

Figure 4.8: Impressions of artistic type and *shi gu* type produced by English and Chinese-English speakers. Adapted from Hoffman *et al.* (1986)

favourable or *good*, are expected to go together, as are negative traits. Negative and positive traits are not expected to occur together. *Evaluative bias* is common in impression formation and the *halo effect*, as it has been termed, affects our perception of even objective characteristics of another person. By far the most persuasive aspect of the halo effect is that associated with physical characteristics. It appears that the saying 'beauty is only skin deep' does not apply, as beautiful people are subject to positive evaluation bias. Eagly *et al.* (1991) in a review of research, found that whatever constitutes our judgement of what or who is beautiful, also influences our evaluation of what is good. Applying this phenomenon to the legal system, a number of researchers (e.g. Downs and Lyons, 1991) found that attractive defendants, both male and female, were given lighter sentences than physically unattractive defendants. Physical attractiveness has also been related to perceived competence. Jackson *et al.* (1995) found, in both adults and children, that attractive people were perceived as more competent than less attractive people. The effects were stronger for males than for females, and also when actual information about competence was absent than when it was present. One of the problems of this type of research is arriving at an agreed, objective set of criteria for an attractive and unattractive person. This differs depending on whether you perceive yourself to be attractive or unattractive in the first place!

4.6.4 Cognitive algebra and impression formation

Following the influential work of Asch (1946) in relation to central and peripheral traits in impression formation, Anderson (1981) generated three other models focusing on the positive and negative values assigned to the attributes of the target person. Anderson believes that the overall impression made of a person is either a cumulative sum of each piece of information called the *additive model*, or an average of the ratings attributed to each trait called the *averaging model*.

Using a rating scale of +5 (most positive) to –5 (most negative), each trait is given a specific rating. For example, if you are told that a person is *honest* (+4), *intelligent* (+3), *warm* (+5), but *boring* (–1), the person would gain a score of 11 using the additive model. However, using an averaging model, the score would be 2.75. The implications of this are that in order to project a favourable impression using the averaging model a person should present only very few positive traits. In the above example, *honest* and *warm* would be the best combination. Alternatively, using the additive model, any marginally positive trait will add to the overall positive impression, hence a large number of traits should be presented. Research has shown that the averaging model has been the favoured approach, but it has its limitations. When assigning ratings for any specific trait it is likely to depend on the context in which the impression is being made. You value different traits depending on whether the person is a potential friend, work colleague or merely an acquaintance. For instance, 'efficient' and 'organised' are valued traits in a work colleague, whereas in a potential friend such traits may imply that the person lacks spontaneity.

The fact that context affects how we value particular traits when forming an impression led to the development of the *weighted averaging model*. The difference that weightings make to the overall impression, depending on the context in which this impression is being made can be seen in Figure 4.9. This shows that using the averaging model an overall impression of the person is moderately favourable (+2.67). However, notice what happens when we put this in a particular context, a long-term partner or work colleague, where we provide a weighting or evaluation of the desirability of each trait. For example, with the long-term partner honesty is given the highest rating (5), while reliability is slightly negatively weighted (–1). As Figure 4.9(b) shows, this results in a final figure of 7.33 representing a positive evaluation. By contrast, notice that for the work colleague all three traits are desirable with efficiency receiving the highest weighting. On the basis of the overall values resulting from the weighted averaging model, the person would make an equally good work colleague and long-term partner since good, positive evaluations results for each context.

Both the configural model of Asch (1946) and the cognitive algebra model proposed by Anderson assume that the full range of information about an individual is integrated to form an impression of that person. However, they differ in how this integration is achieved. Asch, using a Gestalt perspective, proposed that in order to get a coherent whole, some aspects of the individual have to be modified during the impression

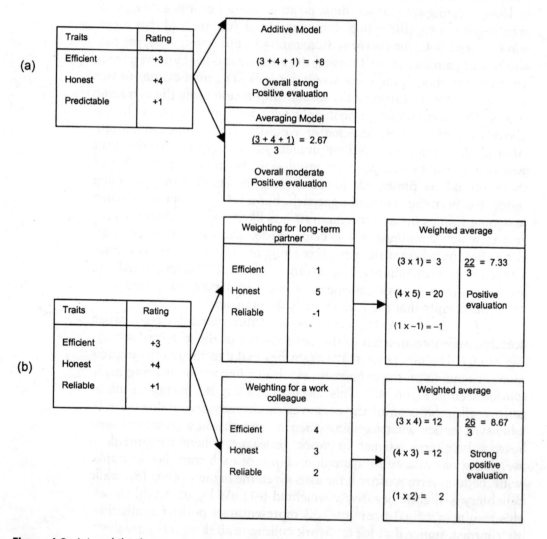

Figure 4.9: (a) and (b) depicting worked examples of the additive, averaging and weighted averaging models of impression formation

formation process. He emphasised that the meaning of individual features and their inter-relationship with each other must be taken into account. Anderson, on the other hand, believes the perceiver assesses the implications of each known piece of information about the target person separately. The perceiver then combines them algebraically into an impression. While the process is different, there are similarities between the two approaches in that both show some traits to be more influential in the final impression than others. In fact, Pavelchak (1989) proposed that rather than these models conflicting, they are complementary. He based this judgement on the results of a study designed to include both processes. First, student participants were asked to rate 50 personality traits, and 35 subjects (such as Mathematics, English) on a scale of likeability. These were used as comparisons for a second part of the experiment carried out a few days later. Half of the same participants were asked to rate their likeability for a person described as bright, studious, precise and methodical and then suggest what subject of study he or she might be taking (piecemeal group).

Other participants were asked to guess the subject of study *before* making their evaluation of likeability (category group). Pavelchak proposed that if the participants were making categorical based judgements (based on Asch), the likeability ratings for the person would match the likeability of the suggested subject study made in the first part of the experiment. If the participants were making their judgements 'piecemeal', then the evaluation of the person would match the average of the scores for the four traits used in the second experiment. The results showed that two different processes of impression formation were operating, depending on which instructions were received from the experimenter.

4.6.5 Continuum model – Fiske and Neuberg (1990)

As a result of these findings Fiske and Neuberg (1990) developed the *continuum* model of impression formation. We initially categorise a person on the basis of information we have about them. This may be a salient cue to categorisation such as skin colour, gender or occupation. If there is no personal involvement or the person is of little relevance to us, the process is unlikely to continue any further. For instance, this might apply to somebody we fleetingly meet on a train or in the street. However, if we enter into social interaction with the person, and they are more important to us, we are likely to pay more attention to the information we have of them. This is then checked against the initial categorisation and, if consistent, confirmation of the initial impression is made. This is depicted in Figure 4.10.

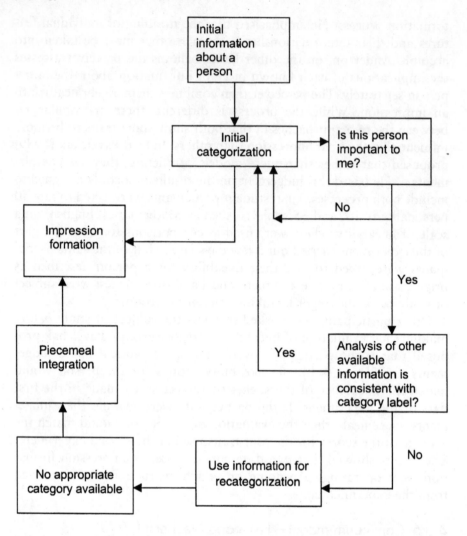

Figure 4.10: Schematic representation of the continuum model of impression formation

If, however, the additional information is inconsistent with the category label used, an alternative category is sought using a process of categorisation as shown in Figure 4.10. If no suitable categories are available, an *attribute-focused* piecemeal process of impression formation is adopted.

Fiske and Neuberg (1990) regarded *category-based* processes (the initial categorisation) and *attribute-focused* processes (impression formed following additional information) at either end of a continuum, with *category confirmation*, *re-categorisation* and *piecemeal integration* being used between the two extremes, depending on the situation. This seems to be a plausible explanation, if we accept that category-based impressions take priority when there is little time or motivation to attend to further information. In situations when it is vital that an accurate impression is made, as in a job interview, the piecemeal-based process should be initiated, as conflicting or inconsistent information is likely to be present. It therefore needs a balanced view and variable weightings attached to particular traits in order to make as accurate a judgement as possible. It seems that individuals always engage in a *serial* step-by-step process with a category-based process first, perhaps automatically. They only apply an attribute-focused process if they are highly motivated, or the nature of the attribute or trait resists re-categorisation of the individual as belonging to any particular group.

Using further developments in cognitive processing, Kunda and Thagard (1996) have proposed an alternative approach, *the parallel – constraint – satisfaction model*. They suggest that instead of serial processing, stereotypical (category-based) information and individuating information are processed simultaneously and both have equal effect on the final impression. In order to outline the major issues related to the model Kunda and Thagard (1996) used the earlier research by Duncan (1976). Duncan demonstrated the effects of stereotypes by interpreting the behaviour of a person observed elbowing another person. He showed that when this behaviour was performed by a black person it was interpreted as a *violent push*, but when performed by a white person it was seen as a *jovial shove*.

Using a parallel – constraint – satisfaction theory to explain this, when a white person sees a black person push somebody, it activates both violent push and jovial shove. The stereotypical belief about black people activates 'aggressive' which then activates violent push and deactivates jovial shove. However, if a white individual observes a white person pushing somebody, 'aggressive' is not activated, which means that violent push is deactivated and jovial shove is activated. This is shown in Figure 4.11. The basic premise of the theory is that stereotypes do not necessarily dominate impressions, as the serial models imply, but that individuating information and stereotypical information operate simultaneously, depending on how conspicuous the stereotype and the perceiver's goals are.

4.7 Biases in forming impressions

Forming impressions of other people often leads to erroneous or biased impressions and judgements being made. At times when we have little information about a person we may make an automatic categorisation

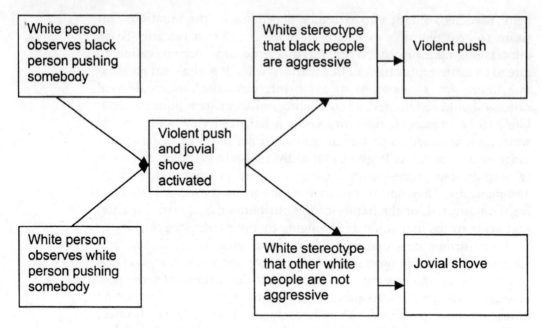

Figure 4.11: Parallel–constraint–satisfaction model of impression formation

and leave matters there. At other times we have a large amount of information available but only a limited capacity for processing this information. Terms like *cognitive miser* together with the use of cognitive heuristics (see Section 4.5) may often lead us to form a biased impression. In this section we look at three main causes of bias: the primacy effect, positive and negative information about a person, and the self-fulfilling prophecy.

4.7.1 Primacy effect

The order in which information is presented can have a profound effect on the subsequent impression made of that person. Asch (1946) in a series of experiments, used six traits to describe a hypothetical person to participants. For half the participants the person was described as *intelligent, industrious, impulsive, critical, stubborn* and *envious*, i.e. positive traits first. For the other half of the participants the order in which the traits were given was reversed. It was found that the person was evaluated more favourably by participants when the positive traits were given first, showing strong evidence for a *primacy effect*. There are two major reasons for the primacy effect. The first is the attention decrement hypothesis. Individuals tend to believe that they have made an accurate impression of somebody, and then pay less attention to subsequent contradictory information. Belmore (1987) found that when people were asked to read a series of statements about a person, they spent less time reading as they proceeded through the list, thus giving greater attention to material appearing early on. A second reason for primacy is that once a person has formed an impression, all further inconsistent information is interpreted in the light of the impression made. This can be illustrated with the use of the trait 'proud'. If the initial impression made is positive, *proud* can be interpreted as self-respecting but, if negative, it could mean conceited (Brehm and Kassin, 1996).

Luchins (1957) demonstrated both a primacy and recency effect in an early classic study on impression formation. A recency effect is where information presented last has the strongest influence over the impression formed. Luchins presented participants in his experiment with two one-paragraph descriptions of a person. One paragraph portrayed the person, Jim, as an extrovert and the other as an introvert. The paragraphs used are given.

Extrovert paragraph

Jim left the house to get some stationery. He walked out into the sun-filled street with two of his friends, basking in the sun as he walked. Jim entered the stationery store which was full of people. Jim talked with an acquaintance while he waited for the clerk to catch his eye. On his way out, he stopped to chat with a school friend who was just coming into the store. Leaving the store, he walked toward school. On his way he met the girl to whom he had been introduced the night before. They talked for a while, and then Jim left for school.

Introvert paragraph

After school Jim left the classroom alone. Leaving school he started on his long walk home. The street was brilliantly filled with sunshine. Jim walked down the street on the shady side. Coming down the street towards him, he saw the pretty girl whom he had met on the previous evening. Jim crossed the street and entered the candy store. The store was crowded with students, and he noticed a few familiar faces. Jim waited quietly until the counterman caught his eye and then gave his order. Taking his drink, he sat down at a side table. When he had finished his drink he went home.

Instead of providing ratings to adjectives, participants were asked whether they liked Jim and whether they would talk to him. Luchins also asked participants to imagine what Jim would do in the following situation: 'Jim was waiting his turn in the barber's shop. The barber's overlooked him to call in another customer who had just come in. What did Jim do?'

Luchins reported a primacy effect when the two paragraphs were read one immediately after the other, but a recency effect when there was a time delay between reading the paragraphs and the delay was filled with a distracting task (reading a comic).

4.7.2 Positive and negative information

Negative information about somebody, or the presence of negative traits, tends to take on more importance in impression formation than positive information (Fiske, 1980). It is also significant that once a negative impression is formed, it is less likely to change even in the light of new positive information. Skowronski and Carlston (1989) in a review of explanations for this, believe that as negative information is more distinctive and usual, it attracts more attention in situations when, on the whole, we like to assume the best of people. Alternatively, it could be that negative information tends to signal potential danger, so to be aware of it has survival value for the individual. However, it can have very important implications for the person being judged, as will be seen in the next section.

4.7.3 Self-fulfilling prophecy

The self-fulfilling prophecy is a process by which one's expectations about a person eventually tend to make that person behave in ways that confirm those expectations. Rosenthal and Jacobson (1968) carried out a very influential study called Pygmalion in the classroom. Teachers in a San Francisco school were told that 20 pupils in their class were about to have an *intellectual growth spurt* (bloomers). The experimenters cited IQ scores, but in fact the 20 pupils were randomly selected. The teachers very quickly rated the two groups of pupils differently, with the non-bloomers being considered less curious, less interested and less happy than the bloomers. The results of the IQ tests over the two-year period showed a significantly greater IQ gain in the pupils assigned to the 'bloomer' group. The implications of the research, that positive teacher expectations influence student performance, caused some disquiet. Critics could see that if this was so, negative teacher expectations of pupils could similarly affect performance of students negatively.

While one might say that the original research is dated, Rosenthal (1985) has since found after analysing over 400 experiments designed to test the original hypothesis, that in 36 per cent of them teacher expectations significantly influenced student performance. The effect has been seen to operate in contexts other than the educational setting. For example, using the same paradigm, Eden (1990) sampled 29 platoons of Israeli soldiers, consisting in total of over 1000 men. Some platoon leaders were told to expect their group of trainees to have greater potential than the others whereas, in reality, they were only of average ability. After ten weeks, the performance of all the trainees was assessed, and those who had been assigned to the high expectation groups obtained higher scores in the written examinations and on a weapon operation test. Brehm and Kassin (1996) provide a fairly simple account of why and how people turn expectations into reality. This is shown in Figure 4.12.

However, although these effects are well established, they are not automatic. When perceivers are highly motivated to find out what a person is really like because, for instance, they know that the other person is likely to be important to them, they probe more deeply and often fail to confirm the prophecy. Also, when there is a power differential between perceiver and target, those in a position of low-power or subordinates do not confirm expectations as they are more motivated to

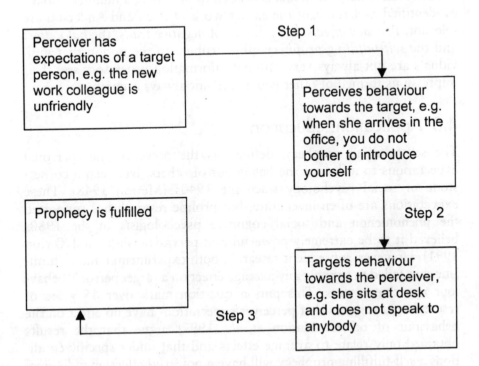

Figure 4.12: A three-step process leading to the self-fulfilling prophecy

present themselves in a way that will cause them to be liked (Copeland, 1994). A third limitation is when the perceiver's expectations clash with a target person's self-concept.

In summary, four models of impression formation have been introduced in this section. The holistic model of Asch assumes that a global impression is made of a person, and that verbal evaluation influences how specific characteristics of the individual are interpreted. This constitutes top-down information processing, whereas Anderson (1990) applied a bottom-up processing to his model. He proposed that the impression of an individual is made by a mathematical integration of evaluative ratings of each trait associated with the person. Fiske and Neuberg (1990) developed a continuum model, believing that the two previous models could be complementary to each other, depending on the context in which the impression is being made. Finally, the model by Kunda and Thagard (1996) again integrates both earlier models, but disputes the idea by Fiske and Neuberg, that processing of information is serial, and that stereotypical information takes precedence. They believe that both category-based and attribute-based information is processed in parallel and again, depending on the situation, there is parallel constraint on either type of information.

However, whichever model is utilised or favoured, a number of biases identified as a result of the earlier work of Asch and Anderson are relevant. *Primacy effects*, the salience of *negative traits*, the *halo effect* and the *self-fulfilling prophecy* all contribute to the notion that individuals are not always very rational information processors and their impressions formed of other people are not always accurate.

4.8 Application: education

The self-fulfilling prophecy, defined as the power of interpersonal expectations to influence the behaviour of others, has been a cornerstone of social psychology since the 1940s (Merton 1948). These expectations are often inaccurate, but prolific research has supported the phenomenon and social cognitive psychologists in the 1980s believed it to be extremely powerful and pervasive (Fiske and Taylor, 1991). However, subsequent research, both experimental and naturalistic, has failed to support any average effect on a target person's behaviour or achievements. This puts a question mark over 45 years of research and suggests that perceiver expectations have no effect on the behaviour of others. Madon *et al.* (1997) argue that the results obtained only relate to average effects and that under specific conditions a self-fulfilling prophecy will have a powerful effect on individual target behaviour. Using a naturalistic educational setting involving the transfer of pupils from an elementary to a junior high school in 12 school districts in one state of the USA, they posed four research questions:

1　Are negative or positive expectations more powerful self-fulfilling prophecies?
2　Do teacher expectations produce more powerful self-fulfilling prophecy effects if they match the pupil's self-concept in a specific subject domain?
3　Are pupils with negative self-concepts more vulnerable to the effects of a self-fulfilling prophecy than pupils with positive self-concepts?
4　Are pupils with poor academic records more susceptible than those with good records of achievement?

The overall results of the research showed that the self-fulfilling prophecies were more potent when they were over-estimation of achievements. This was considerably more powerful when the over-estimation was in relation to low achievers, where substantial gains in achievement were seen. This is depicted in Figure 4.13. This shows the gradient above 0 (zero) is steeper for both high and low achievers and less so below zero. The effect can be seen to be very marked in low achievers.

In the present educational climate in Britain, where a school's position in the league tables is considered to be a reflection of a 'good' or 'bad' school, it would be useful to take note of such results. Jussim *et al.* (1996) demonstrated powerful self-fulfilling prophecies among students from stigmatised groups, so in schools where there is a high proportion of different ethnic groups, teachers' perceptions could have a powerful effect on pupil achievement. Over the last five years GCSE results have consistently shown a positive bias towards girls. It would now seem that boys are under-achieving and not reaching their true potential. Policy that encourages perceivers, both teachers and parents, to have realistic but high expectations for boys, could be beneficial.

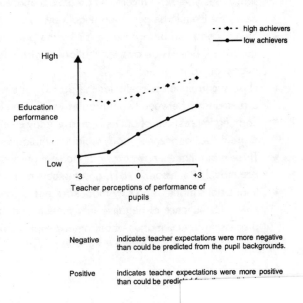

Figure 4.13: Self-fulfilling prop⌐ pupil achievers. After Madon *e*⌐

4.9 Summary

- Social cognition can be defined as the manner in which we interpret, analyse, remember and use information about our social world.
- There are two basic components of social thought: schemas and prototypes, which can be defined as mental structures that allow large amounts of diverse information to be organised efficiently.
- Categorisation is a process by which stimuli are grouped on the basis of similarity. Prototypes are the most typical representations of a category and are therefore easier to process.
- A schema is similar to a prototype but less typical. Four main types of schema have been identified, all serving similar functions in information processing. These types are self schema, person schema, role and event schemas.
- Schematic processing refers to how schema affect all the main social cognitive processes, namely attention, encoding and retrieval.
- When there is information overload, strategies are used to reduce cognitive effort. These strategies, referred to as heuristics, are simple 'rules of thumb', which individuals use to make complex inferences as quickly as possible, without too much cognitive processing.
- The three most commonly used heuristics are the representative, availability and encoding/adjustment heuristics.
- A stereotype has all the properties of a schema, especially when applied to a role or person. Stereotypes have received a great deal of attention in social psychology, due to the tendency for them to be perceived negatively.
- Stereotyping can be accounted for by the principle of accentuation. As a result of categorisation, there is an over-estimation of intra-category similarity and over-estimation of inter-group difference.
- Illusory correlation perpetuates the process of stereotyping as it involves a perception of a relationship between two variables when none actually exists.
- Forming impressions of others is an everyday event and the process involved has received a great deal of attention from social psychologists over the past 50 years.
- Three main models have evolved: the configural model (Asch, 1946), the cognitive algebra model (Anderson, 1981), and the continuum model (Fiske and Neuberg, 1990).
- Impressions made using any model are not always accurate. Biases such as the primacy effect, the salience of negative information and the self-fulfilling prophecy all distort the processing of information about other people, especially in relation to first impressions.

4.10 Suggestions for further reading

Fiske, S. T. and Taylor, S. E. 1991: *Social Cognition*. 2nd edition. New York: McGraw-Hill.
The authoritative text in the area, reasonably up-to-date providing plenty of detail about theory and research on person perception.

Hewstone, M., Stroebe, W. and Stephenson, G. M. 1996: *Introduction to Social Psychology.* 2nd edition. Oxford: Blackwell Publishers.
Chapters 5 and 6 provide an up-to-date European perspective on social cognition and person perception. Many of the theories and concepts dealt with in this chapter appear in the Hewstone book but with an interesting and different slant.

Wyer, R. S. and Srull, T. K. (ed.) 1996: *Handbook of Social Cognition*. 2nd edition. Hillsdale, NJ : Erlbaum.
Advanced and up-to-date text containing numerous chapters written by authorities in the field. This book should only be read by those who already have a good foundation and understanding of social cognition.

5

Social cognition II:
The attribution approach

5.1 Introduction

In the previous chapter we saw how perceptions and impressions guide the judgement we make about ourselves and other people. In this chapter the attribution approach in social psychology is considered in some detail.

The central concern of the attribution approach is to understand and explain how people attribute *causes* to their own and other people's behaviour. For example, suppose you have just had an interview for a job, and you performed very poorly at the interview; consequently you were not offered the job. How might you explain to yourself, and to your friends, why you made such a mess of the interview and so did not get the job? That is, what causes might you attribute to your poor performance? A host of possibilities present themselves, for example, you may have been very anxious, or had a late night, or found the interviewer aggressive and patronising. Doubtless you can think of other possible causes which all offer some explanation and justification for the poor performance. Take another example, suppose this time you are walking along a busy shopping precinct and a stranger collapses on the pavement just in front of you. You may automatically go to the person's assistance but at the same time you will probably be speculating about what caused the person to collapse. How you *perceive* the behaviour to be caused may affect the quality of help you are willing to offer. Take two extremes: if the person was dressed shabbily and smelt of alcohol you may attribute the cause of collapse to the person being drunk. By contrast, if the person was smartly dressed, did not smell of alcohol, and appeared to you rather 'old for his age', you may think the cause to be a heart attack. None of this can be known for certain at the time, the point is though that you would probably be less willing to help if you attributed the cause to drunkenness than if you attributed the cause to a heart attack.

The perception of the cause of another's behaviour also has consequences for the degree of responsibility attributed to the person for his or her actions. The distinction between murder and manslaughter is a good example of this. Somebody who, in cold blood and premeditation, plans to kill somebody and then goes out and commits the deed is held to be highly responsible for that act (excepting, of course, when that person is judged to be insane). On the other hand, a woman who has a violent drunkard for a husband and in a fit of temper and exasperation kills him will most likely be convicted of manslaughter, or an even lesser offence perhaps. This may be so since the killing of her husband is not perceived to be entirely caused by her, as his violent drunkenness reduces her responsibility for the act.

These examples serve to demonstrate three points about the attribution approach: first, in many circumstances people *seek* to explain their own and other people's behaviour. This is because attributing causes to behaviour serves the important function of *reducing uncertainty* about how that person is likely to behave in the future. People need to feel that they can predict and have some control over the world in which they live. Second, both examples demonstrate how people *search for and use information* when attributing causes. Information about the person in question and the social context in which the behaviour takes place is used to make a causal attribution. Third, in characterising people as seeking to explain and understand social behaviour we may regard them as *naïve scientists*. We may think of scientists searching for the cause of physical events such as the weather, electricity, etc. Psychologists, as scientists, attempt to explain why people behave as they do by constructing theories then testing and investigating predictions (see Chapter 1). In a similar, but much less rigorous way, the lay person may be viewed as a naïve scientist (Heider, 1958), Figure 5.1 summarises these key features.

This chapter develops the ideas and themes introduced above by first looking at the fundamental concepts and when attributions are made. The chapter then examines four models of attribution, and then moves on to consider errors and biases that people often make. Some consideration is given to how the child develops in terms of attributing causes to behaviour, then moves on to consider the wider social and societal

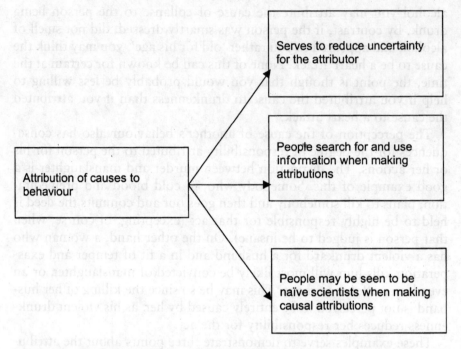

Figure 5.1: Key features of the attribution approach in social psychology

context in which attributions are made. The chapter concludes by look-ing at personality and attributional style, and the application of the attribution approach to the understanding and treatment of clinical depression.

5.2 Basic considerations

Before looking at theory and research in the attributional approach, it is important to have a good understanding of the underlying concepts, when we are most likely to make attributions, and when attributions of cause are made automatically or only after some deliberation (Gilbert, 1989).

5.2.1 Fundamental concepts

The conceptual foundation on which theories of attribution have been built was provided by Heider (1944) who offered three principles:

1 behaviour is perceived as being caused;
2 perceptions are important;
3 the locus of the cause(s) of behaviour is perceived to be with the person, the situation, or some combination of both.

We will deal with each of these points in turn. Claiming that people perceive behaviour as being caused may seem rather obvious and trite on first acquaintance, however, the important point is that we attribute causes to virtually *all* human behaviour. People appear to be ill at ease or loath to admit or believe that behaviour happens because of chance events. Everything that others and ourselves do is believed to result from one or a number of specific causes.

How behaviour is perceived to be caused, rather than how it is actually caused (if this can ever be known), is of interest to attribution theorists. Consider again the example, given earlier, where you were asked to imagine you performed poorly at a job interview. Possible causes you might offer such as being anxious, having a headache from being up late, etc. were suggested. However, the reasons for your bad performance might be perceived in an entirely different way by the person who interviewed you, for example, the interviewer may regard you as incompetent and inarticulate. Discrepancies in perceptions of the causes of behaviour happen frequently in our social life. Attribution researchers are concerned to discover if there are distinct patterns in the different ways in which people, from different perspectives, attribute causes to behaviour. If you think back to what was said in the previous chapter, on social perception, it is not hard to see why different people with different perspectives may offer different causal attributions for the *same* behaviour. In Chapter 4 we saw that perception is an active process in which we selectively attend to only limited features of our social environment. Heider (1958) claimed that perceptions of the causes of behaviour, as with our perception of physical objects, depends on three things:

1 the characteristics of the perceiver;
2 the features of the behaviour perceived; and
3 the social context in which the behaviour takes place.

The third point made by Heider, and one of central importance, which will be encountered again and again this chapter, is that people attribute causes, primarily, to either *the person or the situation*. Consider the example, given earlier, of the distinction between murder and manslaughter. For a person to be convicted of murder the cause of the behaviour has to be attributed entirely to the person by referring to such things as personality traits, motives, intentions, etc. Such attributions are known as *internal causes* since they refer to causes of behaviour located within the individual whose behaviour we are concerned to explain. By contrast, our example of the circumstances under which a person may be found guilty of manslaughter tend to emphasise *external causes*. Generally, these are forces located outside the person and in the social situation which, as it were, compel or incline a person to act in such a way. External causes are those which most people think would compel them to act in a similar way in such a situation. In our example of manslaughter, the external cause was a violent drunkard for a husband. This is summarised, with examples in Figure 5.2.

The distinction between internal and external causes is of fundamental importance to the attribution approach. Theories have been developed to predict when people make internal attributions and when they make external attributions. The internal–external distinction is a relative one, and it is important to bear this in mind. An example, discussed by Ross (1977) highlights this. Suppose we are interested in knowing why Jack has just bought the house that he has. One person might say that Jack bought the house 'because it was so secluded', implying that it is something about the house (external attribution) that caused Jack to buy it. Another person, however, might say that Jack bought the house 'because he wanted privacy' emphasising something about Jack's need for seclusion (internal attribution) that caused him to buy the house. Notice, however, the latter implies that the house is secluded and the former implies that Jack likes privacy (he would be hardly likely to buy such a house if he did not!). An internal attribution may, then, have external implications and vice versa, but of interest is the emphasis a particular person gives when attributing the cause of behaviour. A further problem for psychologists in their search for when people make internal or external attributions is that in certain contexts

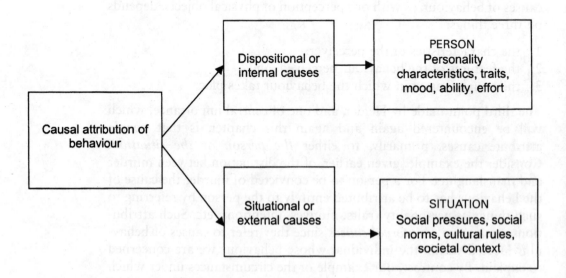

Figure 5.2: Internal and external causes in the attribution of behaviour

people use both. This has been found when people are attributing causes to extreme events, such as terrorist bombing (Kelley, 1973) or between partners in intimate relationships (Fincham, 1985). Weiner's (1986) model of attribution, which we shall consider in Section 5.3.4, overcomes the problem of making an internal–external distinction by offering a multi-dimensional approach.

5.2.2 When attributions are made

In the previous section the claim was made that we attribute causes to all behaviour. While this may be true, over time it is clear that we do not spend all our time thinking about and making attributions of causes of behaviour. Weiner (1985) identified two main conditions under which people are most likely to produce attributions. First, when something unexpected or surprising happens, for example, your best friend behaves in a way that you regard as completely out of character. Second, failure to achieve a desired outcome, for example, passing an examination such as a driving test. Other circumstances when attributions are most likely to be made are when a person loses control or is in a bad mood or experiencing a negative emotion (Bohner *et al.* 1988).

5.2.3 A two-stage model

At times we may offer a spontaneous causal attribution, at other times deliberation, thought and gathering of information takes place before an attribution is made. Gilbert (1989) developed a two-stage model in which *spontaneous,* initial reactions are distinguished from responses resulting from *deliberation.* In the spontaneous stage the behaviour, situation and person are categorised and identified and immediately available information used to make an attribution. For example, Jane (person identification) comes home in a bad mood and is very irritable (behaviour identification) after a difficult day at work (situation identification). One of two attributions, depending on your previous knowledge of Jane, might be spontaneously made. Either work was very stressful that day (external attribution) or Jane cannot cope with the demands of the job (internal attribution). This example shows that we try to interpret ambiguity to make an internal or external attribution. By contrast, unambiguous behaviour, for example, someone acting cruelly, usually results in internal or person attributions being made (Carlston and Skowronski, 1994). Spontaneous attributions are more likely to be dispositional (something about the person) than situational (Jones, 1990).

When a spontaneous attribution cannot be made, for example, if the behaviour is ambiguous, unexpected, or the first impression of a cause of behaviour needs adjusting, a *deliberative* stage is entered. In this stage further information about the behaviour is considered in relation to how that person behaves at different times, how other people will behave in that situation, effects of the behaviour and the emotional impact of the behaviour (Lord, 1997). This information is used to adjust an initial, spontaneous attribution that was made. To continue with our example of Jane coming home from work in a bad mood, we may know that Jane rarely comes home from work like this, in fact she enjoys her job and is regarded as very competent. This deliberation over such information would most likely lead you to make an external attribution – Jane's boss expected too much of her at work that day. Figure 5.3 summarises this two-stage model of attribution. The deliberative stage requires further thought and information gathering and is represented in different ways by the four models of attribution that we will now consider.

5.3 Models of attribution

Four models of attribution will be looked at in this section: the first three are not to be seen as offering different explanations of behaviour but apply depending on what information is available to the attributor. The *causal schemata* model (Kelley, 1972) is used when we have information about a person behaving on a single occasion only. The *covariation*

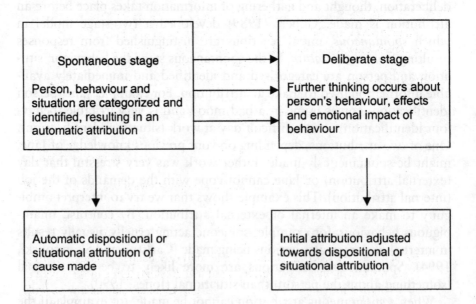

Figure 5.3: Two-stage model of the attribution process

model (Kelley, 1967; 1973) applies when there is considerable information available about the person and other people's behaviour in similar situations. The *correspondent inference* model (Jones and Davis, 1965) is concerned solely with understanding when and under what circumstances people make internal or dispositional attributions. The fourth model is that of Weiner (1979, 1986) which is concerned with how we attribute the causes of success and failure to behaviour and how this might affect self-esteem.

5.3.1 Causal schemata model

In many everyday social situations we make attributions about the cause of a person's behaviour based on no more than a single observation of that person behaving. Take the example, given earlier, of the stranger collapsing on the pavement in front of you; uppermost in your mind, perhaps, will be attempting to explain why the stranger collapsed. What information can be used to assist you in making an attribution? Since you do not know the person you cannot think back to how he behaved in the past; to make an attribution you have to rely on your existing knowledge or *schema* of how people behave in general. To continue with the example, you might infer the person collapsed through being drunk because he was shabbily dressed, smelt of alcohol, etc. In a sense, making attributions based on single acts means that people often draw on stereotypes, implicit personality theory, cultural or societal expectations, etc. These are the kind of things meant by Kelley's term 'causal schemata'. A causal schema is defined by Kelley (1972) as 'a general conception the person has about how certain kinds of causes interact to produce a specific kind of effect'. However, as the above example also demonstrates, we need some guidelines to tell us how we arrive at one type of causal explanation (drunkenness) rather than another (heart attack). Further deliberation and thought are now needed to help decide what specific causal attribution to make.

One of the main strategies used, Kelley (1972) suggests, is the *discounting* principle; this is where other causes are discounted if one is known to be present. For example, suppose I have an accident in my car, on a bend in the road, and this happens late at night. You might be tempted to say I had been drinking since it was about the time the pubs shut. However, you might well discount this causal explanation if you also knew that it had been snowing and the road was very slippery. Given you know one cause to be present (road conditions), you are likely to discount other causes (drinking). The discounting principle demonstrates the tendency people have towards *simplicity* in social perception. While it may be the case that the accident was a result of both of these factors, people often give just one causal explanation when possible. Kelley also proposed an *augmentation* principle, which is the opposite to discounting and where an adjustment is made towards a situational attribution. Using the same example, you might augment the 'road conditions' explanation with further information about the road, such as the accident happened on a bend where many other people had had accidents.

5.3.2 Kelley's covariation model

Kelley's (1967, 1972) covariation model has been highly influential and applies when a considerable amount of information is available to the attributor about how the person in question and other people have behaved in similar social situations. Three types of information about behaviour – consistency, distinctiveness and consensus – are used when making a person or situation attribution.

Suppose we were interested to explain why someone we know, called Steven, behaved in an aggressive way to another person called Peter. Table 5.1 provides a summary description of each type of information

Type of information	Question asked about behaviour	Examples
Consistency	Does the person behave in the same way to the other person at different times?	*High consistency:* Steven usually behaves aggressively towards Peter *Low consistency:* Steven rarely behaves aggressively towards Peter
Distinctiveness	Does the person behave in a similar way to other people?	*High distinctiveness:* Peter does not behave aggressively towards other people *Low distinctiveness:* Peter behaves aggressively to most other people
Consensus	Do other people behave in a similar way to the person?	*High consensus:* Most other people behave in an aggressive way to Peter *Low consensus:* Other people do not behave in an aggressive way towards Peter

Table 5.1: The covariation model of Kelley showing the three types of information – consistency, distinctiveness and consensus – people use to make a person or situation attribution

with examples. As you can see, *consistency* information is about whether the person, in this case Steven, behaves in the same way to the other person, Peter, at *different times*. High consistency is where similar behaviour has been shown at different times and low consistency where past behaviour has been different. *Distinctiveness* is concerned with how the person behaves with other people; highly distinctive behaviour or, in our example, where Peter does not behave aggressively to other people. Behaviour low in distinctiveness is where the person behaves in the same way to everybody else. Consensus information is to do with how other people act towards Steven. That is, in our example, are other people aggressive towards Steven (high consensus) or not (low consensus)?

This is called a *covariation model* since the attribution of a person or situation cause depends on how these three types of information covary to give an overall picture. Table 5.2 shows when an internal (person), external (situation) or circumstance attribution will be made. A *circumstance* attribution is where there are a combination of special factors that are operating at that time only.

Attribution	Type and category of information	Example
Internal dispositional 'Steven is an aggressive person'	High consistency	Steven is almost always aggressive to Peter
	Low distinctiveness	Steven is aggressive to most other people
	Low consensus	Nobody else acts aggressively with Peter
External or situational 'Peter causes Steven to be aggressive'	High consistency	Steven is almost always aggressive to Peter
	High distinctiveness	Steven is not aggressive to most other people
	High consensus	Most other people act aggressively with Peter
Circumstance attribution 'Steven was in a bad mood because his marriage had just broken up'	Low consistency	Steven has never been aggressive to Peter before
	High distinctiveness	Peter is rarely aggressive to other people
	High consensus	Most other people act aggressively with Peter

Table 5.2: Kelley's covariation model showing types of attributions made with examples

McArthur (1972) experimentally investigated Kelley's covariation model by giving participants different combinations of the three types of information. Overall, McArthur found support for the combinations of information specified by Kelley under which people make internal, external and circumstances attributions. However, there were findings not quite in accord with the model and which have been important for later research on attributional biases (see Section 5.4). McArthur found more internal than external attributions were made overall. Also, distinctiveness information was perceived to be the most important type of information, consistency the second most important, and consensus the least important. The covariation model says that people use all three types of information equally, but McArthur's work suggests this not to be the case. More recent research by Alloy and Tabachnik (1984) suggests that people are not that good at assessing and using covariation information.

The covariation model misleadingly suggests that people use only these three types of information, Garland *et al.* (1975) showed that when people are allowed to ask for *any* information they wish, only 23 per cent of requests were for consistency, distinctiveness and consensus information. Some 29 per cent of requests were for other types of dispositional (personality traits) information. Garland *et al.* also found that 25 per cent of requests were concerned with requests for information about the other person. While the covariation model may accurately characterise how we use consistency, distinctiveness and consensus information, it fails to include other information that people may use or seek when making attributions. Much of the research on the covariation model has used short descriptions of behaviour and hence the findings may not generalise to the complexities of 'real' behaviour.

In summary, the covariation model is an elaborate theory of how people perceive the causes of behaviour; it does require a lot of information about the person's past behaviour and about the behaviour of other people. The model also attempts to predict when we will make internal, external and circumstances attributions. However, if we are solely concerned with the more detailed factors regarding when an *internal* attribution is made, the correspondent inference model of Jones and Davis (1965) is best to consider.

5.3.3 Correspondent inference model

The *correspondent inference* model of Jones and Davis (1965) attempts to discover the conditions under which a person's behaviour corresponds to their dispositions (personality, intention, attitude, temperament, etc.). This model attempts to account for how behaviour corresponds to enduring and stable aspects of personality. Such attributions serve the functions of reducing uncertainty, enhancing prediction of future behaviour and increasing our sense of control over the world. Figure 5.4 summarises the five types of information that are thought to be used when making a correspondent inference (Jones and McGillis, 1976).

The two factors that have received the greatest attention are the non-common effects of behaviour and social desirability. To highlight the former, suppose, for example, you are trying to make your mind up about which of three universities you will attend to study psychology. You focus on four factors: location of the campus, academic status, distance from home, and sports facilities. You make enquiries and obtain the information summarised in Table 5.3.

If you decide to go to University A, it is unlikely to be because it is far from home or of good academic status – all three universities have this in common. The non-common aspect of your choice is that University A is on an isolated campus. By contrast, if you choose to go to University C, the non-common aspect or effect is its location in a large city. Making the latter choice might lead to an attribution of *gregariousness*, however,

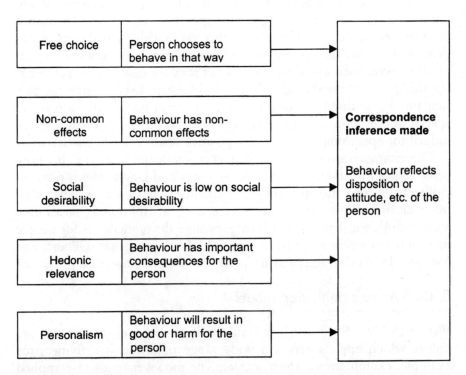

Figure 5.4: Five factors determining whether or not a correspondent inference is made

Factors	University A	University B	University C
Location of campus	Isolated	Small town	Large city
Academic status	Good, high	Good, high	Good, high
Distance from home	Distant	Distant	Distant
Sports facilities	Poor	Good	Good

Table 5.3: Common and non-common consequences from choosing which of three universities to attend

social desirability would need to be taken into account first. If everybody else wants to go to University C, then we cannot say a lot about your choosing to go to this university. By contrast, if this university was unpopular, i.e. not socially desirable, then we could be more confident in our attribution of a gregariousness disposition. To generalise, a correspondent inference is most likely to be made when a behaviour has few non-common effects and is low in social desirability.

The importance of these and other factors given in Table 5.3 was experimentally investigated by Jones and Harris (1967). In this study, students were asked to give a positive speech about someone that they did not have a high opinion of (in this case Fidel Castro). Other students were then asked to make attributions after watching the speeches. They were then asked to assess what they thought the person making the speech really thought about Fidel Castro. Even though the participants knew that the students had been required to make a positive speech about someone they did not like, the observers of the speech judged the speechmakers to hold a positive attitude towards Castro.

The characterisation of when a correspondent inference between behaviour and personality is made by Jones and Davis (1965) requires deliberation and thought about numerous social cues and personal information. When we come to consider attributional biases (see Section 5.4), we shall see just how pervasive the tendency is for people to make dispositional attributions, to the extent that Gilbert and Malone (1995) characterise this as the *correspondence bias*.

5.3.4 Weiner's attribution model

Weiner (1979, 1986) developed an attribution model for success and failure which applies across a wide range of different activities; for example, examinations, sport, career. The model may also be applied in a clinical setting to depression, as we shall see in Section 5.8, because of its implications for future behaviour and the self-esteem of a person.

In explaining success or failure, Weiner claims that we attribute it to one (or more) of four basic causes: ability, effort, task difficulty and luck. How a person arrives at one of these four causal attributions depends on the categorisation on each of three dimensions; internal–external, stable–unstable and controllable–uncontrollable. The internal–external dimension should already be quite familiar to you since it is to do with the *locus* of the cause; something about the person (internal) or about the situation (external). The stable–unstable dimension refers to whether the cause is changeable or likely to change, or whether it is enduring and a permanent feature. For example, in an educational context ability in say, mathematics is regarded as a stable disposition of a person, whereas mood may be regarded as unstable. The third dimension concerns the extent to which we may regard a person as having control over a cause. Thus effort put into revision is controllable, whereas being set a really difficult examination paper is uncontrollable. Table 5.4 summarises how the four basic causes are categorised according to each of these three dimensions.

This model has received considerable application to the education context. For example, Dweck *et al.* (1993) show that adults and children who attribute failure in a task to an internal, stable cause, such as a character defect, are not likely to persist in the task. Making an external attribution for failure serves to protect a person's self-esteem. For example, attributing failure to get a job to other people's discrimination and ignorance means the person will continue to apply for jobs in the future (Crocker and Major, 1989). Our emotional reaction to the plight of a victim will differ according to whether we think the victim was able to control or not control the circumstances. Betancourt (1990) showed that pity is aroused if we regard a cause as uncontrollable, whereas anger is aroused if the cause is perceived as controllable.

While there is considerable empirical support for Weiner's model, there are concerns about whether people actually use these three

	Internal		External	
	Stable	**Unstable**	**Stable**	**Unstable**
Controllable	Typical effort	Unusual effort	Help from a friend	Help from a stranger
Uncontrollable	Ability	Mood	Task difficulty	Luck

Table 5.4: Weiner's (1979) model for attribution of success and failure showing possible causes related to each of the three dimensions

dimensions and if so, whether such a detailed and logical approach is adopted. Krantz and Rude (1984) asked participants to classify the four common causes mentioned above along each of Weiner's three dimensions. Only a minority classified a cause in the same way as Weiner, for example, a good proportion of participants classified ability as unstable. Individuals perceive human attributes differently; intelligence is seen as stable by some people and unstable (liable to change) by others. However, Weiner's model does enjoy considerable success and has recently been extended to provide an analysis of how we judge responsibility and blame (Weiner, 1995), thus offering a widely applicable theory of social behaviour.

5.4 Attributional accuracy and error

These four models of causal attribution assume that people operate in a rational and logical way in characterising cause and effect in human social behaviour. However, since we rarely are disinterested, detached and objective when making attributions, these models ought, perhaps, to be regarded as *normative*. That is, they prescribe how attributions may be made on a rational basis. For example, Kelley's covariation model tells us which combinations of information (consistency, distinctiveness and consensus) *should* result in an internal or an external attribution being made. Research in social cognition demonstrates that when describing what people actually do, short cuts or heuristics are used (Fiske and Taylor, 1991). Processes involved in social perception (see Chapter 4), may mean that self-interest, a person's strongly held beliefs, focus of attention, etc., may introduce bias or error when people make causal attributions. In this section we shall look at four errors or biases that people are commonly found to make. These are: the correspondence bias, actor–observer differences, self-serving biases and group-serving biases.

5.4.1 Correspondence bias

Thirty years of research by social psychologists into how people attribute causes to social behaviour has time and time again demonstrated the strong tendency for people to attribute behaviour to dispositions (Gilbert, 1995; Jones, 1990). People making attributions too readily assume a person's traits, attitudes, beliefs, intentions, etc., *correspond* with what a person does or says. A study by Jones and Harris (1967) provided an early demonstration of this. In this study, students read an essay about Fidel Castro, the President of Cuba, which they were told was written by another student. The student readers of the essay read either a pro- or anti-Castro essay and were told the student who wrote it either had no choice (they were instructed to do so), or freedom to choose whether or not to write the essay. The experimenters asked the students who read the essays to estimate the attitude towards Fidel Castro of the student who wrote the essay. Where students chose to write the essay, a positive attitude to Castro was attributed. However, a dispositional attribution, i.e. positive attitude, was also attributed to students who were instructed to write the essay. These findings are summarised in Figure 5.5.

Gilbert and Malone (1995) suggest four main reasons to explain the pervasiveness of the correspondence bias. First, people do not take sufficient account of situational constraints, and this is known as the fundamental attribution error (Ross, 1977). Second, when making attributions people wrongly assume that what a person says and does is always consistent with their attitudes and intentions (see Chapter 4 for more on the attitude–behaviour link). Third, the link between the person and the behaviour is over-emphasised because people make spontaneous trait attributions (see Section 5.2.3). Fourth, spontaneous attributions are taken at face value and not adjusted sufficiently when further deliberation is made (Gilbert, 1991). Figure 5.6 summarises these four contributions to the correspondence bias.

The fundamental attribution error was investigated in a study by Ross *et al.* (1977). In this experiment, participants were either assigned the role of 'questioner' or 'answerer' in a general knowledge quiz game. The questioner was asked to make up a number of questions from his or her general knowledge. These questions were then put to the participant allocated the 'answerer' role. The answerer is at a strong disadvantage here since the questioner can draw on his or her own idiosyncratic general knowledge. Another group of participants observed this quiz game and were instructed to pay attention to both the questioner and answerer when observing. When the quiz was over, the questioners, answerers and observers were all asked to rate the general knowledge of the questioner and answerer. It was found that both answerers and observers rated the questioner as having *superior* general knowledge to the answerers. The findings are summarised in Figure 5.7.

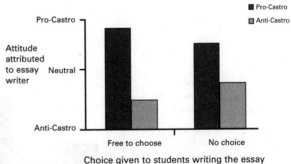

Figure 5.5: Attributions made by students reading essays of other students who were instructed or free to choose whether they wrote a pro- or anti-Castro essay. Adapted from Jones and Harris (1967)

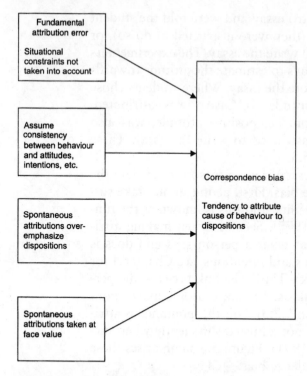

Figure 5.6: Four reasons suggested by Gilbert & Malone (1995) to explain the correspondence bias

These findings represent the fundamental attribution error since, as Ross *et al.* (1977) argue, the perceivers (answers and observers) ignored the situational determinants (structure of the game) which gave power to the questioners. Too much emphasis was placed on the personality characteristics of the questioner. The fundamental attribution error has been shown to extend to where people fail to recognize the power they themselves have over a situation (Gilbert and Jones, 1986). Barjonet (1980) reports research demonstrating a tendency to over-attribute road accidents to the driver rather than situational factors such as the state of the car or road conditions.

The second explanation for the correspondence bias concerns unrealistic expectations that we have at times of other people and ourselves. We tend to assume greater consistency between attitudes, intentions and behaviour (see Chapter

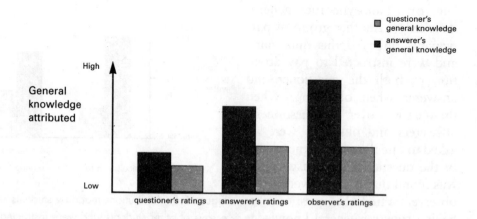

Figure 5.7: Attributions of general knowledge made by questioners, answerers, and observers in Ross *et al.* (1977) Quiz Game

4) with the consequence that when attributing a cause to behaviour, we too readily assume consistency and offer dispositional attributions. Further, Reeder *et al.* (1989) demonstrated that unrealistic expectations are held about what a person is able to do. For example, Sherman (1980) showed that college students wrongly think that people will not agree to write an essay counter to their own beliefs or attitudes. Bierbrauer (1979) asked participants to watch a re-enactment of the famous Milgram (1963) experiment on obedience to authority. Participants were asked to indicate the percentage of disobedience they thought would occur at various levels of electric shock. Results showed a consistent *under-estimate* of how 'teachers' would yield to situational forces demanding obedience. Other explanations of the correspondence bias include, focus of attention, differential forgetting, developmental changes, cultural factors and linguistic factors. For example, Kassin and Pryor (1985) regard the tendency to make dispositional attributions as acquired in childhood. Children, it would seem, have to learn *not* to make situational attributions (Higgins and Bryant, 1982) and to discover that a person is responsible for his or her behaviour. This may well be due to parental influences, since Dix *et al.* (1986) found that parents were more likely to use dispositional attributions to explain their child's behaviour as the child grows older. This may also be cultural, since Miller (1984) showed that Hindu children became increasingly 'situational' in their attributions as they get older. This may reflect different cultural norms (Morris and Peng, 1994).

On a critical note, Harvey, Town and Yarkin (1981) argue that in order to say an attribution is biased or in error, we first need to know what is the correct attribution for the cause of a behaviour. As Locke and Pennington (1982) point out, people from different perspectives may emphasise different reasons for the behaviour which may be *justified* given the perspectives and interests of the attributor. For example, Kulik (1983) demonstrated that people make situational attributions when behaviour is inconsistent with prior expectations.

5.4.2 Actor–observer differences

When looking at the fundamental attribution error we saw that situational factors tend to be ignored. This applies when we are making attributions about another person's behaviour. However, when we attribute causes to our own behaviour, situational factors tend to get over-emphasised. This has become known as the actor–observer difference (Jones and Nisbett, 1972); the actor or self is the person attributing causes (mainly external or situational) to his or her own behaviour; the observer or other is the person attributing causes (mainly internal or dispositional) to another's behaviour. Nisbett *et al.* showed this in an experiment where participants were asked to explain, both for themselves and a friend, reasons for their chosen course of study at a college. Attribution of reasons for their own chosen course of study gave as much emphasis to their own interests and personality traits (dispositional) as to the quality of the course (situational). By contrast, when explaining why a friend had taken a certain course of study, participants emphasised dispositional factors. Three main explanations, summarised in Figure 5.8, have been offered to account for this difference. First, the difference may arise simply because we have more *privileged information* when explaining our own rather than another person's behaviour.

Each of us know a lot more about how we have acted in the past than how another person has acted (even a close, long-standing friend). Second, the *salience* or *focus of attention* of causal factors is different for actors and observers. The observer finds the individual more salient

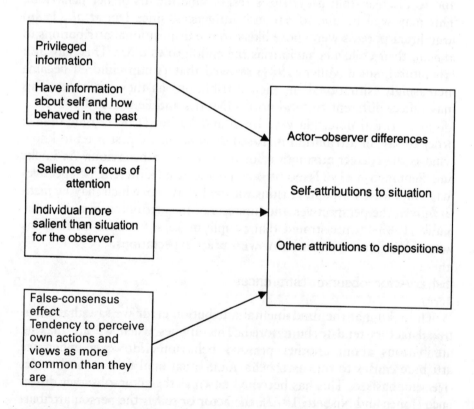

Figure 5.8: Explanations for the actor–observer differences in the attribution of causes to social behaviour

since attention is focused more on the person than the surrounding situation (in Gestalt psychology the individual is the *figure* and the social situation the *background*). By contrast, the individual is more sensitive to forces in the environment than his or her personality when making a self-attribution (Fiske and Taylor, 1991). If this line of argument is valid, we would predict that *any* technique which changes salience for actor and observer should result in a corresponding change in attributions made. Storms (1973) demonstrated that actor–observer attributions could be *reversed* by showing the actor a videotape of himself or herself. In this experiment, two participants took part in a conversation and two observers watched – each observer watched one of the participants in the conversation. Storms videotaped the conversation and played it back to the participants in one of two ways. Half the participants (actors who were the participants in conversation and observers) saw the same videotape to that which they saw live. That is, the actor saw a videotape of the person he was in conversation with, the observer saw the person he was originally assigned to watch. This is the *same orientation* condition of the experiment. The other half of the participants saw a videotape from the *opposite* orientation, that is, actors watched *themselves* in conversation, and observers watched the person they had been instructed *not* to watch initially in the 'live' conversation. There was also a control group of participants who watched only the live conversation, but not the video playback. All participants were then asked to rate the extent to which friendliness, nervousness and dominance of the person they watched initially or themselves was due to either dispositional or situation factors.

Results showed that first, the traditional actor–observer difference was present in the control condition as expected. Second, participants who saw the videotape in the *same* orientation produced even greater actor–observer differences (actors gave more external and observers more internal attributions). Third, and most importantly, participants who were in the *opposite* orientation for the video playback *reversed* the traditional attributional difference. Actors tended to see their behaviour strongly in dispositional terms and observers in situational terms.

The third main explanation for actor–observer differences is the *false consensus* effect; this is the tendency to view our own actions, attitudes and choices as more common than they actually are (Marks and Miller, 1987; Wetzel and Walton, 1985). A classic study by Ross, Greene and House (1977) demonstrated this. In this experiment students were asked if they would walk around the campus with a sandwich board with the word 'repent' written in large letters. Students who agreed to do this estimated that about 60 per cent of people asked would also agree, while students who refused estimated that over 75 per cent of other people asked would also refuse. In attributing causes to others this study demonstrates that people underestimate situational constraints and see their own choice as much more common than it actually is. In a similar way, we may see our friends and acquaintances as more like ourselves in terms of attitudes and personality traits. This demonstrates that the false consensus effect has wider application than in just explaining actor–observer differences. More recently, Buehler, Griffin and Ross (1995) have shown that people are over-optimistic about their abilities at certain tasks and pessimistic about other people in relation to the same tasks. This may reflect self-interest and the need to preserve our own self-esteem. This takes us to consider self-serving biases.

5.4.3 Self-serving biases

A self-serving bias is where a person attributes causes to their own or others' behaviour in such a way as to enhance their abilities and/or their self-esteem (Snyder *et al.* 1977). For example, people who experience success at some task might attribute that success to person (internal) characteristics such as ability and effort. In Weiner's (1985) model of attribution, attribution of success is due to internal, stable and controllable causes (see Section 5.3.4). By contrast, people who experience failure may attribute the failure to external factors such as task difficulty and bad luck (i.e. external, unstable, and uncontrollable). With the former, a person is saying he or she is responsible for that success, but with the latter the person is saying that failure is not his or her fault. If you had just failed an exam your self-esteem would be 'dented', so to bolster your opinion of yourself it would be self-serving to think and claim that the examination paper was a particularly hard one that year and that you had bad luck with the questions that came up, thus making an external attribution.

Initial support for a self-serving bias in attribution came from Johnson *et al.* (1964), who used educational psychology students as participants and asked them to teach arithmetic to two pupils. The students were subsequently told that one pupil had performed well and one had performed poorly on a test. Students were then asked to teach more arithmetic to the same two pupils. Subsequently the participants were told that the pupil who had done well the first time had continued to do so, but the pupil who had done badly the first time had either (a) continued to perform badly or (b) improved. Students were then asked to account for the performance of the two pupils. It was found that the student teachers attributed improved performance in the initially poor pupil to themselves and continued poor performance to the pupil. However, research using experienced rather than student teachers failed to produce consistent findings. Ross *et al.* (1974) had professional teachers coach 11-year-olds to spell words correctly which are often misspelt. Teachers were then informed that the pupil had done very well or very badly on a subsequent spelling test. The teachers were then asked to indicate how important they thought teaching ability and scholastic ability of the pupil were in determining the pupil's test performance. It was found that teachers who were told their pupil performed badly thought teaching ability *more* important that scholastic ability of the pupil. By contrast, teachers who were told pupils had done well thought the pupils' ability to be more important than the teaching they received. Explanations for self-serving biases centre on motivational (Zuckerman, 1979) and cognitive factors (Miller and Ross, 1975). Subsequent research has found difficulties in making a clear distinction between these two factors (Tetlock and Manstead, 1985). However, the ego-enhancing and self-preservational self-serving biases do have important enhancing functions for the individual and may well lead them to persist at a task or try again at an examination or driving test, for example. Otherwise ego-deflating attributions would be made.

5.4.4 Group-serving biases

The idea that attributions may act as self-serving biases for individual enhancement may be extended to inter-group attribution (Hewstone, 1989). Such attributions are typically ethnocentric in that they serve to enhance the in-group (the group you identify yourself as being a member of) and denigrate the out-group. Pettigrew (1979) suggested that negative behaviours of an out-group are attributed to negative dispositions of the group members, whilst positive out-group behaviours are attributed to situational factors such as luck. Hewstone and Ward (1985) showed that Malays who lived in Malaysia demonstrated an ethnocentre bias, but this was less marked for Malays living in Singapore. By contrast, Chinese participants did not show an ethnocentric bias. Islam and Hewstone (1993) showed that a majority group (in this case Muslims) displayed an ethnocentric bias favouring their own group and attributed negatively to a minority group (in this case Hindus). However, the effect does not seem to apply to majority and minority groups generally, since Hindus did not display a strong in-group bias. Cultural differences may be present in the way attributions are made (Fletcher and Ward, 1988) with Western cultures placing more value on dispositional attributions generally.

Two explanations for ethnocentric attributional biases have been identified. First, the process of *social categorisation* itself creates expectations and stereotypes for in-groups and out-groups (Hogg and Abrams, 1988). Second, *social identity theory* (see Chapter 10) states that people gain a sense of identity and enhanced self-esteem from belonging to certain social groups (Turner, 1982). Thus the group to which a person belongs is 'protected' by making positive, internal attributions about desirable outcomes and negative external attributions about undesirable outcomes. Table 5.5 provides an example of possible attributions in the context of a sport competition involving two teams.

5.5 Attribution and the social context

In our consideration of attributional biases and error, reference to cultural differences has been made a number of times, especially in relation to inter-group attributions. In this section we take a look at the influence of the social context, in terms of cultural differences, on causal attribution. Cross-cultural research in social psychology has paid particular attention to individualistic versus collectivist cultural norms (Triandis, 1994). In the attribution context, Bond and Hwang (1986) for example, found Hong Kong Chinese students to focus more on collective responsibilities (external) than American students. There does seem to be general support for the idea that non-Western cultures are less likely to make internal or dispositional attributions for behaviour than Western cultures (Morris and Peng, 1994). The explanations offered for this difference are to do with the influence of social roles in non-Western collectivist cultures (Fletcher and Ward, 1988) and a more holistic world-view. Miller (1984) compared North American and Hindu children in the 8-year-old to 15-year-old age range and found that at age 8 both groups offered relatively infrequent dispositional attributions for social behaviour. However, as age increased, North Americans came to make more dispositional attributions compared to Hindus.

Attribution	Own team wins	Other team wins
Internal	We are good at the sport Trained well in advance Natural aptitude for the sport	Not good at the sport Did little training before the game No natural aptitude for the sport
External	Competition was strong Referee was fair	Had lots of luck and lucky breaks Referee was biased

Table 5.5: Intergroup biases in a game of sport between two teams

Smith and Bond (1993) identify what they call *cross-cultural misattribution*. This is where an attribution made by someone foreign to a particular culture differs from that made by a person who is a member of that culture. An example may help clarify what is meant here; imagine a culture X where men openly express emotions and you come from a British culture where men have a 'stiff upper lip' and regard it as weak to display feelings. In culture X, people may perceive you as rude and violating social norms by behaving 'coldly', and hence an attribution of 'uncivilised' may be made about you (Burgoon, 1989). Thus to behave in ways appropriate to your own culture may result in a misattribution; in our example here it is negative. Burgoon also demonstrates that misattribution may also be positive, for example, closer personal distance, more touching and higher levels of eye-contact from a person of another culture to ours are generally positively received.

Cross-cultural differences have also been found in the attribution of success and failure. For example, Fry and Ghosh (1980) took matched groups of white Canadian and Asian-Indian Canadian children aged between eight and ten years. The self-serving bias was present in the white Canadian children who attributed success to effort and ability, and failure to bad luck and other external factors. However, Asian–Indian children rated luck as important for success and ability as an important factor in failure. Cross-cultural differences in causal attribution may often lead to misunderstanding between people and groups from different cultures. Referring back to the two-stage model (see Section 5.2.3), the importance of avoiding spontaneous attributions and being more deliberative when making attributions about the behaviour of somebody from another culture should be obvious. Deliberation may avoid negative (and positive) misattributions and help avoid misunderstandings.

5.6 Personality and attributional style

So far, this chapter has been concerned to discover the conditions under which people make internal and external attributions. At the beginning of the chapter we saw that people attribute internal and external causes in an attempt to make the social world a more predictable place in which to live. Being in a position to predict how other people will behave has the implication that a certain amount of *control* over the future is possible. The two themes of control and internal/external attributions are claimed to constitute a single personality dimension suggested by Rotter (1966), and called *locus of control*. Rotter suggested that some people perceive behaviour (both theirs and others) to be largely under external control called *external locus of control*. This means that those who fall towards the 'internal' end of the locus of control personality dimension perceive their own behaviour as under their own personal control, hence the consequences of certain behaviours such as success or failure at an examination, joy or despair, are seen as under their control and resulting from their own actions. By contrast, people who are 'external' perceive themselves as having little control over how they are, what they do and the consequences which follow their actions. Here, success or failure at an examination would not be attributed to effort and ability (internal) but more to other people's behaviour (good teachers) and chance or luck (the right questions came up), which are both external attributions.

A personality questionnaire was developed by Rotter (1966) which consisted of 29 items, five of which are given in Table 5.6. You may wish to see if you are an 'internal' or 'external'; to do this, circle the option in each question, either (a) or (b), which most accurately represents your views. The notes given in Table 5.6 tell you how to score each item and how to find out where you might be on the locus of control scale (remember this is only an indication).

The theory Rotter used in developing the idea of locus of control was not derived from the attribution tradition of Heider but from the *behaviourist* approach in which all behaviour is seen as a product of

---

Items on the locus of control scale

1. <u>a</u> Many of the unhappy things in people's lives are partly due to bad luck.
   b People's misfortunes result from the mistakes they make.
2. <u>a</u> In the long run people get the respect they deserve in this world.
   b Unfortunately, an individual's worth often passes unrecognized no matter how hard he tries.
3. <u>a</u> In the case of the well-prepared student there is rarely, if ever, such a thing as an unfair test.
   b Many times exam questions tend to be so unrelated to coursework that studying is really useless.
4. <u>a</u> In my case getting what I want has little or nothing to do with luck.
   b Many times we might just as well decide what to do by flipping a coin.
5. <u>a</u> Sometimes I can't understand how teachers arrive at the grades they give.
   b There is a direct connection between how hard I study and the grades I get.

Table 5.6: Examples of items from Rotter's (1966) Locus of Control Scale questionnaire. To reach a score, simply add up the number of times you agreed with an underlined statement (a) or (b). A score of 5 (maximum here) indicates *external* locus of control, a score of 0 (minimum) indicates *internal* locus of control

either *reinforcement* or *punishment*. Rotter originally called the scale the 'internal versus external control of reinforcement', emphasising the point that it is the internal or external control of reinforcement that was of central concern. The idea of locus of control has readily lent itself to the attribution approach. In the next section we shall see how it has been applied to the understanding and treatment of clinical depression where Seligman *et al.* (1979) developed an attributional style questionnaire.

The concept of attributional style and locus of control as a personality variable has enjoyed considerable attention in the field of health psychology (Taylor, 1991). Research indicates that healthier people are those who are more internal (Strickland, 1974). Seeman *et al.* (1985) report that internals are more likely to engage in behaviours that will keep them healthy. Internals are reported to be more likely to be successful at stopping smoking (Shipley, 1981). Putting this into an attributional framework means that a smoker who scores as an internal on the locus of control scale will predict his or her likely success at giving up smoking as due to ability, effort and other dispositions. By contrast, an external may say things like 'the time is right' for me to give up smoking and other external attributions. Hence, when situational difficulties arise, the external may revert back to smoking because the situation has changed.

Wallston and Wallston (1978) have shown that people who suffer from a chronic disease such as diabetes are generally healthier if they believe they can control their condition (as opposed to control lying with health professionals or powerful others). This idea relates to Bandura's (1977a) concept of *self-efficacy*. This is the extent to which a person believes he or she can successfully perform a certain behaviour (such as dieting, giving up smoking, etc.).

Paulhas (1983) refined the general idea of locus of control and developed a questionnaire designed to measure three different aspects: control over personal achievements, control over interpersonal encounters, and control over wider social and political matters. Paulhas found that people differ in their perception of control in these three different aspects. Scoring 'internal' on two of these aspects does not necessarily mean a person would score as internal on the third aspect. This refinement means that personality differences in attributional style may be specific to one of three particular domains.

The main criticism of individual differences with respect to attributional style is that high levels of cross-situational consistency are not found. This means that a person scoring high as an internal does not consistently act in this way across a wide range of different social situations. The work of Paulhas, mentioned above, may throw some light on why cross-situational consistency is low for attributional style.

5.7 Application: attribution and depression

Depression is something we all suffer from at times – it varies in intensity from just having the 'blues' or feeling a little down to chronic states where a person sees the whole world as a useless, evil place in which to live and has little or no self-esteem or feeling of self-worth. Attribution theorists and clinical psychologists have developed a model and therapy for understanding and treating depression (Abramson and Martin, 1981). At this point, it is important to bear in mind that the approach applies only to what is called *unipolar* depression, not *bipolar* depression. Bipolar depression is where an individual *alternates* between periods of depression and mania; unipolar depression is where somebody only has depressive episodes with *no* history or indication of mania.

The approach has been developed from the *learned helplessness* model of depression (Seligman, 1975) which states that depressed people believe themselves to have little or no control over what happens to them in their lives. This makes people feel helpless, becomes a normal way of viewing oneself, and results in people being unable to help themselves. However, lowered self-esteem is also an important aspect of depression which the learned helplessness model fails to account for on its own. A reformulation in attribution terms by Abramson *et al.* (1978) suggested that *how* people make attributions for this lack of control over what happens to them in their lives has important consequences for their depressive state in general and their self-esteem in particular.

Weiner's (1979) attribution model for success and failure, which we looked at in some detail in Section 5.3.4, has been modified on one of the three dimensions. Applying the model to depression maintained the two dimensions of internal–external and stable–unstable, and introduced a third dimension of global–specific. A global attribution is where a person perceives the cause as being related to many different behaviours in their life, or specific to just that behaviour. An example may help clarify how the model applies to depression. Imagine that you have just broken up with your boyfriend or girlfriend and you have become very depressed about this. How you attribute the cause of the relationship failure, your attribution style for negative events, may cause you to become very depressed. Abramson and Martin (1981) suggest that a person who was chronically depressed would make an internal, stable and global attribution which might be as shown in Figure 5.9.

This negative attributional style has the consequences of lowering self-esteem (I am not worth knowing since I always cause arguments), making the person believe he or she is unable to control the future (I'm

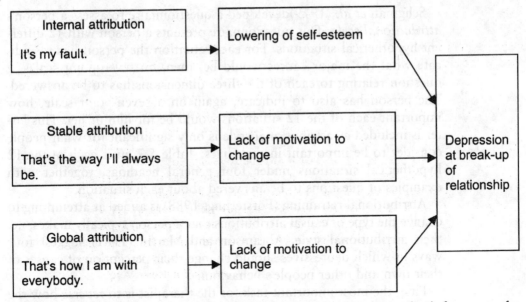

Figure 5.9: Weiner's three dimensions demonstrating a negative attributional style for causes of a relationship breaking up

never going to be worth knowing because I will always cause arguments), and that this happens no matter who the person is with (I'm like this with everybody). Sweeney *et al.* (1986) reviewed a large number of studies and found a reasonable correlation between attributional style and depression. However, as was discussed in Chapter 1, correlation is not causation and from this we could equally infer that depression causes a negative attribution style. Nolen-Hoeksama *et al.* (1992) provide evidence that attributional style predicts certain depressive symptoms. This provides some indication that attributional style may cause depression.

The example we have looked at above is for a negative event, but how would a depressed person with a negative attributional style attribute the cause of a *positive* event? For example, consider the attributions for a person successfully forming an enduring relationship, a negative attribution style would be to make an external, unstable and specific attribution. The external attribution could be 'the relationship works because she always gives in to me'; the unstable attribution 'good things only happen when she is in a good mood'; and the specific attribution 'this relationship would not work with anybody else'. Put together, these attributions result in the person perceiving him or herself to be helpless to bring about positive events in life and possessing low self-esteem.

Seligman *et al.* (1979)developed a questionnaire to assess a person's *attributional style*. This questionnaire presents a person with 12 different hypothetical situations. For each situation the person has to indicate what the major causes would be, then, on seven-point scales, a question relating to each of the three dimensions has to be answered. The person has also to indicate, again on a seven-point scale, how important each of the 12 situations would be for him or her. This latter is included as attributional style is only significant for what people consider to be important in their lives. Table 5.7 gives each of the 12 hypothetical situations under four general headings, together with examples of questions to be answered about each situation.

Attributional retraining (Försterling, 1988) is aimed at attempting to change the type of causal attributions that a person typically makes, i.e. their attributional style. Abramson and Martin (1981) suggest four ways in which depressives should change their perception of causes of their own and other people's behaviour.

First, the most important task for the therapist is to *reverse* how the person perceives control over the outcomes of his or her behaviour – the person has to be encouraged to think and believe that he or she *can control* what happens. This should result in a change in attributional style from, for example, internal, stable and global for negative events to external, unstable and specific. The change from helplessness to believing one can help oneself is crucial. Second, depressives must set themselves *realistic* goals in life rather than unattainable goals – a person often does the latter since it serves to perpetuate feelings of helplessness. Third, the importance of unattainable, but often desirable, goals must be *decreased*; the therapist must try to make the person find attainable goals rather than unattainable goals desirable and attractive. Fourth, in feeling helpless the depressive perceives other people to have control; this has to be changed to a more healthy balanced position whereby the amount of control another is perceived to have is equal to the amount of control one perceives oneself to have.

Attributional retraining for someone with an established negative attributional style may be difficult to achieve since research has shown that learned helplessness may have an onset in early childhood (Dweck, 1991). Fincham *et al.* (1987) have shown that this may lead a child to exhibit negative emotions and depression, and that this is relatively stable in late childhood (Fincham *et al.*, 1989). How children develop such an attributional style is not really known and is an area in need of research.

The application of Weiner's (1979) model of attribution to understanding and treating depression has proved valuable for clinical psychologists. However, it has been suggested that not all three dimensions

Attributional-Style Questionnaire

Hypothetical situations

Positive achievement items
(i)   You become very rich
(ii)   You apply for a job (college place) that you badly want and get it
(iii)   You get a raise

Negative achievement items
(iv)   You have been looking for a job unsuccessfully for some time
(v)   You give an important talk in front of a group and the audience reacts negatively
(vi)   You can't get all the work done that others expect of you

Positive interpersonal items
(vii)   You meet a friend who compliments you on your appearance
(viii) Your spouse (boyfriend/girlfriend) has been treating you more lovingly
(ix)   You do a project which is highly praised

Negative interpersonal items
(x)   A friend comes to you with a problem and you don't try to help him
(xi)   You meet a friend who acts hostilely toward you
(xii)   You go out on a date and it goes badly

Questions asked about each of the above situations

(i)   Write down *one* major cause

(ii)   *Is the cause of your friend's compliment due to something about the other person or circumstances?*
        Totally due to the other person   1   2   3   4   5   6   7
        Totally due to me or circumstances

(iii)   *In the future when you are with your friends, will this cause again be present?*
        Will never again be present   1   2   3   4   5   6   7
        Will always be present

(iv)   *Is the cause something that just affects interacting with friends or does it also influence other areas of your life?*
        Influences just this particular situation   1   2   3   4   5   6   7
        Influences all situations in my life

(v)   *How important would this situation be if it happened to you?*
        Not at all important   1   2   3   4   5   6   7
        Extremely important

Table 5.7: Examples of items from the attributional-style questionnaire developed by Seligman (1979)

are of equal importance. The internal–external dimension is seen as the most important since it relates directly to controllability of behaviour. Reversing attributions for positive events from external to internal, and for negative events from internal to external has been found to be the most effective way of raising self-esteem and alleviating depression (Försterling, 1988).

5.8 Summary

- The attribution approach is concerned to understand how people attribute causes to their own and other people's behaviour.
- Heider (1944) laid conceptual foundations in claiming that people perceive causes of behaviour as either to do with the person (dispositions/internal) or to do with situational forces (external).
- People are most likely to attribute causes when behaviour is unexpected or a desired outcome is not achieved.
- The two-stage model distinguishes between causal attributions made spontaneously and attributions made after deliberation where further information is sought and used.
- The four main models of attribution are the causal schemata model, Kelley's covariation model, the correspondent inference model and Weiner's model of attributions for success and failure. All four models may require deliberation before an attribution is made.
- The attributions that people actually make reveal four common errors or biases. First, the correspondence bias where attributions to dispositions/the person tend to be made. One explanation of this is the fundamental attribution error where situational forces are ignored. Second, actor–observer differences where people attribute their own behaviour to external causes and others' behaviour to internal causes. Third, self-serving biases and, fourth, group-serving biases.
- Cross-cultural research in attribution has investigated individualistic versus collectivist cultural norms resulting in the former tending towards internal attributions and the latter towards external attributions. Cultural misattribution may result from different cultural norms and not understanding the norms of a different culture.
- Rotter developed the concept of locus of control and suggested that a personality difference exists where some people perceive behaviour to be caused by internal factors and others perceive behaviour to be caused by external factors.
- The attribution model of Weiner has been applied to the understanding and treatment of depression. The learned helplessness model was reformulated to the three dimensions of internal–external, stable–unstable and global–specific. Depressives demonstrate a negative attributional style and attributional retraining attempts to reverse, for example, the attribution of internal, stable and global to negative events.

5.9 Suggestions for further reading

Durkin, K. 1995: *Developmental Social Psychology: From Infancy to Old Age*. Oxford: Blackwell.

Very well-written text book that has a good chapter on attribution and child development, also good, short summaries of main areas of attribution theory and research.

Fiske, S. T. and Taylor, S. E. 1991: *Social Cognition*. New York: McGraw-Hill.

Good coverage of attribution theory and research together with the inclusion of areas concerned with social perception. Reasonably advanced text that looks at the development of attribution theory from the work of Heider. Needs updating to take account of more recent research.

FÖRSTERLING, E. 1988: *Attribution Theory in Clinical Psychology*. Chichester: Wiley.

Detailed account of the application of attribution to help understand and treat clinical disorders such as depression. A more accessible article by the same author can be found in the *American Psychologist*, 1986, volume 41, pp. 275–85.

Hewstone, M. 1989: *Casual Attribution: From Cognitive Processes to Collective Beliefs*. Oxford: Blackwell.

Good general coverage of attribution theory and research, although in need of updating. Especially useful for social, group and cross-cultural aspects of theory and research.

Weiner, B. 1995: *Judgements of Responsibilities*. New York: Guilford.

Up-to-date, if advanced text, summarising research and the critical developments of this author's important contribution to attribution applications in many contexts, especially education.

6 Non-verbal communication and interpersonal behaviour

6.1 Introduction

We spend much of our social lives interacting, face-to-face, with another person or small group of people. This occurs via the medium of both spoken language and *non-verbal communication*. Verbal communication may be defined as the actual words spoken, whereas non-verbal communication includes both *vocal* and *non-vocal behaviour*. Vocal behaviour refers to aspects of speech such as intonation, pitch, speed and hesitations, and non-vocal behaviour includes other communicative behaviour. This includes physical contact (touch), body language, gaze and facial expressions, personal space, appearance, and environmental factors (Hargie *et al.*, 1994) (*see* Fig. 6.1).

We may regard these two types of communication as serving different functions. However, it is important to bear in mind that non-verbal communication can substitute for language; the best example of this is sign language used by deaf people. Functionally, verbal communication, in the form of language, is used to convey logical or abstract ideas, whereas non-verbal communication serves a much broader range of functions (Hargie *et al.*, 1994).

Early research on non-verbal behaviours tended to concentrate on 'channels' of communication in isolation. Each different type of non-verbal behaviour, e.g. contact, proximity, touch, etc. was regarded as a different channel, just like television channels. However, more recent

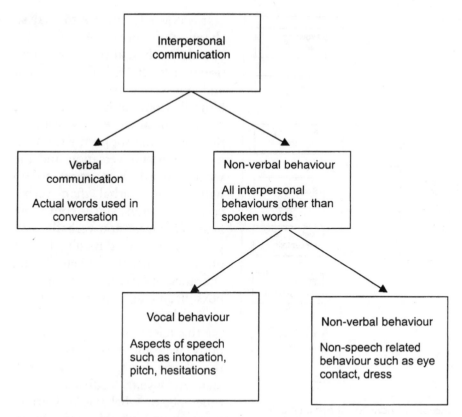

Figure 6.1: Components of interpersonal communication showing how non-verbal communication consists of both vocal and non-vocal behaviour

research has developed an 'across channels' approach which makes it possible to identify the functions served by different combinations and patterns of non-verbal behaviour (Patterson, 1990). Three basic functions of non-verbal behaviour originally identified by researchers in the late 1960s and early 1970s were: (a) providing information to another person or other people; (b) regulating interaction between two or more people; and (c) expressing intimacy, especially with our loved ones.

More recently, Patterson (1987) has proposed four additional categories, which include: *social control* – to gain influence over an interactant partner; *self-presentation* – to create a preferred identity; *effect management* – which regulates and modifies the experience, for instance negative reactions might be shown by avoidance techniques and reduced gaze. The fourth additional function is the *service–task* function, which relates to exchanges with professionals, such as doctors or dentists, in which there might be higher levels of touching. This is summarised in Figure 6.2.

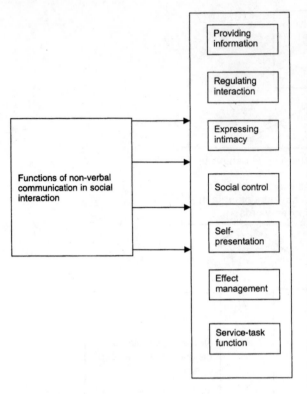

Providing information

Regulating interaction

Expressing intimacy

Functions of non-verbal communication in social interaction

Social control

Self-presentation

Effect management

Service-task function

Figure 6.2: Functions of non-verbal communication including categories proposed by Patterson (1987)

It is not only difficult to analyse channels of non-verbal behaviours in isolation but, at times, the functional distinction between verbal and non-verbal behaviour is also blurred. Communication can take place in the absence of, or with little, non-verbal support, such as in a telephone conversation and the written word. It is easier to do without non-verbal than verbal communication since conveying abstract ideas non-verbally can prove extremely difficult. This is illustrated very well when playing charades. Alternatively, while it is possible, it can at times be difficult to conduct a smooth interaction on the telephone, or with somebody wearing dark glasses, and the reason for this is to do with lack of visual feedback of the other person's behaviour. Current research reflects this difficulty of making a functional distinction between verbal and non-verbal behaviours and tends to focus on the relationship between them (Cappella and Palmer, 1990).

In what follows we begin with a discussion regarding the degree to which non-verbal behaviours are necessarily considered to be communication. It is then appropriate briefly to identify the main channels or types of non-verbal behaviour before looking in more detail at the functional approach. Gender and cultural issues relevant to both verbal and non-verbal behaviours will also be addressed. The chapter continues with a discussion of how non-verbal behaviours interact with conversational speech in relation to interruptions and floor management, deception, politeness and self-disclosure. Finally, application of some of this work is made to health professional–client interaction.

6.2 Animal communication

Charles Darwin proposed that there are some features of human non-verbal behaviour that are common across cultures and may have parallels in the animal kingdom. Darwin suggested that there are six universal expressions of emotion in the human face: happiness, surprise, anger, fear, disgust and sadness. Sub-human primates, for example, exhibit elaborate and complex non-vocal behaviours associated with territoriality, mating and dominance hierarchies. Territoriality can be likened to the idea of personal space in humans, which we shall consider later in this chapter. Van Hooff (1967), tracing the evolutionary significance of smiling and laughter in humans, claimed that the majority of primates have a 'bared-teeth' and 'relaxed-open mouth' display, as shown in Figure 6.3.

In humans, Van Hooff suggests that the silent bared-teeth display is similar to smiling, and the relaxed open-mouth display to laughter. Further evidence of the shared evolutionary roots of humans and non-human primates comes from the observation that chimpanzees often reciprocate human laughter with a relaxed open-mouth display.

Perhaps the most important difference between humans and other animals is that we possess language. Language allows us to think, talk, write about what we see, feel and imagine in order to represent the world in which we live and interact with other people. Animals other than humans possess communication systems but none as elaborate, well-developed or formally learned (Hockett, 1960).

Among invertebrates the 'dance' of the honey bee, first described by Von Frisch (1954), stands out as the most elaborate system for communicating the direction and distance of nectar or pollen to other bees. The 'figure of eight' dance, shown in Figure 6.4, communicates direction by

Figure 6.3: The 'bared teeth' and 'relaxed open mouth' displays of the chimpanzee. The former occurs when threatened, the latter in play and mock fighting. Adapted from van Hooff (1967)

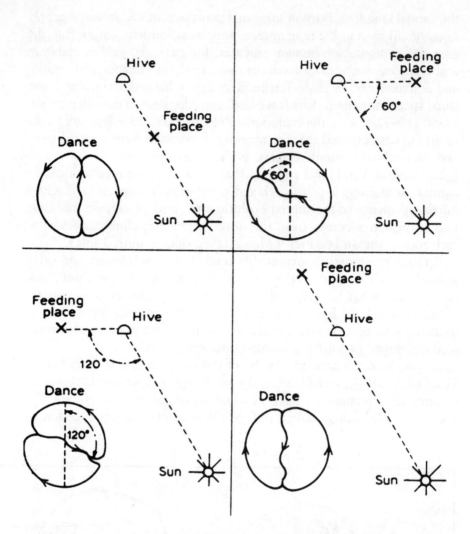

Figure 6.4: The dance of the honey bee used to communicate the direction of a food source to other bees in the hive. Notice how the overall orientation of the dance changes to indicate direction of the food source in relation to the hive and the sun. Distance of the food source from the hive is indicated by the vigour with which the bee performs the dance. From von Frisch (1954)

the bees dancing at an angle to the vertical which then has to be transmitted to other bees in relation to the position of the sun outside the hive. Distance is communicated by the vigour of the dance; the more vigorous, the further away the source of nectar or pollen.

This brief look at two non-human species demonstrates how non-vocal behaviour can act as a means of communication and may be inherited as a product of evolution. Similarities between non-human, especially primate, and human non-vocal behaviour exist. We now turn to consider human non-verbal and non-vocal behaviour.

6.3 Non-verbal behaviour

6.3.1 Non-verbal behaviour and communication

Research into linguistics has suggested that interaction between two people requires three features to be present – an encoder, a code and a decoder (Weiner *et al.*, 1972). One person (the encoder) conveys a message through a system (the code) mutually understood by both people, and this is interpreted by the second person (the decoder). Early researchers in the area assumed that this process was similar to non-verbal communication. However, Radley (1996) considered such behaviour to be very narrow and limited, and claims that most studies in the field concentrated solely on the interpretation of the behaviour by the decoder. This has evolved as there is some ambiguity in the encoding intentions of the sender which are not always clear and, in some instances, absent. Non-verbal codes are not well defined, and have emerged as shared social and cultural norms, usually implicitly adhered to. Perhaps one of the best ways of becoming aware of such 'unwritten rules', is to break them or behave in ways unexpected by others in a given situation. For example, if you get on a nearly empty bus and see one person sitting in a double seat on his own with plenty of other double seats being empty; go and sit next to the lone person!

The difficulty of definition was acknowledged by Posner (1989). He defined three kinds of non-verbal behaviour: communication, signification, and indication, which are summarised in Figure 6.5. Posner suggested that any complete interaction involves a sender, a code, a sign, a context and a recipient. Spoken language can be defined in this context, with the sender and recipient sharing a code and sign system. However, non-verbal behaviour does not always fit these criteria, as we shall see later in the chapter. *Signification* is when a code is used to interpret signs that are 'given off ' by a movement or expression. The person doesn't necessarily intend to send a message by their non-verbal behaviour, but the decoder interprets the behaviour, using a shared code. Even when others try to conceal emotions or attitudes there can be 'leakage' through the non-verbal channels, which are not always under the control of the individual (De Paulo, 1992). *Indication* is when a gesture or expression is made which is not recognisable within a code system. Various glances, postures and expressions might be used to

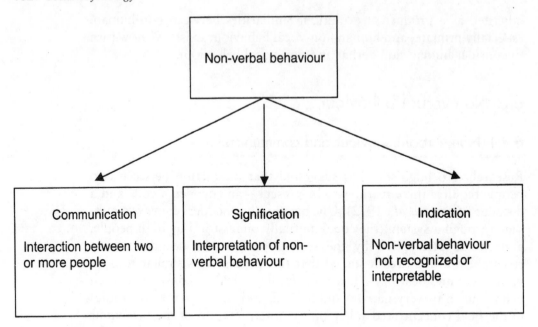

Figure 6.5: Three types of non-verbal behaviour: communication, signification and indication. Defined by Posner (1989)

convey a specific impression but without a shared code, it is unlikely to have any effect on the decoder. Therefore, the term *non-verbal behaviours* will be used throughout this chapter, rather than non-verbal communication.

It is convenient to identify the main non-verbal channels but important to remember that one rarely occurs in isolation from all others. It is also important to acknowledge that some non-verbal cues are more salient and informative than others. For example, in normal everyday interaction we are more likely to spend time looking at another person in the region of the face, especially the eyes, rather than at their feet! The context or nature of the interaction also determines the cues that we are likely to pay most attention to. For instance, telephone conversations only allow paralinguistic cues to be used, so attention has to be directed at the pitch and tone of the voice, and these are then related to timing and pauses in the conversation.

6.3.2 Gaze and eye contact

Gaze and eye contact have often been considered to be the most important types of non-verbal communication. *Gaze* can be defined as when one person looks at another in the region of the eyes, whether the other person is looking back or not. *Eye contact* occurs when both people are mutually looking in the region of the eyes. This enables the other person's non-verbal signals, especially their facial expressions, to be received and decoded (Argyle, 1994). A high level of eye contact can be decoded as a sign of liking or intimacy (Kleinke, 1986). A continuous gaze, which may be maintained regardless of what we do, can be defined as a 'cold stare' and is often interpreted as a need to dominate. Dovidio *et al.* (1988) found that the level of eye contact can be related to status and dominance. In a series of studies investigating the relationship between visual dominance and social power Dovidio *et al.* found that, in general, dominant people look more while speaking and lower status people look more when listening. Looking and eye contact are also used to synchronise speech, especially in floor apportionment, that is, who takes the 'floor', so to speak. This will be discussed in more detail later in the chapter.

6.3.3 Facial expressions

Certain expressions have been found to be easily recognisable signals of specific emotions (Carroll and Russell, 1996). In everyday interaction we are continuously monitoring the emotional state and reactions of other people. While the English language has many words to describe emotions and their nuances, only a small number of such emotional states can be labelled in the absence of any social context. Six basic emotions have been found to be universally recognised: these are happiness, fear, surprise, sadness, anger and disgust (Ekman *et al.*, 1987). Subsequent studies have differentiated between disgust and contempt, which has also been found to be universal (Izard, 1994). However, much of this research was experimental and laboratory-based involving carefully controlled conditions. Carroll and Russell (1996) criticise this type of research as being too simplistic, since it fails sufficiently to address situational contexts. In the traditional experimental setting an observer receives a still photograph of a specially posed facial expression paired with a verbally described situation. The observer is then required to choose from a pre-determined list of possible emotions, which have been selected by the researcher. This constitutes a forced-choice format and excludes the specific meaning that the expression might have for the observer in relation to the situation. Carroll and Russell acknowledge that laboratory experiments obviously have their place in giving insight into what can happen, but they need to be supplemented with studies which demonstrate what actually happens in everyday encounters. An attempt to address the forced-choice format is evident in a recent study conducted by Rosenberg and Ekman (1994). They asked participants to view slides of strangers showing various facial expressions. Participants were then required to label the expressions by either: (a) choosing one of seven labels provided by the researcher; (b) one of seven stories also provided; or (c) give their own description of the emotion shown. There was a high degree of accuracy, irrespective of how the judgements were made.

Early research tended to give the impression that people's facial expressions are simply 'books to be read'. This is mistaken since social constraints and norms operate to regulate emotional expression. For example, it might be considered inappropriate for men to cry in public. Similarly, although you may be bored with talking to somebody you are unlikely to express this feeling, either verbally or non-verbally, and will wait for a suitable cue to end the interaction in a polite way.

6.3.4 Body language

Body language is a generic term which includes the non-verbal behaviours of touch, body orientation, posture, hand gestures and head nods. How a touch is interpreted is dependent on the context and the nature of the relationship between the interactants. Jones and Yarbrough (1985) analysed 1500 bodily contacts between people and identified five discrete categories of touch. These include *positive affect*, which at its most extreme would signify sexual interest, playfulness, control, ritualistic and task-related behaviours. The latter denotes a professional function, for example, when taking a pulse or other examination which might be necessary during a medical consultation. Burgoon *et al.* (1995) added two more categories: *negative effect*, which includes gently pushing an annoying hand away; and *aggressive touch*, such as slaps, kicks, shoves and punches. Table 6.1 summarises these and provides examples.

Categories	Examples of behaviour
Positive affect	Caress of hand upon another person's face
Playful	Body contact when playing 'tag'
Control	Restraining a person by holding their hands together
Ritualistic	Kissing back of hand of religious person
Task-related	Doctor takes a patient's pulse
Negative affect	Push somebody away with your hands
Aggressive touch	Punch somebody on the nose

Table 6.1: Categories of touch suggested by Jones & Yarbrough (1985) and Burgoon *et al.* (1995)

Posture can be discussed in relation to its functions. These include the differential status between interactants, a positive or negative attitude, and the emotional level of the interaction and persuasion (Hargie *et al.*, 1994). For example, in a standing position a high status individual is likely to adopt a relaxed stance often with hands in pocket, while a low status person will generally have a more rigid and 'straighter' posture (Mehrabian, 1972). A positive attitude towards the person and the topic of conversation can be conveyed by leaning forward, as opposed to leaning backwards. It has been noted earlier that facial expression denotes certain emotions but it is bodily posture which conveys the intensity of that emotion (Ekman, 1982). For instance, Fisch *et al.* (1983) found that posture was a significant indicator when differentiating between severely depressed and nearly recovered patients during doctor–patient interviews.

Gestures can be distinguished functionally with those which are linked to speech, called illustrators, and those that are oriented towards self (Feldman and Rimé *et al.*, 1991). Illustrators are intended to communicate, while gestures directed at yourself may be interpreted as a sign of tension or tension release. For example, fiddling with a ring or wringing your hands are both signs of nervousness or anxiety. Harrigan *et al.* (1991) observed that the greater the number of behaviours involving one part of the body touching another, the higher the level of arousal or nervousness being felt by the person, for example, constantly rubbing your ear lobe between thumb and fingers.

An interesting phenomenon reported by a number of researchers is *postural mirroring* or *postural congruence* (Bull, 1983). This is when two interactants display the same posture at the same time. The researchers suggested that this is likely to occur with positive speech and will help in establishing rapport between people. Some examples are depicted in Figure 6.6. Synchronised body posture and movements can also be functional. Lynn and Mynier (1993) conducted a field experiment in restaurants. They arranged for waiters and waitresses to either stand upright or to squat near their customers when taking their orders for drinks. By squatting more eye contact is possible, so the researchers predicted that larger tips would be received from customers when the servers took up this position. The results supported this, irrespective of whether the server was male or female. However, a general sex difference was evident in that the waiters received larger tips than the waitresses!

It should be noted, however, that the waiters were serving at a different restaurant to the waitresses, so a confounding variable exists with this study. The clientele, quality of the environment, the type of food being served, could all have affected the results. In spite of this the

Figure 6.6: Examples of 'postural mirroring' or postural congruence in social interaction (from Bull, 1983)

results were interesting, and the next time you are eating out, take a closer look at the non-verbal behaviour of those who take your order and serve your meal and observe what tip you feel like giving!!

Head nods occur frequently when two people are in conversation; they function as feedback to the speaker, indicating for example, that what is being said is understood or agreed with, and provide reinforcement for the speaker to continue. Head nods might also be used to indicate to the listener that he or she is being offered the 'floor' (i.e. it is their turn to speak).

6.3.5 Personal space

The study of personal space is often referred to as *proxemics*. It is the area with invisible boundaries surrounding a person's body into which intruders may not come (Sommer, 1969). The crucial variable is what counts as an intruder, since this determines whether we feel our personal space has been invaded. Early research by Hall (1996), on a North American society, showed that distance between interactants could be classified into four main zones, depending on the nature of the relationship and the purpose of the interaction, this is shown in Table 6.2.

It is important to take into consideration the status differences between the interactants. Zahn (1991) found that people of equal status tend to take up a closer distance to each other than people of unequal status. For example, it is unlikely that a person of lower status would approach a higher status person with the same degree of closeness as those of equal status. Invasions of personal space initiate threat with the likely response of flight, or varying level of anxiety, but see Section 6.5 for compensatory measures.

Garfinkel (1964), and Felipe and Sommer (1966) demonstrated the effects of violating personal space in a series of field experiments. These experimenters violated personal space in public places such as libraries and benches in parks, and found people to show embarrassment and bewilderment in their facial expressions. For example, sitting right next to somebody on an otherwise empty park bench caused the person to either move further along the bench, thus restoring an appropriate level of personal space, or get up and walk away!

6.3.6 Paralanguage

Paralanguage is commonly referred to as *that which is left after subtracting the verbal content from speech*. *It's not what you say, but the way that you say it.* How often have you heard this said or said it yourself? Paralinguistic aspects of speech include prosody (pitch, stress, timing and pauses), an emotional tone of voice, accent, and speech errors (such as 'stuttering', 'ums', 'ers', etc.). The speed at which a person

Zone	Description
Intimate zone	Those who have an intimate relationship with each other interact at distance of 50cm or less
Personal zone	Those who have a personal relationship, friends, will take up a distance of between 50cm and 1 metre
Social/consultative zone	2–3 metres may be appropriate for work colleagues to interact, perhaps with a desk between them
Public zone	Speakers on public occasions will stand at a distance of 3–4 metres from their audience

Table 6.2: Four main zones of personal space after Hall (1996)

talks is often interpreted as a sign of anxiety, if speech is very rapid. People who suffer from speech impediments, such as stuttering or speech that is difficult to understand after a person has had a stroke, often get frustrated by an insensitive 'normal' talker. The latter often interrupt or attempt to complete what the other person has started to say. Finally, we often stereotype people who speak in an abnormal way, especially very slowly and with a flat voice, as being of low intelligence. Aspects of speech, called paralanguage, may have dramatic effects on social interaction and social categorisation.

6.4 Gender and cultural issues relating to non-verbal behaviour

6.4.1 Gender

Hall (1984), in a literature review, found a number of consistent sex differences in non-verbal behaviours. For example, women tend to smile and gaze at other people when in social interaction more frequently than men. The interpretation of this research is quite confusing, as smiling is assumed to be part of the female role. Deutsch *et al.* (1987) showed that women who were not smiling were given more negative evaluations: they were rated as less happy and less relaxed both in comparison with men, and with other women who were smiling. This assumes that it is a social norm for women to smile, and that people will react negatively when women fail to perform this part of their 'normative' female role. Women are also more comfortable than men with closer interpersonal distances.

In relation to eye contact, as opposed to gaze, it has been shown that visual dominance (that is, engaging in high levels of eye contact), has been related to power. It might be expected that males are more visually dominant in mixed sex pairs socially interacting. Dovidio *et al.* (1988) investigated this relationship when she assigned college students to *mixed-sex dyads* and each dyad was requested to discuss three topics in sequence. The first scenario was a natural situation with no manipulation of power, the second topic involved one member of the pair evaluating the other and awarding extra credit points on the basis of their evaluation. In the third experimental condition the roles were reversed. The results showed that in the control condition, the males looked at their partners more while speaking and women looked more while listening, which reflects the assumed differential status between men and women. However, when women were assigned to the more powerful role in the interaction, they looked more than men when speaking, and men looked more when listening. Therefore, when women are ascribed social power they become more visually dominant in mixed-sex dyads. This is depicted in Figure 6.7.

Hall and Veccia (1990) found that gender and age interact to show differences in touching behaviour. Amongst younger couples, males are more likely to touch females first, but as age increases, especially over the age of 40 there is a reversal when it can be seen that females initiate the touching more. Hall (1996) attempted to explain these results in relation to the stability of a relationship. With younger couples, the relationship is possibly not so well established, so it may be that the stereotypical gender roles prevail, with the males using touching as a visible sign of possessiveness to other males. As the relationship

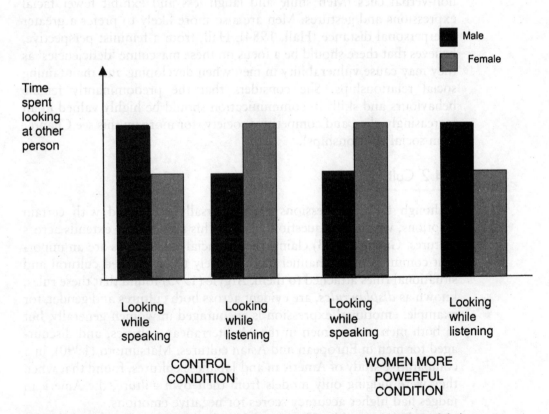

Figure 6.7: Time women and men spent looking while speaking, and looking while listening where male and female in each dyad are of equal status (control) and where female is in a more powerful position in the dyad than the male. Adapted from Dovidio *et al.* (1988)

matures, females might similarly need to demonstrate the visible signal of possessiveness, which would account for their increased level of touching. Nevertheless, when age groups were combined there were no overall gender differences.

Smith, Archer and Costanzo (1991) supported previous research, which found that women are more accurate in decoding non-verbal cues. Using an Interpersonal Perception Task (IPT) test, which involves objectively correct answers to questions posed about videotaped sequences of naturalistic behaviour, they found that women performed significantly better than men. Within the experiment, the researchers also asked the participants to estimate how many correct answers they thought they had made. The estimates made by males were higher than those made by females, suggesting that either women in general under-estimate their performance or that men overestimate theirs.

Overall, research has found that men, compared to women, have less skill sending and receiving cues of emotion, and are less sensitive to non-verbal cues. Men smile and laugh less and exhibit fewer facial expressions and gestures. Men are also more likely to prefer a greater interpersonal distance (Hall, 1984). Hall, from a feminist perspective, believes that there should be a focus on these masculine 'deficiencies' as they may cause vulnerability in men when developing and maintaining social relationships. She considers that the predominantly female behaviours and skills in communication should be highly valued in an increasingly alien and competitive society (for more on this see Chapter 7 on social relationships).

6.4.2 Culture

Although facial expressions are universally associated with certain emotions, we need to question whether this universality extends across cultures. Gallois (1993) claims that as facial expressions are an important communicative channel there is likely to be marked cultural and situational rules attached to them. Argyle (1995) found that these rules, known as *display rules*, are evident across both cultures and gender, for example, emotional expression is encouraged in women generally, but in both men and women in the Mediterranean cultures, and discouraged for men in European and Asian cultures. Matsumoto (1990), in a comparative study of American and Japanese cultures, found that when they were judging only models from their own culture, the American judges had higher accuracy scores for negative emotions.

In relation to this, Hogg and Vaughan (1995) also noted that in Japan people are socialised to control facial expressions which are associated with negative emotion. They use smiling or laughing to cover up for anger or grief. These results are consistent with norms for collectivist societies, of which Japan is one. Collectivist societies strive to avoid conflict and achieve face-saving strategies at all costs (Kitayama *et al.*, 1995). Schimmack (1996) in a re-analysis of cross-cultural studies on the recognition of facial expressions of emotions, found that Caucasian judges recognised emotions better than non-Caucasian judges. Methodological flaws could have accounted for this in that there were culturally biased stimulus sets used in the studies and display rules previously considered by Argyle are more rigid in Caucasian cultures (Ekman and Friesen, 1972).

With regard to gestures, some *emblems*, defined as gestures used to replace or symbolise the spoken word, are culturally understood, whereas others are culture specific. Morris *et al.* (1979), demonstrated this when they analysed how 20 emblems were used in Western, Southern European and the Mediterranean areas. For example, a specific emblem used in Italy known as the 'cheek-screw' involves pressing and rotating a straightened forefinger against the cheek; it is a gesture of praise only used in that culture. Another example of cultural difference is that of a sideways nod of the head, which means 'no' in Britain, but 'yes' in India. In Turkey 'no' is indicated by moving the head backwards and rolling the eyes upwards (Rubin, 1973). It would therefore seem that decoding non-verbal behaviours across different cultures could be as problematic as decoding facial expressions.

Anthropologists have distinguished between 'contact' cultures such as North Africa and 'non-contact' cultures such as Europe, India and North America (Argyle, 1994). Similarly, there are cultural differences in orientation and interpersonal distance. A European or Asian interacting with an Arab or Latin American may feel uncomfortable because they may feel their personal space has been invaded. In such situations they are likely to back away to compensate, only to find that the person they are interacting with will move closer! Hall (1996) suggested that this might be due to Latin American and Southern Mediterranean people relying more on tactile and olfactory information, whereas Britons are more dependent on visual cues.

Subsequent research on interpersonal distance, observed in naturally occurring interactions in England, France, Italy, Greece, Scotland and Ireland, found that in Irish and Scottish dyads, the interactants stood closer than did the French, English, Italian and Greeks, when interacting (Remland *et al.*, 1995). This refutes the findings of Hall (1996), which made the distinction between contact and non-contact cultures, and would therefore predict that the Greeks and Italians would stand closer than the non-contact cultures of England, Ireland, Scotland and the Netherlands. This would suggest that the cultural explanation is too simplistic. Other variables which cannot be controlled in field studies, such as relationships between interactants, topic of conversation and personality of individuals, are possibly as, or more important than, cultural norms. It could also be that cultural norms simply change, which may be reflected in the almost 30 year time difference in the conducted research.

6.5 Functions of non-verbal behaviour

In the introduction to this chapter we briefly considered different functions that non-verbal behaviour might serve for the individual. We now look at these functions in a little more detail.

6.5.1 Regulating interaction

The function of regulating interaction is concerned with the role of non-verbal behaviour in helping conversations to flow in a smooth, orderly fashion. A number of general patterns relating to the behaviours of both the speaker and the listener have been identified. Early research by Kendon (1967), which used a pictographic system, and involved frame by frame analysis of the conversation between two people, found a number of regularities. He found that during long utterances (5 seconds or more), the listener looks at the speaker, but the speaker looks away, especially when unsure of content. When a speaker wishes to end an utterance, the speaker engages in eye contact which is interpreted as 'offering the floor' to the listener. This would lead to the new speaker looking away, while the former speaker looks at the new speaker.

Later research by Duncan and Fiske (1977) identified other cues that signal a speaker's readiness to yield the 'floor'. These combine both verbal and non-verbal cues. They include a rise or fall in pitch at the end of a clause, a cessation of gestures and a drop in voice volume. Duncan and Fiske also found that if a speaker continued to use hand gestures, it virtually eliminated an attempt by the listener to take the flow and speak. The general transitional process from listener to speaker is, in general, characterised by increased gesturing, an audible intake of breath, and over-loudness of the first few items of speech (Harrigan, 1985). All these non-verbal cues come together to facilitate a smooth transition from one speaker to another in everyday social interaction.

6.5.2 Providing information

The informational function relates to both decoding and encoding. Referring to the decoding process first, it is evident from the discussion concerning the individual channels that taken alone they have informational value to the observer. Not only can facial expressions be universally decoded as expressions of emotion, but vocal cues such as pitch, loudness and rate of speech can also be used to identify specific emotional states reasonable accuracy. When taken together, the accuracy level is greatly enhanced.

Wallbott and Scherer (1986) varied the medium through which emotions were expressed. They found that decoding accuracy was generally higher when the observer is able to use combined audio-visual cues or visual-only channels than it was for the audio channel alone. These results demonstrate the importance of visual interaction. Specific functions of looking and eye contact have been well researched, but it is the availability of social cues gained from being able to see another person when we interact with them which is most informative (Rutter, 1984). Rutter predicted that as the number of social (non-verbal) cues available decreases (the degree of cuelessness), the conversation should become more depersonalised and task oriented. This is suggested by the *cuelessness* model of Rutter (1984), shown in Figure 6.8. The model states that the fewer social cues available to a person, then the greater will he or she experience a feeling of psychological distance. This will affect the

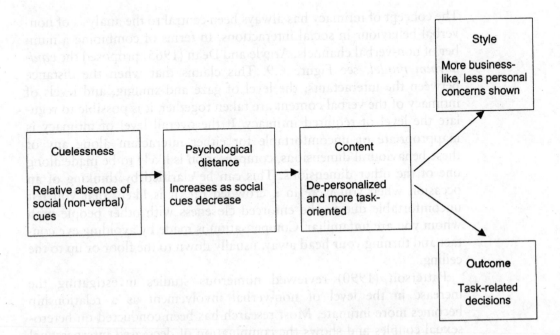

Figure 6.8: The cuelessness model proposed by Rutter (1984)

content of what is said (more depersonalised and task oriented), which in turn will affect the style of speech (a less spontaneous conversation), and the outcome of interaction.

The effects of cuelessness can be seen in the research by Rutter and Robinson (1981), who compared the content and style of Open University tutorials conducted either face-to-face or over the telephone. Tutorials in both conditions were task oriented and impersonal, but telephone tutorials were characterised by tutors seeking more contributions from students and students responding more. Also, style of conversation was less spontaneous and more structured in telephone tutorials.

While there is less research directly relating the informational function to the encoding process, one theory which does apply is Bem's *self-perception theory* (Bem, 1967). You will recall from Chapter 3, that this states individuals use their own behaviour to make attributions about their feelings and attitudes towards another person. They observe their own behaviour and use it as an indication of their feelings or judgements. For example, John might use the knowledge that he smiled and gazed at Jane a great deal and to infer that he likes her (I'm smiling at Jane, therefore I must like Jane).

6.5.3 Expressing intimacy

The concept of intimacy has always been central to the analysis of non-verbal behaviour in social interactions. In terms of combining a number of non-verbal channels, Argyle and Dean (1965) proposed the *equilibrium model,* see Figure 6.9. This claims that when the distance between the interactants, the level of gaze and smiling, and levels of intimacy of the verbal content are taken together, it is possible to regulate the level of required intimacy. If the overall level of intimacy is inappropriate or uncomfortable for either interactant along any of these behavioural dimensions, compensation is likely to be made along one of the other dimensions. This can be clarified by thinking of an occasion when you were in a crowded lift. It is likely that you felt uncomfortable due to the enforced closeness with other people with whom you are unfamiliar. Compensation is made by avoiding eye contact and turning your head away, usually down to the floor or up to the ceiling.

Patterson (1990) reviewed numerous studies investigating the increase in the level of non-verbal involvement as a relationship becomes more intimate. Most research has been conducted on heterosexual couples and shows the combination of decreased interpersonal distance, increased frequency of touch and increased mutual gaze, as a reflection of intimacy, this is shown in Figure 6.9(b). Studies of intimate, same sex interactions show that males typically initiate far lower levels of involvement than females (Greenbaum and Rosenfeld, 1980). This may illustrate the stereotypical caring and nurturing functions attributed to females, giving greater licence to engage in more touching behaviour without incurring disapproval from other people.

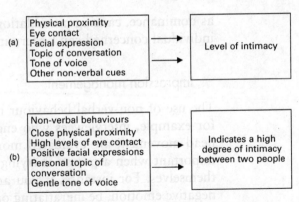

Figure 6.9: Showing the general intimacy model of Argyle & Dean (1965) (a) and equilibrium between different types of non-verbal behaviour in a close relationship (b)

6.5.4 Social control

Social control has been looked at in terms of: dominance and submission; persuasion and compliance; and impression management. We shall look briefly at each of these types of control.

■ Dominance and submission

Argyle (1994) considers that dominance or power is communicated by a non-smiling, frowning face, standing to full height, with the chest expanded, hands on hips, gesticular pointing, touching but not being touched back, and increased gaze. Dominance or assertiveness signals are an important social skill. Kalma (1992) demonstrated that when in a group of three people, a leader will control who speaks by giving a prolonged gaze at one member of the group. There have been mixed results from encoding studies, but they do suggest that higher status allows greater flexibility in how much non-verbal involvement a person is able to initiate. Lower status individuals, on the other hand, do not have this choice and have to take their cues from the higher status person.

■ Persuasion and compliance

Studies have consistently shown that simple requests for help, like donations to charity or signing a petition, are more successful if increased gaze, minimal contact and a close physical proximity accompany the request (Patterson, 1986). Patterson interprets these findings to be due to the higher involvement of the requester, leading to them being perceived as more attractive. Alternatively, it could be perceived as dominance, causing intimidation with resultant stress which for the individual concerned can be terminated by compliance to the request.

■ Impression management

The use of non-verbal behaviour to create an impression is common, for example, interviewees who engage in increased gaze, smiling and head movement are evaluated more positively. Smiling is particularly important when a person is trying to convey a positive impression of themselves. For instance, if you are either trying to be polite, hide a negative emotion, be ingratiating or trying to initiate some interest in a person, you usually smile more. However, Ekman and Friesen (1972) noted that a genuine smile can be distinguished from a phoney smile by the sequence in which facial muscles are activated, and the onset and duration of the smile.

6.5.5 Presenting identities and images

Patterson (1987), drawing upon the work of the dramaturgical approach of Goffman (1972), considered that we use presentational patterns in order to create a preferred identity or image to a third party observer. Goffman described these as *performances* which may be directed towards a partner or to a wider audience. They may also be self-presentational or designed to create a preferred image of a relationship. Patterson (1987) suggests that there may be partner co-operation in that there is an investment for both people to support a particular relationship. For example, a married couple who are in the middle of an argument when they join a social gathering with friends, might want to portray an impression of marital harmony. In order to do this they are likely to over-play the intimacy cues. Therefore, presentation patterns can show exaggerated or decreased levels of involvement with a partner to present a specific image or identity to an audience. This is an aspect of how we may use non-verbal behaviour to manage the impression we want other people to have of us.

6.5.6 Affect management

Embarrassment is a common negative affect. When it is anticipated in an interaction, avoidance techniques are activated; these involve gaze avoidance and an increase in gesticular movement and smiling. Positive affect is often shown by an increase in touch. For instance, unexpected success, intense happiness or good fortune, are often accompanied by hugs and kisses, increased smiling and laughter. Success in athletic activities is often followed by increased touch amongst team members, and public displays of intimacy frequently occur in team sports. Ritualised patterns of touching are often shared between competing teams, for instance, the congratulatory handshake and exchange of shirts after the game are common.

6.5.7 Facilitating service and task goals

This function is evident in professional service exchanges such as those with doctors, dentists and hairdressers. In these situations, interpersonal distance is close, increased touch and intense visual scrutiny are common. This high level of involvement is a necessary part of the service offered to the client rather than elements of a personal relationship. The non-verbal behaviours often follow a prescribed 'script' or set of professional norms. Non-verbal behaviours may be restricted by task goals, for example, tasks which involve cognitive complexity, or are of a confidential nature, will be carried out in relative isolation. Alternatively, working on an assembly line involves enforced close contact with others. As there is little choice of the non-verbal behaviours available in these contexts, it may be the personality of an individual which is likely to determine the choice of job. For instance, extroverts, rather than introverts, would be more likely to choose work situations which involve close interpersonal distances and/or high levels of gaze.

6.6 Interaction of verbal and non-verbal behaviours in conversation

6.6.1 Interruptions and 'floor' management in conversation

Some form of turn-taking is necessary to enable conversation between two or more people to flow smoothly. The role of non-verbal cues in the smooth exchange of floor apportionment has already been discussed earlier in the chapter, and what follows is related more to the underlying implications of verbal *interruptions*. Interruptions are often mistakenly defined and are really just overlaps of conversation between two interactants. Turn-taking in conversation usually involves short moments of silence between speakers, but overlap often occurs if the second speaker begins to speak simultaneously without the first speaker stopping. This type of verbal behaviour is often defined as an interruption whereas it should be considered as overlap, since there is no attempt to stop the speaker or to take control of the conversation (Irish and Hall, 1995).

Beattie (1983) highlighted the strategic use of interruptions and overlap as a social skill used by some politicians when being interviewed, for example, Margaret Thatcher, when Prime Minister, developed a particular interview style which enabled her to maintain the 'floor' for long periods, force the interviewer to interrupt her, and not allow interruptions to result in floor changes. Beattie found that Margaret Thatcher rarely 'butted in' when being interviewed, but had a skill which made people think that she had come to the end of an utterance, indicated by clause completion and change in voice pitch, when in fact she had not. She used simultaneous speech much longer than is usual in order to maintain control of the interview. Table 6.3 highlights these findings.

Irrespective of definition, the early research, which associated interruptions with power differentials among speakers, has been more or less refuted. Since the research by Zimmerman and West (1975), which found that in cross-sex conversations 96 per cent of interruptions were made by men, it had been commonly accepted that men interrupt women when in mixed sex pairs. Subsequent research shows no significant gender differences, which suggesting that conversational style can no longer be supported or accepted as a form of domination and control by men (Carli, 1989).

In relation to some of these variables, Irish and Hall (1995) conducted an interesting study of interruptive patterns in medical visits. Results refuted the status theory; it was found that patients used more interruptions and overlapping speech than did physicians. However, when the content of the interruptions was analysed, it was found that patients used statements, whereas physicians used questions when interrupting. There was also no difference in the use of interruptions by senior or junior physicians and no significant sex differences, both in relation to female physicians or female patients. Female patients were equally able to give their story and female physicians were not undermined in respect

Speaker	Smooth speaker switches	Interruptions when speaking			
		Simple interruptions	Overlap interruptions	Butting In	Silent
Margaret Thatcher	17	19	4	4	11	0
Interviewer	16	10	1	8	1	0

Table 6.3: Interruptions made of speaker and type of interruptions. Note that the interviewer mostly butted in to interrupt Margaret Thatcher speaking. Adapted from Beattie, 1983

of verbal domination by male patients. However, it is both misleading and over-simplistic to analyse interruptions solely in relation to gender and power. This suggests that more research is necessary to determine consistent variables and the full range of factors that need to be taken into consideration.

6.6.2 Deception and lying

The identification of behaviours exhibited by liars has traditionally focused on non-verbal signals, as researchers previously believed that liars are able to control and manipulate their verbal behaviours, but find it more difficult to control their non-verbal behaviours (Knapp and Hall 1992; Miller and Stiff, 1993). This was indicated by De Paulo *et al.* (1983), who considered that the non-verbal behaviours associated with lying are relatively uncontrollable and believe that the more important the lie is to the deceiver, the easier it is to detect through non-verbal channels. A famous quotation from Freud's case study of Dora serves to make the point very well indeed:

> He that has eyes to see and ears to hear may convince him-
> self that no mortal can keep a secret. If his lips are silent, he
> chatters with his fingertips; betrayal oozes out of him at
> every pore.
>
> (Freud, 1905)

However, it has now been acknowledged that the interaction of verbal and non-verbal behaviours need to be explored in greater depth. Current research shows that liars often smile less, hesitate and make more errors in their speech, and demonstrate a higher voice pitch. Avoidance of eye gaze has typically been associated with lying and therefore liars consciously seek to control it. As a result, eye gaze becomes exaggerated and the liar ends up staring or engaging in inappropriately high levels of eye contact.

In the absence of a universal set of behaviours associated with lying, it is easier to study the underlying psychological processes of arousal and cognitive difficulty. An inexperienced liar, who knows the consequences associated with their lying, is likely to experience both of these states, which can be detected by both verbal and non-verbal behaviours. Non-verbally, pupil dilation, blinking and higher voice pitch are taken as signs of lying. Significant verbal signals include the common use of responses like 'why do you always have to question me', to seemingly non-threatening questions, as well as curt responses or extremes in language usage. The cognitive difficulty may be manifested in the hesitations, shorter responses and a lack of co-ordination between verbal and non-verbal behaviours. Stiff *et al.* (1989) use the term *sentence repairs* to account for instances when people who are lying, start a sentence, interrupt it and then start again.

Burgoon, Butler and Guerrero (1995) have proposed the Interpersonal Deception Theory (IDT), which suggests that there is a difference between socially skilled individuals and unskilled individuals, when attempting to deceive others. Based on the work of Riggio (1993), they put forward a model which identified these differences. The model is based on three key skills, each of which have a verbal (*social*) and a non-verbal (*emotional*) component. The basic dimensions are summarised in Table 6.4.

Burgoon *et al.* conducted research which supported the model and found that the level of individual social skills influences deception and success in detection. Having the skill of emotional control helps senders and receivers to hide the discomfort, anxiety and general negative effect which occurs when you deceive somebody or detect deception in others. Similarly, decoding skills of social and emotional sensitivity are likely to help receivers to detect deception or lying in others.

6.6.3 Politeness and conversational strategies

Brown and Levinson (1987) proposed *politeness theory,* which was developed solely on the basis of use of language. This theory suggests that the verbal strategies adopted by individuals will depend on the nature and context of the relationship between the interactants. Speakers are likely to be more polite when the social and power distances are high between them and the target, and when the degree of imposition the request places on the target increases.

Holtgraves and Yang (1990) suggest there are five possible strategies which people might use, which can be identified in an increasing order of politeness. First, the speaker could boldly state facts which, if bad news, is likely to reduce the self-esteem of the target. Second, the speaker could use positive politeness by showing solidarity with the target. For instance, news of a job rejection might be conveyed with

Expressiveness	Ability to encode messages
Control	Ability to regulate the flow of interaction
Sensitivity	Ability to decode messages

Table 6.4: Three key skills claimed by Burgoon *et al.* (1994) to be involved in deception

statements such as 'it is their loss, but it might be useful to do some work on your interviewing techniques'. The third strategy is negative politeness in which the speaker is formal and self-effacing, but respecting the other person's freedom of action in relation to them. An example of this is when informing one of your parents that you have failed a driving test; you might blame yourself, and so allow them to withdraw future help. Fourth, it is possible to state the news off-the-record by hinting, and this might be illustrated when you are trying to end a relationship. This is often done by a partner suggesting that they are not worthy of you, and that you need to find somebody who would appreciate you more. The fifth and final strategy is when the 'no' message is not conveyed at all.

Cross-cultural universality of the politeness theory was demonstrated by Holtgraves and Yang (1990) using Americans and Koreans. Later, Ambady *et al.* (1996), in an attempt to extend the theory, posed the question as to whether cultural universality might also apply to the non-linguistic channels of communication. They investigated politeness in the communication of good and bad news in two different cultures using two different studies. The first involved employees at a firm of Korean money brokers, and the second used American graduate students. Both sets of participants were video-taped communicating either good or bad news related to their work situation, either to a superior, subordinate, or peer. The results showed both similarities and differences across the two cultures. Linguistic and non-linguistic similarities showed that three main types of strategies were used. These were:

Other-oriented: attentive, concerned, seeking agreement, empathic, encouraging;
Affiliative: open, joking and positive;
Circumspect: uncertain, indirect, avoidant, and apologetic.

In both cultures, affiliation was used in a similar way as both Americans and Koreans were affiliative towards peers and more circumspect towards superiors. When giving good news, irrespective of power differences, they were both more affiliative and less circumspect. Circumspection, in both cultures was more evident from non-verbal behaviour, rather than through what was actually said. The differences across the two cultures were most evident in the other-orientation. This is a strategy which involves both positive and negative politeness strategies. Koreans used different levels depending on the status of the target, and showed more other-oriented behaviour towards their superiors. Alternatively, the Americans were equally other-oriented to all three target groups (i.e. superior, subordinate and peer). Another difference was that the Americans used other-oriented strategies when conveying good news rather than bad news, but Koreans showed no difference in strategy in relation to message content.

These differences are consistent with the general communication differences between individualistic, low context cultures and collectivist, high context cultures (Hofstede, 1980). In spite of some methodological flaws, such as differential status of the two groups of participants, this study does demonstrate that politeness, irrespective of culture, is conveyed through both language and non-verbal channels, but some cultural differences do exist (Gallagher, 1987).

6.7 Verbal communication and questioning

Strack and Schwartz (1992) suggest that 'a communication that is structured by questions and answers is probably the most important form of human interaction' (p. 173). Although a question can be both initiated by the verbal and non-verbal channels, most questions in social interaction are verbal, and the non-verbal behaviours act as a support, for instance, raising or lowering of verbal inflection at the end of a question, head nods, raising eyebrows and direct eye contact, are all signals that the utterance requires a response.

A consistent research finding is that the higher status person is in control and, in some instances, causes stress to the person being questioned. However, in interactions made up of people of equal standing questions serve a number of functions, for example, they can be used to obtain information, to arouse discussion regarding a specific subject, or to ascertain attitudes, feelings and opinion of the other person.

Questions can be of a number of types, each type serving a different purpose. Probing questions are used to encourage somebody to expand on their previous response. A rhetorical question is one that does not require an answer. This is either because the speaker intends to provide the answer or the question is being used synonymously with a statement. It is a common technique in public speaking to stimulate interest amongst the audience. Similar to the wide variety of questions that can be asked, there is also a variety of possible responses. Dillon (1986) identified the main types used by individuals. They include silence, verbal refusal to answer, changing the topic, deflecting the question with humour, or merely giving a false answer. Other techniques used to avoid answering the question are evading, stalling, selective ambiguity and distortion which means that you give the answer you feel the speaker wants to hear. However, the most common response is to give a direct, truthful answer.

A large amount of material has been introduced in this chapter with the focus on the role of non-verbal behaviours in social interaction, both in relation to different channels and the functions which they serve. It is often difficult to distinguish functional difference between the verbal and non-verbal channels, examples of which are reflected in the discussion relating to interruptions, politeness strategies, deception, self-disclosure and questioning/responding strategies. We now consider the application of what social psychologists have found out about non-verbal communication to the health professional–client interaction.

6.8 Application: health professional–client interaction

The relationship between a health professional (doctor, physiotherapist, clinical psychologist, etc.), and his or her client is regarded as a key for achieving therapeutic goals (Roter and Hall, 1992). The communication which takes place between, for example, doctor and patient also relates to patient satisfaction. When communication is good and effective, and based on a trusting relationship, patients report high degrees of satisfaction, even when a life-threatening illness is being talked about. When communication is poor and little trust exists, patients report dissatisfaction (Ley, 1988). Much of the research in this area has focused on the doctor–patient relationship, and this is what we will concentrate on here.

Ong *et al.* (1995) identify three different functions of doctor–patient communication: (a) to develop and sustain a good relationship; (b) to exchange information; and (c) to make recommendations and decisions over how the patient should be treated. However, if a good relationship does not develop, the latter two functions will be impeded to the detriment of the patient (Dimatteo *et al.*, 1994). Communication, then, is of fundamental importance and, as we have seen earlier in this chapter, will rely heavily on the non-verbal communication that takes place between the doctor and patient. Larsen and Smith (1981) demonstrated that patient satisfaction may be influenced by the type of non-verbal communication that takes place. Larsen and Smith analysed doctor–patient consultations using three categories of non-verbal behaviour: (a) *immediacy* – which gives an indication of the degree of closeness in the relationship; (b) how *relaxed* the two were in interaction; and (c) the *responsiveness* of each person to what the other was saying. The types of non-verbal behaviour associated with each of these three categories is summarised in Figure 6.10.

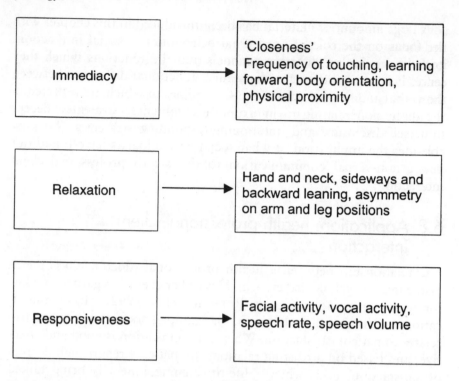

Figure 6.10: Three categories of non-verbal behaviour used by Larsen & Smith (1981) to assess levels of patient satisfaction

With respect to immediacy, for example, closeness in the relationship was evidenced by occasional touching, each leaning forward with body orientation towards each other, and close physical proximity. A 'distant' relationship was characterised by the opposite of these non-verbal behaviours. A relationship characterised by *responsiveness* was observed to have high levels of facial activity (providing feedback), variation in tone and pitch of voice (showing interest) and an appropriate level of speech.

Larsen and Smith (1981) found that the types of behaviours associated with immediacy were strongly related to patient satisfaction (distant or non-immediate relationships were characterised by low levels of patient satisfaction). They found the other two categories to also play a role in patient satisfaction, but not as strongly as that of immediacy. From this research it should be clear that the non-verbal behaviours of *both* the doctor and the patient are vital to the effectiveness of a consultation with a health professional.

These findings may also help to explain the *behavioural style* of the doctor and patient. Byrne and Long (1976) analysed tape-recorded consultations and suggested the style of the consultant could be classified either as doctor-centred or patient-centred. Patient-centred behavioural styles resulted in higher patient satisfaction. Many of the patient-centred behaviours identified by Byrne and Long (1976) were similar to those shown in Figure 6.10.

Finally, you might ask why patient satisfaction has been researched so widely and regarded as an important factor. Apart from being desirable for its own sake, research consistently demonstrates that high levels of patient satisfaction are strongly associated with a patient's adherence to medical advice and treatments (Ley, 1988).

6.9 Summary

- Communication can be both verbal and non-verbal. Verbal refers to the actual words spoken and non-verbal communication includes both vocal and non-vocal.
- Early research concentrated on the channels of non-verbal communication in isolation but an 'across-channel approach' is now preferred as it allows a more accurate analysis of function.
- Functions of non-verbal behaviours identified in early research include providing information about the emotional state of the interactants, regulating the interactions and expression of emotion.
- Non-human animals communicate using non-vocal behaviour. Such behaviour is a product of evolution and certain specific primate behaviours are similar to smiling and laughter in humans.
- Resulting from subsequent research, social control, self-presentation, effect management and service task functions have also been identified as functions of non-verbal behaviour.
- Differentiation of functionality between verbal and non-verbal communication can be too simplistic and current research focuses on their interaction.
- Major channels of non-verbal communication include gaze and eye contact, facial expressions, and body language.
- Personal space or proxemics, which is the area around the body which each individual likes to keep free from others, can vary according to status, culture and the relationship between the interactants.
- Aspects of speech such as pitch, stress, timing, pauses, the emotional tone of the voice, accent or dialect and speech errors, are also informative within the communication process.
- There are gender differences in the use of, and decoding of, non-verbal behaviours. On the whole, women have been found to be more accurate and sensitive in their decoding of these than men.
- Decoding of many non-verbal cues is culturally universal but there are some culturally specific behaviours which could make decoding difficult.

- The interaction between verbal and non-verbal behaviours can be analysed in relation to interruptions, 'floor' management, deception and lying and in politeness strategies.
- Early research associated interruptions with gender and power, but this assumption has now been refuted and more research is necessary to determine consistent variables.
- In relation to deception, it is believed that associated non-verbal behaviours are difficult to control, Burgoon *et al.* (1995), proposed the Interpersonal Deception Theory, based on three skills, each with its verbal (social) and non-verbal (emotional) component.
- The Politeness Theory has been extended to include non-linguistic channels of communication.
- Self-disclosure is an important element in communication. It has a number of functions, but in order to be effective, the timing and context of the disclosure need to be carefully monitored.
- Questions and answers form an important part of human interaction. Questions used in interactions between people of equal standing can serve a number of purposes.

6.10 Suggestions for further reading

Argyle. M. 1994: *The Psychology of Interpersonal Behaviours.* Fifth edition. Harmondsworth: Penguin.

> Now classic text in its fifth edition. Readable and up to date and the best book to go to if you wish to pursue matters dealt with in this chapter in more depth.

Knapp, M. L. and Hall, J. A. 1992: *Non-verbal Communication in Human Interaction.* Third edition. Fort Worth: Harcourt, Brace Jovanovich.

> Another good text, not quite so up to date and an American text reflecting research more from that perspective. Nevertheless, well written and detailed.

Hargie, O., Saunders, C. and Dickson, D. 1994: *Social Skills in Interpersonal Communication.* London: Routledge.

> Practical-based text with lots of exercises to help people enhance their social skills and deals with the societal and conceptual side as well. Now in its third edition, it has proved a popular text for practitioners in a range of professions dealing with people.

Miller, G. R. and Stiff, J. B. 1993: *Deceptive Communication.* Thousand Oaks, California: Sage Publications.

> Readable, accessible and well-written text dealing with theory and research in social psychology on lying and deception. Gathers together a wide range of research in a short text of just over hundred pages.

7

Social relationships

7.1 Introduction

Imagine for a minute what life would be like without social relationships: not swapping news with your family at the end of the day, not gossiping with your friends about the party you went to last night, not chatting with colleagues at the coffee machine, not having any close relationship involving mutual support and caring. Imagining this kind of life is so difficult as to be almost impossible, which neatly illustrates the importance of social relationships in our lives. In Chapter 2, the development of attachment was discussed at length. You will recall that from the moment of birth, babies seek to establish an enduring social relationship with their main carer, extending their circle of relationships outwards as skills and circumstances permit. From the earliest age humans want to belong to their world and to feel a sense of connectedness with it. This need for belongingness is known as *social motivation*, and it is this form of motivation that can be observed in infants through their earliest interactions with others. Later, as social skills develop, children accommodate their behaviour to others in order to fit in and affiliate with other people.

Wanting to belong is thought to be a basic need (Buck, 1985), and is often referred to as the *affiliation motivation*. This term reflects our propensity and need to set up, keep and repair, when necessary, good social relations with others. It has been proposed that affiliation takes place for four main reasons: to enable us to compare ourselves with others, thereby reducing uncertainty; to obtain the reward of stimulating company; to be valued; and to gain emotional support (Hill, 1987). Fox (1980) asked people to specify the conditions under which they would like to be with others. He found that people preferred the company of others in pleasant conditions such as enjoying a music concert, when happy or in the work environment. Company was also preferred in threatening conditions, such as when afraid or in danger. In unpleasant conditions, such as when tense or having just failed a test, people preferred to be alone, as they did in conditions requiring them to concentrate, such as solving a complicated problem or making a decision. Section 7.2 of this chapter examines the conditions and circumstances of affiliation in more detail. Section 7.3 considers interpersonal attraction; Sections 7.4 and 7.5 look at the development of close and intimate relationships, and the final sections consider factors affecting development and breakdown of close relationships.

7.2 Affiliation

Early research on affiliation saw it as an innate process, with seeking the company of others as akin to the herding instinct in animals (McDougall, 1908). However, with the advent of Behaviourism, Watson (1913) rejected explanations such as the herding instinct on the basis that they simply described behaviour rather than providing an explanation for it. One way of examining the importance of affiliation is to look at the effects of social isolation, where affiliation does not take place. We have all heard stories of amazing courage when people have been shipwrecked or left isolated from some other natural catastrophe. In circumstances like these, though, it is hard to disentangle the effects of social isolation from the effects of hardships such as lack of food, water and shelter. One study reports the case of Admiral Byrd, who in 1938 set out to spend six months without the company of others in the Arctic, compiling meteorological reports. For the first two or three weeks Byrd reported no ill effects. However, after 24 days his diaries show that he began to experience a terrible loneliness that intensified as his period of solitude lengthened. He began to imagine that he was with people he knew, and after nine weeks he became obsessed with religious questions and pondered on the meaning of life. He also sought ways of convincing himself that despite his isolation he was not alone, writing that he was part of a family of man scattered throughout the universe. After three months he began to suffer from depression, hallucinations and disordered ideas. His experiences are familiar to Inuit people, who take long fishing trips in groups to prevent the detrimental effects of social isolation (Hogg and Vaughan, 1995).

Studies of institutionalised infants have also demonstrated the dramatic effects of social deprivation. Spitz (1945) examined babies who had been left in a crowded institution for two years while their mothers were unable to care for them. The babies had their physical needs met, but they were only rarely handled, and were left in their cots for long periods of time without the company of a caregiver. Spitz found that these unfortunate infants were less intellectually and socially advanced than their non-institutionalised peers, and suffered from a high mortality rate. There are similarities here with the desperate plight of children left in Romanian orphanages during the recent past. The discovery of feral children such as Anna and Isabelle, noted in Chapter 2, and their intellectual and social deficits, lend support to the importance of affiliation for healthy psychological development.

7.2.1 Why affiliate?

In his classic study on shared stress, Schachter (1959) led female psychology students to believe that they were to receive electric shocks. Group A was told that the shocks would be painful, while Group B was told that the shocks would be mild. Both groups were then told that they would need to wait while the shock equipment was set up. The women were given the choice to either wait alone, or wait with another participant. Once they had made their choice, the experiment ended and no shocks were given. Their choice was between waiting alone or with others expecting to receive painful shocks, or waiting alone or with another student not involved in the experiment. Table 7.1 summarises results from this study.

Schacter found that participants in the high anxiety condition (those told they would receive painful shocks) preferred to wait in the company of another participant. Low anxiety participants (those told they

Group	Type of shock	Anxiety state	Choice
A	Painful	High	Wait with another
B	Mild	Low	Wait alone

Table 7.1: Preferences for waiting alone or with others in stressful situations. Adapted from Schachter (1959)

would receive mild shocks) were less likely to take this option. In addition, participants preferred to wait with others who were in the same boat. Why should this be? According to social comparison theory (Festinger, 1954), waiting in such an ambiguous situation would produce uncertainty, which could be reduced by comparing one's own reactions to the situation with others facing it. In a more recent study Buunk *et al.* (1991) found that people who were unsure about the stability of their marriage preferred to talk to others in a similar position. Both Schacter's and Buunk's findings suggest that being with others in a similar situation to yourself helps, because you can compare your reactions with those of others and decide whether your anxiety is justified. However, contrast Schacter and Buunk's findings with results from a study carried out by Sarnoff and Zimbardo (1961). They led participants to expect to have to suck on a large feeding nipple or on a child's pacifier. Sarnoff and Zimbardo found that participants preferred not to wait with others while the equipment was set up. At first reading this is puzzling; why should those who are fearful choose to wait with others, while those who are embarrassed prefer to wait alone?

7.2.2 Utility of affiliation

Rofé (1984) argues that the answer to this puzzle lies in the utility or value of affiliation. He claims that being stressed will increase affiliative behaviour only when the company of others is thought to be useful in reducing stress, and that the perceived utility of affiliation depends on the kind of stress experienced. In Schacter's study the other person provided the means for *social comparison* against which participants could measure their own uncertainty. Thus participants would be able to decide whether their fear was justified. However, in the Sarnoff and Zimbardo study no such utility accrued from waiting with others. Embarrassment is a type of social anxiety, and is likely to be enhanced in the company of others. As well as providing a means of social comparison, waiting with others could serve to reduce anxiety if the others approached the situation in a relatively unworried way. Gerrard (1963) attached dummy electrodes to the hands of participants in his experiment, and rigged an 'emotionality index' so that participants recorded either stable or erratic responses. He found that participants in the erratic condition preferred to wait with others in the same condition. Furthermore, they preferred to affiliate with others who showed less emotion, probably because such people provided reassurance that the situation was not as threatening. Thus affiliation can serve as an *anxiety reduction* strategy. A third motive for affiliation is *information seeking*. Shaver and Klinnert (1982) proposed that just as infants and young children refer to their parents for information in new or ambiguous situations as part of the attachment process, adults will also seek out someone with more information when faced with a difficult situation. This proposal was borne out in a study by Kulik and Mahler (1989) who discovered that hospital patients facing an operation the next day preferred to spend the night with others who had already had the operation. They would rather spend time with someone who could provide information about the potential danger than with someone else who faced the same operation.

Individual characteristics also influence the need to affiliate under stress. First-born children and females are more likely than other individuals to affiliate, perhaps as a result of parenting practices. The perception of others as able or unable to help also influences the decision to affiliate; research by Kulik *et al.* (1994) shows that we both look at and ask questions more of those we think can help compared with those we perceive as unable to help. Table 7.2 shows the conditions where affiliation while stressed is most and least likely to occur.

7.2.3 Cultural differences in affiliation

While all of us appear to have an innate need for belongingness, the type of relationship that we form is to some extent culturally bound. For example, in collectivist cultures where the importance of the community and the family is paramount, relationships are characterised by quality rather than quantity, and there is an expectation that relations between people will be meaningful, extremely long-lasting and characterised by commitment. In contrast, individualist cultures tend to

Factors influencing perceived utility of affiliation	Factors eliciting affiliation under stress	Factors deferring affiliation under stress
Type of stress	Manageable activity	Unmanageable anxiety Social anxiety
Characteristics of stressed person	First born child	Later born child
	Female	Male
Characteristics of affiliates	Similar to stressed person Able to cope effectively with situation	Dissimilar to stressed person Unable to cope effectively with situation

Table 7.2: Factors influencing affiliation under stressed conditions. Based on Rofé (1984)

reflect the tendency to form many friendships which are not close and intimate and may seem rather superficial when compared with other cultures (Triandis *et al.*, 1988). It is true to say then that people are social animals and actively seek out the company of others and the establishment of good social relationships. The next section traces the development of such relationships.

7.3 Interpersonal attraction

7.3.1 Factors affecting interpersonal attraction

Most of us are able to establish a rewarding variety of social relationships with others, from acquaintanceship through deep friendship and intimate sexual relationships. How does this happen? What are the processes we go through in establishing good relationships with others? When we move to a new environment, leave home for university, take up a new job or move to a different area, how do we make new friends? In this section we will examine several factors which have been found to influence the progression of social relationships. We will look at the factors which change relationships from consisting of superficial interactions, such as smiling when you pass one another, into deep friendships or even intimate partnerships. Initial moves in establishing a relationship are often provoked by feelings of attraction to another person (Moghaddam *et al.*, 1993). Attraction takes place when one person experiences positive feelings towards another.

7.3.2 Physical attractiveness

Attraction or liking for others is strongly influenced by what we consider to be physically attractive; people are drawn to those whom they consider to be physically beautiful. This is partly because we confuse the two concepts of beauty and goodness, and believe that what is beautiful is good (Eagly *et al.*, 1991). We automatically consider attractive people to have positive characteristics and see them as happier, more stable individuals who are socially skilled, assertive, friendly and warm (Feingold, 1992). Such stereotypical views of attractive people do have some basis in fact, since from early life attractive people are likely to have received more attention from others and to have become more self-confident as a result – and the 'beautiful is good' belief becomes a *self-fulfilling prophecy*.

Luckily for those of us who are not blessed with movie star looks, the notion of physical beauty is both culturally and temporally variable, for example, in most Western cultures slimness is considered attractive. However, in other cultures being plump or even what Western observers would consider obese is deemed attractive. In the 1950s researchers sought examples of physical beauty from over 200 non-Western societies and found that not a single characteristic was considered attractive everywhere (Ford and Beach, 1951). Even in our own century there have been several shifts in what is considered physically attractive. In the 1930s the 'ideal' female shape was one of boyish slimness, while in the 1940s and especially in the 1950s (think of Marilyn Monroe) a more voluptuous figure was considered desirable. Later both men and women preferred a quite androgynous look which persisted for some years, and currently thinness is culturally preferable in Western society.

Whether we like a person or not can affect our judgements of how physically attractive we find them. Owens and Ford (1978) carried out a study in which participants were asked to rate the physical attractiveness of females from photographs, having previously read favourable or unfavourable accounts of the females' personality. The researchers found that participants in the experiment rated females who supposedly had an attractive character as more physically attractive. However, when Klentz *et al.* (1987) replicated this experiment using photographs of males they found no effect of character description on the perceived physical attractiveness of males, which suggests that for females at least personality counts!

The effects of physical attractiveness are very wide-ranging and being attractive definitely confers an advantage. Cash *et al.* (1977) found that among a group of supposed candidates for employment (actually confederates of the experimenter), physically attractive applicants were preferred, and in a simulated courtroom situation Kulka and Kessler (1978) found that physically attractive defendants were treated more leniently. In education too, appearance counts. Landy and Sigall (1974) asked male students to mark two essays of different standards. They paired each of the essays either with a photo of an attractive female or with a less attractive female. Perhaps you can guess the results of the study. Predictably, better grades were given to the attractive female. Results from this study are summarised in Figure 7.1.

Even in childhood the influence of physical attractiveness is discernible. Dion *et al.* (1974) found that children prefer to have physically attractive playmates and assume that less attractive children have unpleasant character traits. In choosing a sexual partner, physical attractiveness is very important. Walster *et al.* (1966b) carried out a seminal study of the effects of physical attractiveness in the dating situation. She randomly paired students for an evening of socialising. While the students got to know each other, researchers covertly rated

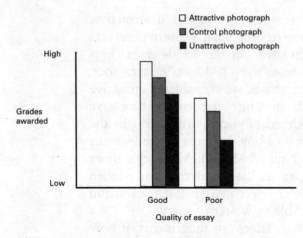

Figure 7.1: Effect of pairing attractive and unattractive photographs with essays of different quality. Adapted from Landy and Sigall (1974)

them for physical attractiveness and social skills. The researchers also obtained the student's IQ scores and their results on personality tests. At the end of the evening, each student was asked to rate how satisfied he or she had been with their date. Walster found that the strongest determinant of satisfaction was the physical attractiveness of the partner, above all other factors, including intelligence, personality and social skills. Next time you are accused of being vain, you could argue that paying attention to your looks is a sound investment.

7.3.3 Sex differences in ratings of physical attractiveness

While both men and women prefer their partners to be physically attractive, attractiveness is more important for males than for females. In a cross-cultural study of 37 societies, Buss (1989) found that although both sexes identified physical attractiveness as important, the effect was stronger for men. Stroebe *et al.* (1971) gave participants completed attitude surveys paired with pictures of others of varying levels of attractiveness. They found that both sexes preferred others with similar rather than dissimilar attitudes to their own, and physically attractive people over less attractive people. However, the effects of physical attractiveness were more pronounced for men.

The sex differences observed in ratings of physical attractiveness are in accordance with *socio-evolutionary theory*. Socio-evolutionary theory proposes that we act on the basis of mainly unconscious processes which are rooted in human evolution and which serve to increase the chances of producing viable offspring and successfully raising them to adulthood. According to this theory, men will be attracted to women who appear to be highly fertile and capable of producing healthy children, and they will be attuned to search for signs that indicate fecundity such as youth, health and reproductive capacity. Research has indicated that men find women with childish faces (large wide eyes, small features) indicative of youth more attractive (Cunningham, 1986). Also, men prefer women with a small waist to hip ratio, a factor which is both a signal of good health and of reproductive value (Singh, 1993).

If men prefer 'cute' women, what do women look for in a man? Historically the female has been responsible for caring for and feeding her children. Females would have a better chance of their offspring (and themselves) surviving if there was a man around who could provide food, shelter and other resources. According to the socio-evolutionary perspective, women would look for signs of status, strength and dominance in a man (Buss, 1994). A number of studies have shown that women prefer men who demonstrate dominant and assertive non-verbal behaviour (Sadalla *et al.*, 1987). Physically, women prefer tall, muscular men (Hatfield and Sprecher, 1986) and well-dressed men with strong, pronounced facial features (Cunningham *et al.*, 1990). These preferences echo the evolutionary inheritance of the search for someone who is able to provide for the woman and her offspring.

Figure 7.2: Physical attractiveness is a key determinant of interpersonal attraction

So, why do we like being with physically attractive people? Partly, of course, the reason is that we enjoy looking at them, and earlier we noted that we are prone to confusing what is beautiful with what is good, often believing the two attributes to be indissolubly entwined. Eagly *et al.* (1991) showed that beautiful people are commonly perceived to be confident, approachable and warm. An earlier study (Snyder *et al.*, 1977) provided evidence for the existence of this belief. Snyder showed male participants photos of a female they were supposedly about to have a telephone conversation with. One group saw a photo of an attractive female, and the other saw a photo of a less attractive female. Both groups then held a conversation with a woman who knew nothing of the photos they had seen. When the taped conversations were listened to later, it was found that the men's behaviour differed according to the photo they had seen. Men who they thought they were talking to an attractive female were more sociable and confident. Interestingly, these attributes were reflected by the supposedly attractive women who also acted more sociably and confidently. The researchers concluded that when we perceive people as attractive, we expect them to have desirable personality characteristics and we treat them in a way that draws out such positive features. Thus the perception that what is beautiful is good becomes a self-fulfilling prophecy.

7.3.4 Similarity

You will probably have heard two conflicting proverbs, one being 'birds of a feather flock together' and the other 'opposites attract'. In social psychological terms, the former statement is the more accurate, since similarity has been found to be one of the most important factors affecting interpersonal attraction, especially for women (Feingold, 1991). When you take up a new job, you will probably spend time with those who work most closely with you, but over time you may discover other people in the company who seem more like 'your type' and gravitate towards them. This section addresses three main types of similarity and considers the role of similarity in the attraction process.

▆ Similarity: personal characteristics

There is a strong correlation between friends, partners and spouses on variables such as age, education, race, type of background, religious beliefs and socio-economic status (Warren, 1966). Correlations, however strong, cannot prove a causal relationship between similarity and attraction. Nevertheless, Newcomb (1961) provided strong support for this link. In a classic study he allowed male students to live in college accommodation rent-free for a semester. He measured demographic variables such as age and background among the students prior to the start of their course, and then measured attraction among the students over the length of a semester. He found that during the first couple of weeks, liking was based on proximity (dealt with in a later section of this chapter). However, over time he found that attraction was more strongly related to pre-existing demographic variables. Similarity provides obvious keys for attraction, since shared interests give us the opportunity to interact with others, and those shared interests increase the likelihood of the interaction being positive. Later research has shown a diminution of the effects of demographic similarity, however, with people from different races and backgrounds being more likely to marry than previously (Smolowe, 1993).

Attraction between people is, perhaps not surprisingly, associated with similarities in personality (Caspi and Harbener, 1990). Also, there is an association between mood and attraction. Locke and Horowitz (1990) paired students with others in similar mood states (either depressed or not depressed). The researchers found that these students reported more satisfaction with the short interaction than other pairs whose moods differed. This suggests that being with people of a similar mood, even a negative mood, can aid attraction. It is important to note that the interactions were short; long-term interaction with negative mood states does not facilitate attraction, and married couples where one or both partners are depressed report a reduction in marital satisfaction (McLeod and Eckberg, 1993).

▨ Similarity: physical appearance

Think of your reaction when you see a couple who are physically mismatched, one being very attractive and the other much less so. Usually, we expect couples to be about equal in attractiveness and if they are not we tend to think that the less attractive partner must bring wealth or some other advantage to the relationship, in accordance with equity theory (see Section 7.4.3). Psychologists expected that the *matching hypothesis* (the idea that people prefer those similar to themselves) would also apply to physical attractiveness, but results from studies to examine this hypothesis have been quite mixed. For example, a study by Walster *et al.* (1966b) found no support for the matching hypothesis of physical attractiveness, while Berscheid *et al.* (1971) did find support for the hypothesis. Studies of real-life situations have consistently shown evidence for the matching hypothesis among dating, engaged and married couples (Feingold, 1988).

Why should laboratory studies provide such inconsistent results while observational studies of real couples find such consistent results? There are at least two possible explanations. The first is that long-term partners simply grow to look alike, either as a result of factors like shared environment such as diet, exercise and beliefs about personal appearance, or as a result of reflecting each other's facial expressions (Zajonc *et al.*, 1987). However, support for this argument is not strong (Tambs and Moum, 1992). The second explanation is more pragmatic. In real life, approaching someone who is highly physically attractive carries with it the threat of rejection. In the laboratory, this risk is not present. So in the laboratory situation people could simply be choosing the most attractive person, regardless of their own appearance, because there is no possibility of being rejected, say, by a photograph. Life, then, may be a compromise between choosing to approach someone who is physically attractive and fearing the possibility of rejection.

Similarity: shared attitudes

If you were a keen supporter of the Labour Party and new to town, it is highly unlikely that you would go along to the next meeting of the local Conservative Club. Instead you would probably go along to the next meeting of the local Labour group, because you would expect to meet people who shared similar attitudes to your own. There are two types of similarities of attitude: *perceived similarity* and *actual similarity*. Newcomb's research with the experimental college environment can help untangle the effects of the two. At the beginning of the study, he found that perceived similarity in attitudes was strongly correlated with liking among the students. Since it was impossible for students to know each other's true attitudes at this point, attraction was the key to liking. Marks and Miller (1982) showed that when we are attracted to others, we presume that they share our attitudes. This perceived similarity of attitude increases liking. As the academic year progressed and students had a chance to get to know each other better, Newcomb found an increasingly strong relationship between actual attitudinal similarity and liking. Byrne (1971) later underpinned results from Newcomb's study in a study. In the first stage of his study, he gave students an attitude questionnaire to complete. In the second stage participants received an attitude questionnaire supposedly completed by a fellow student but in fact manipulated by Byrne to express similar or dissimilar attitudes to the student's own. Results showed that students preferred people with similar attitudes to theirs, and it is now a well-documented fact that the more attitudes people share, the more they are attracted to one another – this is known as the *law of attraction*. Yet perhaps similarity of attitudes is less important than dissimilarity. Imagine how hard it would be to get along with someone who does not share the same attitudes as yourself. You would constantly need to explain and argue your position, which is not a very comfortable way for a relationship to get started, or to progress. Rosenbaum (1986) argues that it is because we find attitudinal dissimilarity so repellent that we seek to avoid it, and, therefore, dissimilarity is a more potent predictor of not liking than similarity is of liking. Byrne *et al.* (1986) disagree with this standpoint and propose a model of attraction which takes into account a refinement of attitudinal similarity: high and low similarity. The model is pictured in Figure 7.3. The model states that we avoid those who are dissimilar to ourselves as a first stage. At the second stage, we consider those who are left and are attracted to those who are most similar to ourselves.

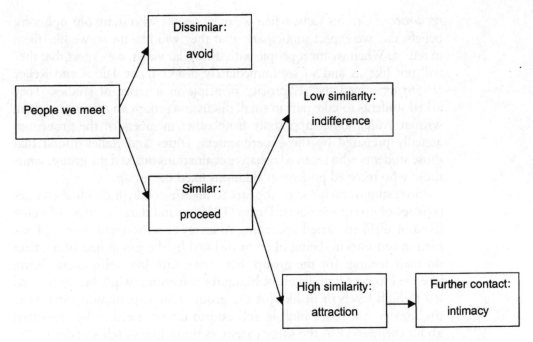

Figure 7.3: Two-stage model of similarity in the attraction process. Adapted from Byrne *et al.* (1986)

7.3.5 Explaining the effects of similarity

In the preceding section we discussed how both similarity and dissimilarity act as influences on attraction. Byrne and Clore (1970) argue from the perspective of classical conditioning, that similarity is rewarding to us because it is reassuring to know that there are others who see the world as we do and share our beliefs. Conversely, dissimilarity is not rewarding since it threatens our perception of the world and our self-esteem. Wetzel and Insko (1982) proposed a theory related to similarity. Here the search for similarity actually represents the search for someone who meets our ideals. Our ideals are closely related to our self-perception but better, and we seek someone who meets those ideals. Wetzel and Insko found that people preferred those who met their ideals more than those who were similar to them.

7.3.6 Reciprocity

An opposing view espouses the *reciprocity principle*, the idea that we usually like people who like us and dislike people who dislike us. Aronson and Worchel (1966) propose that we act according to *anticipatory reciprocity*. On this view, when we meet people who share our opinions, beliefs, etc. we expect (anticipate) that they will like us, so we like them in return. When we meet people with dissimilar views, we expect that they will not like us and so we immediately dislike them. Dittes and Kelley (1956) examined the reciprocity principle in a series of studies. They asked students to take part in small discussion groups and then gave them written evaluations, supposedly from other members of the group but actually prepared by the experimenters. Dittes and Kelley found that those students who received negative evaluations disliked the group, while those who received positive evaluations liked the group.

Interestingly, reciprocity appears to be affected by individual characteristics of group members. Dittes (1959) found that the effect of being liked or disliked varied according to levels of self-esteem. For students high in self-esteem, being liked or disliked by the group had little effect on their feelings for the group. For those with low self-esteem, being liked led to very high levels of liking for the group, while being disliked led to high levels of dislike for the group. One explanation for Dittes' findings is that those high in self-esteem do not need to be reassured about themselves to the same extent as those low in self-esteem.

7.3.7 Proximity

Usually we like the people we come into contact with on a regular basis. One of the most important factors in attraction is *proximity* (sometimes referred to as propinquity), and several studies have shown the effect of this variable. The most famous of these is a study carried out by Festinger, Schacter and Back (1950). These researchers looked at relationships among married student couples in a university housing complex, which consisted of 17 buildings of 10 apartments spread over two floors. Couples were assigned from a waiting list to apartments as they became vacant. After some months, Festinger *et al.* found that there were ten times as many friendships between couples who lived in the same building than between couples who lived in different buildings. Within buildings, proximity was also important. More friendships developed between couples on the same floor than on different floors, and between couples who lived closer together on the same floor. Those whose apartments were located next to stairs or mailboxes reported more friendships than did other couples located elsewhere. The effect is shown in Figure 7.4.

The effect is not limited to location within a building. Newcomb (1961) found that students placed together as roommates developed friendships, and the effect of proximity has been noted in the classroom too. Segal (1974) asked students at a police training academy to list their three closest friends and found an extremely high correlation between the initial letter of the student's surname and those of his friends. The seating arrangements at the academy were in alphabetical order, placing those with names close in the alphabet in close physical proximity.

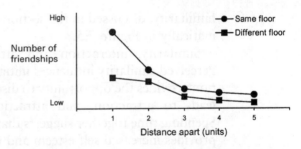

Figure 7.4: Effect of proximity on friendship relationships. Based on Festinger *et al.* (1950)

Why should proximity have such a pervasive effect on attraction? There are several possible explanations. First, it requires much less effort to interact with those close to us; even climbing a flight of stairs represents expending effort. Second, interacting with someone regularly gives us the opportunity to discover more about them, and usually proves to be an interesting and rewarding experience. Third, proximity can lead to attraction because we become more familiar with those we see regularly – this is known as the *mere exposure effect* (Bernstein *et al.*, 1987). Moreland and Beach (1992) demonstrated the effect of mere exposure even when no interaction had taken place. They recruited four women who resembled typical college students. All of them had their photograph taken, and then three of the four attended a large Psychology lecture course for either 5, 10 or 15 times out of a possible 40 lectures. When the real students on the lecture course were shown the photos and asked to make judgements about the person pictured, the more classes the woman had attended, the more positively she was perceived *even though they had never spoken to the woman*.

At the beginning of this section we noted that proximity usually leads to attraction. But does proximity always have a positive effect? While neighbours may prove to be the best of friends, they may also become the worst of enemies. Ebbesen *et al.* (1976) found that while the most liked people lived in close proximity, so did the most disliked people. Negative interaction, for example, having to spend time with someone who is racist, aggressive or plain unpleasant leads to more dislike.

Generally, interaction more often leads to attraction than to annoyance (Rosenbaum, 1986) and there are a number of reasons for this. First, interacting with others provides us with a sense of mastery (Smith and Mackie, 1997) by providing the opportunity to solve personal problems (Schacter, 1959) and validate our beliefs (Wheeler, 1974). Second, interaction helps us to achieve a sense of belongingness by providing fun, warmth, acceptance and stimulation (intellectual, social, and sexual). Finally, interaction leads to attraction through simple familiarity, discussed in the section above. This is represented diagrammatically in Figure 7.5.

Similarity, interaction and attraction are mutually reinforcing. Perceived similarity influences initial attraction, and subsequent interaction provides the opportunity to discover further similarities. Interaction leads to attraction, and attraction leads to increased interaction. Spending time together suggests that two people like each other, and this provides increased self-esteem and validation for both. Finally, similarity and attraction are mutually reinforcing since we are attracted to those who are similar to us, we think people we are attracted to are similar to us and we expect that people who are like us will be attracted to us (Condon and Crano, 1988). Figure 7.6 shows this relationship.

7.4 Development and maintenance of close relationships

So far, we have discussed the effects of physical attractiveness, similarity and proximity as factors influencing interpersonal attraction. Even

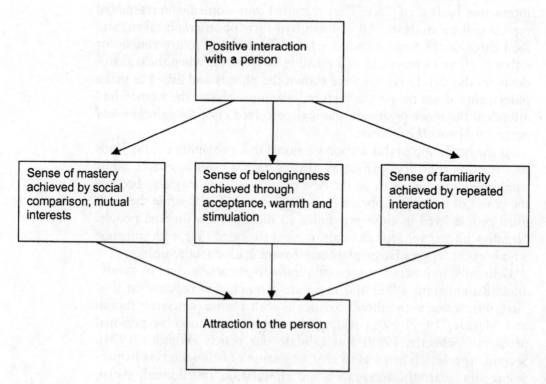

Figure 7.5: Effect of interaction on attraction. Adapted from Smith and Mackie (1995)

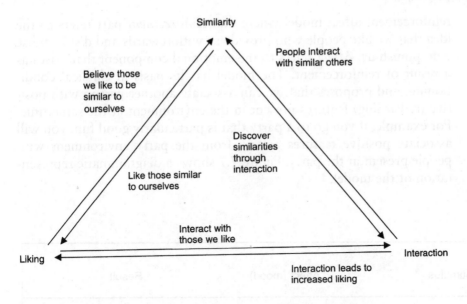

Figure 7.6: The inter-linked effects of similarity, interaction and liking

when optimum environmental conditions exist, a close friendship may still not develop. A close relationship can be defined as one in which there is strong connection involving robust and frequent *interdependence*. Kelly *et al.* (1983) define interdependence as a context in which one person's behaviour, emotions and thoughts affects the other. This section discusses theories that attempt to account for the development of close relationships. The most important rules of friendship (Argyle and Henderson, 1985) are offering help to a friend in need, respecting a friend's privacy and keeping confidences and operating in a climate of mutual trust.

Social psychologists have attempted to account for the development and maintenance of close relationships by proposing a number of theories that claim to account for attraction between individuals. Three of these, reinforcement theory, social exchange theory and equity theory are discussed below. In addition, the importance of self-disclosure is outlined.

7.4.1 Reinforcement theory

A number of explanations for attraction have been culled from learning theory, the simplest being that we like people who are present when we receive a reward, since this reward provides positive reinforcement for us (Lott and Lott 1972). Byrne and Clore (1970) have presented the reinforcement-affect model where the *reinforcement* part refers to the idea that we like people who provide us with rewards and dislike those who punish us. *Affect* refers to the emotional component that arises as a result of reinforcement. The model has its basis in classical conditioning, and proposes that we can associate another person with positive (rewarding) features present in the environment at the same time. For example, if you go to a party that is particularly good fun, you will associate positive features arising from the party environment with people present at the party. Figure 7.7 shows a diagrammatic representation of the model.

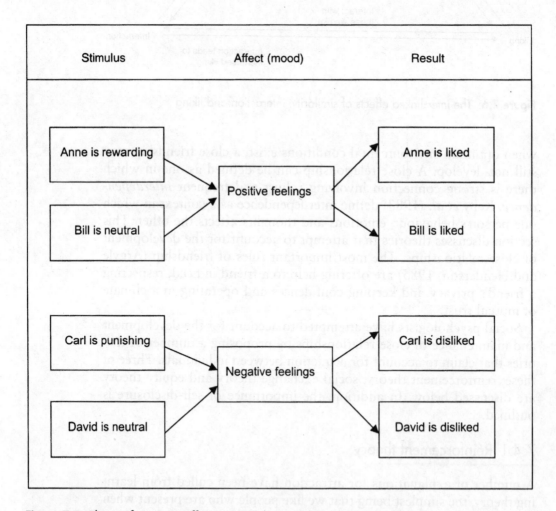

Figure 7.7: The reinforcement-affect process showing that attraction is based on principles of classical conditioning. Based on Byrne and Clore (1974)

The reinforcement-affect model assumes four basic principles:

- Stimuli provided by others are either rewarding or punishing, and we seek out rewarding stimuli while avoiding punishing stimuli.
- Rewarding stimuli evoke positive feelings (affect), while punishing stimuli evoke negative feelings.
- If a stimulus arouses positive feelings, it will be evaluated as good. If a stimulus arouses negative feelings it will be evaluated as bad.
- Any neutral stimuli (e.g. a person) present in the background that are associated with the positive stimuli will arouse positive feelings. Neutral stimuli associated with negative stimuli will arouse negative feelings.

According to Byrne and Clore's model, people are liked if they are associated with positive feelings and disliked if they are associated with negative feelings. This prediction has been supported empirically. Griffit and Veitch (1971) gave people statements from strangers in one of two conditions: either hot and crowded (negative condition) or comfortable (positive condition). They found that in the negative conditions, the stranger was liked less. It appears that the strangers' statements (the neutral stimulus) became associated with the negative feelings aroused by physically uncomfortable conditions. In a further experiment (Griffit and Veitch, 1971) the same effect was observed when people listened either to a broadcast of bad news or one of good news and later met a stranger. Those who had heard the bad news disliked the stranger, while those who had heard the good news liked the stranger. However, the model describes human relationships in two dichotomous terms: like and dislike. In real life this distinction does not hold, since most people provide a mixed bag of rewards and punishments. In Byrne and Clore's view the balance of positive and negative feelings is crucial. Relationships which are characterised by more positive feelings than negative feelings are likely to develop and succeed, while those where negative feelings outweigh the positive are likely to fail.

7.4.2 Social exchange theory

Social exchange theory can be considered a behaviourist theory, with one important distinction. As well as the theme of rewards and punishments, social exchange theory addresses the fact that a relationship consists of interaction between at least two people who exchange rewards with one another. According to this approach, what determines whether a relationship will develop and thrive or stagnate and cool depends on the perceived rewards each person derives from the relationship. This theory has some currency, since in everyday life we seek to gain or exchange things we value with others. Some of these exchanges are economic and may be relatively meaningless, but others are more important to us, especially those involving emotions. The basic idea of social exchange theory is that since rewards are dependent on the actions of another person, we seek to develop ways of interacting that are reciprocal and beneficial to both partners. Foa and Foa (1980) list six examples of interpersonal relationships involving the exchange of different kinds of resources:

- Goods: produce or objects
- Information: views, instructions or counsel
- Love: affection, emotional support and warmth
- Money: a token with an associated value
- Services: activities undertaken for the other person's benefit
- Status: relationship confers esteem

Thibaut and Kelley (1959) were the major proponents of social exchange theory. They proposed that human relationships progress according to a series of business-like deals or strategies, with each person in the relationship attempting to minimise costs to themselves and maximise benefits – the so-called *minimax* strategy. A relationship will cease to develop when the costs exceed the rewards for remaining in the relationship. Costs include financial expenditure without adequate recompense, or emotional expenditure such as (for example) embarrassment, disappointment and irritation. Rewards include pleasure, comfort and warmth. Thibaut and Kelley's social exchange theory represents a reduction of human relationships to a basis of profit and loss, with each person trading in cost and benefit to themselves, albeit unconsciously. They suggest the following stages of social exchange as a relationship develops, as shown in Table 7.3.

Stage	Description
Sampling	When we first meet someone we scan potential costs and rewards of the relationship and compare with other relationships available
Bargaining	When interaction begins rewards are swapped and decision made whether or not to develop relationship further
Commitment	Both sampling and bargaining reduce. Costs of interaction also reduce, becomes easier to understand the other person, and easier to gain rewards from them
Institutionalization	Relationship develops its own unique pattern of costs and benefits which is recognized by each partner

Table 7.3: Stages in relationship development according to social exchange theory

Thibaut and Kelley propose that social exchange theory has a further component, *comparison level*, a term that refers to our tendency to judge all relationships against a personal baseline measure. Our personal comparison level is made up from the average value of all outcomes of past relationships, our experiences in similar contexts, our general expectations about relationships, and what we know of other people's relationships. It provides a baseline measure against which new relationships can be judged, but it can change over time and in different contexts. If we perceive that a new relationship exceeds the comparison level, we will be attracted to that person. However, if the comparison level is not exceeded, it is unlikely that the relationship will succeed. Consider going out on a date with a new partner. The outcome of the date consists of the rewards (enjoying yourself, developing satisfactory interactions) less the costs (social embarrassment, spending too much money). The perceived outcome will depend on how your date compared with other dates in similar contexts you have had in the past, your general expectations of dates, together with what you know of other people's dates.

A further feature is the *comparison level for alternatives*. Suppose you are in a committed relationship, and then meet an attractive new person. If you consider leaving your existing relationship, you will do so on the basis of comparing what you have with a potential increase in rewards from a relationship with the new person. If an increase in rewards is anticipated, the existing relationship will both founder and break up or suffer from a decreased level of intimacy. However, if a relationship with the new person suggests an increase in costs, then the existing relationship will continue. The main criticism of social exchange theory is that it provides a rather barren account of human relationships which reduces them to a process of trade and barter. However, one of the strengths of social exchange theory is that it acknowledges the impact of individual differences in interpersonal attraction.

7.4.3 Equity theory

Equity theory is an explicit proposal for how social exchange theory works in interpersonal relationships (Walster *et al.*, 1978). The equity model proposes that people expect resources to be distributed fairly, and was first introduced by Adams (1965). According to Adams, people are satisfied in a relationship if the ratio between what they obtain from the relationship (benefits) to what they give to the relationship (inputs) is similar for both partners in the relationship. In evaluating equity, an individual compares the ratio of his or her total input to the relationship to the benefits accrued from it. The resulting ratio is then compared with the ratio of inputs to benefits for the other person, as shown in Figure 7.8.

Equity theory is not the same as equality, i.e. it is not necessary for both partners to contribute an equal amount of input. If one partner contributes more than the other but also benefits more, the relationship is equitable. However, if one person receives less benefit than required by his or her contribution level, that person is *under-benefited*. If someone receives more benefit compared to his or her contribution level, that person is *over-benefited*. In either case the relationship is inequitable. The more people are under-benefited, the less satisfied they will be with a relationship, though being over-benefited also causes distress (Adams, 1965). In an inequitable relationship, we can either change the amount we input or the amount we benefit so as to restore equilibrium, or we can change our perceptions about the costs and benefits of the relationship to restore the appearance of equilibrium. However, if the ratio falls below an individual's comparison level the relationship will probably be terminated. An American survey of married women found that those who perceived their marriage as inequitable believed they were more likely to be divorced than those who perceived their marriage to be equitable (Katzev *et al.*, 1994). Interestingly, women who were under-benefited felt that divorce was more likely than did those who were over-benefited.

Deciding whether a relationship is equitable involves some complicated calculations, taking into account your own benefits divided by your inputs, and comparing the result with your partner's ratio of benefits and inputs. If this process seems unlikely to you, you may well be right, since research has shown that less complex calculations can be

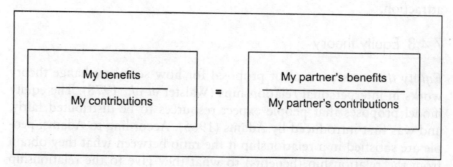

$$\frac{\text{My benefits}}{\text{My contributions}} = \frac{\text{My partner's benefits}}{\text{My partner's contributions}}$$

Figure 7.8: Equity theory: evaluating the ratio of costs and benefits from each partner in a relationship

used. Cate and Lloyd (1988) found that the level of rewards from a relationship was a greater determinant of satisfaction than equity. Feeney *et al.* (1994) examined equity theory in various family contexts. They found that for married couples who were either childless or had all of their offspring still living with them, equity and high reward level were key indicators of marital satisfaction. In families where some of the children had left home, level of rewards determined satisfaction, while parents with an empty nest expressed satisfaction dependent on equity in the relationship. Thus equity theory may fail to predict relationship satisfaction because it fails to take account of variance in relationship contexts.

In addition, there are gender differences in the salience of equity theory. Prins *et al.* (1993) found that among Dutch couples, males who perceived inequity neither expressed the desire to have an affair nor reported that they had done so. However, women who perceived inequity in their relationship both expressed the desire to have an affair and reported more affairs than the men, especially those women who believed that they were over-benefited by the relationship. Also, women are more likely to believe that resources should be distributed according to an equality norm (i.e. that everyone should get an equal amount) while men are more likely to focus on an equity norm (i.e. where benefits should be roughly proportional to costs) (Kahn *et al.*, 1980; Major and Adams, 1983).

7.4.4 Self-disclosure

If a relationship is progressing well, this will be reflected in the level of *self-disclosure* between the partners. Self-disclosure refers to our willingness to reveal intimate facts about ourselves and contributes to the development of intimate relationships (Derlega *et al.*, 1993). The term refers to facts that the other person could not have known if we had not told them. The theory of social penetration (Altman and Taylor, 1973) proposes that relationships progress from minor disclosures between the participants to more and more intimate disclosures. At first, people are content to have superficial exchanges with others, but if the relationship proves rewarding then disclosures become both broader, encompassing other areas of life, and deeper, becoming more intimate. This is shown in Figure 7.9.

Social penetration has been described above as a linear process, with more self-disclosure taking place the longer people interact (Altman and Taylor, 1973). However, this strictly progressive pattern is not always the case. Derlega *et al.* (1993) showed that three other patterns were possible:

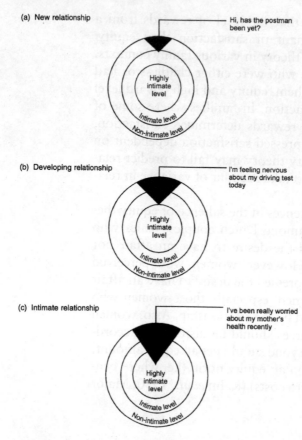

(a) New relationship

Hi, has the postman been yet?

Highly intimate level

Intimate level

Non-intimate level

(b) Developing relationship

I'm feeling nervous about my driving test today

Highly intimate level

Intimate level

Non-intimate level

(c) Intimate relationship

I've been really worried about my mother's health recently

Highly intimate level

Intimate level

Non-intimate level

Figure 7.9: The level of self-disclosure deepens as a relationship develops and becomes more intimate

- rapid intimacy followed by an equally rapid decline in intimacy;
- rapid intimacy followed by intimacy stall which does not progress;
- steady growth in intimacy followed either by intimacy stall or decline.

The amount of self-disclosure also varies according to the stage of the relationship. When we first meet someone, the unwritten rule is to match the level of self-disclosure of the new person (Cunningham *et al.*, 1986). Not to do so would stall the relationship in its tracks and prevent the development of trust, while too much self-disclosure can be threatening or embarrassing. As a relationship matures, strict matching no longer occurs (Altman, 1973). Among partners in a declining relationship, there are two kinds of self-disclosure patterns. In the first, both the breadth and depth of self-disclosure decrease as one might expect (Baxter, 1987). In the second, while breadth of disclosure decreases, depth actually increases as private matters designed to hurt the other person are disclosed and angry bitter words are exchanged (Tolstedt and Stokes, 1984).

More self-disclosure is associated with greater satisfaction in intimate relationships (Rubin *et al.*, 1980; Hansen and Schuldt, 1984). The level of self-disclosure influences the quality of the relationship; we disclose to those whom we like, we like people who disclose to us and we like those we disclose to (Collins and Miller, 1994). Increased self-disclosure leads to a sense of intimacy and commitment in relationships. Intimacy has been defined as psychological closeness (Sternberg, 1986) and involves acceptance, warmth and regard for the well-being of the other. Commitment permits a relationship to endure and involves being able to rely on the other person, taking responsibility for him or her when necessary and offering support and help when required (Kobak and Hazan, 1991). Self-disclosure is the lifeblood of relationships. If we were not to disclose intimate facts about ourselves we would never achieve close and meaningful relationships with others.

7.5 Intimate/sexual relationships

We have discussed the strong need for affiliation in humans and considered some of the factors that influence interpersonal attraction. We have also considered the factors that influence the development and maintenance of relationships. However, we have focused on relationships involving *liking*. The experience of *love* is one that feels qualitatively different from liking, and it is to this topic that we now turn. Rubin (1973) demonstrated the existence of a qualitative difference between liking and loving. He found that people rated intimate partners more highly on certain items (e.g. I would do almost anything for this person) than for friends, and from this developed a 'liking and loving scale' to measure the difference between these two types of interpersonal relationship.

You may well be of the opinion that love is simply too exotic and incomprehensible an experience to be successfully explained by social psychological theories, and indeed as you can imagine, love is a very difficult concept to examine empirically. Most work on the concept of love has been carried out using survey and questionnaire methods. Most social psychologists agree that love takes several different forms (Brehm, 1992). Perhaps the most common distinction is between *companionate* love and *passionate* (romantic) love.

7.5.1 Companionate love

Companionate love involves closeness, intimacy and mutual concern for the well-being of the other person. It is marked by trust, warmth and respect and exists between friends as well as between lovers. It has been argued (Walster *et al.*, 1977) that companionate love is based on equity theory outlined in Section 7.4.3 above, i.e. the belief that relationships prosper or founder according to the equity of benefits to costs for each partner. Companionate love has been regarded as a feature of middle age, especially among couples long married. Grote and Frieze (1994) found that companionate love was strongly associated with relationship satisfaction among middle-aged married couples. However, in a younger context, Murstein *et al.* (1991) reported that American college students showed higher levels of companionate love than did French students. Companionate love is sometimes referred to as *storgic love*, which is characterised by attachments that develop slowly and are enduring. In addition, Hendrick and Hendrick (1993) discovered that accounts of love written by students contained more storge-like features than passionate descriptions of love.

7.5.2 Passionate love

Passionate (romantic) love is the thrilling stuff of Romeo and Juliet, Antony and Cleopatra (played on-screen by two real-life passionate lovers Elizabeth Taylor and Richard Burton) and Liam Gallagher and Patsy Kensit. It is characterised by intense emotional and physical longing for the other person, feelings of unbounded joy and happiness when the relationship flourishes and anguish and despair when it goes wrong (Hatfield and Rapson, 1993). Perhaps the magical qualities of passionate love are best demonstrated by considering what happens when despite your best efforts, you cannot find that vital spark with which to ignite a relationship into love, even though the other person might initially appear to be suitable in every way.

There are some cultural differences in the appreciation of romantic love. Most Western societies expect romantic love to be a feature of enduring sexual relationships, and welcome the emotional disruption it brings. However, in China passionate love is disdained as inferior and even dangerous, and variables such as a high income are preferred over this type of love (Dion and Dion, 1988).

Given the importance of physical attractiveness to interpersonal attraction, it is perhaps not surprising that passionate love is often immediate and intense – the phenomenon of love at first sight. However, after the initial burst of emotional turmoil, passion seems to become less important (Sternberg, 1986) and intimacy and commitment become more important in a relationship. This means that the relationship alters over time from one characterised by a turbulent 'roller coaster ride' of emotional content to a more settled and equally rewarding partnership. Perhaps because we often feel that passionate love is uncontrollable, that it 'just happens', those who feel that events are largely beyond their control (i.e. have an external locus of control) are more likely to feel passionate love (Dion and Dion, 1988).

Shaver and Klinnert (1988) showed that people with anxious attachment styles are more likely to experience the intense peaks and troughs of passionate love, as are adolescents who are anxious (Hatfield *et al.*, 1989). Unfortunately parents who disapprove of their children's choice of partner can sometimes intensify the passionate attachment to an (reputedly) unsuitable other by arousing feelings of anger and resentment which only serve to increase passionate feelings towards the partner (Driscoll *et al.*, 1972). The mechanism by which this happens is outlined below.

Sometimes we attribute the source of the excited anticipatory feelings we experience as passion to the object of our affections. However, this is not always correct, as it seems that almost anything that causes arousal can be interpreted as passion. When we are with the object of our passionate love, we may feel an almost overwhelming flood of sexual desire. We are aware of this arousal and account for it by the proximity of the loved one. However, arousal can be misattributed; a process known as *excitation transfer* (Zillman, 1978; 1984) where arousal from one stimulus is added to arousal from a second stimulus, but perceived as coming only from the second stimulus. Even a negative stimulus such as fear can be misperceived as sexual attraction. Dutton and Aaron (1974) carried out a test of this on two bridges across a canyon in Vancouver. One of the bridges was a low, stable bridge. The other was a 450-ft-long narrow suspension bridge that moved in the wind above the rocky canyon floor. The researchers had either a male or a female research assistant approach every unaccompanied young male who crossed the bridges. The research assistants carried out a short mock experimental study consisting of a few questions, then mentioned that they could be contacted at home if the young man wanted more information about the experiment. Young men met by a female research assistant on the suspension bridge were far more likely to call. The fear caused by crossing the bridge had increased attraction to the research assistant; the negative arousal was misattributed. Perhaps that is why males who wish to move relationships on to a further level take their dates to frightening movies! Zuckerman (1979) and White *et al.* (1981) found that strenuous exercise or watching a comedy film also increased the amount of passion felt towards attractive others. These findings demonstrate how passionate love can be explained in terms of social exchange theory, since the costs of passionate love (unpleasant or emotionally painful experiences) are actually interpreted as benefits and increase love.

7.5.3 Sternberg's triangular theory of love

Robert Sternberg (1986) proposes a more complex division of love than the dichotomy of companionate love and romantic love. According to Sternberg's triangular theory of love, there are three basic components of love: *passion*, *intimacy* and *commitment*, which combine in different degrees to form several different types of love, as illustrated in Figure 7.10.

For example, romantic love involves both intimacy and passion, but does not include commitment. In contrast, companionate love includes both intimacy and commitment, but excludes passion. In Sternberg's

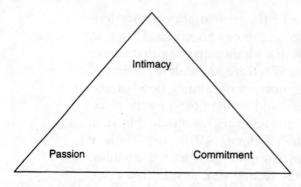

Figure 7.10: Sternberg's (1986) triangular theory of love

view consummate love, involving all three components, passion, intimacy and commitment, is the most complete form of love. It is also likely to be the most satisfying form of love in a relationship. Most relationships in real life are a blend of these types, and partners within a relationship may each have a different style of loving. It is also important to note that feelings of love between two people can change over time, for example as discussed above when passionate love turns to companionate love. The different types of love are given in Figure 7.11.

7.6 Rewards of building good relationships

Social support is one component of successful interpersonal relationships. The term refers to the feeling of being supported by others (Buunk, 1995) and is generally separated into four strands (House, 1981):

- Emotional support: being loved, cherished and nurtured;
- Appraisal support: being guided on evaluating issues; receiving feedback;
- Informational support: being advised on dealing with issues;
- Instrumental support: being given concrete help and assistance.

Emotional, appraisal and informational support are in line with affiliation under stressful conditions, discussed in Section 7.2.2. Numerous studies have shown the benefit of social support in stress reduction with many different stressors, including becoming a parent, financial concerns, job worries and health problems (Buunk, 1990; Cutrona and Russell, 1987; Wills, 1991). Social support appears to ameliorate the physical effects of stress too. Cohen and Hobernman (1983) found that among those who rated their lives as highly stressful, those who had high social support suffered fewer physical symptoms of stress such as headaches, sleeplessness and weight loss (*see* Fig. 7.12). This is known as the *buffer effect of social support*.

Social support provides the opportunity for rewarding interactions with others, including feelings of companionship, warmth and respect. In addition, enjoying good relations with others provides the

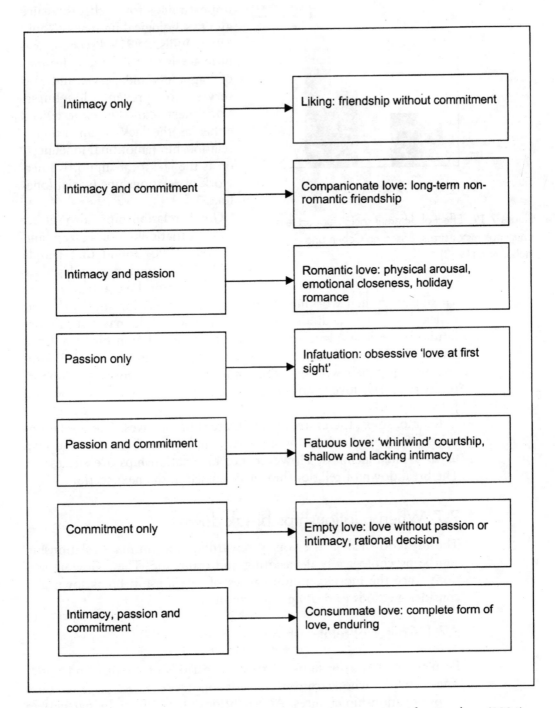

Figure 7.11: Types of love based on intimacy, passion and commitment. After Sternberg (1986)

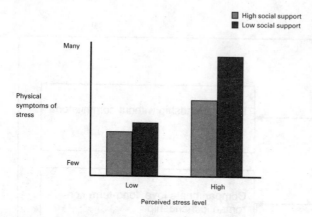

Figure 7.12 legend: High social support / Low social support

Axis labels: Many / Physical symptoms of stress / Few / Low / High / Perceived stress level

Figure 7.12: Effect of different social support levels on symptoms of stress. Based on Cohen and Hoberman (1983)

opportunity for self-disclosure and psychological intimacy (Rook, 1987; Wills, 1991). Psychological intimacy helps to promote feelings of happiness and peace, and also serves to prevent loneliness. Loneliness can be experienced either as the lack of an intimate relationship (emotional loneliness) or as the lack of a supportive network of relationships (social loneliness).

Good relationships also affect work situations too. Hazan and Shaver (1990) found that people with secure attachment styles place great value on love and work, are satisfied with their working life and enjoy good relationships with their colleagues. Those with an avoidant attachment style may put in more hours in the workplace to avoid confronting relationship problems, and are less satisfied with their working lives. Anxiously attached individuals enjoy their work less than other people, use work as an opportunity to receive love from others and are constantly fearful of rejection for poor work.

Relationships, therefore, affect all areas of our lives. Good relationships offer opportunities for support, happiness and comfort and help us to avoid loneliness. However, not all relationships are successful. The breakdown of relationships is discussed in the next section.

7.7 When relationships break down

The breakdown of a previously rewarding and intimate relationship can be psychologically devastating and traumatic. The following sections trace the most common causes of relationship breakdown and consider methods of dealing with conflict.

7.7.1 Causes of relationship breakdown

Even the best relationships go through periods of conflict and upset. Those couples who learn to deal with conflict adequately are the ones whose relationship endures. As a relationship matures, the partners in it become more and more *interdependent*.

While interdependency has its rewards in terms of intimacy and closeness, it also has costs, since any change affecting one partner will inevitably affect the other. Suppose your partner stopped taking part in a sport that you had both played together, or had a major disagreement with a close friend of both of you. Other possible changes such as changes in health or financial status can affect the way one partner can continue to meet the needs of the other. Social norms, such as the assumption that women should carry much of the burden of housework and childcare, can also lead to conflict. Conflicts about responsibilities in the home (who does the cooking and cleaning, etc.) are important determinants in the breakdown of relationships (Blumstein and Schwartz, 1983; Nettles and Loevinger, 1983).

7.7.2 Relationship conflict

Couples who deal successfully with conflict are able to communicate openly with each other about the causes of conflict. They are able to separate negative feelings about the source of the conflict from their feelings for one another, and weather the storm. However, in relationships where conflict is not handled well, couples fail to communicate effectively, resorting to destructive methods of communication. One of these is *negative affect reciprocity* (Gottman and Levenson, 1988) when couples take the opportunity to express negative affect (mood) by swapping complaints and insults. Another destructive means of communication involves a demand/withdraw interaction pattern (Christensen and Heavey, 1983) comprising of three stages:

1 Initiation: the demanding partner tries to begin a discussion of the problem(s) and the withdrawing partner tries to avoid the discussion.
2 Interaction: once discussion is initiated, the demanding partner makes a series of requests and the withdrawing partner remains silent.
3 Criticism: the demanding partner criticises the withdrawing partner, who responds by becoming defensive.

In general, less satisfied couples tend to use the demand/withdraw pattern of communication, with women more likely to be the demanding partner and men the withdrawing partner (Brehm and Kassin, 1996).

As in other aspects of interpersonal relationships, attachment styles (discussed in Chapter 2) affect the process of dealing with conflict. Those with secure attachment styles tend to have high levels of commitment to a relationship, are able to give and receive love adequately and show a high degree of satisfaction with the relationship. Such people are usually able to take a constructive approach to conflict (Simpson, 1990). Levy and Davis (1988) argue that those with anxious or avoidant attachment styles are less able to deal with conflict constructively, often resorting to negative coping strategies such as those outlined above.

7.7.3 Attributions

A key component in relationship maintenance or breakdown is the attributions people give for their partner's behaviour (see Chapter 5 for detailed consideration). If people give positive attributions for their partner's behaviour, conflict is likely to fade away. However, negative attribution leads to an escalation of conflict (Fletcher and Fincham, 1991).

Fincham and O'Leary (1983) had married couples who were either satisfied or dissatisfied with their relationship read a short passage detailing positive or negative behaviours. They were then asked to imagine that their partner had carried out the behaviour in question and to give reasons for the behaviour. The researchers found that happily married couples consistently gave positive attributions for their partner's imagined actions, seeing positive behaviours as an expression of their partner's better characteristics and negative actions as unimportant mistakes. Conversely, unhappy couples saw negative acts as an expression of their partner's character and positive acts as resulting from external events. Fincham and Bradbury (1993) argue that beginning to give negative attributions for a partner's behaviour is often the first indication of marital discord and relationship dissatisfaction, though the relationship between attribution and satisfaction could be bi-directional with each influencing the other. Figure 7.13(a) and (b) gives examples of positive and negative attributions.

Conflict does not always lead to relationship breakdown, and couples who successfully negotiate conflict situations may find their relationship is strengthened. However, Levinger (1980) identifies four factors that signal the end of a relationship:

- making a new start seems to be the only solution;
- another partner is available;
- the current relationship is expected to fail;
- commitment to the relationship has decreased.

Schullo and Alperson (1984) found these reasons to be valid in homosexual relationships too. The next section addresses the effects of relationship breakdown.

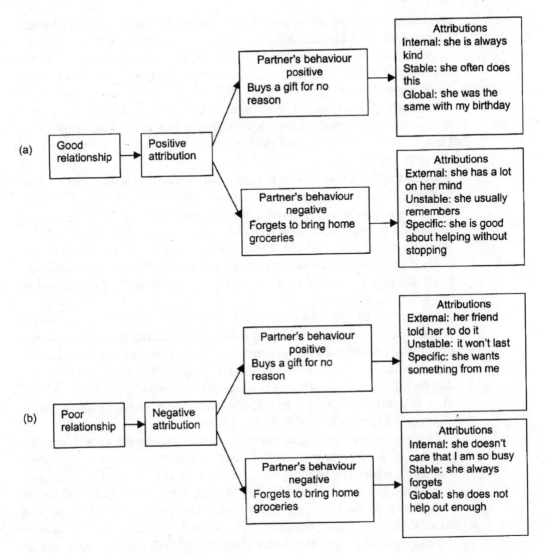

Figure 7.13: Examples of positive (a) and negative (b) attribution styles in good and poor relationships. Adapted from Brehm and Kassim (1996)

7.8 Consequences of relationship breakdown

If a relationship finally breaks down, the consequences can be far-reaching. Women initiate break-up more often then men (Hill *et al.*, 1976), perhaps as a result of their being affected by conflict more (Surra and Longstreth, 1990). Hill *et al.* also found that the more one partner was affected by the breakdown of the relationship, the less the other was. Breakdown of a relationship is rarely clear-cut, and often there is a repetitive sequence of reconciliation and subsequent break-down (Cate and Lloyd, 1988).

As we have seen, relationships are psychologically crucial, so the breakdown of a significant relationship is certain to be traumatic in most cases. The exception to this rule is when couples have experienced decreased intimacy and commitment over a long period of time, since there very little sense of loss is involved when the relationship ends. Harvey *et al.* (1978) showed that excessive rumination on the causes of the split might occur.

Perhaps the most traumatic end to a close relationship is that brought about by the death of a partner. McCrae and Costa (1988) see death of a spouse as the most stressful event one can experience. The death of a partner leads to serious deficits in physical and mental functioning, which may last for a prolonged period in some people, especially if the death was sudden and unexpected. In these cases social support, discussed earlier, has a vital role to play in the rehabilitation of the bereaved partner.

It is ironic that the factors which contribute most effectively to the development and maintenance of a close relationship (interdependence, psychological intimacy, expecting to stay together and experiencing the relationship as important to one's own self-identity) are the ones which increase distress and suffering if the relationship ends. In short, the end of a relationship can be physically and psychologically devastating (Weiss, 1975; Stroebe and Stroebe, 1986).

Divorce as well as bereavement has serious consequences. Divorced people suffer from worse mental health than married people, widows and those who have never married. However, the effect of this variable is confounded since mental health problems may well have led to the breakdown of the marriage (Buunk and Van Driel, 1989; Stroebe and Stroebe, 1986). Partly the stress of a divorce results from the adjustments required to live alone, the absence of friends that people saw as a couple, and lower social status. The psychological effects of divorce include negative feelings of failure and rejection. People who are high in self-esteem and independence are likely to suffer less than others, as are those who quickly establish a new partnership and network of friends.

7.9 Application: social support and health

Some of the beneficial effects of relationships have been discussed in this chapter. However, researchers have discovered that social support is as important to good physical health as medical treatment and a healthy lifestyle. Social support can be defined as 'emotional and physical coping resources provided by other people' (Smith and Mackie, 1995, p.475). If you have suffered a stressful life event such as the death of someone close or the loss of a job, you will know that talking to friends and family helps to get you through. Social support acts as a buffer against ill health. A meta-analysis of studies investigating the relationship between social support and health found that social support underpins good health, especially for women and particularly when the support is provided by family and friends (Schwartzer and Leppin, 1989).

People with terminal and other illnesses who belong to support groups for fellow sufferers have stronger immune systems and survive for longer than those who do not have such support (Goleman, 1990). Berkman and Syme (1979) carried out a longitudinal study involving 6928 residents of California. They questioned participants about the their personal health practices (smoking, alcohol consumption, diet and exercise), the level of social support (also known as social ties) they had (marital status, friendships and family bonds) and their socio-economic status (education, occupation, income). Nine years later the researchers looked at death rates from all causes among their sample. They found that people who enjoyed the highest levels of social support had the lowest death rates, and those with the lowest number of social ties had the highest death rate. Berkman and Syme also found that people with many close social ties were not only less likely to get cancer but less likely to die if they did contract the disease. Results from the study are shown in Figure 7.14.

It has been argued (Rook, 1987; Saranson *et al.*, 1990; Wills, 1991) that social support benefits ill people by offering them the opportunities to share worries, have pleasant interactions with others and gain feelings of closeness and companionship. For healthy people, being able to talk about very upsetting events to those who love us raises both psychological and physical health (Pennebaker, 1990). A close marriage or other intimate relationship that includes psychological intimacy has health benefits too, especially for men. Angier (1990) found that married men aged between 45 and 64 had only half the death rate of unmarried men, even after the effects of financial status and lifestyle were controlled for.

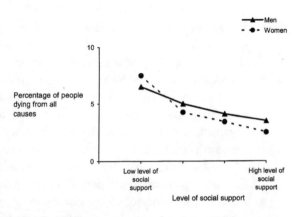

Figure 7.14: Influence of levels of social support on incidence of death. After Berkman and Syme (1979)

Further studies have shown that positive interactions with others can reduce high blood pressure in Type A individuals (Burg *et al.*, 1986), and that good interpersonal relationships can strengthen the immune system (Glaser *et al.*, 1987). The key attribute of those skilled in giving social support seems to be empathy (Thoits, 1986). Empathy involves understanding how another person is feeling and responding appropriately to that person. Empathetic social support enables people both to express and accept their feelings of distress and fear, reducing tension and inducing a calmer state (Green and Shellenberger, 1991).

7.10 Summary

- The need for belongingness is known as *social motivation*. Wanting to belong is thought to be a basic need (Buck, 1985), and is often referred to as the *affiliation* motivation. Lack of opportunity for affiliation among adults has serious consequences, including depression, hallucinations and disordered ideas. Socially deprived infants have been found to be less intellectually and socially advanced than other babies and to suffer from a higher mortality rate.

- Affiliation provides us with the means for *social comparison, anxiety reduction* and *information seeking*.

- Attraction is strongly influenced by physical attraction. The sex differences observed in ratings of physical attractiveness are in accordance with *socio-evolutionary theory*.

- Similarity on a range of variables including personality characteristics, physical appearance and shared attitudes has been found to be one of the most important factors affecting interpersonal attraction. Reciprocity and proximity also affect interpersonal attraction.

- Three theories of attraction, reinforcement theory, social exchange theory and equity theory have been advanced to account for interpersonal attraction, attraction between individuals. In addition, self-disclosure is important.

- The experience of love feels qualitatively different from liking. Most social psychologists agree that love takes several different forms and the most common distinction is between companionate love and passionate (romantic) love.

- Companionate love involves closeness, intimacy and mutual concern for the well-being of the other person. Passionate love is characterised by intense emotional and physical longing for the other person, feelings of unbounded joy and happiness when the relationship flourishes and anguish and despair when it goes wrong.

- According to Sternberg's triangular theory of love, there are three basic components of love: passion, intimacy and commitment, which combine in different degrees to form several different types of love. Consummate love is the most complete form.

- Social support appears to ameliorate the physical effects of stress. This is known as the buffer effect of social support.
- Breakdown of a previously rewarding and intimate relationship can be psychologically devastating and traumatic. The death of a partner leads to serious deficits in physical and mental functioning, which may last for some time.

7.11 Suggestions for further reading

Argyle, M. 1994: *The Psychology of Interpersonal Behaviour* (5th edition). London: Penguin Books.

A comprehensive and readable review of the factors affecting interpersonal communication.

Buss, D. M., 1994: *The Evolution of Desire: Strategies for Human Mating.* New York: Basic Books.

Provides an account of socio-evolutionary theory and romantic attraction in an accessible way.

Duck, S. 1992: *Human Relationships.* 2nd edition. London: Sage.

Provides detailed analysis and description of important aspects of human relationships.

Saranson, B. R., Saranson, I. G. and Pierce, G. (eds), 1990: *Social Support: An Interactional View.* New York:

Gives an engaging review of all aspects of social support.

8

Social influence

8.1 Introduction

Throughout our lives attempts are made, either directly or indirectly to influence the way we think, feel and behave. Similarly, we spend much time in social interaction attempting to influence others to think, feel or act as we do. Indeed, the continuance of any society demands a degree of *conformity* to social norms; society demands people *comply* with requests and *obey* authority at times. Yielding to social influence of whatever type or form is often counter to maintaining a sense of identity. An individual is often placed in a conflicting situation of needing to maintain his or her own sense of identity and independence while at the same time being required or expected to conform, obey or comply with other people's wishes, prevailing norms, or standards. Failure to fall in with the 'crowd' or one's peer group may incur painful penalties – ranging from ostracism to imprisonment if a law has been broken; while failure to achieve and maintain a sense of identity may result in low self-esteem, low self-confidence and, in more extreme cases, depression and apathy. Social influence may be either readily accepted by a person, both consciously and unconsciously, or yielded to reluctantly or resisted.

The act of allowing oneself to be influenced by others should not necessarily be seen as negative or over-coercive. A person who conforms to something for which they had no strong beliefs may be saving themselves effort. The source of influence may not be from other people but the demand characteristics of the situation, for example, entering a church or a library elicits a particular behavioural response with no direct influence or pressure from others (Howitt *et al.*, 1989). Experimental research, primarily from North America in the 1960s and early 1970s, emphasised processes involved in majority influence. More recently, European social psychologists have raised awareness regarding the processes operating in minority influence (Moscovici, 1976). It is possible that an individual or social grouping of people, holding opposing views to the majority, can influence majority opinion.

This chapter will address all these types of social influence, the theoretical explanations for these processes and factors which operate to increase or decrease the degree of influence. This will include the interaction between cultural factors, the social situation and the psychological make-up of the person.

8.2 Compliance

Compliance may be defined as a change in overt (public) behaviour after exposure to other people's 'opinions' (Hewstone *et al.*, 1996). Compliance does not necessarily involve private acceptance, it may change behaviour, which can be observed and measured, whereas acceptance can only be elicited by honest self-report. Compliance-gaining strategies which have real-life application have been widely researched, three of which will be discussed; these are the *foot-in-the-door* technique, the *door-in-the-face* technique, and the *low ball*.

The *foot-in-the-door* technique, where a person first makes a small request followed by a large request, is often effective in getting people to comply with the large request. Freedman and Fraser (1966) asked home owners if they would display a very *large* sign in their front garden which read 'DRIVE CAREFULLY'. There were two experimental conditions and a control group. The control group were simply asked to display the large sign without a prior smaller request. Experimental group A were first asked to display a *small* sign reading 'DRIVE CAREFULLY' (same type of request); experimental group B were first asked to sign a petition about a conservation matter (different type of request). Greatest compliance for the large request (displaying the very large sign) was found when the small request was of the same type – here 75 per cent complied. When the smaller request was different compliance dropped to around 50 per cent, and in the control group compliance was only 17 per cent. The most likely explanation for the success of the foot-in-the-door technique is that people like to think of themselves as helpful and do not mind complying with small requests. Having complied with the small request and attempting to be consistent with their self-image of being helpful, people feel impelled to go along with subsequent requests. This is consistent with the self-perception theory of Bem (1967). Numerous replications of variations of the Freedman and Fraser study support these results (Dillard *et al.*, 1984).

Cialdini *et al.* (1975) has demonstrated a contrary approach to be effective in getting a person to comply with a request. Termed *the-door-in-the-face* technique, a large unreasonable request is made first, and then followed by a more reasonable request, which is the one that you would really wish the person to comply with. This technique appears only to work when the same individual makes both requests, whereas the *foot-in-the-door* technique works equally well when the same or different individuals make the small and large request (Cann *et al.*, 1978).

A third technique, the *low ball*, is a common sales tactic and possibly one we have all fallen prey to at one time or another, for example, people initially committed to buying an item at an unrealistic price but, before the final deal is completed, discover a mistake in the price and a higher one substituted. Having initially committed to buy makes the individual vulnerable and more likely to agree to the new price. Cialdini *et al.* (1978) initially demonstrated this effect when students were requested to participate in a small study. Some 56 per cent agreed, but after giving commitment, the students were told that the experiment would take place at 7 a.m. In a control situation when students were informed of the time in advance of the commitment, only 24 per cent agreed to participate. Joule (1987) demonstrated that this effect is not just transient. Participants, all smokers, agreed to participate in a concentration test for a modest incentive. After agreement they were told that they were required to stop smoking for 18 hours and that the incentive was to be reduced. In spite of this, 90 per cent honoured their commitment. Beyond this, when requested to take part in a further study some weeks later, 90 per cent of the original group volunteered to participate. This highlights the relationship between compliance and acceptance. If this effect is seen to be effective it could lead to eventual acceptance and a more permanent change in smoking behaviour.

Other explanations of compliance include reciprocation and low self-esteem. People are more likely to comply with requests from another person if that other person has done them a favour in the past. Lowering of self-esteem, for example, by getting people to do foolish acts, also results in high levels of compliance (Apsler, 1975). These different and often complementary explanations of compliance are summarised in Figure 8.1.

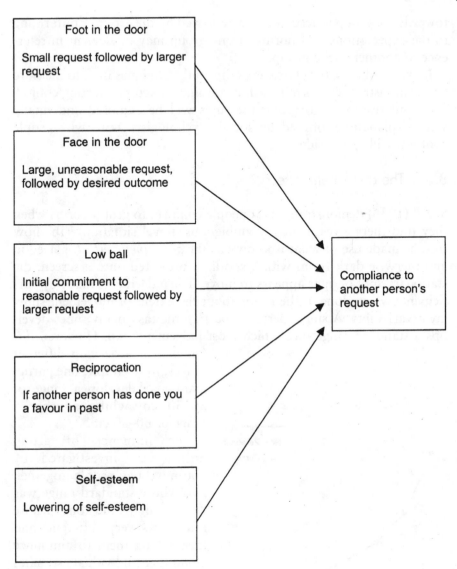

Figure 8.1: Explanations for compliance

8.3 Conformity or majority influence

Conformity differs from compliance in two ways: it involves (a) a change in behaviour *towards* a group or social norm; and (b) pressure from a *group of people* rather than a request from an individual. Conformity or majority influence can be defined as a social influence resulting from exposure to the opinions of a majority or the majority of one's group (Hewstone *et al.*, 1996). This implies that the change towards the group is accepted and approved by the group. Conforming to the expectations and norms of one group may be deviant in reference to another social group.

In what follows, the classic experimental techniques used to measure and demonstrate conformity will be outlined. Factors affecting conformity and resistance to group pressures will be explored and finally some explanations offered by social psychologists as to why people conform will be considered.

8.3.1 The autokinetic effect

Sherif (1936) demonstrated that people conform to group norms when they find themselves in highly ambiguous, novel situations. To show this, he made use of what is known as the *autokinetic effect*: placed in an otherwise dark room with a spotlight projected onto a screen, the stationary spot of light appears to move. The judgements made by participants when alone in the room about the extent of movement show great variability. A single person repeating the task many times develops a standard range into which most judgements fall. However, *different* people develop different ranges, for example, one participant may develop a range of 20–30 cm whilst another a range of 60–80 cm.

The influence of group norms was investigated by putting three people together, two whose standard range was very similar and one whose range was very different, and then asking them to announce aloud their individual estimates of movement of the light. Sherif found that over numerous trials at this task in these conditions, the group converged on a common range and the range was very similar to that of the two initially sharing a similar range. In effect, the 'deviant' person conformed to the group norm. This is shown in Figure 8.2. In a further study, Sherif found

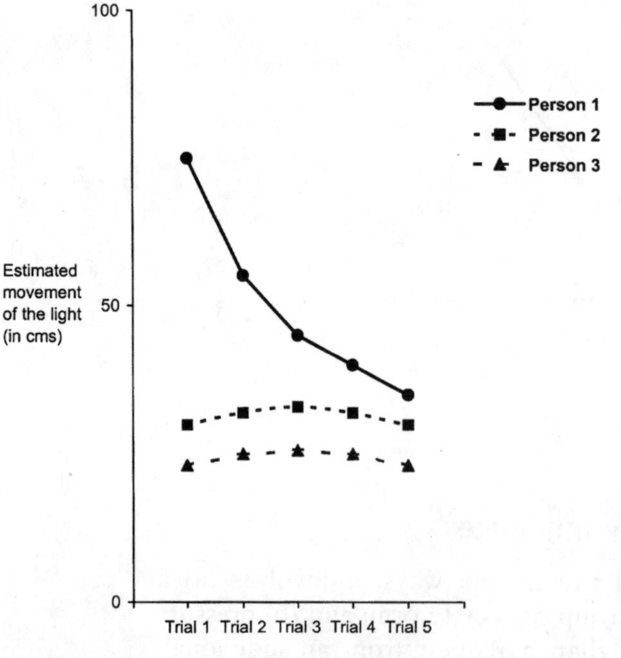

Figure 8.2: Convergence of three different people's estimate of light movement with the autokinetic effect. After Sherif (1936)

conformity to the majority group judgement to occur much more quickly when they had no prior experience of the task and hence had not developed a 'frame of reference'. In such a situation, where an inexperienced participant sat in a darkened room with two experienced participants and sharing the same standard range of movement of the spotlight, the group norm becomes the frame of reference for the person new to the situation. Generally, the more ambiguous the situation and the less experience a person has had in such a situation, the more powerful will be the influence of a group with pre-existing, established norms.

8.3.2 The Asch paradigm

Asch (1951) devised an experimental set-up to investigate conformity which has been used and modified by numerous subsequent researchers. The basic experiment involves presenting a participant with a standard line and three comparison lines. The participant then has the seemingly simple task of judging which comparison line is closest to the standard line in length. Figure 8.3 gives an example of the stimuli typically used by Asch; as you can see the task is an *unambiguous one*. In order to study conformity, Asch put a participant in a room with seven other people who were confederates of the experimenter but thought to be other participants by the naïve participant in the room. Things were arranged so that the naïve participant sat at the end of the row. Each person in the room had to state publicly which comparison line was most similar to the standard line. Since the naïve participant sat at the end of the row, he or she had to listen to the judgements of the confederates before giving his or her judgement.

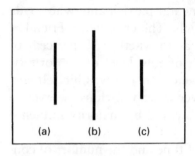

Comparison lines

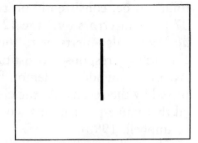

Standard line

Figure 8.3: Example of the line judgement task used by Asch (1955). Note how easy the task is

A typical experiment would proceed as follows: each person in the group would be presented with 18 pairs of cards similar to those shown in Figure 8.3. On the first two of these 18 trials, all confederates would give the *correct* response. Thereafter, on 12 of the remaining 16 trials, *all* confederates would give the same *incorrect* response. A control group of participants performed the 18 judgement trials on their own and hence in the absence of group pressure. Asch was interested in whether participants would conform to the unanimous but incorrect majority.

Participants in the control group conditions made correct judgements 95 per cent of the time. In contrast, in the presence of unanimous, incorrect judgements, 80 per cent of participants agreed at least once with the incorrect majority. Some 8 per cent of the participants agreed with the incorrect majority all of the time, and on average participants conformed between four and five times on the critical 12 trials. Asch interviewed each participant after the experiment: those who agreed with the majority most of the time gave various reasons for their behaviour. For example, that the group was actually correct, that they did not want to spoil the experimenter's results, and that they went along with the majority to avoid creating disharmony and conflict. Participants who did not conform gave the following reasons for maintaining independence: confident their judgement was correct, and thinking the majority was correct but could not agree with them since that was not what they saw.

The Asch experiments are frequently misrepresented as demonstrating high levels of conformity. Friend, Rafferty and Bramel (1990) draw attention to the fact that in the original study, almost two-thirds of the naïve participants resisted group pressure to conform (Asch, 1951). In spite of this, a review of nearly 100 American Social Psychology texts published between 1953–85, showed that the emphasis was, and continues to be, consistently on the experimental participants who made 37 per cent errors over the 12 critical trials. The critique by Friend *et al.* (1990) also alerts us to the dilemma as to whether 37 per cent of conforming responses constitutes a high or low level of conformity. Asch had intended to demonstrate independence and was himself surprised by the results. As the correct answer was so obvious, he expected that naïve participants would not be swayed by majority influence (Campbell, 1990).

The Asch paradigm is costly in terms of time and the number of confederates needed, and requires good acting from the confederates. Crutchfield (1955) devised an alternative experimental model: he had five participants sit in separate booths, side by side. In front of each participant was a box with lights and switches on it, as shown in Figure 8.4.

The stimulus material (which varied from line judgement, dot counting, statements of opinion) was presented on a screen in front of the participants. Using a remote control device, the experimenter then turned on the lights of participants A to D, according to a pre-arranged schedule. The participants sitting in the individual booths would then be required to indicate their choice by flicking one of five switches.

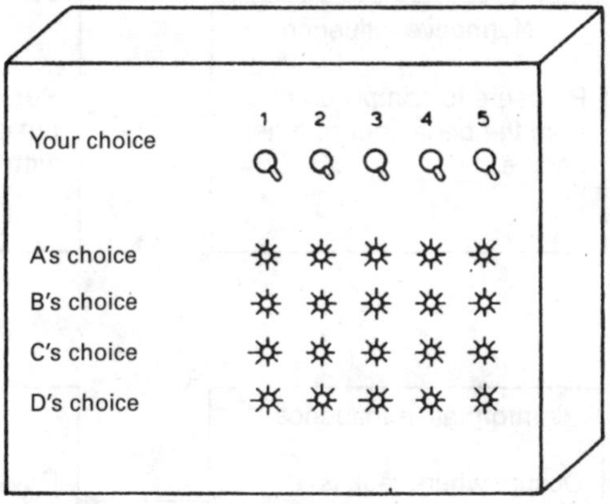

Conformity using this procedure was found to be lower than in the Asch paradigm, for example, only about 50 per cent conformed to a wrong judgement where the task involved estimating whether a particular circle had a larger area than a star. With statements of opinion, conformity was found to be even lower. For example, only 37 per cent of participants (military men in this case) agreed with the statement, 'I doubt whether I would make a good military leader', when given cause to believe four other people had agreed with this statement.

Figure 8.4: The Crutchfield apparatus which was placed in front of a participant who was in an individual booth

Comparison of the Asch and Crutchfield procedures suggest different processes might be operating since participants in the former procedure are required to state publicly their judgements – in the latter this was done in private. This is explained by Kelman (1958), who distinguishes between public compliance and private acceptance (internalisation). *Public compliance* is where somebody publicly conforms to group norms but privately maintains a different opinion; here the individual is said to be under *normative* pressure to conform. Internalisation or *private acceptance* is where the person believes the group to be correct and believes those opinions him or herself. Conformity here is due to *informational* pressure – the group provides information about how reality is to be interpreted. Generally, the more ambiguous a situation, the greater the informational pressure to conform; the less ambiguous the situation or task the greater will normative pressure exert a conforming influence (see Section 8.3.5). This is summarised in Figure 8.5.

8.3.3 Factors affecting conformity

Many factors and variables have been experimentally investigated and their effect on levels of conformity determined. Below we look at a

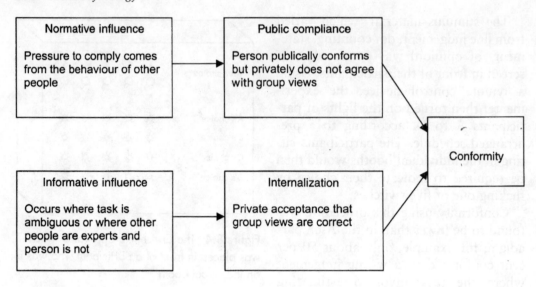

Figure 8.5: Normative and information influences as explanations of uniformity

small range of those that have received attention from social psychologists.

Non-unanimous majority

Asch (1995) investigated the effect of an incorrect, non-unanimous majority on the line judging task. A number of different experiment conditions were employed: where one of the confederates always gave the correct judgement (an ally); when a confederate first gave a correct judgement but subsequently defected to the incorrect, majority view (defector); and where one confederate gave an even more inaccurate answer than the other confederates (extreme dissenter). The results are shown in Figure 8.6 and it can be seen that conformity levels in all these three conditions were lower than with a unanimous, incorrect majority. Asch (1995) also looked at the size of the unanimous, incorrect majority and found that little difference in conformity levels was observed beyond a group of five. With groups of only two or three (i.e., one or two confederates) conformity dropped to 10 per cent or lower.

The attractiveness of the group to the individual

The more attractive the membership of the group is to the individual, the greater will be conformity to the group norms (Festinger *et al.*, 1950).

▨ Self-esteem of the individual

Stang (1973), using the Crutchfield model, found that individuals with high self-esteem conformed less than people with moderate or low self-esteem.

▨ Competence and skill at certain tasks

Skill or experience of a task reduces the likelihood of an individual conforming (Weisenthal *et al.*, 1976). This is particularly rel-evant to research relating to gen-der. In early research it was a com-mon assumption that women are

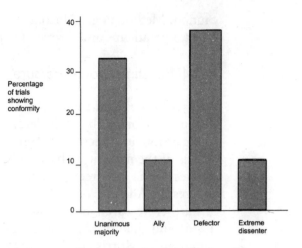

Figure 8.6: Effects on levels of conformity of a non-unanimous majority. After Asch (1955)

more susceptible to social influence than men. Eagly and Carli (1981) reviewed the results of studies over a 30-year period. When statistically combined the assumption was supported. However, on closer analysis, women only conformed more than men when the experimental tasks were sex-typed in favour of males. When using experimental tasks which showed no sex bias there was no apparent sex difference. (Endler, 1966; Sistrunk and McDavid, 1971). Eagly and Chrvala (1986) have subsequently concluded that rather than either men or women having a natural advantage in social influence contexts, any sex difference is like-ly to be due to the attributions of competence of the others (the confed-erates in the standard experimental set-up).

▨ Culture

Smith and Harris Bond (1993), in a review of conformity studies from 1957 to 1985, were able to identify differences in levels of conformity based on whether participants were in a collectivist or individualistic soci-ety. The former, predominantly Latin American and Asian countries, are characterised by members defining their identity on the characteristics of the collective group to which one is permanently attached. Alternatively, members in individualistic societies such as those in European and North American countries, define their identity by personal choices and individ-ual attachments. The studies showed that conformity is higher in collec-tivist societies where group harmony is a priority. An additional finding was that conformity was higher in non-student populations. Comparisons such as these, while interesting and informative, should be viewed with caution. Methodological inconsistencies were apparent in terms of experimental paradigms and degree of experimenter/participant contact.

8.3.4 Resisting group pressure

Asch (1995) almost obliterates all social influence by including a lone dissenter amongst the confederates. It seems that having one dissenter in the group, irrespective of their judgement, destroys the apparent consensus of the majority. This encourages the individual to develop alternatives to the incorrect judgement. Subsequent research has replicated this result (Allen, 1965; 1975).

Further research has shown both the timing (Morris and Miller, 1975) and quality (Allen and Levine, 1971) of that support to be of importance. Morris and Miller (1975), using the Crutchfield technique, had one condition in which the supporter (confederate giving the correct judgement), made the correct response before a majority gave the same incorrect response. In another condition, support was given after the majority opinion had been expressed. A control group of participants was exposed to an incorrect unanimous majority. It was predicted that conformity would be least when the supporter responded *after* the incorrect majority. Results, shown in Figure 8.7, were in the opposite direction: conformity was least when the supporter responded *before* the majority. Morris and Miller explained this by suggesting support before the majority judgements provides the participant with immediate confirmation of his or her own judgement upon first viewing the stimulus material.

Allen and Levine (1971) looked at the effect of either credible or non-credible social support. The task was one involving visual perception and the supporter was presented in one of two ways to participants: where (a) he wore glasses with thick lenses and said he had a sight problem; or, (b) the person did not wear glasses and made no reference to his sight. Results confirmed predictions: conformity was lowest when the supporter's credibility was doubtful – condition (a).

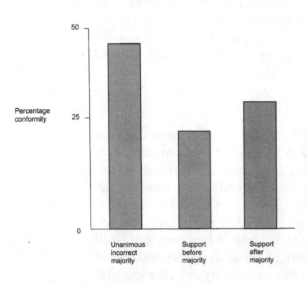

Figure 8.7: Effect of social support, given either before or after a majority, on conformity. Adapted from Morris and Miller (1975)

The above two experiments demonstrate: (a) timing and credibility of support help people resist group pressure; and, (b) any support, ill-timed or of doubtful credibility, is better than none at all since it results in less conformity than where there is a unanimous incorrect majority.

8.3.5 Explanations

Why do people yield to majority influence and conform? Experi-mental social psychology has attempted to address this question for the last 50 years. Sherif (1936) and Deutsch and Gerard (1955) distinguished between *informational* and *normative* influence. Both involved interpersonal dependence. Informational influence occurs when the views of others are considered valid and reliable. This is the most preferable explanation when there is uncertainty and no objective evidence with which to evaluate the stimulus. This was demonstrated in the autokinetic effect used by Sherif. Normative influence arises when there is a need for approval, liking and maintenance of a positive self-image.

Informational and normative influence involve the process of *social comparison* (Festinger, 1954) with other group members. In more recent research an overlap between the two explanations has been demonstrated. Abrams *et al.* (1990) demonstrated that social comparisons made for both informational and normative needs were dependent on perceiving the source of the influence as belonging to one's own category or in-group. Using the Asch paradigm, students on an Introductory Psychology course were given the background of the confederates giving the false answers. The accomplices were either described as other psychology students or students of ancient history from a neighbouring prestigious university. Levels of conformity were higher when the confederates were believed to be psychology students, even though rationally there is no reason why they should be thought to be more able to judge line lengths correctly. The results could therefore be attributed to the influence of the reference group, a group to which they desire to belong and hence conform to norms and values. Turner (1982) terms this *referent informational influence*.

8.4 Group polarisation

Both the Asch and the Crutchfield techniques involve individuals making judgements, expressing opinions, and becoming aware of what others think in the absence of social interaction. Neither discussion of, nor talk about how such a judgement was arrived at takes place or, indeed, is even permitted in these studies. In many respects this is unrealistic, especially for reference groups, as discussions and exchanges of views are often an important means of social influence. It is of importance, then, to enquire into the effects of group discussion upon individual and group opinion and to discover whether other social influence processes occur in such contexts.

8.4.1 The polarisation phenomenon

Research on group decision-making (looked at in more detail in Chapter 11) had, up until the early 1960s, found groups to be conservative and cautious in comparison with individuals. Stoner (1961) investigated risk taking by individuals and groups and found, much to his and many other social psychologist's surprise, that groups took riskier decisions than the average individual group member. This became known as the *risky shift* effect. Stoner's procedure will be described since much subsequent research has been based on it.

Groups of six people were given a number of dilemmas (called choice dilemma questionnaires or CDQs), in which a person is portrayed as having to choose between a risky or cautious alternative. The risky alternative would lead to a desirable outcome if successful, but a highly undesirable outcome if unsuccessful. Participants were first asked, as individuals, to indicate the advice they would give the person in the dilemma by stating the lowest probability of success acceptable before advising the person to take the risky option. The following is an example of a CDQ used by Stoner.

> Mr A, an electrical engineer, who is married and has one child, has been working for a large electronics corporation since graduating from college five years ago. He is assured of a lifetime job with a modest, though adequate, salary and liberal pension benefits upon retirement. On the other hand, it is very unlikely that his salary will increase much before he retires. While attending a convention, Mr A is offered a job with a small, newly founded company which has a highly uncertain future. The new job would pay more to start and would offer the possibility of a share in the ownership if the company survived the competition of the larger firms.
>
> Imagine you are advising Mr A. Listed below are several probabilities or odds of the new company's proving financially sound. *Please check the lowest probability that you would consider acceptable to make it worthwhile for Mr A to take the new job.*
>
> (a) The chances are 1 in 10 that the company will prove financially sound.

(b) The chances are 3 in 10 that the company will prove financially sound.

(c) The chances are 5 in 10 that the company will prove financially sound.

(d) The chances are 7 in 10 that the company will prove financially sound.

(e) The chances are 9 in 10 that the company will prove financially sound.

(f) Place a check here if you think Mr A should not take the new job no matter what the probabilities are.

After indicating their responses individually, participants would be brought together in a group and instructed to discuss each dilemma in turn until they had reached a *unanimous* decision on each. Finally, participants were required again to indicate their own individual decision in light of group discussion and the decision reached by the group. The experimental procedure is summarised in Figure 8.8. Stoner compared the *average* individual pre-discussion choice with the group decision and found the latter to be riskier than the former. Comparison of the average individual pre-discussion and post-discussion decision showed the latter also to be riskier, but less so than the group decision. Numerous studies replicated these findings and the idea that groups take *riskier* decisions than individuals quickly became accepted. This became known as the risky-shift (Kogan and Wallach, 1967).

However, right from the start Stoner had noticed that some CDQs consistently produced shifts in the opposite direction, that is, shifts towards caution, as a result of group discussion. The following is an example of one such CDQ:

Roger, a married man with two children of school age, has a secure job that pays him about £10,000 a year. He can easily

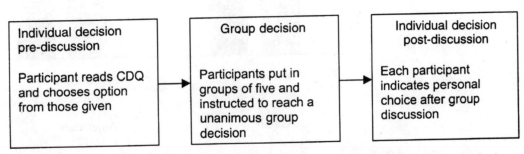

Figure 8.8: Summary of experiment procedure used by Stoner (1961) in looking at individual and group decision-making

afford the necessities of life, but few of the luxuries. Except for a life insurance policy he has no savings. Roger has heard from reliable sources that the stock of a relatively unknown Company X, might triple its present value if a new product currently in production is favourably received by the buying public. On the other hand, if the product is unfavourably received, the stock might decline considerably in value. Roger is considering investing his life insurance money in this company.

However, subsequent research by Moscovici and Zavalloni (1969) also showed a different decisional shift. Using Stoner's procedure of pre-discussion opinion, discussion consensus and post-discussion opinion, they found that there was a shift, but on average towards the initially favourable pole. Figure 8.9 provides the results of this early research in

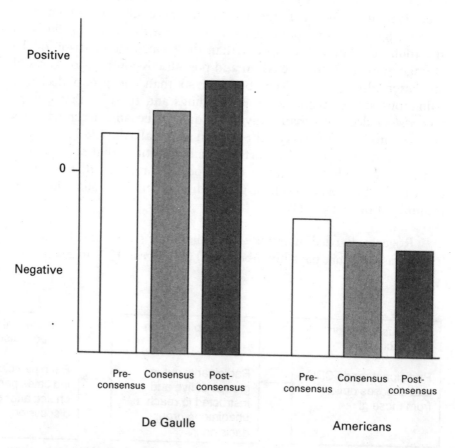

Figure 8.9: Polarization of attitudes towards De Gaulle and Americans. Adapted from Moscovici and Zavalloni (1969)

relation to attitudes to De Gaulle, and towards North Americans: attitudes towards De Gaulle, which were slightly positive pre-discussion, became more positive post-discussion. Attitudes towards Americans, slightly negative at first, became more negative after discussion.

In view of this, Moscovici proposed a *group polarisation* hypothesis, defined as the tendency for groups to make decisions that are more extreme than the mean of individual member's initial position (Myers, 1982; Isenberg, 1986). Group polarisation is so termed because the collective decision tends to move from the average, towards one of the two extreme poles.

8.4.2 Explanations

It became apparent that there was more to group polarisation than the shift towards risk, consequently, many early explanations had to be dropped. Viewing group polarisation as a product of social influence, similar explanations can be offered to account for the phenomenon. Research over the last three decades has produced many different theories but it seems that three major perspectives dominate: (a) normative or social comparison perspective; (b) persuasive-information perspective; and (c) self-categorisation theory.

■ Normative or social comparison perspective

People are motivated to seek social approval and enhance their self-image, and this may result in the social comparison process being biased towards viewing oneself as 'better' or 'more correct' than others. Therefore, if during group discussion you find that others hold opinions nearer to the valued alternative, you will become more extreme in order to distance yourself from the others (Jellison and Arkan, 1977). Sanders and Baron (1977) provided support for this by showing that if you knew the others' position on an issue without having heard their arguments, it would be enough on its own and without group discussion to provide a polarisation effect.

■ Persuasive-information perspective

The persuasive-informational perspective proposes that discussion produces numerous different arguments. If these happen to be the same as those you have already considered, they are likely to strengthen your own position. Additionally, novel arguments might be produced which favour your position and result in making your own choices even more extreme. The discussion then becomes one of mutual persuasion, whereby the degree of shift represents the proportion, novelty and cogency of arguments, favouring one side as opposed to the other. Burnstein and Vinokur (1973) tested this assumption by randomly allocating a position from which to argue to each participant irrespective of their true position. Participants were unaware of each other's true position. Burnstein and Vinokur predicted a change in opinion if participants were arguing from their true position, with no shift in opinion when arguing from their assigned but not true position. The results strongly supported this prediction. People in general are able to put forward more cogent and persuasive arguments if they really believe in something.

Evidence for either the normative or social comparison explanation and the persuasive-information perspective is mixed. Isenberg (1986) proposes that both can be seen as correct and have a contribution to make in explaining group polarisation. Which explanation to adopt depends on different circumstances. Wetherell (1987) considers the social context in which opinions are given or decisions made to be more important than both the different arguments produced for a position and the original position a person holds.

Self-categorisation theory

Self-categorisation (Turner *et al.*, 1987) is the process whereby one identifies with a group and group identification produces conformity to that group, called the in-group (see Chapter 10). The group norm is not necessarily an average position of the group members, but the position which most ideally represents the prototype of the group (see Chapter 4 on social cognition). This is the position corresponding to what the group has in common and what distinguishes it from another group. Therefore the position held by the most prototypical member is adopted as the normative point of reference. The arguments put forward by this person will be perceived to be highly informative and persuasive. This position will vary according to the context of the argument or decision to be made, and the salience of the out-group. The theory assumes that greater group polarisation will occur in the presence of an out-group, or when a different, as compared with a similar, out-group is present. Hogg, Turner and Davidson (1990) demonstrated that the direction of polarisation can be reversed if there is a change in the social context. If an in-group is confronted by a riskier out-group, their perception of their in-group norm is more cautious. Alternatively, members of an in-group perceive an already risky choice to be even more risky when confronted by a cautious out-group.

8.5 Obedience to authority

A dramatic offshoot of Asch's work on conformity was the work of Stanley Milgram, who focused on obedience to authority and carried out a series of experiments between 1960–63, the results of which were published in 1974 (see Milgram, 1974). Obedience is accorded to a person in authority in a hierarchical situation. This may be in the form of parental authority or institutionally based as with the police or army. Generally, for people to obey, the authority or authority figure must be perceived as legitimate. In everyday life, most obedience is benign and constructive and necessary to maintain social order in society. However, 'blind obedience' is often destructive, and it is this that motivated the work of Milgram. Initially, it was the mass slaughter of millions of Jews by the Nazis during the Second World War which influenced him. Since then, there have been other atrocities such as those in Cambodia, Kosovo and Rwanda. These horrendous acts stem, in part, from pre-existing social, racial, ethnic, religious, economic or class conflicts which implies that the individual involved is not necessarily evil but controlled by overwhelmingly strong situational pressures which cause individuals blindly to obey orders. A series of highly controversial experiments conducted by Milgram aimed to measure concrete instances of the act of obeying authority when individuals thought they might be endangering the life of another person.

8.5.1 Milgram's experiments

Milgram recruited participants by placing an advertisement in local newspapers asking for volunteers to take part in an experiment in learning. Respondents were taken to the psychology department of Yale University and told the experiment required one person to act as 'teacher' and another as 'learner'. A coin was tossed in the presence of two participants (actually one was a confederate of Milgram's) and each assigned accordingly to one of the two roles. This was always rigged so the real volunteer, the person who had responded to the newspaper advertisement, was always assigned to the role of teacher. Milgram then explained to the teacher that he had to read a series of word pairs (such as *blue–girl*, *fat–neck*, etc.) to the learner. After this the teacher was instructed to read the first word of each pair to the learner; the learner had to indicate from a set of four words which one was originally paired with the word read by the teacher. If the learner gave the wrong answer the teacher had to give the learner an electric shock. This continued over many trials and each time the learner gave an incorrect response the teacher had to give a shock of *increasing intensity*. A sophisticated-looking piece of equipment was placed in front of the volunteer (the teacher), which he was instructed to use to administer the shocks. On the front panel of this equipment was a voltage scale ranging from 15 to 450 volts with an indication of the severity of the different voltages as follows:

slight shock	15–60 volts
moderate shock	75–120 volts
strong shock	135–180 volts
very strong shock	195–240 volts
intense shock	255–300 volts
extremely intense shock	315–360 volts
danger, severe shock	375–420 volts
XXX	425–450 volts

There were 30 switches on the front panel and the teacher flicked the next one up each time the learner gave the wrong answer. Figure 8.10 shows Milgram with the apparatus and a 'learner' having electrodes attached to his wrists.

Prior to beginning the experiment, participants were given a sample shock of 45 volts (which is quite painful), to give them some idea of what they thought they were inflicting on the learner. In Milgram's original experiments the learner and teacher were put in separate rooms, but the teacher watched while the learner had electrodes placed on his arms. At the same time, the learner informed the experimenter, in the presence of the teacher, that he had a weak heart and was worried in case the shocks were strong. Of course, no shocks were actually given but the teacher did not know this!

Figure 8.10: Stanley Milgram with the 'electric shocks' apparatus (left) and confederate (learner) having electrodes attached to his wrists (right)

Imagine yourself to be the teacher. You have seen the man wired up. He has complained of a weak heart and you are to give him progressively stronger electric shocks as he gets answers wrong. The experiment starts. The learner gets the first few words right and then he makes a mistake. You give the lowest level of shock (15 volts). The learner keeps getting words wrong and you give increasingly stronger shocks. At 75 volts you hear the learner 'grunt' and at 125 volts he says 'that really hurts'. At 180 volts the learner complains of his weak heart, at 285 volts he gives an agonised scream and at 315 volts and beyond there is silence. All the time the experimenter is urging you to continue even though you protest. How far up the 30-switch/450-volt scale do you think you would go before refusing to continue?

Milgram put this question to psychiatrists, college students and middle-class adults and then compared their estimates with what he actually found from running the experiment. The results are shown in Table 8.1. As you can see, predictions fell grossly short of what actually took place. All groups predicted that teacher/participants would not go beyond the 'intense shock' level; in reality, just over 12 per cent refused at this level. Some 65 per cent (26 participants) continued to give shocks up to the maximum intensity. Not surprisingly, there were some criticisms of the basic experimental paradigm. First, it has been suggested that the 'teachers' did not really believe that the learner was

Shock level	Predictions of level at which 'teachers' would refuse to administer shock			Actual shock levels at which subjects refused to continue
	Psychiatrists	Students	Middle-class adults	
Slight shock	10.3	0.0	12.5	0.0
Moderate shock	48.7	25.8	42.5	0.0
Strong shock	92.3	96.8	82.5	0.0
Very strong shock	97.4	100.0	90.0	0.0
Intense shock	100.0	100.0	100.0	12.5
Extremely intense shock	100.0	100.0	100.0	23.5
Danger, severe shock	100.0	100.0	100.0	35.0
XXX	100.0	100.0	100.0	35.0

Table 8.1: Expected and actual behaviour of 'teachers' in Milgram's experiment. Results are shown as cumulative percentages. The column of actual shocks at which subjects refused to continue indicates 65 per cent administered shocks to the maximum level. Adapted from Milgram (1974)

receiving electric shocks. If this were true, Milgram's findings would be invalid. However, detailed extracts of conversations which Milgram had with participants both during and after the experiment lead one to think the 'teacher' believed he was hurting the learner. Debriefing participants gave some indication of their involvement with, and belief in the reality of the experiment, as the following passage from Milgram (1974) shows:–

> *Experimenter*: At what point were you most nervous or tense?
> *Participant*: Well, when he first began to cry out in pain, and I realised this was hurting him. This got worse when he just blocked and refused to answer. There was I, I'm a nice person, I think, hurting somebody and caught up in what seemed a mad situation, and in the interests of science one goes through with it. At one point I had an impulse to just refuse to continue with this kind of teaching situation.

Second, these experiments were considered to be highly unethical (Baumrind, 1964; Rosnow, 1981) as they involve deception and inflicting severe stress and anxiety on participants. Milgram has consistently defended his position by stressing that all participants were followed up by himself and a psychiatrist. He found no evidence of psychopathology and indicated that 83.7 per cent of the participants stated that they were glad they had taken part in the experiment, by contrast only 1.3 per cent were sorry, or very sorry, they had taken part (Milgram, 1992).

Similar experiments could not be conducted now as they fall outside the ethical guidelines for research published by the British Psychological Society and American Psychological Association (see Chapter 1). A third and final criticism is the extent to which these results generalise beyond the laboratory to the real world. Mixon (1972) argues that the results only generalise if we take the roles and the rules that operate in a particular social context. The role of 'teacher' is adopted by the participant, a process which relegates personal identity and personal responsibility to second place. The role of teacher often necessitates punishment when learners do something wrong: giving shocks in the above experimental set-up would be consistent with this. This does ignore, however, the principle of making punishment appropriate to the transgression.

8.5.2 Further findings

Milgram (1974) investigated various situational and social factors affecting people's willingness to obey authority. Using the same learner–teacher paradigm he looked at legitimacy of authority, proximity of the learner to the teacher, proximity of the authority figure, sex of participants and numerous other variables.

Legitimacy of authority was manipulated by using a run-down office in a less respectable part of the city and telling participants the research was sponsored by a private commercial concern. This 'low legitimacy' resulted, as can be seen from Table 8.2, in a lower level of obedience (48 per cent of participants delivered the maximum shock), than when the research was conducted at Yale University, giving 'high legitimacy'. Questionable legitimacy of the authority figure was manipulated by allowing another participant to give the orders rather than a psychologist in a white laboratory coat. Here obedience dropped dramatically, only 20 per cent administered shock to the maximum level.

In Milgram's original experiment the learner was in a different room to the teacher. When both were in close proximity, that is, in the same room, fewer teachers administered maximum shock. This decreased even more when the teacher had to take the hand of the learner and put it on a metal plate for the shock to be delivered.

When the authority figure (the experimenter dressed in a white coat) left the room after instructing the teacher on how to proceed, only 20 per cent obeyed the experimenter's initial request to continue giving increasingly stronger levels of shock. Two authority figures giving conflicting

Situational or social factor	Percentage giving maximum shocks
Legitimacy of authority	
(a) seedy building	47.5
(b) ordinary man giving orders	20.0
Proximity of the 'learner'	
(a) in the same room	40.0
(b) hand on metal plate	30.0
Proximity of the 'experimenter'	
Experimenter leaves the room	20.5
Conflicing commands by two experimenters	0.0
Female volunteers (teachers)	65.0

Table 8.2: Percentage of participants giving maximum shocks under different conditions. In the original experiment with the learner in a different room to the teacher, 65 per cent of participants gave the maximum shock. Adapted from Milgram (1974)

commands (one telling the teacher to continue and the other urging him to stop), resulted in obedience dropping dramatically. No teacher gave maximum shock in this condition, and 19 out of 20 stopped at the 150 volts level – the point at which conflicting commands were given to the participants.

Finally, when females were used as teachers, 65 per cent gave shocks to the maximum level, the same as with male participants. However, Milgram did find greater conflict to be experienced by female than male participants. Kilman and Mann (1974) reported similar findings when they found women tended to resist harming the victim more than men.

8.5.3 Replicating the Milgram paradigm

Despite the ethical outcry about Milgram's experiments, researchers in at least eight other countries have attempted to replicate the experiment. Smith and Harris Bond (1993) have summarised the results of these studies and they are given in Table 8.3. These should, however, be viewed with caution as lack of standardisation of methodological procedures make comparisons difficult. For instance, the Dutch study (Meeus and Raaijmakers, 1986), which showed 92 per cent obedience, was not concerned with giving shocks but used a similar task

Study	Country	Participants	Percentage obedience
Milgram (1963)	USA	Male and female, general public	65
Rosenhaum (Milgram 1974)	USA	Students	85
Ancona	Italy	Students	85
Mantell (1974)	Germany	Male, general public	85
Kilham & Mann (1974)	Australia	Male students	40
		Female students	16
Barley & McGuiness (1977)	UK	Male students	50
Shanab & Yahya (1978)	Jordan	Students	62
Miranda et al. (1981)	Spain	Students	90
Schurz (1985)	Australia	General public	80
Meeus & Raaijmakers (1986)	Holland	General public	92

Table 8.3: Obedience to authority across cultures using variations of the Milgram paradigm. After Smith and Harris Bond (1993)

where participants were instructed to harass and criticise someone when they were completing an application form. Similarly, the rather surprising sex difference shown in the Australian study could be explained by the fact that the Australian women were asked to give shocks to a female victim, as opposed to male victims in the Milgram studies. In spite of these flaws, the subsequent research on obedience demonstrates that it was not isolated to an American population in the early 1960s.

8.5.4 Defying authority

Milgram's studies reveal high levels of obedience even when people are experiencing severe misgivings about obeying a command they believe results in harm being inflicted on another person. Obedience reduces, but still remains relatively high, when the authority seems less than legitimate, or the victim is in close proximity, etc. Only when authority figures are in conflict (giving different orders), does obedience cease. What other factors result in our defying authority?

One of the strongest defiant influences is if our peers show rebellion and resistance. Here, social support from others we perceive to be similar to ourselves may allow us to do what we think is right rather than obey instructions when we think we should not. Milgram (1974), investigated this in an experiment where participants were told that the concern was with 'the effects of collective teaching and punishment on memory' (p.116). Three of the participants, unbeknown to the fourth, naïve participant, were confederates: two confederates and the naïve participant were assigned to teacher roles, the other confederate to the learner role. The three teachers were seated together before the shock generator and proceeded with the experiment giving progressively stronger shocks to the learner as the learner gave wrong answers. At 150 volts one of the confederate teachers rebelled and refused to participate any further. The experimenter urged him to continue but he refused. At 180 volts the second confederate teacher refused to continue, leaving the naïve participant alone.

Most naïve participants continued to give shocks up to the 150-volt level. However, when the first confederate rebelled, 80 per cent continued, but when the second confederate rebelled, over 60 per cent of the subjects rebelled themselves and refused to continue. Some 10 per cent of participants still continued to give shocks up to the maximum level. This experiment demonstrates that social support decreases a person's tendency to obey authority but does not lead to everybody being defiant.

This overall programme of research by Milgram has cast important light on factors affecting people's tendency to obey authority. Two findings stand out: (a) authority exerts a powerful influence over everybody, more perhaps than we realise; and (b) destructive obedience may be reduced by the presence of certain variables, but is rarely eliminated. These experiments have been, and continue to be controversial among psychologists and those studying psychology.

8.6 The influence of roles

So far social influence has been viewed from the perspective of one person or group of people either directly (compliance and obedience to authority), or indirectly (conformity), changing the behaviour of another in a desired direction. Often, social influence operates when a person takes on a role such as the role of parent, teacher, policeman, etc. All have expectations of behaviour associated with them. An important psychological effect of taking on a role is that individual identity is replaced by a group or role identity; this offers a person anonymity. This may lead to *deindividuation* (Zimbardo, 1969), which is the loosening of social, moral and societal constraints upon behaviour.

Zimbardo *et al.* (1973) investigated the deindividuating influence of roles in a controversial study commonly known as the *Stanford prison experiment*. The basement of a university building was converted into a 'prison'; there were three cells – a solitary confinement cell and an observational room for guards. Twenty-one participants were selected from a pool of volunteers. These were judged to be 'stable' (physically and mentally), mature and least involved in anti-social behaviour. Nine were randomly assigned to be prisoners and twelve randomly assigned to be guards. Prisoners were told they 'would be under constant surveillance. Some civil rights would be suspended but there would be no physical abuse.' Guards were instructed to 'maintain a reasonable degree of order within the prison for its effective functioning'.

Participants assigned the role of prisoner were arrested in their homes by the police, brought to the 'prison', stripped and made to take a shower. Then, all were dressed in the same loose fitting smocks and nylon caps. Guards were dressed in khaki uniforms, mirror sun-glasses and each given a wooden baton and whistle. To the surprise and horror of the researchers things quickly got out of hand and the experiment had to be terminated after only six days when it was scheduled to run for two weeks. Observations revealed stable behaviour patterns quickly emerged: prisoners evaluated themselves negatively, became very passive and talked about harming the guards. Guards became increasingly aggressive and sadistic, exercising total control over the prisoners by, for example, making visits to the toilet a privilege rather than a right. Such was the dehumanising effect on prisoners that five had to be 'released' because of depression, crying and acute anxiety. When the experiment was terminated, prisoners expressed great relief, but the guards were unhappy because they found the sense of power exhilarating.

Providing an overall evaluation the researchers commented: 'in less than a week middle class, Caucasians of above average intelligence and emotionally stable Americans became pathological and anti-social' (p.89). Prisoners and guards quickly took on the stereotyped behaviour associated with these roles, displaying personality characteristics and behaviours that were normally alien to them. This study vividly demonstrates how a role can take over a person and relegate personal and ethical standards to second place.

A cleverly conceived study by Johnson and Downing (1979) demonstrated how some roles can have a positive and non-destructive effect and others a negative, destructive effect in a Milgram-type of experiment. Here participants were randomly assigned to dress as nurses or disguises worn by the Ku Klux Klan (an American white, racist group). In each case, half the participants in each group wore clothing that covered their face as well, making each individual anonymous. Participants were asked to decide what level of electric shock to give to a learner who had failed at a task.

As shown in Figure 8.11, participants in the caring and helping profession of nursing selected lower levels of shock than those dressed as members of the Ku Klux Klan. Note that nurses whose faces were covered delivered lower levels of shock than those who had their faces uncovered. The effect of deindividuation is modified by the group membership of a person and the values and norms that membership of that group represent.

8.7 Minority influence

The emphasis to this point has been on majority influence and maintenance of the status quo. Traditionally, social influence demonstrated in the classical experimental research on compliance, conformity and group polarisation was seen to fulfil the normative and informational needs of individual in-groups. Historically, however, social change and innovations have been effected by the power of the minority individual or group, who have converted the majority to their way of thinking. Examples of this can be seen in the work of Galileo, Darwin,

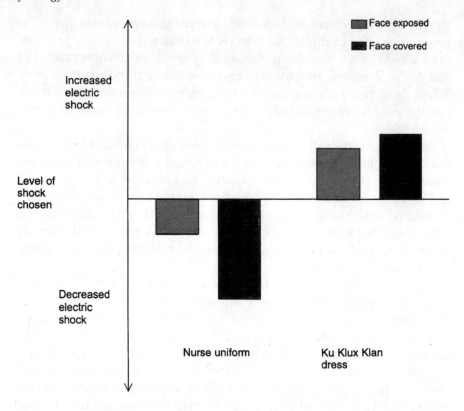

Figure 8.11: Effect of uniform/dress type and whether face is exposed or covered on electric shock levels delivered to a 'learner'. Adapted from Johnson and Downing (1979)

Einstein and Freud, all minority voices at one time but who had profound effects on the world and how we understand and see ourselves. More recent examples can be seen in the acceptance of new forms of art, the women's movement and the success of Greenpeace in the 1980s.

A very illuminating fictional example was seen in the film *Twelve Angry Men*, directed by Sidney Lumet, in the 1950s. Twelve jurors had to produce a guilty or not guilty verdict of whether a young man was guilty of murdering his father. Initially, 11 jurors were convinced of his guilt but one lone juror (Henry Fonda), believed he was innocent. He remained committed, steadfast and persistent in his opinion and gradually persuaded each of the jurors, one by one, to adopt his 'not guilty' decision. There was a final, unanimous decision that the accused was not guilty.

8.7.1 A critique of the classic influence model

In the late 1960s, a French psychologist, Serge Moscovici, started to question the standard approach to conformity research, in which individuals were always dependent on the majority for normative and informational influence (Moscovici and Faucheux, 1972; Moscovici, 1985). In order to understand normative and social change, Moscovici believes that the dynamics of active minorities need to be understood. He criticised the traditional experimental approach as being asymmetrical; the minority was always the target but never the source of the influence, and similarly, the majority was always the source and never the target of influence. The minority were never given the opportunity to persuade the majority of anything which does not really reflect everyday life. Moscovici, in contrast to the traditional conformity research, considered that disagreement and conflict in groups can create any of three social influence modalities: conformity, normalisation or innovation (Moscovici, 1985). An individual can therefore respond in one of the following ways:

1　Conform to the majority opinion to avoid continued conflict.
2　Enter into discussion to effect natural compromise resulting in convergence.
3　Create conflict in order to persuade the majority to adopt their viewpoint.

The success of the minority achieving innovation depends on the *behavioural style* adopted by the individual (Moscovici, 1976).

8.7.2 Behavioural style

The behavioural style of a minority is a critical factor in determining whether a majority will be influenced and come round to adopting the minority view (thus becoming the prevailing or majority view) or whether the minority view will be consigned to history and forgotten. Three main factors have been identified by social psychologists which constitute a behavioural style likely to result in minority influence: consistency, autonomy and rigidity/flexibility.

▩ Consistency

The most important behavioural style is *consistency* – defined as a firm, systematic, coherent and autonomous repetition of one and the same response (Mugny *et al.*, 1984). A consistent minority disrupts the majority norm and causes them to question and doubt their assumptions. The consistency of opinion expressed conveys that there is an alternative viewpoint.

A pioneering experiment by Moscovici, Lage and Naffrechoux (1969) provided empirical support for these contentions. This experiment was in two stages: in the first stage, female participants were formed into groups of six, in which two were confederates of the experimenter, and shown coloured slides which were all blue in colour, but the brightness was varied. In one condition, the confederates said the slides were green on every trial; in the control group there were no confederates in the groups of six. A pronounced influence was found by a minority consistently saying the slides were green: 32 per cent of naïve participants said they saw green at least once. In the control group only a quarter of one per cent of the responses were green. In the second stage of the experiment participants were put into a cubicle by themselves and shown a further sequence of coloured slides. In this sequence, three were obviously blue, three obviously green and 10 were blue/green. Participants exposed to a minority consistently saying green in Stage 1 of the experiment tended to see the blue/green slides as green. This tendency was absent in participants who had been in the control group in the first stage of the experiment. Furthermore, 68 per cent of participants who reported only seeing blue but exposed to a different minority view in Stage 1, saw the blue/green slides as green in Stage 2. The experiment shows consistent minorities effect influence in two ways: (a) at the time at which the minority is espousing its view; and (b) after the minority view has been made and when the minority is absent.

Moscovici *et al.* showed an inconsistent minority to have little effect. In a similar experiment to the one described above, confederates in Stage 1 said they saw green on 24 trials and blue on 12 trials. Overall, participants gave a response of green on only 1.25 per cent of occasions (compared to over 8 per cent with a consistent minority).

Autonomy

Moscovici and Nemeth (1974) point out that consistency of responses alone is not the cause of minority influence. It is necessary that there is a recognition by others that a position is consistent. This suggests others attribute confidence, autonomy and distinctiveness to the minority. Nemeth and Wachtler (1973) demonstrated the effect of autonomy and distinctiveness (focus of attention) in an experiment where groups of five people, four participants and a confederate, had to make 'jury' deliberations. Of interest was the effect of a confederate who put forward a minority view, either assigned (no autonomy) or choosing (autonomy) to sit at the head or side of the table. Figure 8.12 shows the seating arrangements. The seat assigned or chosen was either position Q, R or S. However, when the confederate had chosen his seat, he was highly influential when seated at the head of the table, but not when seated in one of the side positions.

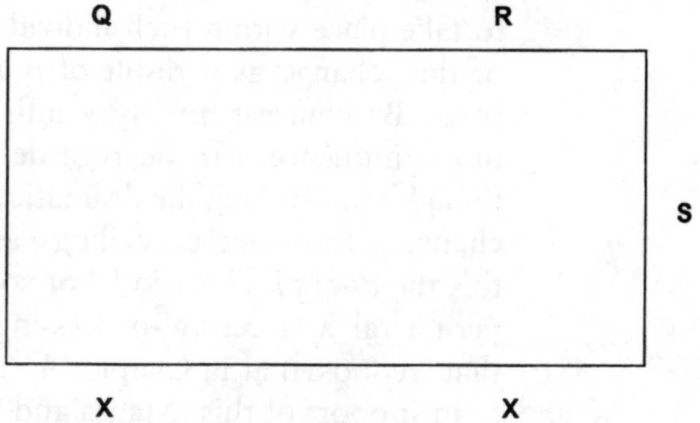

Figure 8.12: Seating positions (Q, R and S) of a confederate adopting a minority view in the group. From Nemeth and Wachtler (1973)

Rigidity/flexibility

If a minority consistently espouses a position without making any concessions to the majority, this may be perceived as dogmatic and inflexible and so reduce minority influence. Mugny *et al.* (1984) have shown, in a series of experiments, that flexibility exerts more influence than dogmatism and inflexibility on the part of the minority. Mugny defines flexibility as 'when some concessions were made to the population so as not to accentuate the conflict, while the break with authority remained consistent' (p.508). Such a strategy prevents the minority from being socially categorised as an out-group. Flexibility stops dissimilarities between the minority and majority being accentuated while at the same time similarities are attended to.

In summary, research confirms that minorities exert more influence when they are perceived by the majority as in-group members (Martin, 1988; Mugny and Pérez, 1991). For instance, heterosexual males holding negative attitudes towards homosexuality are more likely to become more liberal if positive attitudes are put forward by other heterosexual males (in-group members), rather than homosexual males (out-groupers). It is likely that out-group minorities are most likely to be discriminated against and least likely to succeed in attempts at social influence. In-group minorities share the same social identity as the majority which makes the persuasion process easier.

8.7.3 Differential outcomes of majority and minority influence

Conversion or acceptance

For minorities to be successful at social influence Moscovici (1980) proposes that a radical, and often carefully thought-through *conversion* has to take place within each individual in the prevailing majority. Because of this, change as a result of minority influence may be slow to take place. By contrast, majority influence, through normative or informational influence, can be regarded as a passive process requiring little thought and lacking the dramatic change that a person must make when changing from one prevailing view to another. Moscovici (1980) calls this the *dual-process model* of social influence; it can be likened to the peripheral and central-processing model of attitude change proposed that we looked at in Chapter 4.

In support of this, Maass and Clarke (1983) investigated public and private responses to gay rights. They found that the publicly expressed attitudes of people conformed to the majority opinion (pro-gay), while the privately expressed attitudes moved towards the minority, this is depicted in Figure 8.13.

Moscovici and Personnaz (1986) showed strong experimental support for minority influence producing what they called latent internal change. However, other researchers have been less successful in replicating this result. The dual process theory therefore remains controversial (Mugny and Pérez, 1991).

■ Imitation or originality

Nemeth and Kwan (1987) proposed that to disagree with a majority opinion is stressful because one assumes that it is usually correct. Having to decide between our own opinion and that of the majority creates a dilemma as it reduces our options to two (*convergent thinking*). However, when confronted with minority dissent, while the initial reaction is of disapproval and dismissal, if it is consistent and persistent we are forced to take notice, and reappraise the issue. The minority opinion may not necessarily be adopted, but it does open up a number of alternatives from which to choose and encourages *divergent thinking*. The result may be that we stick with our original position, or we may choose one of the alternatives generated. Nemeth was not particularly interested in which position is eventually adopted but the thought processes stimulated

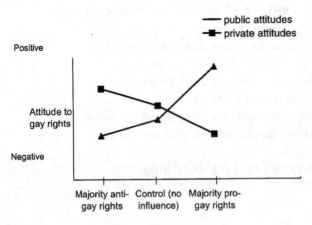

Figure 8.13: Change in public and private attitudes to gay rights following majority or minority influence

by dissent. Nemeth and Kwan illustrated the effect experimentally by presenting participants with unusual sequences of 6 letters, some of which were in capitals and others in lower case (e.g., tNOWap). In groups of four, individuals were asked to form a three-lettered word they perceived. The most commonly produced word was formed from the capitals reading from L to R amongst the six letters. Following five trials, experimenters collected results and then informed participants that either the three (majority) or one (minority) in the group had listed a word formed by reversing sequencing, for example, WON rather than NOW. Participants were then exposed to a new set of letters and asked to make as many words as they could in 15 seconds. The results showed that those participants told that the majority had used reverse sequencing of letters tended to use this strategy consistently, thus reducing the level of their performance. Those told that the minority had used this strategy used a variety of combinations and their performance was enhanced. Nemeth suggests that this demonstrates that minority influence generates divergent thinking and changes the way we think about issues, (Nemeth *et al.*, 1990).

In summary, research on minority influence was neglected in early research by social psychologists on social influence processes. More recent research has tended to focus on minority influence, not least because the dramatic changes in how we view ourselves and our place in this universe have come from individuals adopting a behavioural style resulting in the minority view replacing or prevailing majority view. People like Galileo, Darwin and Freud are good examples of this type of influence.

8.8 Application: group polarisation in a legal context

In Section 8.4 we saw that the group polarisation phenomenon may be explained by normative influence, informational influence and self-categorisation theory. Rugs and Kaplan (1993) categorise group decisions in one of two ways: (a) *intellective* decisions which have clearly correct answers; and (b) *judgemental* decisions which do not have correct answers but reflect a group's beliefs, preferences and values. Hence, group polarisation in the context of judgemental decisions is more likely to result from the normative and self-categorisation explanations.

Kaplan and Miller (1987) investigated the effect of two different decision rules – majority and unanimous – on damages that mock juries awarded to a person in a case of company negligence. In this study intellective decisions were when *compensatory* damages were awarded, and judgemental decisions when *exemplary* damages were awarded.

Exemplary damages are regarded as judgemental in this context since the jury may decide to make 'an example' of the negligent company by awarding the injured person overly high damages. By contrast, compensatory damages are intellective because the negligent company had already offered to pay a set sum for damages.

Kaplan and Miller gave a description of the case to female participants and asked each to give their individual opinion about the level of damages that they would award if fair compensation was exemplary. Groups of six were then put together; half of these groups were asked to reach a majority decision and the other half to reach a unanimous decision.

As can be seen from Figure 8.14, the level of award of damages was quite similar for all conditions except where the jury had to make a

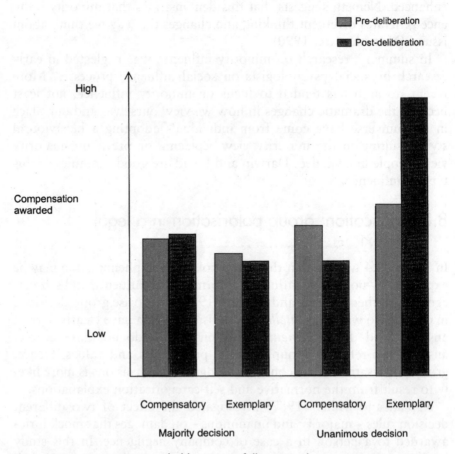

Figure 8.14: Damages awarded by 'juries' following either a majority or unanimous decision rule. Adapted from Kaplan and Miller (1987)

unanimous decision about awarding exemplary damages. The high level of damages awarded, shown in Figure 8.14, demonstrates that group polarisation has occurred. Only in this experimental condition was there a marked change in opinion between each person's individual decision before group discussion and after group discussion. From recordings of the discussions that took place when groups were attempting to reach a decision, Kaplan and Miller reported that normative statements, such as 'do what the majority thinks right', were used more often when exemplary damages were considered in relation to a unanimous decision rule. From this we may conclude that group polarisation is more likely to occur when judgemental decisions are being made by a group that is required to reach a unanimous decision.

8.9 Summary

- Compliance is agreeing to a direct request, where the request is not a command or made by authority. Compliance-gaining strategies which have real life application are 'the *foot-in-the-door*, *door-in-the-face* and the *low ball* techniques'
- Conformity or majority influence is a change in behaviour towards a group norm as a result of a group pressure. Sherif used the autokinetic effect to demonstrate how group norms strongly influence a person in ambiguous or novel situations. Asch investigated the effect of group pressure in an unambiguous situation involving line judgements. A unanimous incorrect majority exerts considerable influence, which decreases when the unanimity is broken and/or if credible social support is provided.
- Conformity can be explained in terms of either *normative* or *informational* pressure.
- Factors affecting the extent of conformity include the size of the unanimous majority, the attractiveness of the group to the individual, the nature of the task, and whether you are a member of a collectivist or individualist culture.
- Group polarisation is where group discussion serves to strengthen or polarise already existing tendencies of the individuals in the group. The phenomenon can be explained from a normative–social comparison perspective, a persuasive-information perspective, or by the self-categorisation theory.
- Milgram investigated obedience to authority by getting subjects to administer what they believed to be increasingly strong electric shocks to a learner when he answered wrongly. Some 65 per cent of participants gave maximum shocks when urged to do so by the experimenter. If the authority was of dubious legitimacy, the learner was in close proximity to the teacher or rebellion was shown by peers, obedience levels were reduced. Only conflicting commands resulted in all participants refusing to carry on giving electric shocks.

- Zimbardo investigated the deindividuating properties of roles in the Stanford prison experiment. Guards and prisoners took on roles so realistically that the experiment had to be stopped. Guards became aggressive and inhuman, and prisoners submissive and distraught.
- Minority influence can be achieved if an appropriate behavioural style is adopted by the minority. Consistency, autonomy and flexibility of opinion have been shown to be effective.
- Minority influence is more likely to result in conversion whereas majority influence usually results in public compliance. Minority opinion may also change the way information is processed leading to divergent thinking.

8.10 Suggestions for further reading

Cialdini, R. and Trost, M. 1998: Social influence; social norms, conformity and compliance. In Gilbert, D. T., Fiske, S. T. and Lindzey, G. (eds), *The Handbook of Social Psychology,* Fourth edition. New York: McGraw-Hill.

More advanced, but up-to-date review of theory and research in the field of social influence. A good understanding of the themes of social influence discussed in this chapter needed before reading.

Milgram, S. 1974: *Obedience to Authority.* New York: Harper Row.

Classic text in which Milgram gives detailed report on the range of controversial experiments he conducted in the 1960s which are briefly summarised in this chapter.

Mugny, G. and Pérez, J. A. 1991: *The Social Psychology of Minority Influence.* Cambridge: Cambridge University Press.

Good account of the theory and research, much developed and conducted by these authors, on minority influence.

9   Pro-social and anti-social behavior

9.1 Introduction

If you read the papers or watch the television news, you will see and hear reports of extraordinary violence among human beings such as brutal wars, cruel rapes, attacks on the elderly, physical and sexual abuse of young children; the list is long. The media rarely report the other side of the coin, the selfless acts of courage and kindness that people do for one another. Consider the career of Mother Theresa of Calcutta, and her caring work with the poor, rejected and homeless of India, or the work of volunteers from relief agencies who offer help to the victims of flood, famine and other natural disasters, for instance to those caught up in the devastation caused by Hurricane Mitch in late 1998. It may surprise you to know that the same variables underlie acts of both pro-social and anti-social behaviour. For example, our perceptions and interpretations of situations influence both pro-social and anti-social behaviours. Both are influenced by modelling from others, both are dependent on social norms and both can offer rewards to the person carrying out the behaviour. This chapter examines the factors that underpin pro-social and anti-social behaviour. The question of whether pro-social and anti-social behaviour is genetically determined is also considered.

9.2 Defining pro-social and anti-social behaviour _____

Every day we casually label behaviour as aggressive or altruistic, often without thinking whether the terms are really appropriate. For example, should we label the pushy double glazing salesman who calls at the door 'aggressive'? Can we justifiably call the local big businessman who bankrolls our hometown rugby team 'altruistic'? As social psychologists, our answers to these questions depend on the *motives* of the actor.

Suppose you are out shopping with a new friend whom you would like very much to impress, and a *Big Issue* seller asks you to buy her magazine. You immediately agree and pay well over the odds for the magazine. You want to help homeless people, but you also want to impress your new friend. Since your action involves an intention to help, it counts as an example of pro-social behaviour. However, you have an ulterior motive, to impress your friend, and so the action cannot count as an example of *altruistic* behaviour. Altruism is motivated by the wish to help someone else rather than yourself (Batson and Coke, 1981). It is a subcategory of *helping* behaviour, which involves an intentional act to benefit someone else (Hogg and Vaughan, 1995). Helping is in turn a subcategory of pro-social behaviour, which consists of any act that carries a positive value in society. This is a very loose definition, since as you can guess there are some societies that have fewer sanctions against violent behaviour (Elkin, 1961).

To an extent, anti-social behaviour is culturally defined and there are interesting debates to be had on the topic of what counts as aggression. However, generally speaking, aggression depends on the motive of the actor. Accidentally tripping up an opposing player in a hockey match is not aggression, but yelling insults at their team captain is. Aggression consists of *emotional aggression* and *instrumental aggression*. An example of emotional aggression is lashing out at another person (physically or verbally) under provocation. In contrast, instrumental aggression involves causing harm in order to achieve a goal, such as falsely insinuating that an acquaintance's lover has been unfaithful, so that you can step in and date her when the relationship ends.

9.3 Pro-social behaviour _____

The impetus for research on when and why people help others was sparked by a tragic event that happened over 30 years ago. In March 1964, Kitty Genovese was returning home from work late at night. As she walked through a respectable residential area of New York City, a man attacked her with a knife. Kitty's attacker repeatedly stabbed her, she screamed and struggled then he ran off. When no one came to help Kitty her attacker returned to continue his attack and to sexually assault her. In the half-hour it took him to kill her, not a single person came to help Kitty, despite her increasingly desperate pleas for help. When the police interviewed witnesses the next day, no fewer than 38 people admitted to seeing and hearing the terrible crime. Yet not one of them had attempted to help. The case caused a national outcry, and provoked a wave of research on helping behaviour.

9.3.1 Genetic factors in pro-social behaviour

Sociobiological theories attempt to explain social behaviour in terms of genetic inheritance and evolution. This approach proposes that we have an innate tendency to help others (Barash, 1977), possibly as an evolutionary survival tactic (Krebs and Miller, 1985). At first glance this seems puzzling. One can understand how being helped by other people could increase an individual's chances of survival, but it is less easy to see how helping others might do so. But an alternative to individual survival is to ensure the survival of one's genes, which are present in close relatives who share our genetic heritage. Helping blood relatives, known as *kinship selection*, helps some of our own genes to survive, and Burnstein *et al.* (1994) found that the intention to help in situations of serious danger is stronger between kinsmen (close relatives). So, on closer examination an innate biological drive for pro-social behaviour has evolutionary value (Dawkins, 1989). Of course, relatives do not always help each other, and we often help those who are not related to us at all, so further explanation is needed. Sociobiologists account for helping unrelated people by proposing that helping involves *reciprocity*. If I help you and you help me, both of us increase our chances of surviving long enough to reproduce our genes. Nevertheless, because of the danger of others cheating by not repaying favours, reciprocal altruism is usually limited to close relationships involving mutual trust (Voland, 1993).

Persuasive as it may be, the sociobiological approach does not tell the whole story since there are wide cultural differences in both pro-social and anti-social behaviour (Fiske, 1991). Therefore, pro-social and anti-social behaviour cannot be wholly determined by biological factors, since cultural norms also play a role (Oyama, 1991). For example, in Western cultures it is thought appropriate to retaliate in the face of aggression; in Japan the 'correct' cultural response is to withdraw. In addition, it is not easy to provide a biological account for the Kitty Genovese case.

9.3.2 Social learning approaches to pro-social behaviour

An alternative to sociobiology is the *social learning* approach which proposes that social behaviour is learned through observing the actions and responses of others. On this account, classical conditioning, instrumental conditioning and observation determine pro-social behaviour.

9.3.3 Instructions on pro-social behaviour

Giving instructions to children to act pro-socially actually increases their helpful behaviour (Grusec *et al.*, (1978). However, the instructions must clearly detail appropriate behaviour, so that the child can establish sound knowledge of what is expected in situations where help is required. Vague instructions to be helpful do not work, nor does the incongruent approach employed by some adults of telling a child to behave in one way while acting in another way themselves! For example, children who were told to behave generously but observed an adult acting selfishly displayed less generous behaviour.

9.3.4 Reinforcement and pro-social behaviour

Grusec (1982) showed that if children were rewarded for pro-social behaviour in natural settings, they were more likely to repeat the behaviour, in line with classical conditioning theory. If they did not receive a reward for the behaviour, they were less likely to continue it. Rushton and Teachman (1978) carried out a study that combined both conditioning and observation. They had children observe a person generously donating tokens to someone else. The children spontaneously imitated this behaviour in an experimental play situation, where they were either punished or rewarded for their generosity. Immediately afterwards, those children who had been rewarded for their generosity donated many more tokens than children who were punished, an effect evident at a two-week follow up. Results from Rushton and Teachman's study are displayed in Figure 9.1.

9.3.5 Modelling

Pro-social behaviour can be elicited by the example of others. In ambiguous situations, other people provide cues as to appropriate behaviour, so that if one person runs to help an injured motorist, others usually follow. The first person acts as a *model* to others, by defining behaviour appropriate to the situation. Bandura (1977b) proposed

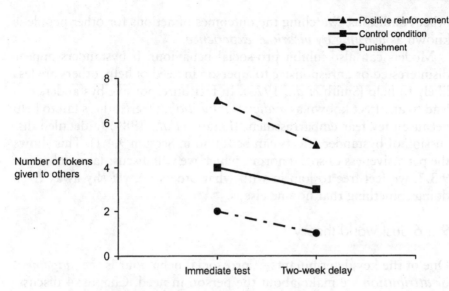

Figure 9.1: Effect of reinforcement and punishment on children's generosity. Adapted from Rushton and Teachman (1978)

that (in accordance with social learning theory) watching pro-social behaviour should encourage similar behaviour in observers. Bryan and Test (1967) demonstrated this in a study. They found that people were more likely to stop and help an apparently broken down car (actually placed at the roadside by the researchers) if they had recently seen another motorist stop and help another stranded driver (again, an accomplice of the researchers). Models elicit helping behaviour because they provide a direct example of behaviour that can be imitated. When models receive rewards for their helpful behaviour, we learn that helping is valued and we are more likely to help in the future. Model behaviour also informs us about cultural standards of what is expected and appropriate behaviour in our society. A model shows us what to do, makes us more certain about helping and gives information about the consequences of providing help (Rushton, 1980).

However, Bandura argues that the modelling process involves more than mere imitation. Crucially, imitation depends on what happens to the model afterwards; if the model is positively reinforced, her behaviour is more likely to be copied than if she is punished. Hornstein (1970) demonstrated this in a study where models returned a 'lost' wallet.' The models appeared either glad to help, resentful of helping or showed no emotion. When participants in the study later discovered an apparently lost wallet, those who had observed the 'happy to help model' were much more likely to return the wallet than people in the other conditions. Watching the outcomes of actions for other people is known as *learning by vicarious experience*.

Models can also inhibit pro-social behaviour. If bystanders appear disinterested or unresponsive to a person in need of help, others are less likely to help (Smith *et al.*, 1973). In fact unresponsive bystanders can lead to an effect known as *audience inhibition*, where others fail to help because they fear embarrassment (Latané *et al.*, 1981) (a detailed discussion of bystander effects can be found in Section 9.4.1). This shows the pervasiveness of social norms, which we will discuss later in Section 9.3.7; we feel free to join in with what others do, yet shy away from doing something that no one else is.

9.3.6 Just world theory

One of the key determinants of pro-social behaviour is the *judgement* or *attribution* we make about the person in need. Chapter 4 discusses attribution theory. Sometimes people do not help, and sometimes they even blame the victim. According to the *just world hypothesis* (Lerner, 1980) people believe that others get what they deserve, in other words, that bad things only happen to people who deserve misfortune and good people encounter only happy events. So powerful is this belief that it has even been shown to adversely affect judgements about innocent victims of rape and sexual assault. One reason for *belief in a just world* is that it provides psychological reassurance against the often random nature of unfortunate events. In the Kitty Genovese case, observers may have explained away her dreadful murder by telling themselves that she deserved it for being out so late at night.

Logically, someone with a strong belief in a just world should refuse to help. Miller (1977) investigated this point in a study during which students were asked to donate their research participant payments to needy families. The study took place just before Christmas, and some students were told that the Psychology Department was raising money for families in need of help over Christmas, while some were told that the fund raising was for families with year-round needs. Students with a weak just world belief gave the same amount regardless of the information they had been given about the recipients. Those with a strong just world belief donated more for the temporary specific need of poor families at Christmas, and much less for those who were (allegedly) always in need of financial assistance. Results from this study are shown in Figure 9.2.

More recent research (Warren and Walker, 1991) has found similar results. Those with a strong belief are much less likely to give in cases of continuous need because they feel that needy people have brought their fate upon themselves.

9.3.7 Norms of pro-social behaviour

We usually feel morally bound to help the distressed child, the frail old person or the stranded motorist. Social norms specify the type of behaviour that is expected and normal. We often help others because we know it is expected of us, and these expectations are socially learned through what others do and say (see Section 9.3.2). Television also influences social norms (Oskamp, 1988) and we will examine its influence on aggressive behaviour in the Application section of this chapter. Almost every society has a norm that looking after others is valued, and self-centred behaviour is not valued. One could argue, therefore, that helping behaviour is *normative* and that behaving pro-socially is rewarded in society while behaving anti-socially is punished.

Two main types of norms have been proposed as determining proso-cial behaviour, *reciprocity* and *social responsibility*. According to the rec-iprocity norm, discussed in connection with the sociobiological approach to pro-social behaviour in Section 9.3.1, we should help those who help us (Gross and Latané, 1974). This seems straightforward, but there are additional influences on reciprocity, for example, if another person does something for us which involves them making a large personal sacrifice (an extreme case would be donating an organ), we feel more strongly bound to repay them than if they simply did us a small favour, such as collecting the dry cleaning. This is in accordance with the norm of *equi-ty*, discussed in the context of interpersonal relationships in Chapter 7. Additionally, in line with social exchange theory discussed in the same chapter, we may feel bound to give help *only* in return for that given in the past or offered in the future.

The social responsibility norm proposes that we should always offer help to those in need, regard-less of the possibility of future repayment (Schwartz, 1975). Giving a donation to a charity col-lector would be one example of this norm. However, as we have seen in Section 9.3.6, other considerations affect the probability of donating and people usually apply this norm only to those they perceive to be in

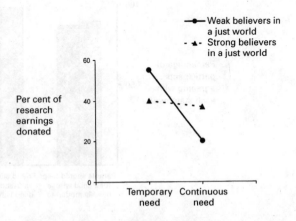

Figure 9.2: Effect of different levels of belief in a just world on donating behaviour. Based on Miller (1977)

difficulties through no fault of their own. So, you may well donate to the NSPCC but be less likely to help someone who is lying on the ground apparently drunk. The norm of social responsibility requires that we give help on the basis of need, but actually applying this norm depends on the norm of *justice*, that is on making judgements about why people need assistance. It can also, as we shall see, conflict with the norm of minding your own business!

Social norms are hugely influenced by the society we live in. Fiske (1991) found that in West African societies, even very valuable resources, including land and water in times of scarcity, is given to those in need. Miller *et al.* (1990) found that residents of the United States of America are much less likely to believe in a moral obligation to help others with a moderate need. In contrast, Hindu Indians do feel this moral obligation; they are not selective about need in the way Americans appear to be. Figure 9.3 summarises results from this study.

Despite the power of social norms, most people place a personal interpretation on them which affects the degree to which they will help others. It is useful to consider the role of *personal norms* in helping behaviour. Those who routinely put themselves at risk for the sake of others act in ways that are in *conflict* with social norms since their behaviour is abnormal. Instead, they conform to their own personal standards. High personal standards of altruism are strongly correlated with parental values about helping. Studies have shown that those whose efforts to help others are truly heroic, such as Oskar Schindler,

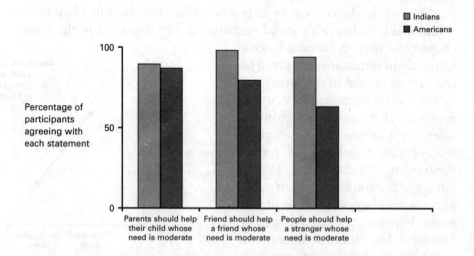

Figure 9.3: Comparison of the norm of social responsibility in Hindu Indians and Americans. From Miller *et al.* (1990)

are strongly influenced by the high standards of their parents (London, 1970; Oliner and Oliner, 1988).

9.3.8 The role of empathy in pro-social behaviour

Discussions so far in this chapter have proposed that helping behaviour results from both genetic factors (the sociobiological approach) and environmental factors (the social learning approach). While most psychological theories assume that helping is at heart an *egoistic* enterprise, guided by self-interest, Batson (1991) believes that some helping behaviours are truly altruistic. On his definition, if your motive is to help another person, then your behaviour is altruistic.

Batson's view is based on the consequences of *empathy*, one of the strongest influences on helping behaviour (Gaertner and Dovidio, 1977; Hoffman, 1981). Empathy can be defined as an emotional response *and* understanding of another person's distress. Sagi and Hoffman (1976) demonstrated that even at a few days old infants respond to another infant's distress, and there is a wealth of research confirming that both adults and children show an empathetic response to distressed others. Most of us find it unpleasant to watch other people suffer.

While debate is ongoing, the general consensus is that empathy consists of both cognitive and emotional components (Eisenberg *et al.*, 1994). The components of empathy include *perspective taking* (the ability to take another person's point of view), *personal distress* (alarm, fear and sadness) and *empathetic concern* (sympathy and compassion). Recent research (Roker *et al.*, 1998) on adolescent altruism and pro-social behaviour found that British adolescents showed a high level of altruistic and helping behaviour, often unbeknown to parents. Altruistic behaviour depends on perspective taking, since this leads to empathetic concern for the person in need. If the perspective of the troubled person is not taken, personal distress results and the motive for helping will be egoistic, since helping is offered purely as a means of reducing one's own distress. Batson's model is shown in Figure 9.4.

Some theorists have argued that when we help others we do so to reduce our own disagreeable feelings provoked by their distress. Piliavin proposed that emergency situations produce unpleasant arousal in observers, from which they seek relief by helping. Therefore, calling this sort of helping altruism is incorrect since it is motivated purely by the wish to reduce our own unpleasant feelings. The question is, how can we determine whether someone is acting altruistically or egoistically?

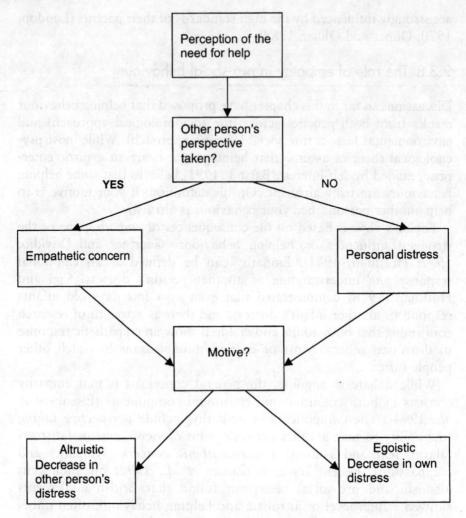

Figure 9.4: Batson's (1991) empathy–altruism and model of pro-social behaviour

Batson *et al.* (1981) devised an experiment to test this question. They believed that separating those with egotistical motives from those with altruistic motives depended on the ease of escape from a person in need. Those with egotistical motivation would leave if there were a chance to do so, thus relieving their personal distress, while those motivated by altruism would stay to help. Participants in Batson *et al.*'s study were led to believe that they were to observe while another person, Elaine, performed a task during which she would receive random electric shocks. Needless to say no real shocks were given. A short time into the experiment Elaine appeared to become distressed and revealed that she had developed a fear of shocks since a childhood accident. The participants were then invited to take Elaine's place. Whether they agreed to do so or not depended on the degree of empathetic concern and the ease of escape that formed the experimental conditions. Half of the participants were told that Elaine was similar to themselves and half were told she was dissimilar to them. Since *similarity* increases empathetic concern (Houston, 1990), those participants who were led to believe that Elaine was similar to them should be higher on this factor. In addition, half the participants were told that they could leave after two trials, and half were told that they must watch all ten trials. Elaine's distress took place after two trials, affording an easy escape route for some participants. As you might expect, those participants in the high empathetic concern condition helped out whether they could leave or not. Low empathetic concern participants were more likely to help Elaine if they had been told to watch all ten trials. They were much less likely to help if they could leave. Results from Batson *et al.*'s study are shown in Figure 9.5.

9.4 Situational factors in pro-social behaviour

In response to the Kitty Genovese case, researchers began to look at helping behaviour in emergency situations. However, as research progressed, its scope widened to include studies of helping in real-life

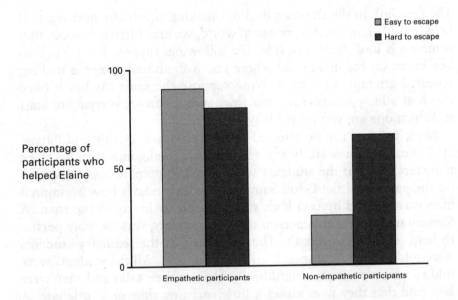

Figure 9.5: Test of the empathy–altruism model. Based on data from Batson *et al.* (1981). Note that with non-empathetic participants in the 'easy to escape' condition Elaine was left to suffer

situations and this section considers factors which affect helping in everyday life.

9.4.1 The bystander effect

Remember that plenty of people saw Kitty Genovese being attacked but simply stood back and did nothing. Research has shown that pro-social behaviour is dramatically influenced by whether one or several people witness a situation; odd as it may seem, your chances of receiving help are far greater if only one person is around than if there are several onlookers. This phenomenon is known as the *bystander effect* and was investigated empirically by Latané and Darley (1970). The researchers doubted that the characteristics of city life provided reasons for the apparent apathy of onlookers in the Genovese incident. They suspected that the presence of others affected the decision to help because individuals were not clear about whether they were responsible for providing help. The researchers provided a five-step model of decision making in helping behaviour. The five steps – attending to the situation, realising it is an emergency, taking responsibility, deciding what is to be done and giving help – are detailed in the following sections.

9.4.2 Attending to the situation

The first link in the chain of decision-making is actually noticing that help is needed. In today's pressured world, we may often not notice that someone is in distress. Consider the following: suppose a car has broken down on the quiet road where you live, and its owner is making repeated attempts to start it. Now suppose the same car has broken down at a busy junction in your town and its owner is trying to start it. Which one are you most likely to notice?

Noticing need can be affected by time pressure. Darley and Batson (1973) carried out a study at a seminary for young men training to be ministers. Half of the students were asked to prepare a short speech on the parable of the Good Samaritan, which relates how an injured man was ignored by two high status people as he lay in the road. A Samaritan, a low status person in Jewish society, was the only person to help the distressed man. The other half of the seminary students were told to prepare a speech on preferred jobs. All the students were told to report to another building to deliver their talk, and they were also told that they were either a little early, on time or a little late. A confederate of the researchers stationed himself on their route, where he lay on the ground groaning. Can you guess how these young ministers behaved? The topic of the speech had no effect on helping behaviour, but time pressure did. Of those who were early, 63 per cent offered help, 45 per cent of those on time offered help, but only 10 per cent of the late students stopped to assist the man. Their own preoccupation had prevented them from noticing the man's need, or at least from attending to it.

9.4.3 Realising it is an emergency

Emergency situations can often appear ambiguous at first glance. Is that man in a diabetic coma or is he drunk? Is that woman shrieking in fear or simply laughing loudly? Clark and Word (1972) found that the more ambiguous a situation is, the less likely bystanders are to help. This can often have tragic consequences. In 1993, two boys abducted two-year-old James Bulger from a Liverpool shopping centre. As they dragged him away, James screamed, cried and lashed out at them. Despite 61 people witnessing the boys' cruelty towards James, no one intervened. He was later found dead. Most people who witnessed James' abduction interpreted it as older boys taking a reluctant younger brother home. Where family members appear to be involved, people are less likely to step in and offer help. Shotland and Straw (1976) found that when people witness disputes between a man and a woman, they interpret the situation as involving husband and wife or dating partners and are unlikely to help. In situations like this the *norm of family privacy* operates and people rarely intervene, preferring to mind their own business.

As in studies of affiliation discussed in Chapter 7, *social comparison* can help to define a situation. Faced with an ambiguous situation, we glance around to see what everyone else makes of it. Unfortunately, often everyone looks at one another for clues as to how to behave, and no one does anything. In these situations the distressed person suffers from what is known as *pluralistic ignorance*. Each person thinks that others are not responding to events because the situation is not really an emergency. Bystanders do not even have to be physically present for pluralistic ignorance to occur. Darley and Latane (1968) isolated students in a cubicle equipped with headphones through which they were led to believe that they could communicate with a variable amount of other people. Shortly after the experiment began, a confederate of the researchers faked an epileptic fit which participants heard through their headphones. Response to the emergency depended on the apparent size of the group. Though all participants were actually alone, the more people they thought were present in other cubicles the less likely they were to help the epileptic. Results from this study are shown in Figure 9.6.

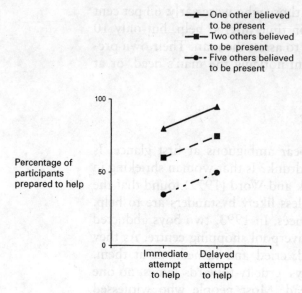

Figure legend:
— ▲ — One other believed to be present
— ■ — Two others believed to be present
— ● -- Five others believed to be present

Percentage of participants prepared to help

100

50

0

Immediate attempt to help   Delayed attempt to help

Figure 9.6: Diffusion of responsibility: the more people participants believed were present, the less likely participants were to help. After Darley and Latané (1968)

9.4.4 Taking responsibility for action

Even when the emergency is noticed and interpreted correctly, a bystander may still not offer help because she is not sure whether or not it is her responsibility to do so. When several potential helpers are present, each of them may assume that the others will take responsibility for helping. This is known as *diffusion of responsibility* and is exactly what happened in the seizure experiment outlined in the previous section. Those participants who thought they were alone could not delegate responsibility for helping the person having a fit, but the more potential helpers, the more responsibility was diffused. Wegner and Schaefer (1978) showed that the presence of a large number of victims and a small number of helpers increases pro-social behaviour.

Two factors can increase the likelihood of bystander helping: a reduction in the *psychological distance* between victim and bystander and a reduction of the psychological distance between bystanders themselves. If victim and bystander know each other, or are related, the probability of receiving help is very high. People who know each other, for example workmates, are more likely to be helpful bystanders than groups of strangers (Rutkowski *et al.*, 1983). Also, social roles such as leadership positions increase the likelihood of taking responsibility for action (Baumeister *et al.*, 1988), as do occupational roles such as nursing (Cramer *et al.*, 1988).

9.4.5 Deciding what is to be done

Unless people have specific training in life-saving procedures or medicine, they are unlikely to try to help the victim in an emergency situation directly. Usually they will help indirectly by calling the emergency services or alerting other people. However, this is not always the case. On a freezing winter day in 1982, an Air Florida jet crash-landed into the icy Potomac River. When a flight attendant lost her grip on a helicopter lifeline and fell back into the freezing water, a heroic bystander dived into the river and rescued her (Clines, 1982). Here the norm of *empathy* overrode any concerns the rescuer had for his own safety and he quickly decided on what had to be done.

9.4.6 Giving help

Many people worry that they will make a fool of themselves if they offer help, or feel too self-conscious to offer help in front of other people. They may experience a *fear of social blunders* which prevents them from public pro-social behaviour. The detrimental effect of others on the decision to help is known as *audience inhibition*, and was mentioned in connection with social modelling in section 9.3.2. Conversely, if people think others will admonish them for not helping, having an audience increases the chances of helping behaviour (Schwartz and Gottlieb, 1980). Emergency situations are unpleasantly arousing, though curiously physiological arousal can decrease on first encountering an emergency. This decrease is an *orienting reaction* and serves to give us thinking time to assess the situation (Piliavin *et al.*, 1981). A rapid increase in arousal levels, a *defence reaction*, follows. According to Piliavin *et al.* (1981) the decision to help is based on:

- becoming physiologically aroused by another person's distress;
- labelling the arousal as personal distress in yourself;
- calculating the costs and benefits of helping and not helping.

This is known as the *arousal-cost-reward* model. The greater the level of arousal, the more likely a person is to help (Piliavin *et al.*, 1981). The greater the potential rewards in comparison to potential costs to both helper and victim, the more likely it is that the victim will be assisted (Dovidio *et al.*, 1991). Piliavin provides a more cynical counterpoint to Batson's view that some behaviours are purely altruistic.

In summary, providing help to someone in distress is not as simple as it might appear at first glance. There are a variety of social phenomena that affect the decision to give assistance, and these are shown in Figure 9.7.

9.5 Personality factors in pro-social behaviour

The preceding sections have examined the effect of the social situation on helping behaviour, but it is important to remember that behaviour is the product both of the environment *and* the individual. *Personal characteristics* can also affect pro-social behaviour, and are generally considered under two categories: mood and personality.

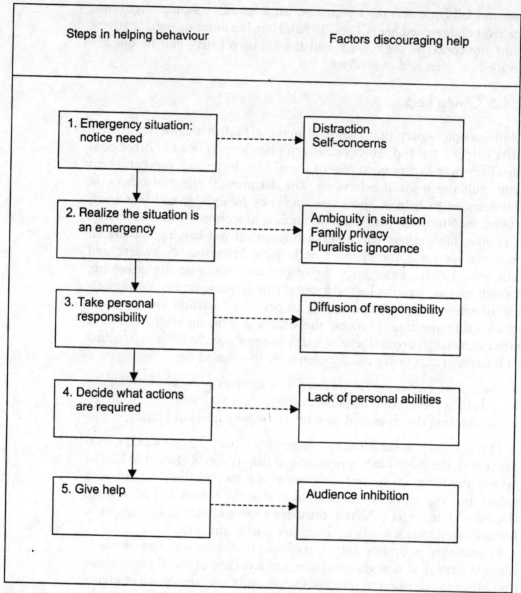

Steps in helping behaviour	Factors discouraging help
1. Emergency situation: notice need	Distraction Self-concerns
2. Realize the situation is an emergency	Ambiguity in situation Family privacy Pluralistic ignorance
3. Take personal responsibility	Diffusion of responsibility
4. Decide what actions are required	Lack of personal abilities
5. Give help	Audience inhibition

Figure 9.7: Five steps to providing help in an emergency situation. After Darley and Latané (1968)

9.5.1 Mood

A body of research has shown that people in an experimentally induced good mood demonstrate higher levels of pro-social behaviour. For example, school teachers who were told that they had performed well on a task donated about seven times as much cash to a fund raising drive than other teachers (Isen, 1970). Isen accounts for this effect by proposing that success leads to enhanced mood, which in turn leads to a focus on the positive (Isen *et al.*, 1976) and an increased sense of optimism (Isen and Stalker, 1982). Even the weather affects pro-social behaviour; people are more helpful on fine sunny days than on cold cloudy days (Cunningham, 1979).

Given the interaction of good mood and helpful behaviour, it is perhaps not surprising that bad mood adversely affects helpfulness. Those in a bad mood focus inwards on their own difficulties and anxieties (Berkowitz, 1970) and they are less concerned about other people's distress and less inclined to help (Weyant, 1978). One exception to this phenomenon is the emotion of guilt. Research has shown that inducing guilt increases the likelihood of the guilty person helping. Regan *et al.* (1972) led participants to think that they had broken an expensive camera, then gave them the opportunity to help someone who had dropped a pile of groceries. He found that 50 per cent of the 'guilty' participants stopped to help while only 15 per cent of control participants did so. This effect has been replicated across many other studies. Why should guilty people help more? Baumeister *et al.* (1994) propose that guilt functions to knit together interpersonal relationships; if we feel guilty about something we take the next available opportunity to strengthen any social relationship we come across. The theory has some currency. All of us can recall some incident when we perhaps unintentionally upset one of our friends. We usually take the soonest opportunity to help them to repair the damage, and we are usually careful in our dealings with other people too. This may be a manifestation of Piliavin's arousal model, where pro-social behaviour is undertaken to reduce personal distress.

9.5.2 Personality

Based on data from twin studies which indicated a correlation in the pro-social behaviour of monozygotic twins ('identical' twins developed from a single egg), Rushton (1981) believes that the *altruistic personality* has a genetic basis. However, Latané and Darley failed to find a correlation between personality measures, including authoritarianism, trustworthiness, need for approval and alienation, and pro-social behaviour. Eisenberg-Berg (1979) found that helpful behaviour is positively associated with an internal locus of control, mature moral judgement and other personality variables, but the evidence remains inconclusive. Perhaps Knight *et al.* (1994) have the best answer to date. They suggest that a number of dispositional traits determine pro-social behaviour, but the dominant traits differ according to the situation. This argument neatly combines both situational and personal influences on pro-social behaviour. At the beginning of this chapter it was noted that both pro-social and anti-social behaviour are affected by some of the same variables. In the following sections, anti-social behaviour is considered in detail.

9.6 Anti-social behaviour

In discussing pro-social behaviour, it was noted that an actor's intentions are critical in determining whether helping behaviour is altruistic. With regard to anti-social behaviour, aggression always includes the intention to cause harm (Smith and Mackie, 1995). Although it is easy to spot examples of aggression in everyday life (rough games in the playground, sports fixtures that turn into violent encounters), the phenomenon is not so easy to study. Many studies of aggression rely on using children as participants. Studies involving adult participants usually centre around participants administering fake electric shocks to confederates of the experimenter and, curiously, little research has been carried out on a very common type of aggression, verbal aggression involving taunts and insults. However, research on aggression has produced some important findings that are tackled in this section. First, however, it is useful to revisit the definition of aggression.

9.6.1 Defining aggression

We are all aware of and affected by the violence in our society. In fact Jones *et al.* (1994) found that fully 20 per cent of a 10,000 strong sample of British women were afraid of walking alone at night for fear of violent attack and there is no doubt that violence has an impact on all our lives. Classifying aggressive acts is not easy, but the general consensus is that aggressive behaviour is intended to injure another person, physically or psychologically. As we have seen with research on pro-social behaviour, discovering another person's intentions is tricky as these are private mental events. Instead, we have to rely on our interpretation of the behaviour, a process that is essentially subjective.

Two main types of aggression have been identified: *emotional aggression* and *instrumental aggression*. Emotional aggression involves the wish to hurt the other person. People in the wild clutches of emotional aggression often lash out at others, seemingly oblivious to the consequences of their actions. You can witness emotional aggression at work in opposing football fans who attack each other with anything that comes to hand, or in the spurned lover who jealously hits out at his former partner. Yet emotional aggression need not take place in such heated circumstances; people who seek revenge on others can often act in a calm measured way with equally devastating results. Consider the case of Lady Moon, who carefully distributed the valuable contents of her errant husband's wine cellar around her home village after he left her for another woman. Instrumental aggression is carried out in order to achieve a specific goal. Robbing someone of a purse or a fashionable jacket are examples of instrumental aggression, as is hacking into a computer system for personal gain. The following sections trace theories that attempt to account for aggressive human behaviour, a task which began many centuries ago (Geen and Donnerstein, 1983).

9.6.2 Genetic factors in anti-social behaviour

As with pro-social behaviour, arguments continue about whether aggression is an innate biological drive. Debate centres on four main approaches: instinct theories, sociobiology, behaviour genetics and gender differences.

9.6.3 Instinct theories

Instinct theories of human aggression propose that the impetus for aggression is an innate force. If this is the case, then we are programmed to respond aggressively to situations, and while aggressive behaviour can be modified, its basis, the drive, cannot. Freud (1930) was the earliest to propose an instinct explanation for aggression. After witnessing the terrible loss of life of the First World War, he came to believe that all aggressive behaviour springs from a destructive death instinct, *thanatos*, the opposing force to the life instinct, *eros*. *Thanatos* represents an unconscious wish to escape the tensions of life by dying, and is originally directed towards the self before being channelled towards others. Freud was heavily influenced by the theories of physics of his age, and believed that tensions arising from *thanatos* built up to unbearable proportions before being unleashed as a powerful aggressive force. Oddly, Freud saw outbursts of aggression as a fleeting victory for *eros*, the drive for self-preservation.

Like Freud, Konrad Lorenz (1966) saw aggression as an innate drive. Lorenz saw self-preservation and aggression as symbiotic. Lorenz observed that animals are much more aggressive to members of their own species, resulting in the best distribution of resources such as food and mates. In addition, he found that aggressive behaviour depends on the presence of certain stimuli, known as *releasers*, in the environment.

In extending his theory to humans, Lorenz proposed that we must possess a fighting instinct. While animals have developed formidable fighting tools such as large sharp claws and teeth, they have also developed a range of *appeasement gestures* that act to limit and eventually stop aggression from another animal. Humans have no such natural tools, nor do we own a range of appeasement gestures to limit violence. An unfortunate consequence is that once people begin to behave aggressively they appear not to know when to stop. Instinct theories of aggression have little current value, mainly because they involve circular reasoning. According to instinct theorists, we behave aggressively because we possess an aggressive instinct. We know we must have an aggressive instinct because we behave aggressively. The claims made by instinct theorists are not empirically testable and are considerably weakened because of this. In addition, claiming that aggression is 'natural' does not mean that it is 'right' and instinct theorists fail to account for moral reasoning, which was discussed in Chapter 7.

9.6.4 Sociobiology

In section 9.3.1, the point was made that people may help one another to ensure the survival of their genes. The same argument is proposed by the sociobiological approach to human aggression. It contrasts with Lorenz's approach since it focuses on *genetic survival* rather than survival of the individual. According to sociobiologists, aggression is an adaptive behaviour that has developed as a means of increasing access to resources. The resource most strongly competed for is access to a mate rather than land or food, since although both of these are necessary for survival, procreation is essential if one's genes are to survive. Blood relatives share our genes. The sociobiological approach would predict, therefore, that we would behave aggressively less against these people. Daly and Wilson (1988) provide some support for the theory. The researchers found that natural parents are much less likely to harm or murder their offspring (who of course share their genes) than stepparents are to abuse their step-children. However, the sociobiological approach to human behaviour is an extremely controversial one. Perhaps the most potent criticism of the sociobiological account of aggression can be levelled at the claim that aggression is innate and *universal* (i.e. applies to all societies). This cannot be the case, since there is a great deal of cultural and historical diversity in the display of aggression (Ruback and Weiner, 1995). For example, over recent years the biggest cause of death among American teenagers is suicide and homicide (Howard, 1990; Ozer, 1998). No other country in the world comes close to these levels. Aggression cannot, therefore, be driven purely by its evolutionary value; social factors must be the primary influence (Lore and Schultz, 1993). Figure 9.8 shows the cultural range of aggressive behaviours.

9.6.5 Behaviour genetics

Research on *behaviour genetics* focuses on the connections between genetic inheritance and behaviour, neatly side stepping the difficult and ambitious task of sociobiology, which attempts to include evolution in the equation. Researchers in the field of genetic inheritance look at differences between individuals or groups of people. The most effective way of examining the consequences of genetic inheritance is to look at twins and adopted children.

In twin studies, monozygotic twins are compared with dizygotic twins. Monozygotic twins develop from the same fertilised egg and share 100 per cent of their genes in common, while dizygotic twins develop from two separate eggs and share only the same amount of

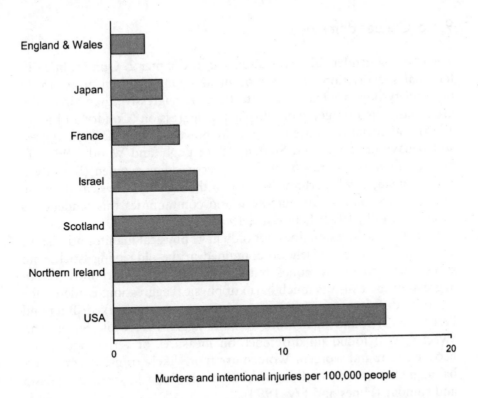

Figure 9.8: Different levels of violence across different countries. From Lore and Schultz (1993)

genes as any other sibling pair. So, if a trait is inherited, monozygotic twins will display more similarity on the trait than dizygotic twins will. Unfortunately, twin studies of aggression have provided mixed results and no firm conclusions can be drawn (Yoshikawa, 1994).

Some interesting research findings are reported from studies of adopted children. In these cases, for any inherited trait, adopted children will be more like their biological parents, who provide their genes, than their adopted parents. Mednick and Kandel (1988) examined the criminal records of adopted children in Denmark, as well as the criminal records of their biological and adoptive parents. Men are more likely to be convicted of crimes than women and for this reason females were excluded from Mendick and Kandel's study. The researchers showed that for property crimes (burglary, etc.) the adopted children's behaviour was positively correlated with that of their biological parents. However, for violent crimes (assault, etc.) there was no relationship. On this evidence, the behaviour genetics approach provides little support for the view that aggression is an inherited part of one's character.

9.6.6 Gender differences

The effect of gender roles was discussed in Chapter 2. Quite subtle differential socialisation processes occur as young children grow up. In our society boys are encouraged to be more aggressive than girls, who are usually discouraged from displaying aggression (Condry and Ross, 1985) and social roles are enormously powerful influences on aggressive behaviour (Eagly and Steffen, 1986; Eagly and Wood, 1991). In general, men are more *physically* aggressive than women (Bjorkqvist and Niemela, 1992) perhaps because of their greater physical strength. However, in some small, remote island communities this tendency is reversed (Cook, 1992; Lepowsky, 1994).

Of course, aggression does not only have physical manifestations; we are all aware of the falsehood contained in the old saying 'sticks and stones may break my bones but names will never hurt me'. *Verbal* aggression can cause as much harm of physical aggression. Evidence for a gender difference in verbal aggression is somewhat mixed; Buss and Perry (1992) found men more verbally aggressive, while Straus and Sweet (1992) found no difference on measures of verbal aggression between men and women. Women are more likely to use *indirect* verbal aggression such as talking behind another's back, spreading gossip and rumour (Hines and Fry, 1994).

How can these gender differences in aggression be accounted for? One possible explanation rests on biological factors including sex hormones and physique. While the male sex hormone testosterone circulates in the bloodstream of both men and women, men have much higher levels than women. The link between testosterone and aggression has been shown in a number of studies. Dabbs *et al.* (1988) found that both males and females imprisoned for violent crime had higher levels of testosterone than prisoners who had not committed violent crime. Berman *et al.* (1993) found that among male students, those with higher testosterone levels acted more aggressively on the experimental task.

However, these studies show a correlation between high levels of testosterone and aggressive behaviour, and correlation cannot prove a causal connection. Some researchers have proposed that aggressive behaviour increases testosterone levels (Baron and Richardson, 1994). In addition, social factors appear to influence the role of testosterone in aggression. For example, Dabbs *et al.* (1990) found that high testosterone levels are more strongly associated with aggressive behaviour among those of lower socioeconomic status. Also, the male physique could account for gender differences in aggression. It is much less risky to be aggressive when you have the muscles and bulk to back up your actions!

9.7 Social learning approaches to anti-social behaviour

In the approaches outlined above, aggression is seen as the inevitable product of factors either in the person or in the environment. However, an alternative view is that like pro-social behaviour, anti-social behaviour can also be learned. In an important series of studies, Bandura and his colleagues investigated the effect of social learning (acquiring and maintaining a behaviour) on aggression. While Bandura accepts the influence of biology on behaviour, his research is directed at examining the influence of experience, either *direct* or *vicarious*. The notion of *learning by direct experience* is derived from Skinner's principles of operant (instrumental) conditioning. If Peter grabs Tony's model car and no adult steps in, having the car now positively reinforces Peter. If Peter subsequently teases Tony and leaves the scene after Tony thumps him, Tony is negatively reinforced by the removal of the negative stimulus, Peter and his teasing. Both Peter and Tony have found that aggression works.

The notion of *learning by vicarious experience* is associated with imitating the behaviour of models. Using a variety of models, Bandura *et al.* (1963) examined the most effective means of learning aggression through observation. The researchers had children aged four and five years old observe a Bobo doll (an inflatable toy popular at the time) being aggressively treated in four conditions:

1 **Live**   An adult model came into the room where the child was playing and after a short while began to hit and kick the doll and strike it with a mallet, all the while keeping up a stream of verbally aggressive comments.

2 **Videotape**   As the live condition, except that the children saw the action on videotape.

3 **Cartoon**   An adult model acted identically to the live condition but wore an animal costume. The room was decorated as if in a cartoon.

4 **Control**   The child was allowed to play with the Bobo doll without witnessing any aggression towards it.

Results from the study are shown in Figure 9.9.

The live condition provided the most effective means of modelling aggressive behaviour, possibly because the child perceived the adult as a useful provider of information about appropriate behaviour. However, the finding that both the videotape and cartoon conditions provided effective models for aggressive behaviours caused concern about the effects of violence portrayed on television. This topic will be discussed in the Application section of this chapter.

Of particular concern is the fear that if violence is learned by imitation, it can be transmitted across generations by this means (Huesmann *et al.*, 1984). A more recent example of the effects of modelling on aggression occurred in 1992 when four white policemen were declared

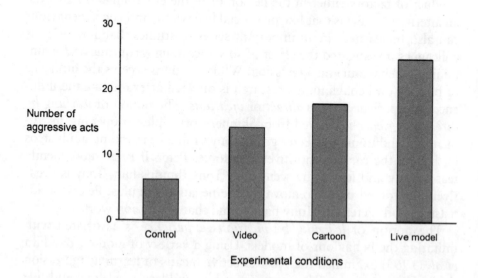

Figure 9.9: Learning to behave aggressively by watching others: effects of watching a violent model on children's behaviour. Adapted from Bandura *et al.* (1963)

not guilty of assaulting an African American, Rodney King. Rioting quickly spread after small-scale scuffles were shown on American television (Mydans, 1992). Equally tragic is the well-documented finding that children from abusive homes often grow up to abuse their own children.

9.7.1 Norms of anti-social behaviour

As with pro-social behaviour, *norms of aggression* also exist. These are pervasive and often the product of a particular subculture. For example, among Chicago adolescents it is wrong to show disrespect to other youths in the neighbourhood (Smith and Mackie, 1995). The normative response to disrespect is extreme violence, including murder (Terry, 1993). Among schoolboys, the popularity accorded to aggressive boys establishes a norm of accepting violence (Price and Dodge, 1989). Norms are not only restricted to young people; often norms promoting aggression are used in the competitive worlds of business among smartly dressed executives too.

Cultural norms often serve to promote aggression. Probably one of the most common is the *norm of reciprocity* that condones retaliation in kind to aggressive behaviour. (Although in Japan retaliation is frowned upon, Alcock *et al.*, 1988). The American constitution contains a popular clause – the right to bear firearms and to use them – which remains hotly defended despite the alarming rates of homicide in that country, especially among young black males (Ozer, 1998). The *norm of male aggression*, prevalent in American and Southern European culture, also endorses aggressive behaviour. In these countries the male is admired much more for being 'macho' than in Northern European countries, including England (Block, 1973). Earlier we noted that the *norm of social responsibility*, tempered by the *norm of justice*, influences whether help was offered. One of the key reasons for avoiding giving help is the *norm of family privacy*. This norm seems to condone aggression in domestic situations by excluding violent behaviour among family members from norms encouraging pro-social behaviour. For example, we often feel unwilling to intervene in an altercation between a couple, because we assume that they are husband and wife. Also, we are unlikely to intervene if we see a woman strike a child in public, assuming she is its mother. Unfortunately the norm of family privacy ensures that violence within the family is not challenged, often supporting domestic violence (Sherman and Berk, 1984).

9.8 Situational factors in anti-social behaviour

Sociobiologists may argue for the existence of an innate biological propensity for anti-social behaviour, and social learning theorists may propose ways in which aggression can be learnt. However, it is also true that situational influences play a role in aggressive behaviour. In this section, the effect of the physical environment, frustration and social status on aggression will be examined.

9.8.1 Environmental conditions

Researchers have found an association between stressful environmental conditions and aggression (Bell, 1992), particularly between temperature and aggression and crowding and aggression. Riots are more likely to happen when there are moderate rather then extreme rises in temperature (Baron and Richardson, 1994) and crowded conditions in prisons lead to an escalation of violence (Paulus, 1988). Other environmental factors also increase aggression, including air pollution (Zillman *et al.*, 1981) and noise (Geen and McCown, 1984). It is interesting to note that in many public houses and bars, all of these noxious environmental conditions are present, together with alcohol. Perhaps it is not surprising that tempers flare on a hot Saturday night.

9.8.2 Frustration

Unless you are a saintly soul, when someone prevents you from achieving a goal, say by driving very slowly in front of you when you are late for a lecture, or playing loud music when the deadline for your psychology essay is one hour away, you will feel *frustrated*. In the 1930s, an influential book, *Frustration and Aggression*, was published by the Yale Group of Psychologists, led by Dollard (1939). The Yale Group proposed that aggression is always the result of frustration, and their work led to the *frustration-aggression hypothesis*. Dollard *et al.* (1939) argued that the motive for aggression is a psychological drive, which is provoked by frustration. Once we experience frustration, we will seek to lash out at the cause of the frustration. The reason we do not always act aggressively in response to frustration, continued Dollard, is either because the source of the frustration is not present (the slow driver may turn off at the next junction) or because we fear retaliation from the other person (the music next door may be emanating from an Arnold Schwarzenegger look-alike). However, the researchers argued that the urge to behave aggressively is not lost but is *displaced* until a more suitable time and target is available. The old saying that you go home and kick the cat at the end of a particularly bad day has been adopted in a more humane way by some Japanese companies, who provide a replica of the boss that workers can take their frustration out on. Activities such as bashing a replica of the boss or watching violent sports provide, it is argued, *catharsis*: an experience during which relief from the stressor is achieved and aggressive tendencies are reduced.

The Yale Group's model of aggression has been heavily criticised on the grounds of providing an over-simplistic account of aggression. In addition, the concept of frustration is loosely specified and does not adequately predict which types of frustrating experiences lead to aggression. Since not all instances of frustration lead to aggression, it is possible that both personal and environmental factors mediate its effects. The cathartic effects of displacement have also been seriously questioned. Observation of violence increases aggressive tendencies (Bandura and Walters, 1963), and while expressed aggression can lower arousal levels, aggressive intentions towards the source of the frustration can still remain to be acted upon later. If a reduction in unpleasant arousal is gained through an aggressive act, the act is negatively reinforcing and, therefore, likely to be repeated. Finally, carrying out minor acts of aggression may lower personal standards restricting violent behaviour.

Zillman (1979) provides a later model of aggressive behaviour. On this account, aggression depends on three variables: learned behaviour; excitation from an external source; and interpretation of the excitation defining an aggressive response as appropriate. Any arousing experience can lead to aggression since excitation from a previous situation can spill over into another. Zillman's theory has much in common with the finding, discussed in Chapter 7, that males made fearful by crossing an unsteady bridge subsequently showed higher levels of attraction to a female researcher. Imagine that a student has just taken part in a strenuous aerobics class. Immediately afterwards, still in a state of heightened physical arousal, another student bumps into her in the corridor, sending her pile of books crashing to the floor. Usually this sort of event would be irritating and no more, but the residual excitation from the aerobics class spills over and the student yells at her clumsy colleague. See the example shown in Figure 9.10.

Zillman's model refers to the combined effect of arousal and emotion. His later model, the *arousal-affect* model (Zillman, 1983), examines the type of emotion and the intensity of physiological arousal in aggression. The researchers found that experiences that elicit negative emotions increase aggression, and if physiological arousal is high, aggression increases further. Experiences that have no strong emotional affect also have no effect on aggression, unless physiological arousal is high, in which case aggression increases. Positive emotional experiences and low arousal decrease aggression, but couple positive emotional experiences with high physiological arousal and either an increase *or* a decrease in aggression occurs, depending on individual responses. Table 9.1 shows the arousal-affect model.

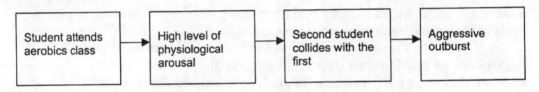

Figure 9.10: The excitation-transfer model of aggression proposed by Zillman (1979)

Physiological arousal	Type of emotion		
	Negative	**Neutral**	**Positive**
Low	Increased aggression	No effect	Decreased aggression
High	Large increase in aggression	Increased aggression	Increased *or* decreased aggression

Table 9.1: The arousal-affect model of aggression of Zillman (1983)

9.8.3 Social status

Those in lower socio-economic groups show a heightened link between testosterone levels and aggressive behaviour when compared with other groups (Dabbs and Morris, 1990). However, the social conditions which people live in can also affect aggression. *Relative deprivation* occurs when people compare their socio-economic status with that of others in their society and conclude that they are badly off. If it is impossible or difficult to redress the balance by legal means, members of the deprived group may act aggressively. Throughout history, many revolutions have begun in this way. It has been suggested that the Los Angeles riots following the acquittal of policemen accused of beating Rodney King were underpinned by a sense of relative deprivation among the rioters (Hogg and Vaughan, 1995).

9.9 Personal characteristics in anti-social behaviour

Behaviour is the product both of the environment *and* the individual; *personal characteristics* can affect anti-social behaviour. Three characteristics – personality, cognitive control and disinhibition – will be discussed here.

9.9.1 Personality

If you think about the people you know, you may consider one or two of them to have an 'aggressive personality'; they seem to react sharply to almost anything and are generally considered to be 'touchy'. Researchers have identified a type of personality known as *Type A* (Matthews, 1982), characterised by extreme competitiveness, over-activity and a sense of time pressure. This personality type is associated with increased levels of coronary heart disease and with a high level of aggression (Carver and Glass, 1978), especially towards peers and subordinates in a business setting (Baron, 1989). Those with established aggressive behaviour patterns may interpret ambiguous situations as deliberately provoking; this is especially true of aggressive children (Dodge and Crick, 1990). Aggressive children typically interpret accidental events in the playground as intentional, and may retaliate violently, thereby perpetuating a cycle of aggressive behaviour.

Deficits in *social reasoning ability* also support aggressive acts. Social reasoning ability, akin to moral reasoning, becomes more sophisticated with age. Krebs and Miller (1985) found consistent individual differences in levels of aggression over time, suggesting that some people are less able than others to think of non-aggressive ways of settling a provoking situation. Children who fail to produce peaceful potential solutions to problem situations show more aggression than children who are able to think up non-aggressive solutions (Huesmann *et al.*, 1987; Dodge and Crick, 1990).

9.9.2 Cognitive control

As noted above, reasoning ability determines aggressive behaviour to a certain extent and perception of intent is critical to the decision to retaliate aggressively or not. Imagine that as you walk through crowds of Christmas shoppers, someone collides sharply with you. You are understandably annoyed, but how do you feel if they apologise? Even though you may still feel annoyed, you are much less likely to respond aggressively following an apology (Ohbuchi *et al.*, 1989). This is because saying 'sorry' provides *mitigating information* indicating that the act was not intentional. In law, mitigating information is used when a person is judged not responsible for their actions by reason of insanity. In everyday situations, we tend to be more lenient towards people who upset us if we know they are experiencing difficult personal circumstances.

In some situations cognitive processing is adversely affected. For example, the arousal-affect model shows that intense emotional states can affect aggression. However, one of the most potent influences on cognitive control is alcohol consumption. Laplace *et al.* (1994) showed that alcohol increases the propensity towards aggression, especially in inexperienced drinkers. The researchers found that intoxicated participants delivered more fake shocks to confederates than non-intoxicated participants. In a similar study Taylor and Sears (1988) found that not only were intoxicated participants more likely to administer shocks, but they were also more susceptible to social pressure to continue the shocks. Alcohol has also been implicated as a cause of sexual assault (Gillen and Muncer, 1995). Alcohol reduces cognitive processing abilities because it leads people to miss cues that would inhibit aggressive behaviour (Steele and Josephs, 1990). Transfer these research findings to a busy bar at the weekend, and it is not difficult to imagine the consequences. However, an alternative theory is that stress contributes both to alcohol consumption and to aggression, and that violent people tend to consume large quantities of alcohol (Bradbury, 1984).

9.9.3 Disinhibition

Part of the reason people serve alcohol at social functions is that in small doses it lowers social inhibitions, allowing people to relax more freely. Large doses of alcohol can lead to complete *disinhibition*. The term refers to a reduction in the social influences that usually restrain people from anti-social behaviour. Disinhibition can occur in three main ways: *deindividuation, dehumanisation* and *collective aggression*.

Deindividuation occurs when individuals see themselves as anonymous components of a large group. In these cases, the possibility of punishment for even seriously aggressive behaviour seems remote. Deindividuation is the product of environmental cues including accountability and anonymity. If people cannot be held accountable for their actions and thus can escape punishment, they are more likely to carry out anti-social acts. Dodd (1985) found that when asked what they would do if they could be invisible for 24 hours, most students said they would rob a bank. A series of research studies have found that guaranteed anonymity leads to increased aggression (Zimbardo, 1970), and that men at women behave aggressively at the same level when anonymous (Lightdale and Prentice, 1994). Deindividuation has led to acts of unspeakable horror, including Japanese atrocities against the Chinese population, attacks on women and children by American troops in Vietnam, and more recently the slaughter of thousands of Tutsi people by the rival Hutus in Rwanda.

9.10 Application: aggression and the media _____

The impact of the mass media, and in particular television and films, has come under intense scrutiny as a potential cause of violence. National newspapers report many cases where murderers, rapists and robbers have claimed to have been inspired to commit their crimes by watching filmed violence. Recently an Oliver Stone movie, *Natural Born Killers*, was implicated as the impetus for two young people to engage in a violent killing spree. But is there any solid evidence to support the claim that watching violent action increases aggression?

Research on this topic has suffered from problems of methodology, since testing for the effects of media violence has typically involved participants viewing mild aggression for a short period of time (Freedman, 1984). Nevertheless, the work of Bandura (1963, 1986) demonstrated that viewing filmed models increases children's aggression, particularly when the model is reinforced for aggressive behaviour or escapes punishment. Heymann (1989) found that American children typically watch three and a half hours of TV per day, seeing an average of 33 incidents of violence in that time. Cartoons are among the most violent programmes, with an average of 20 violent acts per hour (Gerbner *et al.*, 1986). This is worrying considering the effect on children of viewing an aggressive cartoon character (Bandura and Walters, 1963). In addition, aggressors in movies are often the heroes of the action, and the injuries they inflict on others are usually sanitised for the camera, thus distorting the effects of aggression.

Several other types of studies have found an association between viewing violence and behaving aggressively. Singer and Singer (1981) asked parents how much television their young children watched, and then visited the children in school and rated their behaviour. The researchers found that children who behaved most aggressively viewed the most television violence. However, we must be careful about drawing the obvious conclusion here. Perhaps children who watched the most TV were also neglected by their parents, thereby fostering aggressive behaviour. In a study of delinquent boys, Parke *et al.* (1977) found that viewing violent films increased the number of times the boys behaved aggressively. Huesmann and Eron (1986) carried out a longitudinal study in which he traced people's viewing habits across 22 years. They found that the more screen violence a person watched at eight years old, the more likely they were to be convicted of violent crime by age 30.

Sheehan (1983) found that viewing television violence was associated with peer ratings of aggressive behaviour for 8–10-year-old boys.

However, no effect of younger age viewing habits and later aggression was found. The best predictors of later aggression were parenting practices, the child's own ratings of their aggression and the child's use of violent fantasies. So, viewing television violence was simply one of a number of variables contributing to aggressive behaviour. Nevertheless, many studies have shown a general connection between viewing violence and behaving aggressively (Leibert and Sprafkin, 1988; Hearold, 1986), and the effect is long-lasting.

Why should watching violent scenes encourage aggressive behaviour? Berkowitz (1984) provides a *neo-associationist analysis* of this

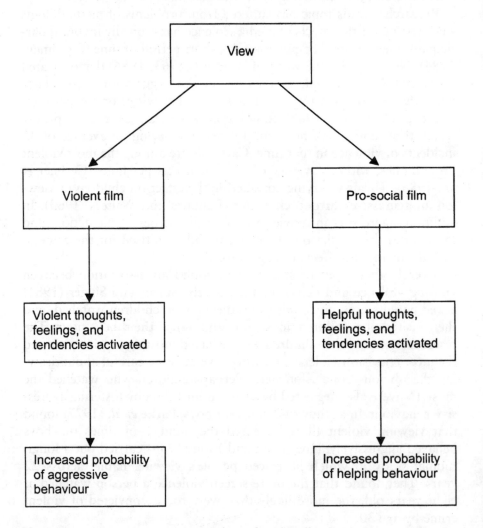

Figure 9.11: A neo-associationist analysis of media effects on behaviour. After Berkowitz (1984)

phenomenon. This theory is based on the belief that as we process information, we automatically react to its content (in this case aggressive acts) and later translate the thoughts elicited by viewing violence into anti-social acts. (It is interesting to note that the neo-associationist theory also proposes that viewing pro-social acts encourages helpful behaviour.) The theory borrows from cognitive psychological theory and proposes that memory consists of a series of nodes, linked via associative pathways. As we think, various nodes associated with the thought are activated. For example, suppose you were watching a film showing a violent murder. As you watch, related thoughts about knives, guns, blood and injuries are likely to be activated automatically, leading to emotional arousal. The probability of committing an aggressive act is elevated (Phillips, 1986). Berkowitz's model is shown in Figure 9.11. However, not everyone who watches a violent movie leaves the cinema and behaves aggressively, so clearly other factors play a role too.

9.11 Summary

- The same variables underlie acts of both pro-social and anti-social behaviour. Perception and interpretation of situations, modelling from others, social norms and influence both pro-social and anti-social behaviours.
- Defining pro-social and anti-social behaviour depends on the *motives* of the actor. *Altruistic* behaviour is motivated by the wish to help someone else rather than yourself and is a subcategory of *helping* behaviour, which involves an intentional act to benefit someone else. Pro-social behaviour consists of any act that carries a positive value in society.
- Aggression consists of *emotional aggression* (lashing out at another person) and *instrumental aggression* (causing harm in order to achieve a goal).
- Sociobiological theories attempt to explain social behaviour in terms of genetic inheritance and evolution. This approach proposes that we have an innate tendency to help others possibly as an evolutionary survival strategy.
- The *social learning* approach proposes that social behaviour is learned through observing the actions and responses of others. Methods of social learning include instructions, reinforcement, observation and modelling.
- Social norms such as *reciprocity, social responsibility, equity, justice and personal norms* influence helping behaviour. *Empathy* is one of the strongest influences on helping behaviour and includes *perspective taking, personal distress* and *empathetic concern*.
- Situational factors such as the bystander effect have a powerful influence on helping behaviour. *Personal characteristics* can also affect pro-social behaviour and are generally considered under two categories: mood and personality.

- As with pro-social behaviour, arguments continue about whether aggression is an innate biological drive. Debate centres on four main approaches: instinct theories, sociobiology, behaviour genetics and gender differences.
- Like pro-social behaviour, anti-social behaviour can also be learned. Research has shown that people can learn to behave aggressively either by *direct experience* or by *vicarious experience*.
- *Norms of aggression* exist and these include *reciprocity*, *male aggression* and *family privacy*. The Yale Group proposed that aggression is always the result of frustration, and their work led to the *frustration-aggression hypothesis*.
- Researchers have found an association between stressful environmental conditions, social conditions and relative deprivation and aggression.
- Personality differences including Type A behaviour patterns, social reasoning and cognitive control affect aggressive behaviour.
- Disinhibition increases aggression and occurs in three main ways: *deindividuation*, *dehumanisation* and *collective aggression*.
- Viewing screen violence encourages aggressive behaviour.

9.12 Suggestions for further reading

Baron, R. A. and Richardson, D. R. 1994: *Human Aggression*. 2nd edition. New York: Plenum.

Engaging introductory level text.

Batson, C. D. 1991: *The Altruism Question: Toward a Social-Psychological Answer*. Hillsdale, NJ: Lawrence Erlbaum.

Develops the empathy altruism hypothesis and provides supporting evidence.

Phillips, D. P. 1986: Natural experiments on the effects of mass media violence on fatal aggression: strengths and weaknesses of a new approach. In Berkowitz, L. (ed.), *Advances in Experimental Social Psychology* 19, 207–50. New York: Academic Press.

A useful review of the effects of mass media on aggressive behaviour.

Tedeschi, J. T. and Felson, R. B. 1995: *Aggression and Coercive Actions: A Social Interactionist Perspective*. Washington, DC: American Psychological Association.

A comprehensive critical review of current research and theory on aggression, and an account of the social interactionist perspective on aggression.

10 Prejudice, conflict and intergroup behaviour

10.1 Introduction

> 'International computer networks must not be used to peddle racist, threatening and abusive material', the Home Secretary said. 'The National Criminal Intelligence Service had a "key role" in bringing Internet racists to justice.'
>
> (*Guardian*, 15 September 1998, p. 4)

Prejudice and discrimination are so widespread in society that the Internet, as the above extract demonstrates, has to be policed to remove offensive, racist material. Religion, race, sexual orientation, gender, mental illness, people with learning or physical difficulties have been and remain objects of negative beliefs, attitudes and behaviour. Pick up any daily newspaper or watch a news programme on television and you will almost certainly come across examples of mistreatment of one person by another or one group by another group of people. Unfortunately history and current times provide numerous instances of mass slaughter, 'ethnic cleansing' and torture arising from prejudice and racial hatred. It seems, depressingly, that bad treatment of one group by another is an unchanging feature of all societies and likely to remain so. Why are people prejudiced and when does prejudice lead to discrimination and conflict? This chapter provides a social psychological perspective in attempting to answer this question and understand such human thought and behaviour. A fundamental assumption is that prejudice and discrimination are unjustified, since neither logical nor scientific grounds exist for one person or group of people to categorise themselves as either superior or inferior to another person or group of people.

This chapter looks at attempts by social psychologists to explain (a) how people become prejudiced; (b) what functions prejudice serves for the individual or group; and (c) how prejudice may be reduced. Consideration is given to explanations at an individual level, however, the emphasis and main focus of the chapter is on the theories of social identity and self-categorisation (Brown, 1995).

It is important to be aware of the distinction between prejudice and discrimination. *Prejudice* may be defined as 'an attitude that predisposes a person to think, feel, perceive an act in favourable or unfavourable ways towards a group or its individual members' (Secord and Backman, 1974). Notice this definition reflects the cognitive, affective and conative components of attitudes looked at in Chapter 3. We usually think of prejudice being about negative attitudes and emotions and while this is the case, prejudice can also be positive in these respects. This is especially so when we think in terms of in-groups and out-groups. As we shall see in Section 10.5, we think and act preferentially to groups we identify with (in-groups) and non-preferentially to groups we do not identify ourselves as members of (out-groups).

Discrimination may be defined as 'the inequitable treatment of individuals considered to belong to a particular social group' (Secord and Backman, 1974). As this definition implies, discrimination is the behavioural acts that usually result from a person's prejudiced attitudes. Discrimination of one group by another often leads to conflict developing between the two groups. Where one group is powerless, for example, the Jews at the hands of the Nazis in the Second World War, actual physical conflict may be at a minimum. Conflict is an extreme form of discrimination where either an intention to harm others or actual harm is carried out.

This chapter concentrates on social psychological approaches to prejudice, discrimination and conflict. Explanations at other levels, to take account of cultural, institutional and economic factors are also important. A sociological perspective sensitizes us to society, cultural and sub-cultural influences, and to understand fully why one group of people is negative towards another group, and in order to be able to do anything about it, the full context must be considered.

10.2 Types of prejudice and discrimination

As we have seen, prejudice and discrimination exist wherever people put themselves into social groupings and are categorised as such by others. In this section we shall look at racism, sexism and tokenism and some ways in which social psychologists have produced evidence of their existence. While this may be obvious from what we see around us in our social world, it is important to provide empirical evidence to support common-sense knowledge. Clearly evidence exists in more extreme types of discrimination since people are harmed and killed. However, prejudice and discrimination operate at many less observable and subtle ways to disadvantage (or advantage) certain groups of people.

10.2.1 Racism

Open or blatant racism is far less evident in modern, Western societies than it was perhaps 30 or 40 years ago; nevertheless it still does exist. Many countries have introduced laws against such behaviour and there is general social disapproval when somebody makes a racist remark. However, some social psychologists argue that what exists now is *modern racism* which is more subtle and less obvious to detect. Surin *et al.* (1995) claim that modern racism reveals itself in three ways: first, denial that minority groups are discriminated against these days; second, impatience and annoyance at the continued demands of minority groups to be treated equally; and third, resentment that minority groups may receive positive treatment or action. This is summarised in Figure 10.1.

Detecting modern racism presents significant challenges for social psychologists, and has mostly been investigated using unobtrusive measures of behaviour (Devine, 1989). For example, Franco and Maass (1996) analysed how people talk about characteristics associated with

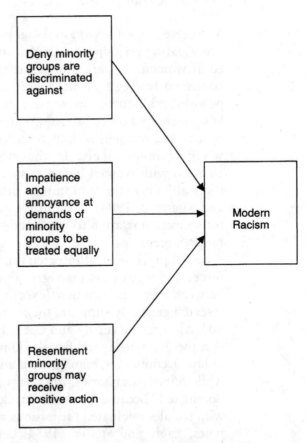

Figure 10.1: Three main components of modern racism – denial, impatience and resentment. After Surini (1991)

people belonging to an out-group that is regarded in a negative way. They found that people use more general and abstract words than when talking about out-group characteristics which are regarded as positive.

Modern racism is likely to be present in our justice system and social psychologists have conducted experiments using people to act as 'mock jurors' in making judgements about a case. For example, Gordon (1993) found that 'jurors' set higher bail for a black man accused of committing a violent crime than a white man accused of exactly the same crime. Pfeifer and Ogloff (1991) found that white university students who read a transcript of a rape case rated a black defendant as more guilty than a white defendant when not reminded to judge free of prejudice.

10.2.2 Sexism

Most research on sexism in social psychology has been concerned with investigating prejudicial attitudes and discriminative behaviour directed at women. Research on sex stereotypes has revealed a reasonably consistent finding that males are viewed as more competent and independent, and females as warmer and more expressive (Deaux, 1985). Sex stereotypes reflect, to some extent, traditional ideas about the roles of men and women, with men pursuing a career and women as housewives or homemakers. In the modern world much has obviously changed with women being as successful as men in careers and 'role reversals' where the man stays at home to look after the children. Eagly and Mladinic (1994) claim that a more positive stereotype now exists for women in relation to work and that women are generally liked better than men.

Social psychological research on, for example, women in the armed forces and women as managers finds little difference in performance between men and women (except on sheer physical strength). The research generally supports the idea that stereotypes about women do not reflect reality (Eagly and Carli, 1981). However, it remains the case that there are male- and female-dominated professions: the professions of law, accountancy, management and engineering are male-dominated, while nurses, secretaries, librarians and restaurant servers are female-dominated. Because of this it is likely that characteristics associated with female-dominated professions are transferred to female sex stereotypes. Eagly and Steffen (1984) demonstrated this in an experiment where male and female students were provided with a description of a male or female, depicting them as either in full-time employment or a 'homemaker'. A control condition was also included whereby the description of the male or female was given without information about employment or being at home. The ratings made were analysed according to degree of femininity or masculinity. As can be seen from Figure 10.2, home-makers were rated as more femi-nine by both male and female stu-dents.

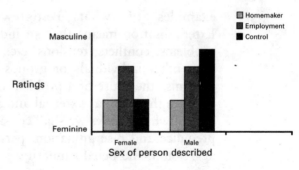

Figure 10.2: Rating of male or female described as either employed or a homemaker by college students. Adapted from Eagly and Steffen (1984)

Sexism may be less in Western societies than it was 20 or 30 years ago, however, it has not disap-peared. Laws prohibiting sex dis-crimination in the workplace have gone some way to help, but gender roles and sex stereotypes remain prevalent.

10.2.3 Tokenism

Tokenism is where positive action is taken by individuals, groups or organisations towards a member of a group to whom they are preju-diced. Having made a token gesture it is then used as an excuse to say that enough has been done to help the discriminated group. Summers (1991) provided evidence to show that people employed as token rep-resentatives of a group are viewed negatively by their fellow workers, thus re-establishing discrimination. Heilman *et al.* (1992) further demonstrated that potential employees who approved of affirmative action for discriminated against minority groups, were seen as less able by a selection panel than people not identified for affirmative action. Tokenism is a form of discrimination that should be avoided.

10.3 Individual explanations

Individual explanations of prejudice and discrimination regard the causes as resulting from emotional dynamics within a person. This ful-fils certain needs for the person, such as reducing tension or satisfying a need for order and control in his or her life. Two types of explana-tion are possible: where prejudice is seen to (a) result from a distinct type of personality; and (b) be rooted in the make-up of *all* people. With the former we search for *differences* in personality; with the lat-ter people are regarded as essentially the same, since frustration is an inevitable feature of daily life for everybody. These two types of expla-nation share an important common feature, though – they are both examples of what Pettigrew (1959) calls *externalisation*. Externalisation means that an individual deals with his or her inner problems, conflicts, tensions, etc., by discharging or projecting them onto other individuals or groups of people. That is, people do not recognise the cause of a problem or conflict as being within them but perceive the cause as external and a feature of the world in which they live. In what follows we shall consider three individual explanations of prejudice and discrimination: personality differences, frustration and aggression, and belief similarity.

10.3.1 Personality differences

Is there a distinct personality style that is strongly associated with prejudiced attitudes? Adorno and his colleagues, 1950) suggested that such attitudes are to be found in individuals with an *authoritarian personality*. The authoritarian personality, they claim, both submits to the authority of others higher in status or power and is, at the same time, authoritarian with those 'beneath' or lower in status than him or her. Authoritarian parents are authoritarian with their children who in turn tend to be authoritarian in bringing up their children. In short, such a personality is characterised by excessive and blind obedience to authority. To establish the validity of these claims two questions need to be answered: (a) does such a personality style exist? and (b) is such a personality style associated with prejudice?

Adorno *et al.* were initially concerned with constructing a questionnaire to measure anti-Semitism. This was in the early 1940s when anti-Semitism was most viciously expressed in Nazi Germany. From an attitude scale measuring a particular type of prejudice Adorno *et al.* turned their attention to constructing an attitude questionnaire measuring prejudice in general, known as *ethnocentrism*. Anti-Semitism, then, is simply one manifestation of ethnocentrism. Research with these two questionnaires led Adorno to propose a link between political ideology and personality. This was the authoritarian personality which was characterised as manifesting itself as anti-democratic and potentially fascist in beliefs and attitudes. Sandford (1956) called this the F-syndrome ('F' standing for fascist) and developed a personality questionnaire, known as the F-scale, to measure authoritarianism. Much of the theory used in constructing the questionnaire derived from Freudian theory. The F-scale is made up of nine components (such as conventionalism, authoritarian submission, superstition, preoccupation with power, puritanical sexual attitudes) with four or five questions to do with each component. Some examples of the questions are given in Table 10.1. The F-scale was

Component of F-scale	Example of question from F-scale
Conventionalism	Obedience and respect for authority are the most important virtues children should learn
Superstition	Some day it will probably be shown that astrology can explain a lot of things
Puritanical sexual attitudes	Homosexuality is a particularly rotten form of delinquency and ought to be severely punished

Table 10.1: Examples of questions from three components of the F-scale. From Sanford (1956)

constructed, as the examples show, such that a positive answer scored a point and was taken as an indicator of an authoritarian personality. The higher the score, the more a person is deemed to have an authoritarian personality.

Adorno *et al*. then looked at the extent to which a person with an authoritarian personality was likely to be anti-Semitic and ethnocentric. Both the original and subsequent research (Christie and Cook, 1958) have shown a consistent positive correlation between the three factors measured by these questionnaires. A strong positive relationship was found to exist between authoritarianism and ethnocentrism, authoritarianism and political and economic conservatism, and authoritarianism and fascist potentials. However, methodological and conceptual problems have questioned the validity of this type of individual explanation of prejudice and discrimination (Brown, 1988).

The major *methodological* problem is that the F-scale (and, for that matter, the ethnocentrism and anti-Semitism questionnaires) is worded in such a way that agreement with an item is taken as an indication of authoritarianism (ethnocentrism or anti-Semitism with the other questionnaires). The danger with this is that it encourages what is known as an 'acquiescent response set' – the tendency people often display of agreeing with whatever is said. Hence we cannot be sure that a high score on the F-scale is a strong indication of authoritarianism; it could simply be a measure of the extent to which a person acquiesces. To some extent authoritarianism and acquiescence are related, but the authoritarian personality, as conceptualised by Adorno *et al*. is also politically conservative, and intolerant of ambiguity. Methodological problems can be overcome by reconstructing the questionnaire in a balanced way, but conceptual problems are less easy to deal with.

One conceptual problem, raised by Hyman and Sheatsley (1954), is that a personality type is *not* needed to explain ethnocentrism since education and socio-economic status offer a more plausible explanation. Hyman and Sheatsley found that the authoritarian personality is more likely to exist amongst the less well educated and those of low socio-economic status. Table 10.2 shows that the percentage agreement with questions from the F-scale decreases as educational levels increase.

A further problem is that the authoritarian personality was assumed to be associated solely with fascism or, more generally, extreme right-wing political conservatism. Rokeach (1960) argued that authoritarianism can as easily be associated with the extreme left as extreme right political wings. Rokeach claims that the important feature of authoritarians of both the left and right is they have *closed minds*, i.e. rigid styles of thought with intolerance of views different from their own. This he calls *dogmatism*. Rokeach hypothesised that *both* Communists and extreme right-wing conservatives should score high on his dogmatism questionnaire. He administered this questionnaire to Conservative, Liberal, Labour and Communist English college students. Results supported the hypothesis that dogmatism is found at both political extremes since he found both Conservatives and Communists to score higher than the other political groups. However, this research is not without its problems since, for example, all 40 items on the dogmatism questionnaire are worded such that agreement indicates dogmatism. The problem of acquiescent response set, as with the F-scale, throws doubt on the validity of the questionnaire. Rokeach

Item from F-scale questionnaire	College	High school	Grammar school*
The most important thing to teach children is absolute obedience to their parents	35	60	80
Any good leader should be strict with people under him in order to gain respect	36	51	45
Prison is too good for sex criminals. They should be publicly whipped or worse	18	31	45
No decent man can respect a woman who has had sexual relations before marriage	14	26	39

Note: *School intermediate between primary and high school

Table 10.2: Percentage of people who agreed with items on the F-scale according to level of education. From Hyman and Sheatsley (1954)

does, though, take an important step forward in the search for a prejudiced personality by separating authoritarianism from political ideology.

The authoritarian personality has remained of consistent interest to social psychologists over the past 50 years, and while there are serious flaws with the approach, it may be that the idea of such a personality type appeals to our everyday explanations of behaviour. For example, you can probably think of a number of people you regard as authoritarian; given this, the approach is intuitively appealing.

Eysenck (1954) proposed that *two* personality dimensions, not one as with Adorno and Rokeach, were needed to characterise similarities and differences between extreme left-wing (radical) and right-wing (conservative) adherents. Eysenck called one dimension *radicalism–conservatism* and the other *tough-minded/tender-minded*. A tender-minded person believes in such things as the abolition of the death penalty, re-education of criminals and pacifism. A tough-minded person, by contrast, is seen as being in favour of, for example, the death penalty, prison and punishment, and compulsory sterilisation of people with serious hereditary defects. With these two dimensions (radical–conservative and tough-minded/tender-minded), Eysenck located the positions of different political parties: this is depicted in Figure 10.3. This shows that while Communists and Fascists are at different ends of the radical–conservative scale, they are both very tough-minded. By contrast, Liberals are presented as rather tender-minded and neither radical nor conservative.

In terms of prejudice and ethnocentrism generally, Eysenck's theory is such that prejudiced attitudes and discriminating behaviour are more likely to stem from tough-minded people. Little research, however, has addressed itself to such issues since the contention that Communists and Fascists are both tough-minded has not received great support. Rokeach's claim that the similarity between the two political extremes is that of dogmatism has enjoyed greater support and favour among psychologists.

In summary, research originally aimed at investigating anti-Semitism suggested a link

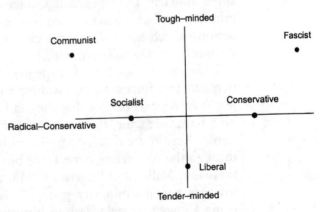

Figure 10.3: Eysenck's two personality dimensions of 'tough-minded/tender-minded' and 'radical-conservative', showing the position of political parties

between ethnocentrism and an authoritarian personality syndrome. Methodological and conceptual problems have cast doubt on this claim. Rokeach and Eysenck have both suggested authoritarianism to be characteristic of the extreme left and the extreme right political wings. The 'closed mind' style of thinking, suggested by Rokeach, and the tough-minded/tender-minded dimension of Eysenck have shown how these two ends of the political spectrum may be related.

Finally, the whole approach of explaining prejudice and discrimination through different types of personality has been questioned by Billig (1976). The main criticism is that such explanations ignore powerful situational, cultural and sub-cultural factors. For example, situational norms often determine how people behave (Minard, 1952). Another criticism is the failure of the approach to explain the existence of widespread prejudice in a particular society. If everybody holds similar prejudicial attitudes then personality cannot be a major factor.

10.3.2 Frustration and aggression

On countless occasions in our lives we experience frustration due to being unable to attain desired goals. Dollard *et al.* (1939) claimed that the occurrence of aggressive behaviour *always* presupposes the existence of frustration and that frustration always leads to some form of aggression. Here our interest is with the extent to which frustration leading to aggression is displaced or targeted on a 'scapegoat'. Berkowitz (1969) argued that frustration *may* result in aggression, and that the less a person who frustrates you is able to retaliate then the more likely you are to be aggressive towards that person. This bears some similarity to scapegoating, since a scapegoat is: (a) relatively powerless to retaliate to acts of aggression; (b) made to take the blame for actions which he or she or the group is not responsible for; and (c) is disliked or hated to begin with.

Experimental studies of scapegoating first attempt to frustrate participants (by, for example, insulting them, stopping them from obtaining desired goals or ensuring they fail at some task) and then measure, on an attitude scale, the extent of prejudice after the frustrating experience. Results are then compared with a control group who did not go through the frustrating experience but just answered the attitude questionnaire. Miller and Bugelski (1948) first asked people their attitudes towards various minority groups. Half were then frustrated by not being allowed to see a desired film they were told they were going to see. The 'frustrated' group were again asked about their attitudes to minority groups. Compared to the control group, the frustrated group showed an increase in prejudice.

In another study, Weatherly (1961) selected two groups of non-Jewish male college students, one group were those who scored high and the other low on an anti-Semitic questionnaire. Half of the group who scored high and half who scored low were 'insulted' while filling out another questionnaire. The other half of the high and low scorers were the control groups since they were not insulted. Later all participants were asked to write short stories about some pictures of men; two of these male pictures were given Jewish names. Two results were obtained: (a) highly anti-Semitic participants who were insulted directed more aggression to the pictures with Jewish-sounding names than did insulted participants who scored low on anti-Semitism; and (b) participants high and low in anti-Semitism who were insulted did not differ in the amount of aggression directed at male pictures with non-Jewish-sounding names. In short, this study supports the idea that highly anti-Semitic people direct their aggression specifically towards Jews and not other groups of people.

Social psychologists generally do not regard frustration as the only or major cause of aggression, but regard it as one of many contributing factors. To reflect this, Berkowitz (1989) provided a reformulation of the frustration–aggression hypothesis which states that frustration may result in aggression because frustration is a negative, unpleasant and aversive experience for a person. This negative emotional state caused by frustration leads to aggression. Hence, with this reformulation (Berkowitz, 1989) is saying that there is a strong link between negative emotional states and aggression and that frustration is just one type of experience causing a person to be in a negative emotional state.

10.3.3 Belief similarity

Rokeach (1968) claims that 'differences in belief on important issues are more powerful determinants of prejudice or discrimination than differences in race or ethnic membership'. Put crudely, the contention is that social discrimination of black people, for example, would not be because of their black colour, but because they believe in different things. This means that people who share the same beliefs, i.e. have *belief congruence*, will be prejudiced towards those who hold different beliefs.

To test this hypothesis Rokeach, Smith and Evans (1960) asked people to rate a number of stimulus persons according to whether or not they thought they would like to be friends with them. The stimulus persons were of either the same or different race and religion as the participants in the study and presented in pairs as follows:

1 (a) A white person who believes in God
  (b) A black person who believes in God
2 (c) A white person who is a communist
  (b) A black person who is anti-communist

Results showed that participants were more likely to say they would like to be friends with someone who believed in the same things as them *regardless* of race. For friendship, then, belief similarity or congruence would appear to be more important than racial similarity.

Rokeach (1968) conducted a field experiment, to test his theory further, in which 26 black and 26 white male job applicants acted as unwitting participants while attending a job interview. Each job applicant was put in a waiting room with four confederates who the job applicant thought were also waiting for interview. The confederates were instructed to talk about treatment of mental patients with the real job applicants and took either a formal or informal approach to treatment. Things were arranged such that the confederates were either different or the same as the participant on race and belief. Two confederates were of the same race but one held different and one the same belief as the participant. The other two confederates were of different race with again one holding the same and one different belief to the participant. After the participant had been talking to the four confederates for about 10 minutes, he was asked to indicate which two out of the four people he would most prefer to work with. Six possible combinations of two from four people to work with were available to the participant to choose from, these are given in Table 10.3. Participants overwhelmingly chose potential workmates who shared the same beliefs as them regardless of race (S + O + in Table 10.3). Also there was some preference for workmates of the same and different race and same and different beliefs (S –, O + in Table 10.3) indicating a tendency for participants to choose mixed groups of people to talk to. Generally, Rokeach's research supports his hypothesis that belief similarity or dissimilarity is a more important factor in social discrimination, positive discrimination for the same beliefs and negative discrimination for different beliefs, than is similarity or difference of race.

There are a number of shortcomings with Rokeach's belief congruence explanation of prejudice, for example, Rokeach says that belief congruence does not apply where prejudice is institutionalised or socially sanctioned. This means that many forms of discrimination are not regarded as relevant to Rokeach's explanation. Also, it is not clear that belief congruence truly exists in the sense of all people in a group sharing the same beliefs. Political parties, for example, are notorious for having different 'wings' representing quite different beliefs.

Combination of partners	Description	Participant choice
S+ O+	Two people who agree with the participant, one the same race and one from the other race	30
S– O–	Two people who disagree with the participant, one the same race and one the other race	3
S+ S–	Two people of the same race as the participant, one agreeing and one disagreeing with the subject	2
O+ O–	Two people of the other race to the participant, one agreeing and one disagreeing with the subject	3
S+ O–	One person of the participant's race agreeing and one of the other race disagreeing	4
S– O+	One person of the participant's race disagreeing and one of the other race agreeing	8
	Total:	50

Table 10.3: Possible combinations of partners participants could choose to work with. 'S' means the same race and 'O' means another race; (+) indicates the same belief and (–) different belief to participant. Figures in the right-hand column show actual choices made by the participants. Adapted from Rokeach (1968, pp. 69–71).

Furthermore, even when people share the same belief it may be held with varying degrees of strength and be seen as different in terms of importance by different individuals in a group.

In summary, individual levels of explanation put forward by social psychologists to explain prejudice and discrimination all suffer quite severe shortcomings, as we have seen. Nevertheless, explanations that focus on the individual remain of interest in research terms and are intuitively appealing to people. Why is this? It may be that this can be explained in part by reference to the attribution approach in Chapter 5, for example, the *correspondence bias* (Section 5.4.1) is where people have a strong tendency to attribute behaviour to dispositions. This bias results in a focus on individual aspects such as personality, beliefs, frustration–aggressive behaviour, which are precisely the types of explanation we have been considering.

10.4 Realistic group conflict

Group membership itself may be an important explanation for prejudice and discrimination. So far we have largely ignored the effects and consequences of belong to a group and how people treat members of their own group compared with members of other groups to which they do not belong or identify with. Social psychologists have looked at this from two perspectives; first, where two or more groups are in *competition* for resources, and, second, how group membership *per se* affects a person's attitudes and behaviour. In this section we consider the former perspective and in Section 10.5 the effects of social categorisation in the absence of competition for resources.

In a series of highly influential and pioneering experiments Sherif (1966) investigated intergroup conflict and co-operation in groups of 11–12 year old boys attending summer school camp in America. The field experiments lasted three weeks and were characterised by three stages each lasting a week:

Stage 1: The boys were put in one of two conditions for the first week. In condition (a) the boys spent a week together where they were involved in various informal activities. In condition (b) the boys spent a week in one of the groups in which they were to be placed in Stage 2, but the two groups were unaware of each other's existence.

Stage 2: The boys in condition (a) were moved to the summer camp and divided into two groups. In condition (b) the two groups were brought together at the summer camp. Sherif arranged a series of competitive events between the two groups with prizes or social advantages for the group which won.

Stage 3: Co-operation between the two groups was encouraged by the setting of *superordinate* goals (goals which could only be achieved by *both* groups co-operating).

Stages 1 and 2 are concerned with the development of conflict, while Stage 3 deals with the reduction of conflict and will be dealt with in more detail in Section 10.8. In the condition where the boys were together in Stage 1, Sherif (1966) divided them into two groups such that about two-thirds of any single boy's friends were in the other group. Sherif then compared changes in friendship patterns in Stage 1 and 2 of the experiment. Table 10.4 shows quite clearly that competition between groups in Stage 2 resulted in boys' friendship patterns changing, ending up with friendships being almost entirely restricted to the in-group.

Friends chosen from	Boys membership			
	Group A		Group B	
	Before	After	Before	After
Group A	35	95	65	12
Group B	65	5	35	88

Table 10.4: Change in percentages in friendship choices before and after group competition. Adapted from Sherif (1966)

In the conditions where the two groups were kept away from each other in Stage 1, Sherif observed dramatic changes in relationships *within* the groups as a result of intergroup competition. For example, the leadership of one group changed from a 'pacifistic' person to a 'bully'. Generally, behaviour and changes in friendship patterns were such as to *increase solidarity in the in-group*.

Relationships between the two groups rapidly escalated into open conflict during Stage 2. This was evidenced by, for example, name-calling, raids on the other group's dormitory, taunting and jeering, refusing to eat with the other group or sit and watch a film with them. At the end of Stage 2, Sherif summarised the situation thus:

> If an outside observer had entered the situation at this point with no information about preceding events, he could only have concluded on the basis of their behaviour that these boys (who were the 'cream of the crop' in their communities) were wicked, disturbed and vicious bunches of youngsters.
>
> (Sherif, 1966, p. 85)

We will return later to see how Sherif attempted to get these 'vicious and wicked youngsters' to be more friendly towards each other. The point to note from this research is that *group conflict arises because of competition between two groups for some prize, goal, resource, etc., that can only be achieved by one group at the expense of the other.* Sherif showed that while intergroup competition may start off in a friendly and sportsmanlike way it rapidly escalates into conflict and open hostility. The out-group became stereotyped, the in-group overevaluated its positive achievements and became more 'tightly knit'.

To explain these findings Sherif (1966) developed a *realistic conflict theory*. This states that to predict whether conflict or co-operation will occur between groups depends on the nature of the goals that the groups are trying to achieve. Group goals requiring *interdependence,* that is, both groups working together, result in groups co-operating with each other. By contrast, group goals which are *mutually exclusive,* that is where one group can only achieve the goal at the expense of the other, result in intergroup competition which often becomes intergroup conflict. The Sherif summer camp experiment is an example of groups trying to achieve mutually exclusive goals thus resulting in realistic intergroup conflict.

When we come to look back at how Sherif attempted to reduce intergroup conflict by the setting of *superordinate* goals for the groups, conflict is reduced and co-operation enhanced (see Section 10.8). Generally, Sherif's realistic conflict theory has been supported and provides a good framework for understanding why groups co-operate and compete.

10.5 Social identity and self-categorisation

In the previous section we saw that Sherif's theory of realistic conflict of intergroup behaviour occurred when the achievement of goals by one group prevented the other group achieving the goal. In such circumstances groups become competitive with each other and prejudice and discrimination often arise. By contrast, Tajfel (1970) demonstrated that group membership itself, in the absence of obvious competition, is a sufficient condition for intergroup discrimination to occur. This initial insight by Tajfel formed the basis for the development of social identity theory (Tajfel, 1978a) and self-categorisation theory (Turner, 1985) which have been a major influence on European, especially British, social psychology.

10.5.1 Minimal group paradigm

The *minimal group paradigm* is central to social identify theory and variations have been used in countless experiments. Tajfel (1970) pioneered the approach using schoolchildren aged between 14 and 15 years and asked them to state their preference for one of two abstract artists, Klee or Kadinsky. The schoolchildren were told that they had been assigned to one of two groups reflecting their preference for one of the two artists. In fact, they were *randomly* assigned to a group. The participants did not know who else had been assigned to their group; no face-to-face interaction took place between group members. No conflict of interest was said to exist between the two groups. Setting up such conditions allows you to understand what is meant by *minimal group membership*. The schoolchildren were then asked to allocate monetary rewards to each of the two groups by deciding one option from a matrix of options presented to them. One such matrix of options used by Tajfel is given in Figure 10.4; imagine you have been allocated to the Klee Group – which option would you choose?

The matrices of options used by Tajfel allowed for different distribution strategies, for example, *maximum joint profit* is where the total rewards obtained by a member of each group are maximised regardless of which group gets the most. In Figure 10.4 this would be option [19, 16]. Another strategy is *maximum difference* where the option chosen maximises the difference in the number of points in favour of your own group (the in-group), this is option [7, 1]. A strategy of fairness would be where rewards are equally distributed to both groups, option [13, 13].

Results showed that choices reflected a strategy of maximising in-group reward or maximising the difference of reward between the two groups in favour of the in-group. The latter strategy was adopted even if this meant that the in-group received less than it could have done. The results clearly showed that people will discriminate against an out-group in favour of an in-group when membership is anonymous and there is no evident self-interest (interdependence of goals) involved. Tajfel and Billig, (1974) found similar results even when participants were made aware that allocation to a particular group had been randomly determined in these experiments by the toss of a coin. Turner (1978) showed that students discriminated even in situations where they had to give up money themselves to favour their in-group and penalise the out-group. Numerous studies conducted over the past 20 years have found this generally to be a robust effect, with in-group favouritism being stronger when the group is meaningful and real for the individual.

While support has been strong, the experimental approach can be criticised, for example, the options in the matrix may prime people towards intergroup competitiveness. Much of the initial research was conducted using schoolboys and it may be that schoolboy culture is such as to enhance interest in group membership and foster intergroup competition. Hogg and Mullen (1998) reported that careful explanation to participants about the different options presented in the matrix reduced discrimination, hence it may be that these artificial matrices have demand characteristics which encourage ingroup favouritism. Research using the minimal group paradigm suggests that there is a general tendency to favour one's own group over other groups. The implications of these findings led Tajfel to develop social identity theory.

Rewards

Group												
To out-group	25	23	21	19	17	13	11	9	7	5	3	1
To in-group	19	18	17	16	15	13	12	11	10	9	8	7

Figure 10.4: Sample matrix used by Tajfel (1970) in the minimal group experiments

10.5.2 Social identity theory

Social identity theory (Tajfel and Turner, 1986) states that social categorisation results in social discrimination because people make social comparisons between in-groups and out-groups. The theory further states that people make social comparisons because they need to provide themselves with a positive identity. Over-valuation of the in-group and devaluation of the out-group facilitate a positive social identity for an individual. Positive social identity is important for a person since it enhances self-esteem and self-worth and gives a sense of 'belonging' in the social world. Comparisons made between in-groups and out-groups in relation to status, value and perceived worth lead to *social competition*. This reflects the desire people have to be members of highly valued, high status and worthwhile groups, and their strivings to put the groups they identify with in such a light as to believe their group to be 'better' than the out-group. The out-group is attributed with false negative or exaggerated stereotypes and negative values, while the in-group is perceived to have positive characteristics and values. Figure 10.5 summarises this and depicts the sequencing of cognitions.

A further, important point about social identity theory is that it is concerned with *social competition* not *realistic competition*. Realistic competition is when groups compete for real resources, and there is interdependence between groups, where one group can only obtain the resource or outcome at the expense of the other group. By contrast, with social competition, no real or tangible resources are being competed for or it is not necessary that they are. Social competition reflects the need people have for a positive self-image which comes from obtaining positive identity and self-esteem from being a member of a valued in-group. To achieve this, the in-group is inappropriately over-valued and the out-group inappropriately devalued.

Finally, social identity theory makes a distinction between personal identity and social identity. *Personal identity* refers to the idiosyncratic or unique features which serve to differentiate one person from another person in a group. *Social identity*, on the other hand, refers to that part of the self-concept resulting from the knowledge that a person is a member of a particular social group and includes the emotional attachment that the person has as a member of the group (Turner, 1982). When social identity is made more salient than personal identity, intergroup behaviour will manifest itself in terms of ethnocentrism, in-group favouritism and out-group differentiation, and this is shown in Figure 10.6.

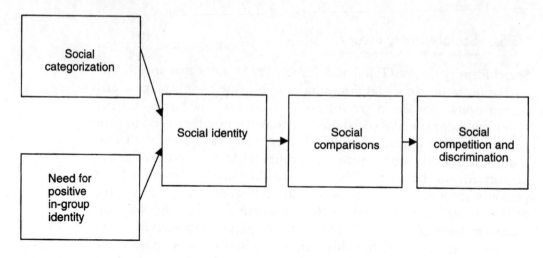

Figure 10.5: Psychological processes underlying social identity and consequences of social comparison for competition and discrimination of out-groups

10.5.3 Social identity and accessibility of group membership

What factors will make group membership salient and to the front of a person's mind? A number of cognitive and social factors have been identified which bring group membership to mind or make it more *accessible*. Four main factors are: direct reminders of group membership; presence of out-group members; being a minority; and intergroup conflict.

Direct reminders include such things as honorary titles, derogatory names, hearing someone who has the same spoken accent as yourself, wearing team uniforms or badges of a club of which you are a member (Wilder and Shapiro, 1991). Making membership of a team accessible often overcomes cross-cultural categorisations where, for example, white and black South Africans play for the same cricket team (Gaertner *et al.*, 1990). The presence of out-group members can serve to emphasise and remind one of our own in-group and the importance we attach to it (Marques *et al.*, 1988). Mullen (1991) demonstrated that if a small number of people representing an in-group are present in the same location as a large number of people from an out-group, your own group membership is made more accessible. This might be seen at a football match where the supporters of the 'away team' are only a handful compared with numbers present to see the 'home team'. This can make the away team supporters attempt to make their presence known very strongly. Take another example, if you are a white person in a setting where you are in the presence of 20 black people, your 'white' skin colour is likely to be something you become acutely conscious of.

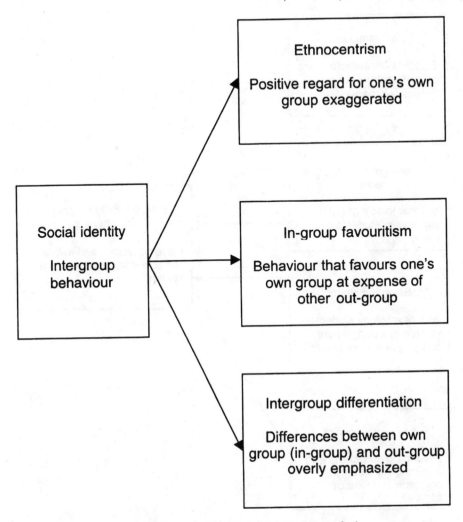

Figure 10.6: Consequences for intergroup behaviour in terms of ethnocentrism, in-group favouritism and intergroup differentiation resulting from social identity salience

Finally, the presence of intergroup conflict is one of the strongest factors making social identity accessible. Whether a person is actually engaged in conflict, for example, or made aware of a continuing conflict through a newspaper headline, group membership will be made more accessible to consciousness. Figure 10.7 summarises all of this.

10.5.4 Self-categorisation theory

Cast your eye over Figure 10.7 again and ask yourself, as a psychology student, why the four factors will enhance accessibility of group

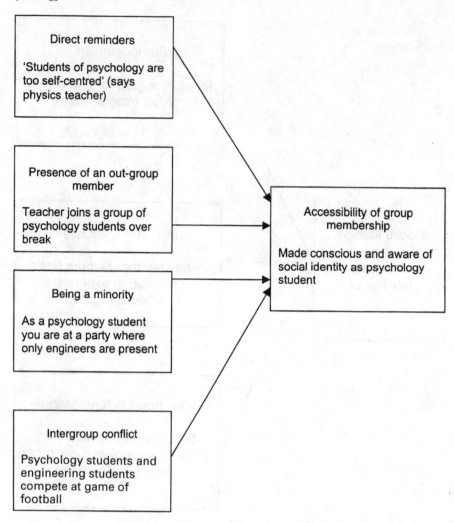

Figure 10.7: Accessibility of group membership as a psychology student, through direct reminders, presence of out-group member, being in a minority and inter-group conflict

membership. This will only work if you classify yourself as a psychology student in the first place or accept the social category provided by other people. By the same token, social identity theory only works if you categorise yourself as a member of an in-group. Turner *et al.* (1987) developed the theory of *self-categorisation* as an extension to social identity theory. People self-categorise themselves both as individuals different from other people and as a member of a social group different from other social groups.

When people self-categorise themselves as a member of an in-group they regard their attitudes, beliefs and behaviour as *prototypical* or representative of the key characteristics they perceive members of the group to have. The prototypical member of a group is the collection of characteristics which no one individual may have, but which is a set of psychological features and behaviours that define the group. When we self-categorise ourselves as a member of an in-group, a degree of depersonalisation takes place since we take on the norms of the group and stereotype ourselves as centrally representative of the group. Self-categorisation theory further states that differences between members of the in-group are minimised while differences from an out-group are maximised. This is summarised in Figure 10.8; you should now understand that self-categorisation is fundamental to social identity and intergroup behaviour. As such, there are important psychological consequences, some of which we examine in the next section.

10.6 Consequences of self-categorisation

Once we have categorised ourselves as a member of a specific group we see ourselves in stereotypical terms: as possessing the typical attitudes, behaviours and beliefs we think the group to have. Turner *et al.* (1987) further demonstrated that when group membership is made accessible (see Section 10.5.3) we see ourselves as even more typical and representative of the group. In what follows we look at three

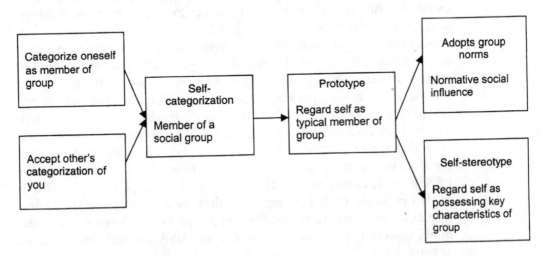

Figure 10.8: Antecedents and consequences of self-categorization as member of social group. Self-categorisation theory. After Turner *et al.* (1987)

important consequences of self-categorisation: stereotypes, illusory correlation and homogeneity of out-groups.

10.6.1 Stereotypes

Stereotypes of out-groups show three features: first, people are categorised on highly visible characteristics such as race, sex, nationality, bodily appearance, dress, etc. Second, all members of that category or social grouping are attributed with possessing the same characteristics – we will look at this more in the section on *homogeneity*. Third, any individual classified as belonging to the social group is attributed with possessing those stereotypical characteristics and the individual's unique personal characteristics are ignored (Rodin, 1987). Stereotypes are grossly over-simplified and over-generalised abstractions about groupings of people, and are usually highly inaccurate even though they may contain a grain of truth.

From this description of stereotypes it can be seen that they are similar to prejudicial attitudes that people hold about social groups. A person holding a stereotype will show a tendency to note and recall subsequent information about the social group which fits the stereotype. This serves to perpetuate and provide greater credence to the correctness of the stereotype (Bodenhausen, 1988). The more a stereotype is used, the more accessible it becomes and the more the stereotype will be used to categorise others (Higgins *et al.*, 1985).

Stereotypes are usually measured by giving people a list of adjectives (such as intelligent, industrious, generous) together with a list of categories of people (categorised by, for example, race, nationality, sex, sexual orientation) and using a Likert-type scale to obtain ratings. There are problems with this approach particularly to do with social desirability – people may not express the strong, prejudiced attitudes that they actually hold since they do not want to present themselves in a negative way. Observational methods may get round this problem to some extent but run into other difficulties such as reliability of measurement. The adjective-rating approach has demonstrated that stereotypes change over time. For example, Dovidio *et al.* (1996) showed that attitudes by whites towards black people in the USA have become less negative over a 60-year period, and this is shown in Table 10.5. However, whether these figures actually reflect true changes in attitudes and the stereotype held is less easy to determine, especially since black people in the USA are still discriminated against.

Recent research has acknowledged that stereotypes have both a cognitive and emotional component feeding into judgements we make

Stereotypical trait	Percentage of white people agreeing with trait in year				
	1933	1951	1967	1982	1993
Superstitious	84	41	13	8	0
Lazy	75	31	26	15	10
Ignorant	38	25	13	14	10

Table 10.5: Changing stereotypical views of white Americans towards African-Americans. Adapted from Dovidio *et al.* (1996)

about social groups. Situations which include strong, negative emotions (such as anger or anxiety) have been found to increase a person's use and reliance on stereotypical thinking (Mackie and Hamilton, 1993). You might think that somebody in a good mood may make a person feel kinder and more positive towards an out-group. Unfortunately, the opposite seems to be the case; Bodenhausen *et al.* (1994) demonstrated that people placed in a happy mood, by asking them to think about happy memories, showed more stereotypical thinking than people in a neutral mood. Bodenhausen *et al.* put this down to the unwillingness of people in a good mood to engage in cognitive effort; stereotypes that are highly accessible do not require much thought. The result of not engaging in cognitive effort is to maintain the happy mood!

What happens if you ask people who hold strong stereotypical attitudes to suppress them for a period? Macrae *et al.* (1994) provided evidence for a *rebound effect* where subsequent expression of the stereotype was stronger than that originally held. Stereotypes, then, are deep-seated evaluations that we make about social groups, are slow to change and are enhanced when we are in a good or bad mood. Stereotypes persist because they serve a positive function of imposing order and structure on our social world. Treating individual members of a social group as the same as the stereotype of the group enhances our own individuality and, as a consequence, positive self-esteem. Stereotypes may also persist and be perpetuated by the social norms and values of the in-groups with which we identify.

10.6.2 Illusory correlation

Illusory correlation refers to 'the perception of a stronger association between two variables than actually exists' (Baron and Byrne, 1997). In the context of prejudice, this is when an out-group is over-estimated in relation to the frequency or number of negative or stereotype-confirming behaviours exhibited by individual members of the group. For example, white people may over-estimate the frequency of crime committed by black people. Social psychologists have explained illusory correlation on the basis of *distinctiveness* (Hamilton and Sherman, 1989). This makes use of the idea that distinctive events, ones that are infrequent or unusual, are paid more attention to, and when judgements are made about a social group in the future the distinctive events come to mind easily. Since many stereotypes and the objects of prejudice are to do with minority groups of one sort or another, negative behaviours by such groups may occur less frequently but because of this be more distinctive to the majority group. Research over a period of 20 years (Hamilton and Gifford, 1976; McConnell *et al.*, 1994) has shown illusory correlation as a basis for stereotypes and prejudice to be a robust phenomenon. Illusory correlation has been found to occur when people are more emotionally aroused, which is consistent with the findings about stereotyping we saw in the last section. However, illusory correlation is more likely to happen when people think automatically rather than deliberating or thinking hard (Stroessner *et al.*, 1992).

10.6.3 Homogeneity

When we considered the self-categorisation theory in Section 10.5.4, it was stated that people see themselves as typical members of an in-group and see an individual who is categorised as belonging to an out-group as the same as all the other members of the out-group. The latter has been labelled *out-group homogeneity*, reflecting the commonly heard phrases made by prejudiced people such as: 'you know what they're like – they're all the same' or 'they're all like that'. This has been called the *illusion of out-group homogeneity* (Linville *et al.*, 1989) and has been used to explain why people tend to see others who are older or younger than themselves as more similar in personality characteristics than people of one's own age group.

There is a reverse side of homogeneity which is called *in-group differentiation*, which is where a person sees members of their in-group as being different from one another. In terms of self-categorisation, while we may see ourselves as typical of the characteristics and attitudes we associate with the in-group with which we identify, we see other members of our in-group as different to ourselves. This maintains personal identity and high self-esteem (as long as the characteristics and attitudes are regarded as positive and of value to ourselves).

The concepts of in-group differentiation and out-group homogeneity apply to face recognition. Here, it is a commonly recognised observation that people say they can distinguish between the faces of people of their own race, but see people of another race as all looking the same. Social psychologists have called this the *cross-race identification bias*. Platz and Hosch (1988) demonstrated this in a naturalistic study where shop assistants in local convenience shops were asked to identify male customers who were actually confederates of the experimenters. Eighty-six shop assistants who were either African–American, Mexican–American or Anglo-American served three confederates, during one day, representing each of these three categories of Americans. The shop assistants were later asked to make identifications and, as Figure 10.9 shows, they were able to make more correct identifications of Americans of their own category.

10.6.4 In-group dislike

Most, if not all people, belong to numerous social groups and in some instances we dislike being identified with a group especially where that group is regarded negatively. The society in which we live may devalue or stigmatise people because of their skin colour, sexual orientation, being overweight, being very short or tall, having a disability, having a bodily disfiguration, or being unemployed. The list goes on and on, and

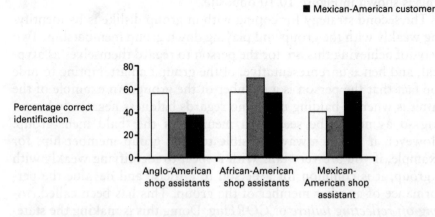

Figure 10.9: Identification of different categories of American customers in convenience stores by different categories of shop assistants. After Platz and Hosch (1988)

it is very likely that you belong to at least one group which you would prefer not be identified with. Social psychologists have investigated three main strategies people employ in such circumstances: maintaining self-esteem, identifying weakly with the group and identifying strongly with the group.

Crocker and Major (1989) showed that people who are members of stigmatised groups have just as high a level of self-esteem as people who do not belong to such groups. The reason this happens is that instead of members of stigmatised groups lowering their self-esteem, they attribute the negative behaviour of others towards them as representing the prejudicial and unfair attitudes that these people hold. However, such a strategy has a cost as well since praise and positive feedback given to a member of a stigmatised group are seen as sympathy or pity from other people rather than recognition of individual achievement (Crocker and Major 1989). This was demonstrated in an experiment by Heilman *et al.* (1987). Here men and women were told that they had been selected for a leadership role either because of their performance on a questionnaire assessing leadership potential or because more of their sex were needed to achieve a better balance in the group. After being given a leadership task to perform, half of the participants were told that they had failed at the task and the other half that they had succeeded at the task. All participants were then asked to rate their own leadership ability. The researchers found that women who were told they were selected on the basis of their sex perceived their leadership ability to be low regardless of whether they were told that they had failed or succeeded at the task. By contrast, men rated their leadership ability as higher in both conditions of the experiment. This is shown in Figure 10.10 opposite.

The second strategy for coping with in-group dislike is by identifying weakly with the group and playing down group membership. Two ways of achieving this are for the person to regard themselves as atypical, and hence unrepresentative, of the group and attempting to hide the fact that the person is a member of the group. An example of the latter is where a balding man who regards baldness negatively buys a wig so as not to be seen as a member of the 'bald men' group. However, it is not always possible to hide group membership, for example, if you are very tall. With respect to identifying weakly with a group, it is common for a person to criticise and devalue the performance of another member of the group. This has been called *cutting-off reflecting failure* or *CORFing*. Doing this is making the statement that you regard another person's performance as unrepresentative of the group. Branscombe *et al.* (1993) related CORFing to the behaviour of sports fans who booed and hissed at their own team

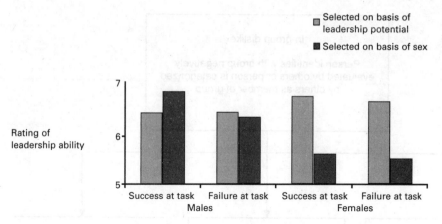

Figure 10.10: Self-ratings of leadership ability by men and women after being told they had failed or succeeded at a task when selected either on the basis of responses to a questionnaire or sex. From Heilman *et al.* (1987)

when performing poorly. Here the fans are showing their disapproval and also distancing themselves psychologically from their team.

The third strategy of identifying strongly with the disliked group is likely to occur when members of the group are trying to alter the negative evaluation of others to a positive evaluation. In a sense this is attempting to engineer social change, for example, the 'black is beautiful' slogan of the 1970s was an attempt by African–Americans to change American society's evaluation of people with black skin colour. Sometimes a negatively valued group will enter into social competition with society. Here in-group members show high levels of solidarity and publicly seek to expose and oppose the prevailing attitudes. Sometimes this may work, but at other times the approach may strengthen the prevailing negative evaluation of the social group.

In summary, we have seen that a person who dislikes a group with which he or she identifies or is categorised by other people as belonging to, may employ a range of strategies to defend individual self-esteem. These are summarised in Figure 10.11.

10.7 Reducing prejudice and discrimination

Up to now this chapter has considered a number of approaches used by social psychologists to understand and explain prejudice and discrimination. In this and the next section, we look at three main ways in which attempts have been made to reduce prejudice and discrimination. These are through: setting superordinate goals where there is realistic conflict; recategorisation; and by contact. Before this it is worth considering how

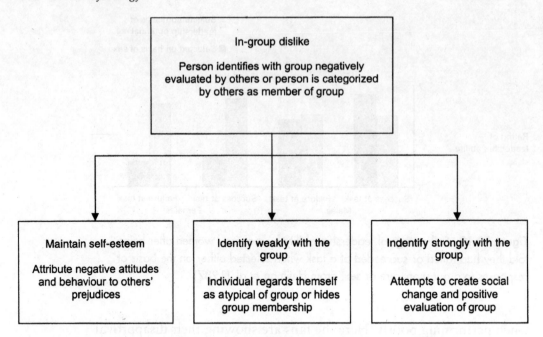

Figure 10.11: Three strategies employed by people who are members of groups that are negatively evaluated and which they dislike being members of themselves

changes may be made to a person's personality to prevent or reduce prejudice.

The authoritarian personality would appear to be self-perpetuating since research has shown (Byrne, 1966) that authoritarian parents tend to produce authoritarian children. However, Table 10.2 showed that the *higher* the level of educational attainment the *less* likely people were to be authoritarian. Clearly, then, it would seem to be in the interests of a more harmonious society for greater provision and access to be made to higher education. Campbell (1971) has shown that attempts to get different races, ethnic groupings, etc. together are more likely to be viewed in a positive way the greater the level of education a person has experienced.

10.7.1 Superordinate goals

In Section 10.4 we saw that at the end of Stage 2 of Sherif's (1966) summer camp experiment that different groups of boys were in competition with each other and this competition had escalated to potentially dangerous levels. In Stage 3 Sherif made attempts to reduce intergroup conflict by setting the groups a series of co-operative tasks. Sherif set the groups *superordinate goals:* objectives which could *only* be achieved by *both* groups working together. Sherif stage-managed superordinate goals in the summer camps by causing, unknown to the boys in the groups, such events as the failure of the water supply and the breakdown of the camp lorry.

Generally, superordinate goals did reduce the intergroup hostility but only when the groups engaged in a *series* of such tasks. Just setting one superordinate goal did not have much effect, each group soon after completing one superordinate task returned to their hostile ways. At the end of the week when the groups had worked together on a number of superordinate tasks intergroup relations were quite friendly. There was a greater tendency for friends to be chosen from *both* groups. Also groups were prepared to share things with each other, and aggressive hostile leadership was frowned upon by the group members. Sherif summarised the position as follows:

> In short, the findings suggest the various methods used with limited success in reducing intergroup hostility may become effective when employed within a framework of cooperation among groups working towards goals that are genuinely appealing and require equitable participation and contributions from all groups.
>
> (Sherif, 1966, p. 93)

Notice Sherif adds two important qualifications: (a) the superordinate goal must have genuine appeal to both groups, i.e. both groups must regard the task as worthwhile; and (b) there must be equitable participation and contribution from both groups – reduction of intergroup hostility will *not* occur when one group is of higher status or in command and one of lower status or subservient.

There are a number of limitations which question the extent to which the setting of superordinate goals can be generalised beyond Sherif's summer camp experiment. First, all the participants in the study were boys who came from similar backgrounds. There was no significant representation of different ethnic, racial or social groups. Second, Sherif conducted the study over a three-week period and outside of a social or societal context. Third, the experimenters were aware of the reasons for each of the three stages of the study and may have unintentionally influenced the competitiveness or co-operativeness of the boys in each of the groups. Nevertheless, Sherif's research does provide important insights into how groups who are in competition behave towards each other.

10.7.2 Recategorisation

Social identity theory (Tajfel, 1978a) as we saw in Section 10.5.2, states that the fact that social categorisation takes place is sufficient to cause discrimination to an out-group. It follows that if strategies are adopted to get people to *recategorise* themselves then the boundaries between in-groups and out-groups may change. Gaertner *et al.* (1993) proposed the *common in-group identity* model which states that when people identify themselves as belonging to different social groups change their views and see themselves as belonging to one, larger social grouping attitudes towards former out-group members become more positive. Gaertner *et al.* (1990) claim that one key factor which brings people to see themselves as part of a larger group is when they work together cooperatively. Gaertner *et al.* (1993) demonstrated this in a field study conducted in a high school in the USA which contained pupils from a range of different ethnic backgrounds. Under circumstances where pupils saw themselves as belonging to one student body, the more positive were their attitudes to pupils from different ethnic groups.

A second approach to recategorisation is to break existing social categories into smaller sub-units, perhaps so small that each individual seems him or herself as unique. This is the opposite to the recategorisation to larger social groups that we looked at above. Emphasising individual uniqueness should result in social groupings becoming less important or salient for the individual. Gaertner *et al.* (1989) investigated this in an experiment where participants were first placed into two groups of three and encouraged them to see themselves as belonging to six one-person 'groups'. While this did reduce in-group bias, the researchers found that participants thought less highly of their original other two in-group members. Strategies that encourage individuals to see themselves as unique rather than as a member of a social group are found to be more critical of others who were originally seen as part of their in-group.

Recategorisation by either getting a person to identify with a larger social group or by seeing himself or herself as unique does result in a reduction in prejudice and discrimination. However, both strategies require self-categorisation, albeit different to normal ways, and as such result in enhanced self-identity (see Section 10.5.4).

10.8 Application: reducing intergroup conflict by contact

Increased contact between social groups through inter-racial mixing, desegregation or any strategy that brings two social groups into contact has been advocated by psychologists, politicians, civil leaders, etc. as a means of reducing prejudice and conflict. The *contact hypothesis*, first suggested by Allport (1954), predicts that under certain conditions negative attitudes held by members of an in-group to an out-group will change to be less negative or more positive as a result of contact. Interpersonally, increased contact should foster and encourage acquaintances and friendships to develop between individuals belonging to different social groups. As a result, this should increase the perception of similarity between members of different groups and reduce the perception of outgroup homogeneity. Research has shown

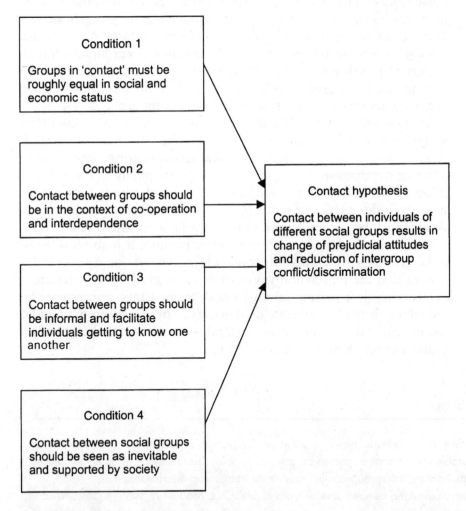

Figure 10.12: Four conditions needed for contact between social groups to result in reduced prejudice and discrimination

that the contact hypothesis reduces prejudice and intergroup conflict when the four conditions shown in Figure 10.12 are met. If one or more of these conditions are absent, then the effectiveness of contact between individuals of different social groups will be reduced or not effective at all.

Aronson and Gonzales (1988) demonstrated the importance of equal status in a school setting using what they called the *jigsaw method* of learning in the classroom. This is where teachers allocate pupils to small groups in which the profile of the group represents the ethnic mix in the classroom. For example, if a class of 30 children consisted of one-third white, one-third Asian and one-third Chinese, then a group of six children would consist of two from each of these categories. The next step with the jigsaw method is for the teacher to give each pupil in the group of six one-sixth of the material or information required to carry out the task. Suppose there to be five such groups in a class, *primary* groups are formed by putting together each child from the group of six having the *same* information. These primary groups meet to talk about how they are going to give the information to the other members of the group of six.

Aronson and Gonzales found that the general classroom environment became less competitive and more co-operative as a result of this technique. Where a class is imbalanced and has a majority and minority group in it, Aronson and Gonzales found that pupils in the minority group gained in self-esteem and attended more at school. Pupils in the majority in the class came to see their classmates as more intelligent and likeable than before implementation of the jigsaw method of contact.

The jigsaw method is particularly effective since it requires different social groupings to come into contact to co-operate on a task. It also ensures that the representatives of each social group in contact are of equal status. Just putting pupils from different ethnic groups together and telling them to co-operate does not result in reductions in prejudice and discrimination. The jigsaw method is not effective when pupils in a mixed group do not have equal status.

10.10 Summary

- Prejudice is an attitude which predisposes a person to act in an unfavourable or favourable way to another person or group of people. Discrimination is the actual behaviour that occurs. Intergroup conflict may result from unfair discrimination.
- Racism, sexism and tokenism are all types of prejudice. Modern racism is subtle and consists of denial, impatience and resentment of one group (usually a majority) to another group (usually a minority).

- Individual explanations have looked at personality differences, frustration and aggression, and belief similarity. Personality differences have investigated the authoritarian personality and Eysenck's radicalism–conservatism and tough-minded/tender-minded dimensions.
- Realist group conflict is where two or more groups are in competition for resources and where a goal achieved by one group is at the expense of the other. Sherif investigated this in the summer school camp study. Realistic conflict theory states that group interdependence fosters co-operation while mutually exclusive goals foster intergroup competition.
- Tajfel stated that group membership itself is a sufficient condition for intergroup discrimination to occur. Tajfel investigated this using the minimal group paradigm. In-group favouritism and out-group discrimination occur under any circumstances of group membership.
- Social identity theory states that social categorisation results in discrimination because people make social comparisons between in-groups and outgroups. Comparisons are made because people need to create a social identity for themselves. Social identity theory is concerned with social competition not realistic competition.
- Self-categorisation theory is fundamental to social identity and intergroup behaviour. Social categorisation results in stereotyping, illusory correlation (over-estimation of negative out-group traits), and out-group homogeneity (members of an in-group see members of out-group as the same or all alike).
- When a person is a member of an in-group which he or she dislikes, three strategies may be used: maintaining self-esteem, identifying weakly with the group, and identifying strongly with the group. All these strategies are designed to defend a person's self-esteem.
- Reducing prejudice and discrimination has been investigated through the setting of super-ordinate goals to competing groups, recategorisation of social group membership and the contact hypothesis.

10.11 Suggestions for further reading

Allport, G. W. 1954: *The Nature of Prejudice*. Reading, Mass: Addison Wesley
Over 40 years old and still highly relevant today. This is the classic social psychology text which had a profound influence on theory and research on prejudice. Covers a vast range of theoretical perspectives.

Brown, R. J. 1995: *Prejudice: Its Social Psychology*. Oxford: Blackwell.
Good, up-to-date text providing a broad coverage of different approaches and explanations of prejudice and conflict. Has a useful chapter on the development of prejudice in children. Adopts an intergroup approach as a general framework.

Fiske, S. T. 1998: Stereotyping, prejudice and discrimination. In Gilbert, D. T., Fiske, S. T. and Lindzey, G. (eds), *The Handbook of Social Psychology*. Fourth edition, Vol. 2. New York: McGraw-Hill.

Another up-to-date overview but this time with a more North American perspective emphasizing a social-cognitive approach. Assumes a certain level of knowledge.

Keneally, T. 1982: *Schindler's List*. London: Sceptre Books, Hodder and Stoughton.

Harrowing account of man's inhumanity to man resulting in the Nazi Holocaust where over three million Jews in Europe were slaughtered. Also see the Oscar-winning film by Steven Spielberg based on this book.

11 Groups and group performance

11.1 Introduction

We all belong to a diverse variety of groups ranging from family groups, work groups, club and friendship groups, and on a large scale, collective groups such as members of society, a football crowd or the audience at the cinema. Most research in social psychology has focused on small groups and this will be the emphasis of this chapter. Paulus (1989) offers a useful definition of small groups: 'A group consists of two or more interacting persons who share common goals, have a stable relationship, are somehow interdependent and perceive that they are in fact part of a group.' This definition highlights four important aspects of groups. First, group members are communicating and interacting; second, groups come together to achieve goals that the individuals have in common; third, a stable set of relationships between group members means that roles, status and norms have usually been established; and fourth, there is interdependence between group members which means that each person in a group relies on the other people in the group and what affects one group member usually affects everybody else in the group.

Our social life is determined by being a member of many different groups and people who shun group activities are often labelled 'loners' or perceived as being odd in someway. Why, then, do we join groups? Four main reasons have been put forward by social psychologists. First, people achieve a sense of *belonging*, thus satisfying social and psychological needs for a person. Second, as the definition given earlier indicates, groups help us *achieve goals* that we regard as personally important. Third, interaction with others serves to provide a greater pool of *knowledge* and information. Finally, a group may provide *security* because we perceive a 'safety in numbers' (Paulus, 1989).

This chapter also considers group performance – how well or poorly groups perform a task. Steiner (1972) identifies two key factors which are called *task demands* and *human resources*. In addition, Steiner (1976) offers a complex classification of tasks that a group might perform. The most salient division of tasks is into unitary and divisible tasks. Unitary tasks are those which cannot easily or sensibly be split up into smaller, component tasks. While divisible tasks can be split up and are often best tackled by a group doing so. Figure 11.1 summarises the two factors and division of tasks suggested by Steiner.

11.2 Individuals and groups

It is commonly perceived wisdom that it is better to have a group of people working at a task rather than a sole individual. In this section

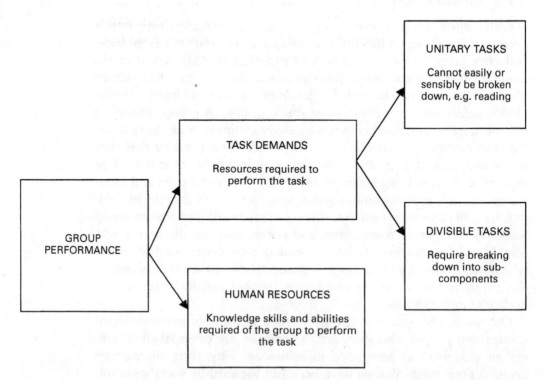

Figure 11.1: Group performance determined by task demands and human resources together with type of task – unitary or divisible. After-Steiner (1976)

social psychological research is presented which investigates both how individual performance may be affected by the simple presence of other people and how group performance may differ from individual performance.

11.2.1 Social facilitation

When an individual is performing a task, such as riding a bike, solving an arithmetical problem or playing a violin, does the mere presence of other people serve to facilitate or inhibit how well the individual performs? This simple question has been investigated for over a hundred years. Triplett (1898) found that racing cyclists were faster when racing with others than when alone. Travis (1925) trained people for several days on a hand–eye co-ordination task, using a pursuit-rota device, until a set standard of performance was reached. These trained people then performed 10 more trials of the task in front of a passive audience. Performance here was compared to their best 10 trials performed alone. Eighteen of the 20 people in the study performed better in front of an audience, with 16 achieving their best scores under such conditions.

Many subsequent studies have shown that social facilitation (enhanced performance in front of an audience) occurs when tasks have been well learned by the person. However, audiences have been found to inhibit performance when an individual has not previously learned the task or where the task is complex. For example, Pessin (1933) had participants learn a series of seven nonsense syllables either alone or in front of an audience. Participants took longer to learn and made more errors in the presence of an audience. Shopping behaviour has been found to be affected by the presence of others; this was shown in a study by Sommer *et al.* (1992) in which researchers observed people shopping in supermarkets and found that people who shopped together spent more time in the supermarket and bought more items than people who shopped alone. Some caution is needed in interpreting these results since we would need to be sure that people who shop alone do not always live alone as this would provide a simple explanation of why they bought less!

Zajonc (1965) offered a theoretical explanation accounting for when facilitation and inhibition were most likely to happen as a consequence of performing in front of an audience. This is called the *drive theory* and the fundamental idea is that the presence of others produces *arousal* and, as a result, the emission of dominant responses from the individual increases. Dominant responses are the behaviour that a person is most able to access, which are simple, well learned and highly practical. Finally, dominant responses may either be correct or incorrect. When a dominant response is correct in relation to a task, social facilitation is found; when incorrect, the person's performance is inhibited by the presence of others. When a task is not well learned and practised or complex, non-dominant responses result. Figure 11.2 depicts Zajonc's drive theory.

To help understand what is being said here take the example of playing tennis. If you are a famous, top-rated tennis player you would be highly practised at all the different tennis strokes. These strokes would be easily accessible to you and dominant when playing tennis in front of an audience at Wimbledon, for example. However, now imagine that you are a relative novice at playing tennis and are asked to play to a full audience at Wimbledon. Because you do not have well-practised tennis skills, such skills are not accessible and not dominant responses. In the former situation social facilitation is likely to occur, in the latter impairment or inhibition.

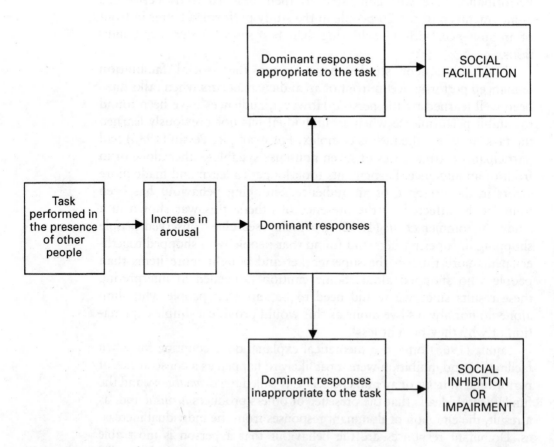

Figure 11.2: Zajonc's (1965) drive theory explanation of social facilitation and social inhibition

Zajonc's (1965) theory does offer an explanation of social facilitation but does not explain why an audience produces arousal in the first place. Geen (1991) summarises theorising on this issue and offers two main explanations: *evaluation apprehension* and *distraction conflict*. Evaluation apprehension recognises the importance each of us places on how we are judged, rated and valued by other people – our self-esteem is highly dependent on what other people think of us. Evaluation apprehension can increase or enhance performance on a simple task but decrease or impair performance on a complex task. This was demonstrated by Bartis *et al.* (1988) in an experiment where participants were asked either to describe different common uses of a knife (simple task) or to think of creative, new ways to use a knife (complete task). In each condition half the participants were led to believe their responses would be individually evaluated and the other half that their responses would be added to a common pool. Figure 11.3 shows the results of this experiment with performance enhanced (facilitated) on the simple task and impaired on the complex task when participants thought their responses would be evaluated.

Distraction conflict states that our attention to the task at hand is distracted by other people since we attempt to think about them, monitor their reactions to what we are doing, etc. Diverting attention away from the task means that we may get concerned or worried about performing poorly with the result that we become anxious and aroused. Figure 11.4 summarises the relationship between evaluation, apprehension and distraction conflict as suggested by Geen (1991). If you link this to Figure 11.2, a full explanation of audience effects on individual performance is achieved.

11.2.2 Brainstorming

Do groups perform better at a task than an individual working alone? Social psychologists have spent over 50 years (Allport, 1924) exploring this question. Here consideration will be given to a technique called *brainstorming* (Osborn, 1957). Brainstorming is an approach to problem-solving that has been widely adopted by industry and business. It is where groups attempt to solve

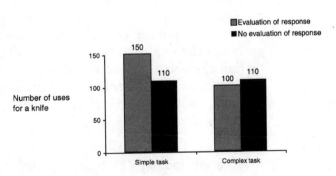

Figure 11.3: Results of experiment by Bartis *et al.* (1988) demonstrating effect of evaluation apprehension on performance at simple and complex tasks

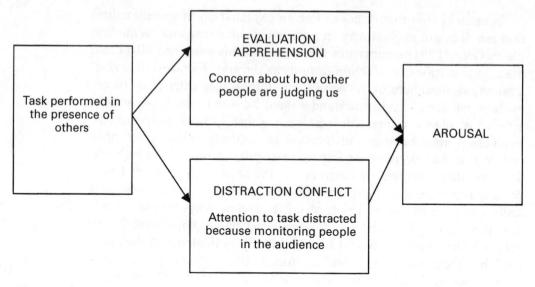

Figure 11.4: Presence of others causes evaluation apprehension and distraction conflict resulting in arousal. After Geen (1991)

problems, come up with new ideas or new solutions by first encouraging each group member to produce as many novel ideas as possible without evaluation. Second, the ideas for the group are pooled and evaluated and some selected for further elaboration. Those selected are first elaborated by all group members but without criticism. Finally, evaluation of the elaborated ideas allows one or a small number to be adopted.

Osborn (1957) claimed that adoption of this technique would result in enhanced group performance over individual performance. However, research has shown that groups who use brainstorming generate fewer ideas and ideas of poorer quality in comparison to having the same number of individuals working independently on the task. Four main explanations have been offered to account for this: evaluation apprehension, social loafing, production blocking and poor group co-ordination. The former was considered in the previous section on social facilitation, therefore we will look briefly at the other three explanations.

▓ Social loafing

Social loafing is when a person puts in less effort when working in a group than when working alone. Ringlemann noticed over 100 years ago, when investigating how much effort different-sized groups of people produce when pulling a rope (similar to a tug-of-war type situation) that there is an inverse relationship between group size and effort. Individuals by themselves exert more effort when pulling a rope attached to a cart than what you might expect from a group. This has been called the *Ringlemann effect* (Kravitz and Martin 1986). Latané *et al.* (1979) demonstrated social loafing in an experimental study where college students were asked to clap or cheer as loudly as they could. Participants did this in groups of either 2, 4 and 6 or alone. It was found that the level of clapping or cheering generated per person decreased as the group size increased. Social loafing has been found to occur less often for tasks that are thought to be interesting and involving (Brickner *et al.*, 1986). By contrast, social loafing is more prevalent when the task does not represent a challenge, individual performance cannot be assessed or if the individual sees his or her contribution to the group as of little value (Karau and Williams 1993).

Production blocking

Production blocking (Diehl and Stroebe, 1987) results from rules operating in an interacting group that only one person can speak at any one time. This is thought to result in some group members participating less because they cannot get 'a word in edgeways' or while waiting to speak forget what they have to say or what idea they had.

Poor group co-ordination

Poor group co-ordination refers to the importance of a group having shared understanding, developed rules for interaction and effective methods of working together. Without this co-ordination of activities needed to be successful at a task may be poor, resulting in the group not performing well at the task. Section 11.3 considers how groups develop to become effective (or ineffective).

11.2.3 Group memory

Clark and Stephenson (1995), following a review of the literature, state that groups not only remember more information than individuals but remember more than the best individual group member. This was demonstrated in a study by Clark and Stephenson (1989) in which university students and police officers were asked individually or in four-person groups to recall information after watching a video tape recording lasting 5 minutes of a police officer questioning a woman alleging she had been raped. Recalled information after watching the recording was categorised according to correct facts, reconstructions, adding information not given, and meta-statements going beyond what was presented in the video. Figure 11.5 shows that groups produced more correct information and made a fewer meta-statements than individuals. This obviously has important potential application to how professionals or lay people question other people.

Moreland *et al.* (1996) extended the notion of group memory to group culture where groups representing a culture have common memory of norms, rules, friends and enemies, etc. A prevailing culture is therefore represented in small groups by 'shared memory'.

11.3 Group composition and performance

Imagine you have been asked to serve on a committee or become a member of a new group. Your first question may be to ask about the purpose of the group, then you will want to know how many other people are on the committee and the profile of each person. *Size* and *membership* are two aspects of group composition that have an impact on group performance.

11.3.1 Group size

We have already seen that as group size increases so does social loafing, and this may be partly as a consequence of the findings that individual satisfaction with the group decreases as the group gets larger

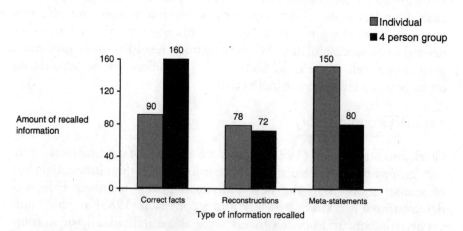

Figure 11.5: Type of information recalled by individuals and group after watching recording of police officer questioning woman alleging rape. After Clark and Stephenson (1989)

(Slater, 1958). Slater found that the greatest level of individual satisfaction with a group was with a membership of five, and beyond this competition between group members increased. Bales *et al.* (1951) (see Section 11.6.3) found larger groups to be characterised by greater disparity in individual contributions: in large groups (10 or more) some people spoke a lot and some hardly at all. By contrast, in groups of four or five individual contributions were more uniform and equal. Kerr (1982) suggests that as group size increases, individual motivation to contribute and perform may reduce. This may result in reduction of effort – social loafing – but also what has been called the *sucker effect*. Here an individual may not contribute to the group because he or she is concerned that others may not work so hard resulting in the view that 'why should I be the sucker who does all the work for the rest of the group?' To avoid being a sucker a person contributes less than he or she could.

Leadership style has been found to change as group size increases: Hemphill (1950) found leaders of large groups (over 30) had greater demands placed on them and were more influential. In large groups the leaders take control more and speak more often than other group members (McGrath, 1984). More generally, large groups rely on the leader to make rules and set standards, while leaders themselves are less tolerant of individual deviations from group norms and more likely to make decisions without consultation with the rest of the group (Hemphill, 1950). We shall look more fully at leadership in Section 11.6.

11.3.2 Group membership

Are groups which are composed of homogeneous or heterogeneous individuals more effective? As might be expected, there is no simple answer. Schultz (1958) found compatible rather than similar pairs to be better at complex problem-solving and no difference between such groups on relatively easy tasks. Compatible groups were where each had different but complementary personality characteristics along the dimensions of need to be included, need to control and need to give affection. A compatible group would be where, for example, person A has high needs to be included, control events and give affection, and person B has high needs to receive inclusion, be controlled and receive affection.

Groups composed of individuals having similar attitudes towards authority show less internal conflict, less disruption and are more productive. A general mix of personalities results in better task performance overall (McGrath, 1984), homogeneity for some traits may be more effective for performance than heterogeneity. A group composed entirely of dominant people is liable to result in conflict amongst members: a group of entirely submissive people is likely to result in poor performance since no one would take initiatives or leadership roles when required.

Overall, the search for consistent correlations between effective group performance and individual abilities, personality and intelligence has been mixed. Groups requiring specialist skills perform less well if those skills are absent; low levels of motivation for achieving group goals result in poor performance. All this suggests factors over and above individual abilities, personality, etc. operate to make groups perform well or poorly. This leads us to look at groups as wholes, not as collections of individual members.

11.4 Group structure and influence

In Chapter 3 we saw how people's attitudes and behaviours could be influenced by others, even when most other people were obviously wrong in their judgements. In the experiments of Sherif, Asch and Crutchfield interaction was not allowed; simply listening to or being informed of other people's views exerts powerful social influences. When individuals in groups are free to interact with each other, a further set of variables operates to influence individual members' behaviour. These variables are properties of the *group structure*, which may be considered to be the relatively stable patterns of relationships that exist among members of the group (McGrath, 1984). Four aspects of group structure, variables influencing member behaviour, will be looked at: *group cohesiveness, group norms, roles and status*, and *communication structure*.

Knowledge of a group's structure will give a good idea of the *dynamics* of that group: the dynamics of a group are processes by which change takes place. Change can be of two sorts: first, at an individual level it refers to changes in attitudes, opinions and willingness or not to conform to group expectations or role demands; and second, at a group level refers to altering patterns of relationships – changes in leadership, membership and morale of the group. Groups that endure over time, even though membership may differ, are continually changing at both individual and group levels to accommodate changes in the environment, the task and pressures within the group.

11.4.1 Group cohesiveness

Group cohesiveness may be regarded as the 'glue of interdependence' that binds a group of individuals together. Traditionally cohesiveness has been seen as the collection of forces (individual, interpersonal, intergroup) that keep members of a group together (Festinger *et al.*, 1950). One way of assessing group cohesiveness is the frequency with which the word 'we' is used by individuals to refer to the group: highly cohesive groups used the word 'we' very frequently. Cohesiveness is important for group performance since, to take an extreme example, if each member of the group disliked the other members of the group and what the group was about, the group is not likely to perform very well or even stay together for very long! However, highly cohesive groups may also perform poorly, as we shall see towards the end of this chapter in the section on 'groupthink' (Section 11.7.3).

What makes membership of a group attractive to an individual and causes that individual to want to remain a member? Early research by Cartwright and Zander (1968) suggested the prime reason to be that the group satisfies individual members' interests. This research suggested that factors which enhance interpersonal attraction such as perceived similarity of group members, co-operation and acceptance of each other result in groups being highly cohesive. This approach has had numerous applications, for example, in sport Widmeyer *et al.* (1985) developed a questionnaire called 'The Group Environment Questionnaire' to measure cohesiveness in sports teams.

More recently, Hogg (1992) has distinguished between personal attraction and social attraction, where the latter is the 'liking component of group membership' while the former does not apply to groups. This is because Hogg claims that the individual characteristics, personality, etc. have little to do with group cohesiveness. Social attraction is based on self-categorisation theory (Turner *et al.*, 1987) (see Chapter 10). Hogg and Turner (1985) demonstrated that cohesiveness or solidarity is shown regardless of whether members of a group thought they would like other members or not. Hogg (1992) produces a general model showing how cohesiveness results from interpersonal attraction, and this is depicted in Figure 11.6. The model emphasises the importance of interdependence, co-operation and satisfaction with the goals of the group.

Highly cohesive groups exert strong influences upon individual members to behave in accordance with group expectations and norms. In an early experiment Schachter (1951) formed groups in which members were told they would get on well with each other (high cohesiveness) or would not (low cohesiveness). Participants had to cut out cardboard shapes in order to make chess boards, they did this working alone in separate rooms. Attempts to influence productivity were made by giving notes to participants who were led to believe these notes had come from other group members. Productivity increased when the notes urged an increase in productivity for both high and low cohesive

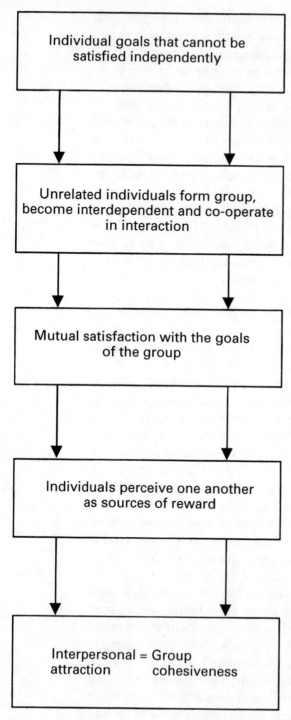

Figure 11.6: Hogg's (1992) interpersonal model of group cohesiveness

groups; however, members of high cohesive groups were much more likely to *reduce* productivity when urged to do so than were members of low cohesive groups. The experiment demonstrates that highly cohesive groups may follow negative injunctions from group members even when this may result in disapproval from people outside of the group. Cohesive groups have been found to react negatively and reject a 'black sheep' of the group and pay greater heed to confirming group members (Marques, 1988). Group cohesiveness, then, is important in influencing people, group performance and providing an individual's satisfaction.

11.4.2 Group norms

When a group first comes together it is unlikely to have a set of standards, values and rules by which to operate. With the autokinetic effect investigated by Sherif (1936) (see Chapter 10) we saw that a group norm developed as a product of the average individual judgement. For a wide range of norms that develop in a group the concept of *convergence* has received wide-ranging support. For example, Hoekstra and Wilke (1972) compared individual management decisions about wages to that of managers in groups of seven and found that the average of the individual recommendations was similar to that made by the groups of managers.

Once a group has established a set of norms, researchers have found them to be resistant to change. This has been established in numerous applied settings including output levels in a manufacturing company (Roethlisberger and Dickson, 1939) to methods of doing a job (Coch and French, 1948).

Norms function to hold a group together and allow new people joining a group to integrate into the group quickly with the result that performance or output is not impaired with change of membership. Wilke and Meertens (1994) propose, in addition, that group norms function to resolve two types of conflict that may arise. These are cognitive conflicts and conflicts of interest. Cognitive conflicts refer to disagreements or differing ideas and opinions and norms guide what should be done. Conflicts of interest arise within a group over status, competitiveness between members, for example, and may reduce effectiveness of group performance. Norms may function to prevent conflicts of interest or indicate how they should be resolved. Norms also help a group to achieve its goal, maintain itself, provide a shared reality and define relationships with other groups and with members within a group (Steiner, 1972).

11.4.3 Roles and status

The behaviour of a person in a group is influenced by the role he or she is expected to adopt and the status of that person in relation to others in the group. A role is usually defined as 'the behaviours expected of a person occupying a certain position in a group'. For example, the roles of father and mother differ in a family group, the roles of leader and expert differ in a work group. Roles are normative in that people occupying them are expected to conform to a set of norms associated with the role.

A tripartite distinction may be made between *expected role, perceived role* and *enacted role* (Shaw, 1981). The perceived role is the behaviour the occupant of the position thinks he or she *should* perform; the enacted role is the *actual* behaviour engaged in by the person occupying the position; and the *expected* role is the behaviour thought appropriate by others in the group. When these three roles are in accord there will be little, if any, conflict between the occupant of the role and other members of the group. However, disparity between any two or all three roles may result in group conflict; if perceived and/or enacted roles differ greatly from member expectations, the person occupying the role may either be put under pressure to conform, asked to vacate the position or, unusually, attempt to change the expectations of other members of the group.

In Chapter 10 we saw how the roles of 'guard' and 'prisoner' in

Zimbardo's (1969) prison simulation study exerted powerful influences over behaviour, so much so that the experiment had to be stopped after only six days. Notice that in Zimbardo's study no external pressure was put on participants to conform to role expectations, their perceived and enacted roles were consistent with stereotypical expectations of prisoner and guard existing in society.

A classic study by Schachter (1951) demonstrates how the role a person adopts in a group affects patterns of communication within the group. Schachter had groups consisting of five to seven members where three were confederates of the experimenter and the others naïve participants. Each member was given a case history of a delinquent to read, after which they had to give their opinions about what ought to be done with the delinquent. The group then had to discuss this for 45 minutes. The confederates adopted one of three roles: (a) *the deviate*, where an extreme and different position from the rest of the group was taken; (b) *the mode*, where the position of the most common view of the group was taken; and (c) *the slider* who first took an extreme and different position to the rest of the group but changed during the course of the discussion to that of the common view of the group. Schachter found that at the start of group discussion communications in the group were mainly directed at people occupying extreme positions (the deviate and slider). As discussions proceeded less and less communications were directed at the slider as his position gradually came to conform to the common group view. However, communications to the deviate, who did not change his position, were high to start with then decreased dramatically; as soon as the group discovered they were not going to change his opinion they ceased attempting to do so and tended to exclude him from further discussion. In reality though, as the Asch studies demonstrate, a lone deviate in the face of an otherwise unanimous group view is unlikely to maintain his or her position for very long, particularly if the person values membership of that group.

Usually a person occupies different roles in different groups: when behaviours demanded of each role differ but occur at the same time there will be *role conflict*. This is resolved by the person enacting the role in the group which has greatest attraction and importance for him or her. Killian (1952) investigated this in policemen when oil refineries in their home city caught fire. Role conflict was between acting as a policeman by serving the community and acting as a father by ensuring the safety of their family. Every policeman whose family lived in the city threatened by the fire resolved role conflict in favour of the role of father. Role conflict is difficult to resolve for an individual and is known to be extremely stressful (Williams *et al.* (1991).

The role or position a person occupies in a group has an evaluation attached to it, and this is the *status* of that position. A distinction is made between *ascribed* and *achieved* status: the former does not reflect individual merit or achievement but comes through, for example, age, sex or social standing of the family into which the person is born. The latter does reflect abilities and achievements (or failures) of the person. The status of a person influences the extent to which he or she conforms to role expectations and group norms. High-status people both conform to, and deviate more from, group norms than low-status people. Greatest conformity to group norms and expectations comes from people occupying the second highest status position (Harvey and Consalvi, 1960). Minority influence may be achieved by a high-status person accumulating *idiosyncrasy credits* (Hollander, 1984).

Status affects the pattern and content of group communications; Beck *et al.* (1950) provided a novel demonstration of this by planting a rumour in a factory with five statuses of workers. The researchers were interested to find who reported the rumour to whom. They found the vast majority of reports were upwards in the status hierarchy, with very few communications of the rumour between people of the same status or downwards to people of lower status. The status of a person can influence both group performance and opinions of group members. Strodtbeck (1957) investigated the effects of socio-economic status of jurors with respect to leadership, participation and influence. Participants acted as jurors and heard a tape-recording of a court case, afterwards they were asked to reach a verdict as a jury. Three findings emerged: first, high socio-economic-status jurors were more likely to be elected as chairperson; second, high-status jurors participated more and had greater influence in pressing their views on others; and third, high-status jurors were better liked than low-status jurors. This has been explained in relation to *expectation states theory* (de Gilder and Wilke, 1994) which takes account of status coming from two aspects in a person: specific and diffuse status characteristics. Diffuse characteristics do not relate directly to the ability or skill needed to be successful at a task but are general and apply across many tasks. Someone perceived to have a high diffuse status tends to be regarded as able in a range of group situations and group tasks. In the Strodtbeck (1957) study, electing a high-status person as foreman of the jury happened because the rest of the jury regard the diffuse characteristics as applicable to effectively enacting the role. In reality, this may not always be the case.

11.4.4 Communication structure

In the preceding sections we have seen how group structure may influence both the pattern and content of communications. Here group members were allowed to communicate freely and face to face; it is of interest to discover how group performance and satisfaction with the group are affected when a communicative structure is imposed and restrictions are placed upon who can communicate with whom. Time, distance and other restraints may not permit a group to come face to face, and communication may take place via the telephone, by computer, through e-mail or a simple letter. In such circumstances allowing each group member to communicate with every other group member may be inefficient in terms of time and duplication. It may then be necessary to impose a certain communication structure upon the group. Bavelas (1950) introduced the notion of communication networks in which individuals in five-person groups were restricted as to who they could communicate with. The most commonly researched networks are given in Figure 11.7, the crucial difference between each is the degree of *centralisation*.

The most centralised network is the wheel since person C can communicate with everyone else, but the four peripheral members (A, B, D and E) can only communicate with person C. The most decentralised network is the circle as each person communicates with two other people, here all members are equally central. The chain and 'Y' networks are moderately centralised positions.

Leavitt (1951) experimentally investigated the effects of these communication networks on performance at problem-solving tasks, member satisfaction and morale. Problems given to groups were to discover which symbol (for example, asterisk, addition or subtraction sign) from a possible six was common for each group member. Each member of a five-person group was given a card with six symbols on it, with a different symbol of the six omitted from each of the five cards. Group members could only communicate to others as dictated by the communication network they worked within, and communication was by written message only. Measures were taken of time to solve problems, number of problems solved, number of incorrect solutions, how much group members enjoyed the task and whether a group was perceived to have a leader.

Two main sets of findings emerged: first, for task performance the more centralised networks solved problems faster and made fewer errors. The wheel produced the fastest and greatest number of accurate solutions, the circle the slowest and fewest number of accurate solutions. Second, satisfaction of individual members was highest in the most decentralised network: those in the circle expressed greatest enjoyment of the task, while peripheral members of the wheel, chain and 'Y' enjoyed the task the least. Person C in the latter three networks was seen as the group leader, no leader was perceived to exist in the

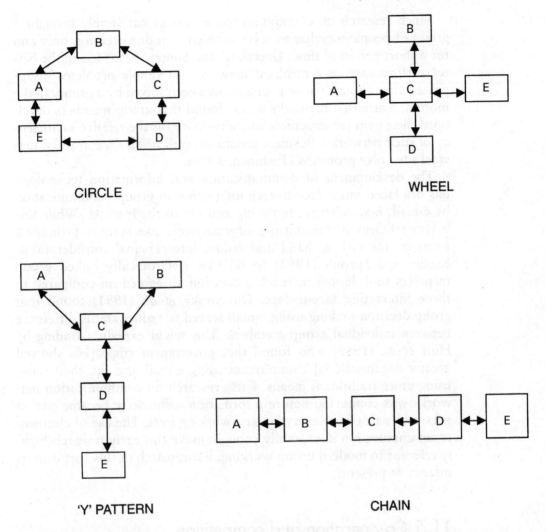

Figure 11.7: Examples of five-person communication networks, boxes represent positions and arrows permissible communication channels between people in the group. The wheel is the most centralised, and the circle the most decentralised network. After Bavelas (1950)

circle network. Subsequent research has confirmed these findings for relatively simple tasks such as those used by Leavitt. However, for more complex problems the more decentralised networks produced superior performance, the circle being the best. Shaw (1981) explains this as due to more complex tasks placing excessive demands or information overload on the central person in centralised networks. Decentralised networks allow a more even distribution of the workload among group members.

Much research on communication networks has simply brought a group of people together to solve problems on one occasion only and for a short period of time. Guetzkow and Simon (1955) found the better performance of centralised networks on simple problems disappeared after about20 or so problems had been solved by a group. In the more decentralised networks it was found that group members developed their own substructures to compensate for the relative inefficiency of such networks. Business groups do well using decentralised networks to solve problems (Tushman, 1978).

The development of communication and information technology has displaced much face-to-face interaction in group communication by e-mail, fax, video conferencing and use of the Internet. While this is very efficient at transmitting information it does seem to promote a focus on the task at hand and reduce interpersonal considerations. Kiesler and Sproull (1992) found that electronically linked group members took longer to reach a decision all agreed on compared to those interacting face-to-face. Dubrovsky *et al.* (1991) found that group decision-making using e-mail served to reduce status difference between individual group members. This might explain a finding by Huff *et al.* (1989) who found that government employees showed greater organisational commitment using e-mail and fax than those using more traditional means. Early research on communication networks was conducted before information technology became such a pervasive part of our everyday and working lives. The use of electronic communication does, oddly enough, make this early research highly relevant to modern group working, but research of this sort is in its infancy at present.

11.5 Co-operation and competition

The issue to be explored in this section is how co-operation and competition affect group performance and which is more effective in helping a group to achieve its goals. Johnson *et al.* (1981) reviewed over 100 studies which had compared competitive with co-operative groups and found only eight in which competition was superior. Research on this goes back over 50 years to the pioneering work of Deutsch (1949), who demonstrated that tasks requiring co-operation of all group members result in high levels of cohesiveness, a commitment to achieving the goals and an atmosphere of helping each other. By contrast, competitive tasks result in group members obstructing and disliking each other, and failing to achieve the goal set. Given these remarkably consistent findings, Brown (1988) wonders why there is such an 'overwhelming emphasis on competitive arrangements in our educational institutions and workplaces' (p. 32).

Social dilemmas are situations where the action of an individual benefits that individual but harms the group as a whole. For example, our use of cars produces pollution in cities and contributes to global warming through the 'greenhouse effect'. As individuals we each seem unwilling to change our pattern of life because it is so beneficial to us. But the net effect for a country or city is damaging to large groups of people or nations (Stern, 1992). Social dilemmas, then, are situations where each person favours competition over co-operation. To overcome social dilemmas strategies for encouraging co-operation are needed. However, this does require people to trust each other not to be selfish. Research on social dilemmas typically uses *resource dilemmas* where individual benefit results in the resource disappearing altogether for the group. Messick *et al.* (1983) identified students who had either low or high trust in other people. The students were then given a resource dilemma in which they were told that a certain number of fish were in a lake. Each participant then decides how many fish he or she will take from the common resource. Following each person deciding, the total number of fish are taken from the lake and the remaining fish are replenished by 10 per cent. This is repeated over a number of trials. Messick *et al.* found that low-trust students took as many fish for themselves as they could. By contrast, high-trust students took less from the lake on each subsequent trial. This allowed the lake to replenish itself so that everybody could have fish over many, many trials. These results are summarised in Figure 11.8.

Social psychologists have produced evidence that social dilemmas may be overcome by first, restructuring the group task to emphasise interpendence between people, and, second, by focusing on interdependence to increased shared identity and commitment to group rather than individual goals (Liebrand *et al.*, 1992). This is not a simple or easy matter – think of how difficult it is going to be to change our patterns of use of the car in order to reduce congestion, pollution and road rage!

11.6 Power and leadership

Social psychology has devoted much effort in attempting to answer such questions as: 'What makes a good leader?', 'Can effective and ineffective leaders be distinguished?', 'Do different situations demand different leadership styles?' Contemporary perspectives suggest the following variables all need to be taken into account: the leader's personality and

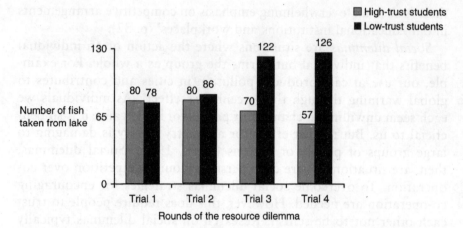

Figure 11.8: Number of fish taken from the lake by high- and low-trust students in the resource dilemma used by Messick *et al.* (1983)

behaviour; composition and function of the group; the situation and group structure; the nature of the task and whether the leader is effective or ineffective; and how and what types of power the leader uses. Early research looked for personality characteristics which might separate leaders from non-leaders, but failure here led psychologists to focus on the situation rather than the person. This too failed and theorising became increasingly complex to encompass all or most of the variables mentioned above. Given the number of variables now acknowledged to be important, you will not be surprised to discover that no one single definition of leadership has been forthcoming. Leadership may be seen as involving at least three components: first, leadership as *social influence* refers to the extent to which a person or persons can direct and control the behaviour of others by changing attitudes and opinions and getting members to conform to roles and group norms; second, leadership *behaviour* refers to what the leader does in terms of clarifying group objectives, making decisions and suggesting ways of achieving objectives. Leadership as *authority* concerns the power the leader is invested with or is perceived to have by other group members in order to achieve the group's goals and institute change when necessary. One shortcoming of attempting to understand leadership along these lines is that it does not tell us what makes leaders effective in some situations and not others. For example, we need to know why Winston Churchill made a good leader during World War II, but not before or afterwards. Before looking in more detail at leadership we shall first examine different types of interpersonal power that social psychologists have suggested leaders may use.

11.6.1 Types of power

The most enduring and influential analysis of power suggests that there are six types: expert power, referent power, informational power, legitimate power, reward power and coercive power (French and Raven, 1959; Raven, 1993). Expert power comes from having specialist knowledge and ability, for example, in documentary or news programmes experts in the field are brought in to give an informed view. Referent power depends on making a common identity or social identity amongst other people in the group, so making people in a group feel part of a team. Informational power is the use of logic, argument and information to persuade others to do a task or do it in a certain way. Legitimate power uses norms, accepted rules and hierarchical structures. Reward power comes from the ability of the leader to reward group members for performing well through promotion, praise or bonuses. Coercive power is where punishment can be used or threatened to achieve the desired outcome. Table 11.1 summarises these six types of power and gives an example of each related to the role of a teacher.

If you think a little more about each of these types of power in relation to your psychology teacher some ideas may come to you about when and under what circumstances each may be used. Frost and Stakelski (1998) showed that top managers in business organisations

Type of power	Description	Example: psychology teacher
Expert power	Has high level of knowledge and/or ability	Teacher has doctorate in social psychology
Referent power	Enhances group or common identity	Teacher makes whole class feel like a group with shared goals
Information power	Uses logic, argument and information to persuade	Teacher persuades you that psychology is worth studying
Legitimate power	Use of norms, rules and status and hierarchies	Teacher expects students to regard her as in charge of the class
Reward power	Able to give or withhold rewards	Teacher praises you for hard work on practical project
Coercive power	Ability to threaten or actually punish	Teacher sends you out of class for talking

Table 11.1: Six types of interpersonal power with an example of each in relation to a teacher of psychology. After French and Raven (1959) and Raven (1993)

tend to use coercive, reward and legitimate power more than middle managers. The latter rely heavily on using referent and expert power in managing other people. In follow-up research, Stakelski *et al.* (1989) showed that the more senior a person is in an organisation and the more people that person has to manage, the more he or she will use coercive, reward and referent power. At the extreme, dictators maintain their position of power by excessive use of coercive and reward power, they also use referent power in an attempt to create a common group identity (think of leaders of religious cults).

11.6.2 'Great man' theory of leadership

Historically and traditionally a leader has been viewed as a person possessing a distinct set of personality characteristics – this view is encapsulated in the saying 'leaders are born not made'. Early research looked for traits distinguishing leaders from non-leaders and found, at best, leaders to be slightly more intelligent than non-leaders! Mann (1959) reviewed over 100 studies seeking to correlate personality characteristics with leadership; some of the findings are summarised in Table 11.2.

From Table 11.2 it can be seen that weak evidence exists supporting the claim that leaders are more intelligent, more extrovert, more dominant and more sensitive than non-leaders. Mullen *et al.* (1989) have added talkativeness to this list, but this may be seen as part of extroversion. McGrath (1984) offers five reasons for why the trait approach has been and always will be unsuccessful: (a) there are no agreed upon personality traits by which to compare leaders and non-leaders; (b) there is no agreed upon definition of leadership – researchers using different definitions may

Traits	Number of findings	% giving a positive relationship	% giving a negative relationship	% yielding no relationship
Intelligence	196	46	1	53
Adjustment	164	30	2	68
Extroversion	119	31	5	64
Dominance	39	38	15	46
Masculinity	70	16	1	83
Conservatism	62	5	27	68
Sensitivity	101	15	1	84

Table 11.2: Percentage of positive and negative relationships between personality traits and leadership. Adapted from Mann (1959)

select different people from the same group as leaders; (c) the trait approach ignores relationships between leaders and followers – are relationships good or bad and are different people more or less effective in different situations?; (d) the situation generally is ignored; and (e) the approach assumes a single leader exists in a group when quite often two types of leaders often emerge.

Lack of success with the trait approach led researchers to focus on the situation and how this affects the person who becomes the leader. Being *appointed* to the position of leader, as opposed to a leader *emerging*, may shape the person's behaviour because of role requirements stemming from that position and different behaviour by group members to the leader than to other group members. In a study by Bell and French (1950), acting petty officers were randomly assigned from a pool of new recruits; they were subsequently found to be retained in that position and perceived to be leaders by their fellow recruits. The study demonstrates that mere occupancy of a role, even if arrived at randomly, results in that person being treated as and perceived to be the leader.

The communication structure, as we saw earlier in this chapter, may determine the leader: Leavitt (1951) found occupants of the central positions in the wheel, chain and 'Y' pattern were perceived to be and became group leaders. Similarly, Sommer (1969) found people who occupied central positions at a table were often treated as and became the group leader. Crisis situations often result in the emergence or replacement of a leader. Hamblin (1958) demonstrated this in an experiment in which college students working in groups of three were asked to play a game in which they had to work out some of the rules of the game for themselves. Upon correctly discovering a rule the experimenter turned on a green light, when wrong a red light was switched on. All groups had to play the game six times; for half the groups the rules to be discovered remained the same throughout, for the other half the experimenter changed the rules after the third game. The latter condition resulted in a crisis for the groups on the fourth game since rules they thought were correct were now wrong. Hamblin took two measures: (a) the frequency of suggestions made by each person in the group; and (b) the frequency with which suggestions made by one person were accepted by the other two group members. Individuals who had been influential in 'pre-crisis' games became much more so in the 'crisis' games – they made more suggestions and had their suggestions accepted more often. The person who emerged as leader in the crisis period was also challenged and criticised less often. In short, a crisis situation resulted in members of a group being more willing to be led and influenced than in a non-crisis situation.

In summary, there is some evidence to suggest situations make leaders; this occurs not because of any inherent personality characteristics of the leader but because the situation demands greater directiveness and clarity of thought, and here group members are more willing to be guided by one person. The emergence of a leader may be because the person talks and contributes the most or may simply be due to the person occupying a central position in the group, or the leader may be more intelligent than other people in the group (Bass and Avolio, 1993).

11.6.3 Behavioural style of leaders

Regardless of whether a leader is appointed or emerges, the *behavioural style* of the person in that role has important consequences for group performance. Leadership style affects task performance, morale and the cohesiveness of the group. Hemphill (1950) conducted a large-scale study in which participants rated leaders' behaviour on over 1000 different aspects. Two important behavioural dimensions emerged: *group-centred* and *directive* behaviours. Group-centred or 'consideration' behaviours included warmth of personal relationships, mutual trust, willingness to listen to followers' suggestions and a democratic approach allowing all members to participate in decision-making. Directive behaviours, called 'initiating structure', included maintenance of standards and performance, assigning tasks to members, ensuring individuals followed rules and conformed to norms and making sure the members understood the leader's role. Consideration behaviours bear a similarity to the behaviours of the socio-emotional leader and initiating structure behaviours to the task-oriented leader found by Bales (1950) who developed a comprehensive and highly influential coding system for all behaviours, verbal and non-verbal, that take place in interacting, small groups. These behaviours are allocated to one of four main areas: positive and negative socio-emotional behaviour, and task-related questions and answers. Each category is then broken down into three specific sub-categories as shown in Table 11.3.

Interaction Process Analysis (IPA) provides a powerful tool for recording individual behaviour in group interaction since it provides measures of both patterns and content of communications as well as participation rates of each person in the group.

Bales and Slater (1955) used IPA to show how role differentiation takes place in problem-solving groups; they found two leadership roles emerged from initially unstructured groups. First, the role of task leader emerges; communications are mainly confined to the two task areas (questions and answers in Table 11.3). Second, the role of group

Area	Behaviour
Socio-emotional (positive reactions)	Shows solidarity, raises others' status, gives help and rewards
	Shows tension release, laughs, jokes and shows satisfaction
	Agrees, shows passive acceptance, understands, concurs, complies
Task area (attempted answers)	Gives suggestion, direction, implying autonomy of the other
	Gives opinion, evaluation, analysis, expresses feelings and wishes
	Gives orientation, information, repeats, clarifies, confirms
Task area (questions)	Asks for orientation, information, repetition, confirmation
	Asks for opinion, evaluation, analysis, expression of feeling
	Asks for suggestion, direction, possible ways of action
Socio-emotional (negative reactions)	Disagrees, shows passive rejection, formality, withholds help
	Shows tension, asks for help, withdraws out of field
	Shows antagonism, deflates others' status, defends or asserts self

Table 11.3: Bales's (1950) Interaction Process Analysis (IPA) scheme for categorizing verbal and non-verbal behaviour of members interacting in a group

harmoniser or socio-emotional leader emerges; this person takes on the role of promoting group cohesiveness and reducing tension and conflict within the group. Bales claimed that different people occupied each of these leadership roles, and that the socio-emotional leader was the best liked member of the group. However, research has produced evidence that one person may occupy both leadership roles (Burke, 1974).

A different, and now classic, set of studies by Lewin, Lippett and White (1939) demonstrated how the behavioural style of a leader affects group performance. Groups of 10- to 11-year-old boys worked in small groups on a task of carving models from bars of soap. The groups were exposed to three different leadership styles: authoritarian, democratic and *laissez-faire*. *Authoritarian* leaders made all the decisions for the group, did not participate in group activities, assigned boys to tasks without saying why and made changes without consultation. *Democratic* leaders made decisions only after consultation with the group, were friendly to group members, participated in group activities, gave reasons for praise and criticism, and offered help when required. *Laissez-faire* leaders played a passive role, did not attempt to direct or co-ordinate the group and made neither positive or negative evaluations of the group.

The democratic style of leadership was found to produce highest morale in the group and greatest friendliness and co-operation. However, groups with this style of leadership produced fewer models than those under authoritarian leadership, though the models were of higher quality. The boys also kept working in the absence of the leader. The authoritarian style resulted in more models being made but misbehaviour occurred when the leader was absent. Poorest performance was under the *laissez-faire* style of leadership; here fewest models were produced and misbehaviour occurred all the time, however, the boys were friendly towards the leader. After the boys had experienced each type of leadership style they were found to prefer the democratic approach most. In summary, group performance in terms of quality of the models made and group cohesiveness was highest with the democratic style of leadership.

More recent research has suggested that leadership behaviour can be accounted for along two dimensions resulting in four leadership styles. The dimensions are autocratic–democratic and directive–permissive (Muczyk and Reimann, 1987). The former relates to that of the above studies, while the latter dimension refers to how much freedom the leader gives to group members when carrying out their task. The four leadership styles to emerge from this conceptual framework are: permissive democrat, directive democrat, permissive autocrat and directive autocrat.

Other research on leadership style has produced consistent evidence for two behavioural styles; these relate to the socio-emotional or consideration style, and task or initiating structure style. The task-oriented leader may adopt any one of the four categories identified by Muczyk and Riemann (1987), but it is unlikely that a socio-emotional leader would have much success as a directive autocrat!

11.6.4 Fiedler's contingency theory

A highly influential theory of leadership *effectiveness* has been proposed by Fiedler (1971), this takes both *leadership style* and *situational factors* into account. There are three situational factors: (a) leader–follower relations: if the leader is accepted, trusted and respected, relations are good, if not relations are bad; (b) task structure: high task structure is where the task set the group is well defined, low is where it is vague; and (c) power of the leader: the leader has strong position of power if the leader's power is both legitimate and can draw on resources to impose rewards and sanctions on members of the group as a whole; position of power is weak if both these are absent. These three situational factors, since they can each take on one of two values, yield eight different combinations or *octants* as Fiedler calls them. For each octant the *overall* favourableness of the situation can be assessed, and favourableness ranges from extremely high to extremely low. Table 11.4 depicts the eight octants and the overall favourableness rating of

	Octants							
	I	**II**	**III**	**IV**	**V**	**VI**	**VII**	**VIII**
Leader–follower relations	Good	Good	Good	Poor	Poor	Poor	Poor	Poor
Task structure	High	High	Low	Low	High	High	Low	Low
Leader position power	Strong	Weak	Strong	Weak	Strong	Weak	Strong	Weak
Overall situational favourableness	Extra High	High	High	Mod. High	Mod. High	Low	Low	Extra Low

Table 11.4: Fiedler's typology of leadership situations and situational favourableness. Adapted from Fiedler (1971)

each. For example, one favourable situation (octant I) is where leader–follower relations are good, task structure is high and the leader's position of power is strong. Favourable situations are ones where the leader has a high degree of situational control; and unfavourable situations (octant VIII) where the leader has low situational control.

In order to predict effective leadership in each of these octants Fiedler says we need to know the *leadership style* of the person. This is measured by asking leaders, or anybody for that matter, to cast their mind over all the people they have worked with in the past and think about the person they least liked – the *least preferred co-worker* or LPC. With this person in mind the leader is asked to fill in a set of semantic differential scales containing such items as 'friendly – unfriendly', 'co-operative – unco-operative'. A favourable attitude towards the LPC would attract a high score (high LPC) and an unfavourable attitude a low score (low LPC). For Fiedler a high LPC score indicates a *relations-oriented* (socio-emotional) leader and a low LPC a *task-oriented* leader.

Task-oriented leaders will be most effective, Fiedler claims, in either very favourable or very unfavourable situations; relations-oriented leaders will be most effective where the situation is moderately favourable, this is shown in Table 11.5. The most important situational factor is leader–follower relations; when this is good (or bad) only one other situational factor needs to be good (or bad) for the overall situation to be favourable (or unfavourable). Accordingly, octants I, II and III in Table 11.4 represent the highly favourable conditions; while octants I, II and III represent the highly favourable conditions; finally,

Leadership style	Situational factors		
	Highly favourable (Octants I, II, III)	Moderately favourable (Octants IV, V)	Highly unfavourable (Octants VI, VII, VIII)
Relationship oriented leader (High LPC)	Ineffective	Effective	Ineffective
Task oriented leader (Low LPC)	Effective	Ineffective	Effective

Table 11.5: Effectiveness or ineffectiveness of different types of leaders according to situational favourableness. Adapted from Fiedler (1971)

octants VI, VII and VIII represent the highly unfavourable conditions. In these cases groups would be effectively led by a task-oriented leader. Octants IV and V are moderately favourable and a relations-oriented leader would be most effective here.

Why should such leadership styles be most effective in these different situations? Fiedler argues that when conditions are unfavourable the group would be willing to overlook interpersonal conflicts and tensions in order to get on with the task, hence the appropriateness of a task-oriented leader. In favourable conditions, the leader can get on with the task in hand since the situation is a positive one with little interpersonal conflict, again a task-oriented leader is most appropriate. When the situation is only moderately favourable, conflict and tension within the group may be the biggest problem; the socio-emotional or relations-oriented leader is needed to sort this out before the group can get on with their task. Matching a leadership style to the situational control is important since research which has investigated 'mismatches' report subordinate dissatisfaction and reduced job performance (Chemers *et al.*, 1985). Socio-emotional leaders trained in task performance have been found to enhance group productivity (Fiedler, 1993).

Thirty years of research on Fiedler's contingency model has provided fairly consistent support and demonstrated a wide range of application, especially in management (Fiedler and Garcia, 1987). However, the approach does not pay sufficient attention to group processes nor explain why leaders are appointed to a position and subsequently removed. For example, how might you use Fiedler's model to analyse the image of President Clinton following the Lewinski sex case? Thinking about this may lead you to wonder why leaders are chosen in the first place, and it is to this we now turn.

11.6.5 Choice of leader

If groups are allowed to choose their own leader, do they choose effective leaders? We saw above how important it is to match the leadership style to the situation. Research has shown that groups often make poor choices of who should be their leader, for example, Sorrentino and Field (1986) showed that the person who talks the most in the group regardless of the quality of what is said is viewed as the leader. Stereotypes also play a role in who we choose to be leader; group members often place too much importance on task-related matters and not enough on socio-emotional matters. Lord *et al.* (1986) claim that the preponderance of white males in key positions is to do with the stereotype of white males as competent and assertive. This suggests that there are aspects of a self-fulfilling prophecy operating here. This leads to the question of whether males and females use different leadership styles.

11.6.6 Male and female leaders

Eagly and Karau (1991) analysed 75 studies of leadership where mixed-sex groups interacted without a leader having initially been appointed. In these studies group members subsequently were asked who they perceived the leader to have been. Men were seen as occupying leadership positions more often than women. These findings seem to reinforce the stereotype of leaders we considered at the end of the previous section. Eagly and Johnson (1990), in another review of a large number of studies, found little difference in leadership style between males and females; females were slightly more democratic but not more socio-emotional as a common stereotype would lead you to think. Eagly *et al.* (1992) investigated how male and female leaders are evaluated by their subordinates. Again, little difference was found; however, female leaders were downrated if male subordinates perceived them to be adopting a masculine style – autocratic and directive. Female leaders were also rated as less effective when they were operating in areas where most other leaders were male. Eagly *et al.* (1992) do report that group members are happier if their leader is female and that women are just as effective leaders as men in getting a job done successfully.

11.7 Group decision-making

Decision-making is a common feature of our lives both domestically and at work. Day-to-day routine decisions are usually made individually.

However, when facing more important decisions which may have far-reaching effects on our lives, such as whether to accept a job in another part of the country, or move house, we often discuss the problem with significant others in order to arrive at the best choice from among the alternatives. Likewise at work, routine decisions we usually make on our own, for more important decisions, such as those of strategy and policy, formal decision-making groups are either constituted or already exist. Industrial organisations have boards and committees; schools and colleges have staff meetings and governments have cabinet meetings or their equivalent. At every layer in society, people come together to make decisions – it is assumed that the collective wisdom of a body of people produces a more informed and a higher quality decision than could be achieved by a single person working alone. Research, as we shall see, has addressed itself to testing the validity of these and related assumptions. In what follows we first look at the use of different types of decisions and rules by groups and their effect on outcomes. This is followed by a comparison of individual and group decision making. Finally, defective group decision-making will be considered by reference to Janis's notion of *groupthink*.

11.7.1 Decision-making rules

Davis (1973) developed the concept of *social decision schemes* as a simple set of rules to predict the final decision reached by a group from knowing the initial views of each group member. Davis proposes five main rules as follows: *unanimity* – here all group members must agree on the decision reached. Next, *majority wins* – the initial majority position is adopted as the final decision. The variation on this is the two-thirds majority rule. The *truth wins* rule states that the correct position or decision will emerge from group discussion. Finally, the *first-shift rule* suggests that the final decision adopted by the group will be consistent with the direction of the first shift in opinion shown by the group members.

Research on these social decision schemes has been conducted in a range of both laboratory and applied 'real-life' settings and has proved remarkably successful at predicting even quite complex decisions (Stasser *et al.*, 1989). Different rules apply to different types of decisions, for example, majority wins predicts decisions taken for judgement or evaluative tasks well, while truth wins predicts better for tasks where there is a correct answer (Kirchler and Davis, 1986).

11.7.2 Individual and group decision-making

Assessing whether groups make better decisions than individuals depends on how the word 'better' is interpreted and used. If there is an objective standard to compare individual and group decisions with, then performance judgements can easily be made. However, most decisions, both domestically and at work, cannot be easily compared to an objective standard. For example, was the decision to make the wearing of seat belts compulsory by law a good or bad one? Research had supported the view that wearing seat belts saved lives, but it may be that the wearing of seat belts causes more accidents, resulting in more non-fatal injuries, since people may feel safer with a seat belt on and be prepared to take greater risks than when they did not wear them.

On problem-solving tasks, comparing individual and group performance shows groups to solve more problems correctly than individuals working alone, but groups are less efficient in terms of the total number of person-hours used. The quality of group problem-solving is better than that of the *average* group member but is rarely better than that of the most able group member (Shaw, 1981). In many circumstances it is best to let an extremely able individual work alone rather than in a group.

A research strategy used by social psychologists to assess whether individuals working alone or groups produce higher quality decisions is to compare performance on a task with expert opinion. Hall and Watson (1970) used the 'moon problem', given in Figure 11.9, to compare individual and group decisions. In the first stage of the experiment participants worked alone in ranking the importance of each item for survival. They were then put in groups of 4–6 persons and told to discuss the rankings and come to a group consensus ranking (the unanimity rule) for the ranking of each item. Individual and group rankings were compared with the rankings given by experts from NASA. Hall and Watson found that groups did perform better than individuals, but not better than the best individual rankings (i.e. those closest to the experts).

Generally, research does support common wisdom that groups produce better decisions than individuals but with two riders: first, the amount of time spent by a group is much greater than the individual working alone when measured in person hours; second, the best individual performs better than a group.

11.7.3 Groupthink

On 17 April 1961 a brigade of 1400 Cuban exiles invaded a swampy part of the coast of Cuba known as the Bay of Pigs. The ultimate aim of this invasion was the overthrow of Fidel Castro's government. However, nothing went as planned: by the first day two of the supply ships had been sunk by Castro's air force and the remaining two supply ships had fled.

The 'Moon Problem'

You are a member of a space crew originally scheduled to rendezvous with a mother ship on the lighted surface of the moon. Due to mechanical difficulties, however, your ship was forced to land at a spot some 200 miles from the rendezvous point. During the crash landing much of the equipment aboard was damaged and since survival depends on reaching the mother ship the most critical items available must be chosen for the 200-mile trip. Below are listed the 15 items left intact and undamaged after landing. Your task is to rank order them in terms of their importance in allowing your crew to reach the rendezvous point. Place the number 1 by the most important item, the number 2 by the second most important item, and so on. Place the number 15 by the least important item.

ITEMS	RANKING
Box of matches	
Food concentrate	
50 feet of nylon rope	
Parachute silk	
Portable heating unit	
Two 0.45 calibre pistols	
1 case dehydrated milk	
2 hundred-pound tanks of oxygen	
Stellar map (of the moon's constellation)	
Life raft	
Magnetic compass	
5 gallons of water	
Signal flares	
First aid kit	
Solar-powered RM receiver-transmitter	

The NASA ranks were as follows: Box of matches – 15; food concentrate – 4; 50 feet of nylon rope – 6; parachute silk – 8; portable heating unit – 13; two 0.45 calibre pistols – 11; 1 case of dehydrated milk – 12; two hundred-pound tanks of oxygen – 1; stellar map – 3; life raft – 9; magnetic compass – 14; 5 gallons of water – 2; signal flares – 10; first aid kit – 7; solar-powered RM receiver-transmitter – 5.

Figure 11.9: The 'Moon problem' together with NASA rankings used by Hall and Watson (1970)

By the second day the brigade of exiles was surrounded at the Bay of Pigs by Castro's army, and by the end of the third day it was all over: what was left of the invasion force was captured and imprisoned. The Bay of Pigs' fiasco, as it came to be called, was approved by President Kennedy and his small group of highly experienced policy and military advisers. Shortly afterwards Kennedy admitted making a dreadful decision and asked,

'How could I have been so stupid as to let them go ahead?' Consequences of the fiasco were far-reaching: less than a year later Russia was installing nuclear weapons and a large military force in Cuba. This led to the Cuban missile crisis of October 1962 which posed the greatest threat of nuclear war in the world's history. This crisis, fortunately, was effectively dealt with by the Kennedy administration.

Janis (1972) proposed that members of President Kennedy's decision-making group exhibited what he called *groupthink*. This occurs in a highly cohesive group which has as its main goal unanimity of opinion rather than a critical and realistic appraisal of the situation. Janis (1982) analysed other 'fiascos' in international decision-making such as the bombing of Pearl Harbor in the Second World War, and the Watergate Affair with President Nixon and found evidence in all these cases of groupthink.

When is groupthink likely to occur, how can it be identified and how does it produce defective decision making? Figure 11.10 shows how the concurrence-seeking tendency, or striving for unanimity, results from five antecedent conditions. The first, high cohesiveness, is perhaps, the most important, isolation of the group from outside criticism and the lack of procedures in the group for evaluating properly different alternatives are also very important. The eight symptoms of groupthink, shown in Figure 11.10, can be illustrated by reference to the major assumptions the group made which all proved to be wrong when deciding to go ahead with the invasion of the Bay of Pigs.

An illusion of invulnerability led to excessive optimism and risk taking – the group was unrealistic about the cover story holding up, unrealistic in assessing the Cuban air force and army to be effective and unrealistic about the morale and willingness of the Cuban exiles to carry out the invasion on their own. Belief in the inherent morality of the group led members to think that what they were doing was right and that because of this it was bound to succeed. Direct pressures on dissenters within the group prevented critical evaluation of the assumptions that were made. An illusion of unanimity in the group led to 'silences' in group discussion to be interpreted as agreement. Finally, and most sinister of all the symptoms of groupthink, is the emergence of self-appointed *mindguards*. These were members of the group who took it upon themselves to protect the group from criticism and dissent and so fostered a false feeling of unanimity. The research method used by Janis was to examine archive material and conduct a content analysis. Subsequent research in the same vein has confirmed that groupthink does play a role in disastrous or poor quality decisions (Tetlock *et al.*, 1992). This more recent research suggests that the main factor is the use of overly restrictive decision procedures by the group.

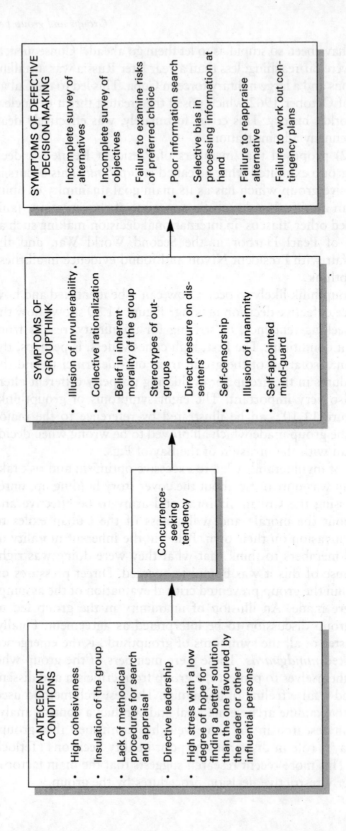

Figure 11.10: The antecedent conditions prevailing in a group which lead to concurrence-seeking tendencies. Such tendencies result in the eight symptoms of groupthink, groupthink results in decision-making being defective in seven major ways. From Janis and Mann (1977)

Investigating groupthink in laboratory experiments has proved more challenging. Turner *et al.* (1992) conducted a series of experiments in which groupthink was induced by fostering group cohesiveness. This was done by giving all members of the group a common identity through giving a name to the group and having each group member wear a label with the group name on it. This research also had groups operating in either high or low threat conditions. Findings showed that high cohesive groups in high threat conditions reached poorer quality decisions than low cohesive groups in high threat conditions. Interestingly, high cohesive groups in low threat conditions arrived at better quality decisions than low cohesive groups in low threat conditions. This implies that groupthink is most likely to occur when a group is in a threatening situation, which is precisely the conditions under which President Kennedy operated with his group in the Bay of Pigs fiasco. Other research conducted through laboratory experiments has not found strong support for the claim that highly cohesive groups produce poor quality decisions.

11.7.4 Preventing groupthink

The Cuban missile crisis, less than a year after the Bay of Pigs, was dealt with by the same group of people but, according to Janis, was characterised by high quality decision-making. The symptoms of groupthink, given in Figure 11.10, tell us which group characteristics are undesirable and should suggest ways of avoiding them. For example, group members should not suppress their doubts (self-censorship); dissent from group opinions should be encouraged rather than suppressed. If the group appears unanimous it would be important to ascertain that this is actually the case rather than assume it to be so. Of course, these and others you may be able to think of introduce conflict and tensions into a group and so *reduce* cohesiveness.

Janis (1982) offers numerous prescriptions for avoiding groupthink: three of the more important ones will be given. First, the leader or chairperson of the group should encourage each group member to express doubts and objections to a proposed course of action. Second, the leader of the group should attempt to be impartial rather than state his or her preferences at the outset, this avoids concurrence-seeking tendencies from other members. Third, the group should, if possible, set up other independent groups to work on the same problem and make their own recommendations, the products of the two groups could then be evaluated and the most soundly reasoned decision taken. Costs are incurred for adopting such procedures – it will take longer to reach a decision, conflict within the group and between individual members will increase, and group cohesiveness will decrease. As you can see, there is no easy, foolproof way of avoiding groupthink, but if decision-making groups are more concerned with the quality of decision than satisfaction with being members of the group, such costs will be accepted. In the end, it must be more satisfying to be a member of a decision-making group producing high quality rather than defective decisions, even if more argument, conflict and greater time are spent reaching decisions.

11.8 Application: management teams and team roles

We have seen in this chapter how group performance may be affected by such factors as group size, cohesiveness and type of leader. The application of various areas in social psychology to understanding behaviour in organisations is recognised as important by many top managers (Robbins, 1998). In this section we look at the composition of management teams and briefly consider profiles of teams that are likely and unlikely to be successful.

Belbin (1981; 1993) produced a highly influential management team model based on the idea that different people may perform different roles or functions in a management team. Furthermore, Belbin states that successful management teams are composed of a balance of different roles or functions. Belbin (1981) claims that, 'What is needed is not well-balanced individuals, but individuals who balance well with one another' (p. 77). Belbin based his model on data collected from training courses run for senior management, and proposes that nine team roles may describe the range of functions that individuals operate in management teams. These are identified and described in Table 11.6. Belbin's original model produced in 1981 identified eight roles, in his 1993 modification two roles were renamed ('chairman' became 'co-ordinator' and 'company worker' became 'implementer') In addition, a ninth role was added – that of 'specialist'. Each role, as you will see from Table 11.6, has what Belbin calls *allowable weaknesses*. By this is meant that for a person effectively to enact the role certain shortcomings are inherent and have to be recognised by other team members and allowances made.

To discover the preferences people have for these different team roles, Belbin (1981) produced a self-report inventory to ascertain a person's primary preference. Belbin claimed that an individual usually had one or two secondary roles that could be enhanced should a team be short of one of the nine roles. One example from the seven items making up this inventory is given below. Your task is to distribute a total of

Role	Description of role	Allowable weaknesses
Plant	Produces ideas, highly creative unconventional, forthright	Not a good communicator, ignores detail, too blunt
Resource Investigator	Enthusiastic and extrovert, looks into opportunities and practicalities, liaises with other people	Too positive at times, may lose interest after initial enthusiasm
Co-ordinator (Chairman)	Good at clarifying goals and carrying out agreed plans, confident and self-disciplined	May delegate too much at times
Shaper	Challenges, drives the team forward, dominant task leader motivator	May be over-challenging and insensitive to others' feelings. Argumentative, easily disappointed
Monitor Evaluator	Evaluates ideas, rational, analytic thinker, sees a range of options	Critical and may not be able to motivate other people
Teamworker	Helps reduce tension in the team, co-operates, listens to other people	May be indecisive, and easily influenced by others
Implementer (Company worker)	Turns ideas into practical workable plans. Implements plans effectively	May be inflexible and slow to take up new ideas and opportunities
Completer	Meets deadlines, attention to detail and conscientious. Checks for errors and mistakes	Worries too much, may not delegate, too much attention to detail
Specialist	Offers specialist knowledge and skills. Dedicated to specialist area	Narrow, technical and misses the 'big picture'

Table 11.6: Nine team roles identified by Belbin (1981; 1999)

10 points amongst the options – you may choose to give all 10 points to just one option or distribute to a number of options. The words in brackets after each option indicate which role it applies to.

When involved in a project with other people:

1 I have an aptitude for influencing people without pressurising them. (Co-ordinator).
2 My general vigilance prevents careless mistakes and omissions being made. (Completer-Finisher).

3 I am ready to press for action to make sure that the meeting does not waste time or lose sight of the main objective. (Shaper).
4 I can be counted on to contribute something original. (Plant).
5 I am always ready to back a good suggestion in the common interest. (Team Worker).
6 I am keen to look for the latest in new ideas and development. (Resource Investigator).
7 I believe my capacity for cool judgement is appreciated by others. (Monitor Evaluator).
8 I can be relied upon to see that all essential work is organised. (Implementer).

Effective and successful teams, Belbin argues, are those where all roles are carried out by the individual team members. In small groups of five or six, for example, one person may take on two roles. Management teams that are composed mainly of Shapers may not be effective since too many people are producing ideas but not enough people in the team are evaluating, exploring resource implications, and implementing the ideas. In such circumstances a team needs to identify that it is 'top heavy' with respect to one or two roles and get some individuals deliberately to take on a different role (one of their second preferences). If this is not possible, Belbin recommends that a special 'project group' is set up which includes some people outside of the management team. This will allow a balanced group to be created.

Belbin claims that some teams will never be effective, and these are characterised by teams who do not have a creative or analytical member (Plant), or where individuals do not slot clearly and predominantly into one of the range of roles. Belbin's management team model has been extremely influential and adopted by many leading international companies to analyse and enhance management team effectiveness. Recent research by Fisher *et al.* (1988) has shown that these team roles fall into *task* and *relationship* categories. Furthermore, if the primary role of a team member was a task one such as Resource Investigator, then their secondary role would also most likely be a task role also.

11.9 Summary

- Small groups consist of interacting individuals who share common goals, are interdependent and perceive they are part of a group.
- Social facilitation is where a dominant (well-learned) response is enhanced in the presence of an audience; non-dominant responses are inhibited in front of an audience. The

presence of others causes arousal because of evaluation, apprehension and distraction conflict.

- Brainstorming is a group approach to problem-solving where individuals first generate, uncritically, ideas; these ideas are selected and evaluated with one or more being adopted. Research has shown that groups produce poorer quality and fewer ideas than individuals working alone due to social loafing, production blocking and poor co-ordination.

- Group composition has been researched in relation to group size and group membership. Generally, as group size increases, individual satisfaction decreases.

- Group structure influences individual member behaviour and has been investigated in relation to group cohesiveness. Group norms, rules and status, and communication structure. Group cohesiveness is the 'glue of interdependence' and holds groups together.

- Co-operative group working has been consistently and overwhelming demonstrated to result in better group performance than competition. Social dilemmas are competitive situations where individuals and group compete for scarce resources.

- There are six types of interpersonal power that leaders may use: expert, referent, information, legitimate, reward and coercive power.

- Research on personality and leadership has generally failed to find differences between leaders and non-leaders. However, evidence suggests leaders are more intelligent, extrovert and talkative.

- The behaviour style of leaders reflects group-centred and directive behaviours as two important dimensions. This is similar to the task and socio-emotional styles of leadership proposed by Bales.

- The most influential theory of leadership has been Fiedler's contingency theory which takes both leadership style and situational factors into account to predict leader effectiveness.

- Group decision-making rules follow social decision schemes which are simple rules such as unanimity, majority wins, truth wins and the first shift. Groups generally make better decisions than individuals but not better than the most able individual in the group.

- Janis attributed defective decision making to groupthink which occurs in highly cohesive groups facing a threatening situation. Groupthink may be countered by encouraging criticism, expressing doubts and bringing in outsiders to work on the problem.

11.10 Suggestions for further reading

Baron, R. S., Kerr, N. and Miller, N. 1992: *Group Processes, Group Decision and Group Action.* Milton Keynes: Open University Press.
 Good general coverage of theory, concepts and research of group performance with an especially thorough look at group decision-making.

Brown, R. 1988: *Group Processes: Dynamics Within and Between Groups*. Oxford: Blackwell.
Highly readable text taking a European perspective. Provides a wider coverage of groups than in this chapter by considering intergroup behaviour and intergroup conflict. Excellent critical commentary in places.

Janis, I. 1989: *Crucial Decisions: Leadership in Policy Making and Crisis*. New York: Free Press.
Enquiry into key international decisions using the concept of groupthink to understand defective and high quality decision-making. Quite fascinating psychological insights into decision-making by world figures.

Wilke, H. A. M. and Meertens, R. W. 1993: *Group Performance*. London: Routledge.
Takes more of a European perspective, providing an up-to-date and thorough text on group performance. Fairly advanced reading.

References

Abelson, R. P. 1981: The psychological status of the script concept. *American Psychologist* 36, 715–729.

Abrams, D. and Hogg, M. A. 1990a: Social identification, self categorisation and social influence. *European Review of Social Psychology* 1, 195–228.

Abrams, D. and Hogg, M. A. (eds), 1990b: *Social identity theory: constructive and critical advances.* London: Harvester Wheatsheaf.

Abrams, D., Wetherell, M., Cochrane, S. *et al.* 1990: Knowing what to think by knowing who you are. Self-categorisation and the nature of norm formation, conformity and group polarisation. *British Journal of Social Psychology* 29, 97–119.

Abramson, L. Y. and Martin, D. J. 1981: Depression and the causal inference process. In Harvey, J. M., Ickes, W. and Kidd, R. F. (eds), *New directions in attribution research.* Vol. 3. Hillsdale, NJ: Erlbaum.

Abramson, L. Y., Seligman, M. E. P. and Teasdale, J. D. 1978: Learned helplessness in humans: critique and reformulation. *Journal of Abnormal Psychology* 87, 49–74.

Adams, G. R. and Jones, R. M. 1983: Female adolescents identity development: age comparisons and perceived child rearing experience. *Developmental Psychology* 19, 249–256.

Adams, J. 1965: Inequity in social exchange. In Berkowitz, L. (ed.), *Advances in experimental social psychology.* New York: Academic Press, vol. 2, pp. 267–299.

Adorno, T. W., Frenkel-Brunswick, E., Levinson, D. J. and Sanford, R. N. 1950: *The authoritarian personality.* New York: Harper.

Ainsworth, M. D. S. 1973: The development of infant mother attachment. In Caldwell, B. M. and Ricciuti, H. N. (eds), *Review of child development research,* Vol. 3. Chicago, University of Chicago Press.

Ainsworth, M. D. S., Blehar, M. D., Waters, E. and Wall, S. 1978: *Patterns of attachment: a psychological study of the strange situation.* Hillsdale, NJ: Lawrence Erlbaum Associates.

Ajzen, I. 1989: Attitude structure and behaviour. In Pratkanis, A. R. Breckler, S. J., and Greenwood, A. G. (eds), *Attitude structure and function.* Hillsdale, NJ: Erlbaum.

Akhtar, N., Dunham, F. and Dunham, P. J. 1991: Directive interactions and early vocabulary development: the role of joint attentional focus. *Journal of Child Language* 18, 41–49.

Alcock, J. E., Carment, D. W. and Sadava, S. W. 1988: *A textbook of social psychology.* Scarborough, Ontario: Prentice-Hall.

Allen, V. L. 1965: Situational factors in conformity. In Berkowitz, L. (ed.), *Advances in experimental social psychology,* vol. 2. New York: Academic Press, pp. 133–175.

Allen, V. L. 1975: Social support for non-conformity. In Berkowitz, L. (ed.), *Advances in expermental social psychology,* vol. 8. New York: Academic Press, pp. 1–43.

Allen, V. L. and Levine, J. M. 1971: Social pressure and personal influence. *Journal of Experimental Social Psychology* 7, 122–124.

Alloy, L. B. and Tabachnik, N. (1984: Assessment of covariation by humans and animals: the joint influence of prior expectations and current situational information. *Psychological Review* 91, 112–149.

Allport, F. H. 1924: *Social psychology.* Boston: Houghton Mifflin.

Allport, G. 1954: *The nature of prejudice.* Reading, MA: Addison-Wesley.

Allport, G. 1985: 'The historical background of social psychology'. In Lindzey, G. and Aronson, E. (eds). *The handbook of social psychology*. Third edition, Vol. 1. New York: Random House.

Allport, G. W. 1935: Attitudes. In Murchison, G. (ed.), *Handbook of social psychology*. Worcester, CA: Clark University Press.

Altman, I. 1973: Reciprocity of interpersonal exchange. *Journal for Theory of Social Behaviour* 3, 249–261.

Altman, I. and Taylor, D. A. 1973: *Social penetration: the development of interpersonal relationships*. New York: Holt, Rinehart and Winston.

Ambady, N., Koo J., Lee, F., and Rosenthal, R. 1996: More than words: linguistic and non-linguistic politeness in two cultures. *Journal of Personality and Social Psychology* 70, 5, 996–1101.

Ancona, L. and Paregson, R. 1968: Contributo allo studio della aggressione: la dinamica della obedienza distincttiva. *Archivio di Psicologia Neurologia e Psichiatria* 29, 340–372.

Anderson, J. R. 1990: *Cognitive psychology and its implications*. 3rd ed. New York: Freeman.

Anderson, N. H. 1981: *Foundations of information integration theory*. New York: Academic Press.

Angier, N. 1990: *Marriage is a lifesaver for men after 45. The New York Times*, 13 December.

Apsler, R. 1975: Effects of embarrassment on behaviour towards others. *Journal of Personality and Social Psychology* 32, 145–153.

Archer, J. and Lloyd, B. 1985: *Sex and gender*. Cambridge: Cambridge University Press.

Argyle, M. 1994: *The psychology of interpersonal behaviour*. 5th edn. Harmondsworth: Penguin.

Argyle, M. and Dean J. 1965: Eye contact, distance and affiliation. *Sociometry* 28, 289–304.

Argyle, M. and Henderson, M. 1985: *The anatomy of relationships*. Harmondsworth: Penguin.

Aronson, E. 1969: The theory of cognitive dissonance: a current perspective. In Berkowitz, L. (ed.), *Advances in experimental social psychology*, Vol. 4. New York: Academic Press.

Aronson, E. and Gonzales, A. 1988: Desegregation jigsaw and the Mexican–American experience. In Katz, P. A. and Taylor, D. A. (eds), *Eliminating racism: profiles in controversy*. New York: Plenum.

Aronson, E. and Mills, J. 1959: The effects of severity of initiation on liking for a group. *Journal of Abnormal and Social Psychology* 59, 177–181.

Aronson, E., Wilson, J. and Akert, R. 1997: *Social psychology*. 2nd edn. New York: Longman.

Aronson, E. and Worchel, S. 1966: Similarity versus liking as determinants of interpersonal attractiveness. *Psychonomic Science* 5, 157–158.

Asch, S. 1951: Effects of group pressure on the modification and distortion of judgements: In Gretzkow, H. (ed.), *Groups, leadership, and men*. Pittsburg: Carnegie Press.

Asch, S. 1955: Opinions and social pressure. *Scientific American* 193, 5, 31–35.

Asch, S. E. 1946: Forming impressions of personality. *Journal of Abnormal and Social Psychology* 41, 258–290.

Aspler, R. 1975: Effects of embarrassment on behaviour towards others. *Journal of Personality and Social Psychology* 32, 145–153.

Axsom, D. and Cooper, J. 1985: Cognitive dissonance and psychotherapy: the role of effort justification in inducing weight loss. *Journal of Experimental Psychology* 21, 149–160.

Bales, R. F. 1950: *Interaction process analysis: a method for the study of small groups.* Reading, MA: Addison-Wesley.

Bales, R.F. and Slater, P. 1955: Role differentiation in small decision making groups. In T. Parsons (ed.), *Family, socialization and interaction processes.* New York: Free Press.

Bales, R. F., Strodtbeck, F. L. Mills, T. M. and Roseborough, M.E. 1951: Channels of communication in small groups. *American Sociological* Review 16, 461–468.

Bandura, A. 1973: *Aggression: a social learning theory analysis.* Englewood Cliffs, NJ: Prentice-Hall.

Bandura, A. 1977a: Self-efficacy: toward a unifying theory of behaviour change. *Psychological Review* 84,191–215.

Bandura, A. 1977b: *Social learning theory.* Englewood Cliffs, NJ: Prentice-Hall.

Bandura, A. 1986: *Social foundations of thought and action: a social cognitive theory.* Englewood Cliffs, NJ: Prentice-Hall.

Bandura, A., Ross, D. and Ross, S. A. 1963: Imitation of film mediated aggressive models. *Journal of Abnormal and Social Psychology* 66, 3–11.

Bandura, A. and Walters, R. H. 1963: *Social learning and personality development.* New York: Rinehart and Winston.

Barash, D. P. 1977: *Sociobiology of behaviour.* New York: Elsevier.

Barjonet, P. E. 1980: L'influence sociale et des représentations des causes de l'accident de la route. *Le Travail Human* 20, 1–14.

Baron, R. A. 1989 Personality and organisational conflict: the Type A behaviour pattern and self monitoring. *Organisational Behaviour and Human Decision Processes* 44, 281–297.

Baron, R. A. and Byrne, D. 1997: *Social psychology.* 8th edn. London: Allyn and Bacon.

Baron, R. A. and Richardson, D. R. 1994: *Human aggression* (2nd edn). New York: Plenum.

Bartholomew, K. and Horowitz, L. M. 1991: Attachment styles among young adults: a test of a four category model. *Journal of Personality and Social Psychology* 61, 226–264.

Bartis, S., Szymanski, K. and Harkins, S.G. 1988: Evaluation and performance: a two-edged knife. *Personality and Social Psychology Bulletin* 14, 242–251.

Bass, B. M. and Avolio, B. J. (1993: Transformational leadership: a response to critiques. In M. M. Chemers and R. A. Ayman (eds), *Leadership theory and research: perspectives and directions.* London: Academic Press.

Batson, C. D. 1991: The altruism question. Hillsdale, NJ: Erlbaum.

Batson, C. D. and Coke, J. S. 1981: Empathy: a source of altruistic motivation for helping? In Rushton, J. P. and Sorrentino, R. M. (eds) *Altruism and helping behaviour: social, personality and developmental perspectives.* Hillsdale, NJ: Erlbaum.

Batson, C. D., Duncan, B., Ackerman, P., Buckley, T. and Birch, K. 1981: Is empathetic emotion a source of altruistic motivation? *Journal of Personality and Social Psychology* 40, 290–302.

Baumeister, R. F., Chesner, S. P., Senders, P. S. and Tice, D. M. 1988: Who's in charge here? Group leaders do lend help in emergencies. *Personality and Social Psychology Bulletin* 14, 17–22.

Baumeister, R. F. and Covington, M. V. 1985: Self-esteem, persuasion and retrospective distortion of initial attitudes. *Electronic Social Psychology* 1, 1–22.

Baumeister, R., Stillwell, A. M. and Hetherington, T. F. 1994: Guilt: an interpersonal approach. *Psychological Bulletin* 115, 243–267.

Baumrind, D. 1964: Some thoughts on ethics in research: after reading Milgram's behavioural study of obedience. *American Psychologist* 19, 421–423.

Baumrind, D. 1971: Current patterns of parental authority. *Developmental Psychology Monographs* 4, (1 part 2).

Baumrind, D. 1979: The costs of deception. *I. R. B. A Review of Human Subjects Research* 6, 1–4.

Baumrind, D. 1985: Research using intentional deception: ethical issues revisited. *American Psychologist* 40, 165–174.

Baumrind, D. 1986: Familial antecedents of social competence in middle childhood. Unpublished monograph, Institute of Human Development, University of California, Berkeley.

Baumrind, D. 1991: Effective parenting during the early adolescent transition. In Cowan, P. A. and Hetherington, E. M. (eds), *Family transition*. Hillsdale, NJ: Lawrence Erlbaum Associates, pp. 111–163.

Bavelas, A. 1950: Communication patterns in task-oriented groups. *Journal of Psycholinguistic Research* 22, 725–730.

Baxter, L. A. 1987: Self disclosure and disengagement. In Derleg, V. J. and Berg, J. H. (eds), *Self disclosure: theory, research and therapy*. New York: Plenum, pp. 155–174.

Beattie G. 1983: *Talk: an analysis of speech and non-verbal behaviour in conversation*. Buckingham: Open University Press.

Beck, K.W., Festinger, L., Hymovitach, B., Kelley, H.H., Schachter, S. and Thibaut, J.W. 1950: The methodology of studying rumour transition. *Human Relations* 3, 307–312.

Beck, L. and Ajzen, I. 1991: Predicting dishonest actions using the theory of planned behaviour. *Journal of Research in Personality* 25, 285–301.

Beck, M. 1992: The new middle age. *Newsweek* 50–56.

Begley, S. 1995: Gray matters. *Newsweek* 48–54.

Belbin, R. M. 1981: *Management teams: why they succeed or fail*. Oxford: Butterworth Heinemann.

Belbin, R. M. 1993: *Team roles at work*. Oxford: Butterworth-Heinemann.

Bell, G. and French, R. 1950: Consistency of individual leadership position in small groups of varying membership. *Journal of Abnormal and Social Psychology* 45, 764–765.

Bell, P. A. 1992: In defence of the negative affect escape model of heat and aggression. *Psychological Bulletin* 111, 342–6.

Belmore, S. M. 1987: Determinants of attention during impression formation. *Journal of Experimental Psychology: Learning, Memory and Cognition* 13, 480–489.

Belmore, S. M. and Hubbard, M. L. 1989: The role of advance expectancies in person memory. *Journal of Personality and Social Psychology* 53, 61–70.

Belsky, J. and Kelly, J. 1994: *The transition to parenthood*. New York: Dell.

Bem, D. J. 1967: Self-perception theory: an alternative interpretation of cognitive dissonance phenomena. *Psychological Review* 74, 183–200.

Bem, S. L. 1981: Gender schema theory. a cognitive account of sex typing. *Psychological Review* 88, 354–364.

Berkman, L. and Syme, L. 1979: Social networks, host resistance and mortality: A nine year follow up study of Alameda County residents. *American Journal of Epidemiology* 109, 186–204.

Berkowitz, L. 1969: The frustration–aggression hypothesis revisited. In Berkowitz, L. (ed.), *Roots of aggression: a re-examination of the frustration-aggression hypothesis*. New York: Atherton Press.

Berkowitz, L. 1970: The self, selfishness and altruism. In McCauley, J. and Berkowitz, L. (ed.) *Altruism and helping behavior*. New York: Academic Press.

Berkowitz, L. 1984: Some effects of thoughts on anti and pro social influences of media events: a cognitive neo-associationist analysis. *Psychological Bulletin 95*, 410–427.

Berkowitz, L. 1989: Frustration–aggression hypothesis: examination and reformulation. *Psychological Bulletin 106*, 59–73.

Berman, M., Gladue, B. and Taylor, S. 1993: The effects of hormones, Type A behaviour patterns and provocation on aggression in men. *Motivation and Emotion 17*, 125–138.

Bernstein, D. A., Clarke-Stewart, A., Roy, E. J. and Wickens, C. D. 1997: *Psychology.* 4th edn, New York: Houghton Mifflin.

Berscheid, E., Dion, K., Walster, E. and Walster, G. W. 1971: Physical attractiveness and dating choice: a test of the matching hypothesis. *Journal of Experimental Social Psychology 7*, 173–189.

Betancourt H. 1990: An attribution-empathy model of helping behaviour: behavioural intentions and judgements of help-giving. *Personality and Social Psychology Bulletin 16*, 573–591.

Bierbrauer, G. 1979: Why did he do it? Attribution of obedience and the phenomenon of dispositional bias. *European Journal of Social Psychology 9*, 67–84.

Biernat, M., Manis, M. and Nelson, T. 1991: Stereotypes and standards of judgement. *Journal of Personality and Social Psychology 60*, 485–499.

Billig, M. 1976: *Social psychology and inter-group relations*. London: Academic Press.

Bjorkqvist, K. and Niemela, P. 1992: New trends in the study of female aggression. In Bjorkqvist, K. and Niemela, P. (eds), *Of mice and women: aspects of female aggression*. San Diego: Academic Press, pp. 3–16.

Block, J. 1973: Conceptions of sex roles: some cross-cultural and longitudinal perspectives. *American Psychologist 28*, 512–526.

Bloomfield, L. 1933: *Language*. New York: Henry Holt and Co.

Blumstein, P. and Schwartz, P. 1983: *American couples: money, work, sex*. New York: William Morrow.

Bodenhausen, G. V. 1988: Stereotypical biases in social decision making and memory: testing process models of stereotype use. *Journal of Personality and Social Psychology 66*, 621–632.

Bodenhausen, G. V., Kramer, G. P. and Susser, K. 1994: Happiness and stereotypical thinking in social judgement. *Journal of Personality and Social Psychology 66*, 621–632.

Bohner, G., Bless, H., Schwartz, N. and Strack, F. 1988: What triggers causal attributions? The impact of subjective probability. *European Journal of Social Psychology 18*, 335–346.

Bond, M. H. and Hwang, K. K. 1986: The social psychology of Chinese people. In Bond, M. H. (ed.), *The psychology of the Chinese people*. Oxford: Oxford University Press.

Bowlby, J. 1951: *Maternal and child health*. World Health Organization Monograph 2. Geneva: World Health Organisation.

Bowlby, J. 1973: *Attachment and loss. Vol. 2. Separation*. New York: Basic Books.

Bradbury, J. 1984: *Violent offending and drinking patterns*. Institute of Criminology Monograph. Wellington: Victoria University of Wellington.

Branscombe, N. R., Wann, D. C., Noel, J. G. and Coleman, J. 1993: In-group or out-group extremity: importance of the threatened identity. *Personality and Social Psychology Bulletin 19*, 381–388.

Brehm J. W. 1956: Post-decisional changes in desirability of alternatives. *Journal of Abnormal and Social Psychology 52*, 384–389.

Brehm, J. W. 1966: *A theory of psychological reactance.* New York: Academic Press.

Brehm, S. S. 1992: *Intimate relationships.* 2nd edn, New York: McGraw-Hill.

Brehm, S. S. and Kassin, S. M. 1996: *Social psychology.* 3rd edn, New York: Houghton Mifflin.

Brickner, M. A., Harkins, S.G. and Ostrom, T. M. 1986: Effects of personal development: thought-provoking implications for social loafing. *Journal of Personality and Social Psychology* 51, 763–770.

Brown, B. B., Clasen, D. R. and Eicher, S. A. 1986: Perceptions of peer pressure, peer conformity dispositions and self reported behaviour among adolescents. *Developmental Psychology* 22, 521–530.

Brown, J. 1973: *A first language.* Cambridge, MA: Harvard University Press.

Brown, P. and Levinson, S. 1987: *Politeness: some universals of language usage.* Cambridge: Cambridge University Press.

Brown, R. 1988 *Group processes: dynamics within and between groups.* Oxford: Blackwell.

Brown, R. J. 1995: *Prejudice and its social psychology.* Oxford: Blackwell.

Bruner, J. and Taguiri, R. 1954: Person perception. In Lindzey, G. (ed.), *Handbook of social psychology.* Vol. 2. Reading, MA: Addison-Wesley.

Bruner, J. S. 1983: The acquisition of pragmatic commitments. In Golinkoff, R. M. (ed.), *The transition from prelinguistic to linguistic communication.* Hillsdale, NJ: Erlbaum, pp. 29–47.

Bryan, J. H. and Test, M. A. 1967: Models and helping: naturalistic studies in aiding behaviour. *Journal of Personality and Social Psychology* 6, 400–407.

Buck, R. 1985: Prime theory: an integrated view of motivation and emotion. *Psychological Review* 92, 389–413.

Buehler, R., Griffin, D. and Ross, M. 1995: It's about time: optimistic predictions in work and love. In Stroebe, W. and Hewstone, M. (eds), *European review of social psychology.* Chichester: Wiley, 1–32.

Bull, P. E. 1983: *Body movement and interpersonal communication.* Chichester: Wiley.

Burg, M., Blumenthal, J., Barefoot, J., Williams, R. and Haney, T. 1986: Social support as a buffer against the development of coronary artery disease. Paper presented at the Society of Behavioural Medicine Meeting, San Francisco.

Burgoon, J. K. 1989: Comparatively speaking: applying a comparative approach to non-verbal expectancy violations theory. Unpublished MSS, University of Arizona.

Burgoon, J., Buller, D., and Guerrero, L. 1995: Interpersonal deception. *Journal of Language and Social Psychology* 14, 3, 289–311.

Burgoon, M. 1994: Message and persuasive effects. In Hargie, O., Saunders, C. and Dickson, D., *Social skills and interpersonal communication.* 3rd edn. London: Routledge.

Burke, P. J. (1974: Participation and leadership in small groups. *American Sociological Review* 39, 832–842.

Burley, P. M. and McGuinness, J. 1977: Effects of social intelligence on the Milgram paradigm. *Psychological Reports* 40, 767–770.

Burnstein, E., Crandall, C. and Kitayama, S. 1994: Some neo-Darwinian decision rules for altruism: weighing cues for inclusive fitness as a function of the biological importance of the decision. *Journal of Personality and Social Psychology* 67, 217–234.

Burnstein, E. and Vinokur, A. 1973: Testing two classes of theories about group induced shifts in individual choice. *Journal of Experimental Social Psychology* 9, 123–137.

Buss, A. H. and Perry, M. 1992: The aggression questionnaire. *Journal of Personality and Social Psychology* 63, 452–459.

Buss, D. M. 1989: Sex differences in human mate preferences: evolutionary hypotheses tested in 37 cultures. *Behavioural and Brain Sciences* 12, 1–14.

Buss, D. M. 1994: *The evolution of desire: strategies of human mating.* New York: Basic Books.

Buunk, B. P. 1990: Affiliation and helping interactions within organisations: a critical analysis of the role of social support with regard to occupational stress. In Stroebe, W. and Hewstone, M. (eds), *European Review of Social Psychology.* Chichester: John Wiley, vol. 1, pp. 293–322.

Buunk, B. P. 1995: Comparison direction and comparison dimension among disabled individuals: toward a refined conceptualisation of social comparison under stress. *Personality and Social Psychology Bulletin* 21, 316–330.

Buunk, B. P. and Van Driel, B. 1989: *Variant lifestyles and relationships.* Newbury Park, CA: Sage.

Buunk, B. P., Van Yperen, N. W., Taylor, S. E. and Collins, R. L. 1991: Social comparison and the drive upward revisited: affiliation as a response to marital stress. *European Journal of Social Psychology* 21, 529–546.

Byrne, D. 1966: *An introduction to personality.* Englewood Cliffs, NJ: Prentice-Hall.

Byrne, D. 1971: *The attraction paradigm.* New York: Academic Press.

Byrne, D. and Clore, G. L. 1970: A reinforcement model of evaluative processes. *Personality: An International Journal* 1, 102–128.

Byrne, D., Clore, G. L. and Smeaton, G. 1986: The attraction hypothesis: do similar attitudes affect anything? *Journal of Personality and Social Psychology* 51, 1167–1170.

Byrne, P. S. and Long, B. E. L. 1976: *Doctors talking to patients.* London: Her Majesty's Stationery Office.

Cacioppo, J. T. and Petty, R. E. 1981: Electromyograms as measures of extent and affectivity of information processing. *American Psychologist* 36, 441–456.

Cacioppo, J. T., Petty, R. E. and Morris, K. J. 1983: Effects of need for cognition on message evaluation, recall and persuasion. *Journal of Personality and Social Psychology* 45, 805–818.

Cacioppo, J. T. and Tassinary, L. G. 1990: Inferring psychological significance from physiological signals. *Scientific American* 45, 16–28.

Campbell, A. A. 1971: *White attitudes to black people.* Ann Arbor, MI: Institute for Social Research.

Campbell, D. T. 1990: Asch's moral epistemology for socially shared knowledge. In Rock, I. (ed.), *The legacy of Soloman Asch: essays in cognition and psychology.* Hillside, NJ: Erlbaum.

Campbell, D. T. and Stanley, J. C. 1966: *Experimental and quasi-experimental designs for research.* Chicago: Rand McNally.

Camras, L. A. 1977: Facial expressions used by children in a conflict situation. *Child Development* 48, 1431–1435.

Cann, A., Sherman, S. J. and Elkes, R. 1978: Effects of initial request size and timing of a second request on compliance. *Journal of Personality and Social Psychology* 38, 382–395.

Cantor, N. and Mischel, W. 1979: Prototypes in person perception. In Berkowitz, L. (ed.), *Advances in experimental social psychology.* Vol. 12. New York: Academic Press, pp. 3–52.

Cappella, J.N. and Palmer, M.T. 1990: The structure and organisation of verbal and non-verbal behaviour. In Giles, H. and Robinson, W. P. *Handbook of language and social psychology.* Chichester: Wiley.

Carli, L. 1989: Gender differences in interaction style and influence. *Journal of Personality and Social Psychology* 56, 565.

Carlston, D. E. and Skowronski, J. J. 1994: Savings in the relearning of trait information as evidence for spontaneous inference generation. *Journal of Personality and Social Psychology* 66, 840–856.

Carroll, J. M. and Russell, J.A. 1996: Do facial expressions signal specific emotions? Judging emotions from the face in context. *Journal of Personality and Social Psychology* 70, 2, 205–218.

Cartensen, L. L. 1992: Motivation for social contact across the lifespan: a theory of socioemotional selectivity. In Dienstbier, R. and Jacobs, J. E. (eds), *Developmental perspectives on motivation*. Nebraska symposium on motivation. Lincoln: University of Nebraska Press, 209–254.

Cartwright, D. and Zander, A. 1968: *Group dynamics: theory and research*. New York: Harper and Row.

Carver, C. S. and Glass, D. C. 1978: Coronary prone behaviour pattern and interpersonal aggression. *Journal of Personality and Social Psychology* 36, 361–366.

Cash, T.F., Kehr, J. A., Polyson, J. and Freeman, V. 1977: Role of physical attractiveness in peer attribution of psychological disturbance. *Journal of Consulting and Clinical Psychology* 45, 987–993.

Caspi, A. and Harbener, E.S. 1990: Continuity and change: assortive marriage and the constituency of personality in adulthood. *Journal of Personality and Social Psychology* 58, 250–258.

Cate, R. M. and Lloyd, S. A. 1988: Courtship. In Duck, S. (ed.), *Handbook of personal relationships: theory, research and interventions*. New York: Wiley, pp. 409–427.

Chaiken, S. 1979: Communicator physical attractiveness and persuasion. *Journal of Personality and Social Psychology* 37, 1387–1397.

Chaiken, S., Liberman, A. and Eagly, A. H. 1989: Heuristic and systematic information processing: within and beyond the persuasion context. In Uleman, J. S. and Borgh, J. A. (eds), *Unintended thought: limits of awareness, intention and control*. New York: Guilford.

Chapman, L. J. 1967: Illusory correlation in observational report. *Journal of Verbal Learning and Verbal Behaviour* 6, 151–155.

Chemers, M. M., Hayes, R. B., Rhodewalt, F. and Wysocki, J. 1985: A person-environment analysis of job stress: a contingency model explanation. *Journal of Personality and Social Psychology* 49, 628–635.

Chomsky, N. 1959: A review of verbal behaviour. *Language* 35, 26–58.

Christensen, A. and Heavey, C. L. 1983: Gender differences in marital conflict: the demand/withdraw interaction pattern. In Oskamp, S. and Constanzo, M. (eds). *Gender issues in contemporary society*. Newbury Park, CA: Sage, pp. 113–141.

Christie, R. and Cook, P. 1958: A guide to the published literature relating to the authoritarian personality. *Journal of Psychology* 45, 171–199.

Cialdini, R. B., Cacioppo, J. T., Bassett, R. and Miller, J. A. 1978: Low ball procedure for producing compliance: commitment then cost. *Journal of Personality and Social Psychology* 36, 463–476.

Cialdini, R. B., Vincent, J. E., Lewis, S. K., Catalan, J., Wheeler, D. and Darby, B. L. 1975: Reciprocal concessions procedure for inducing compliance: the door-in-the-face technique. *Journal of Personality and Social Psychology* 31, 200–215.

Clark N. K. and Stephenson, G. M. 1989: Group remembering. In Paulus, P. B. (ed.), *Psychology of group influence*. 2nd edn. Hillsdale, NJ: Erlbaum.

Clarke, N. K. and Stephenson, G. M. 1995: Social remembering: individual and collaborative memory for social information. *European Review of Social Psychology* 6, 127–160.

Clark, R. D. and Word, I. E. 1972: Why don't bystanders help? Because of ambiguity? *Journal of Personality and Social Psychology* 24, 392–400.

Clarke-Stewart, K. A. and Fein, G. G. 1983: Early childhood programs. In Mussen, P. H. (ed.), *Handbook of child psychology: vol. 2. Infancy and developmental psychobiology*. New York: Wiley.

Clines, F. X. 1982: Plane hits bridge over the Potomac: 12 dead, 50 missing. *The New York Times* 14 January. pp. A1, B6.

Coch, L. and French, J. R. R. 1948: Overcoming resistance to change. *Human Relations* 1, 512–532.

Cohen, A. 1957: Need for cognition and order of communication as determinants of opinion change. In Hovland, C. I. (ed.), *The order of presentation in persuasion*. New Haven: Yale University Press.

Cohen, C. E. 1981: Person categories and social perception: testing some boundaries of the processing effects of prior knowledge. *Journal of Personality and Social Psychology* 40, 441–452.

Cohen, E. G. and Hoberman, H. M. 1983: Positive events and social supports as buffers of life change. *Journal of Applied Social Psychology* 13, 99–125.

Cohn, J. F. and Tronick, E. Z. 1983: Three month old infants reaction to simulated maternal depression. *Child Development* 54, 185–193.

Collins, L. L. and Miller, L. C. 1994: Self-disclosure and liking: a meta analytic view. *Psychological Bulletin* 116, 457–475.

Condon, J. W. and Crano, W. D. 1988: Inferred evaluation and the relation between attitude similarity and interpersonal attraction. *Journal of Personality and Social Psychology* 54, 789–797.

Condry, J. C. and Ross, J. F. 1985: Sex and aggression: the influence of gender label. *Child Development* 56, 225–233.

Cook, H. B. K. 1992: Matricality and female aggression in Margaretino society. In Bjorkqvist, K. and Niemela, K. (eds), *Of mice and women: aspects of female aggression*. San Diego: Academic Press, pp. 149–162.

Cooper J. and Fazio, R. H. 1984: A new look at dissonance theory. In L. Berkowitz(ed.), *Advances in experimental social psychology*. Vol. 17. New York: Academic Press, pp. 229–266.

Cooper, W. H. 1981: Ubiquitous halo. *Psychological Bulletin* 90, 218–244.

Copeland, J. T. 1994: Prophecies of power: motivational implications of social power for behavioural confirmation. *Journal of Personality and Social Psychology* 67, 264–277.

Cotterell, J. 1996: *Social networks and social influences in adolescence*. London: Routledge.

Coupland, J., Coupland, N. and Grainger, K. 1991: Intergrational discourse: contextural variations of age and elderliness. *Ageing and Society* 11, 189–208.

Cramer, R. E., McMaster, M. R., Bartell, P. A. and Dragna, M. 1988: Subject competence and minimisation of the bystander effect. *Journal of Applied Social Psychology* 18, 1133–1148.

Crocker, J. and Major, B. 1989: Social stigma and self-esteem: the self-protective properties of stigma. *Psychological Review* 96, 608–630.

Crutchfield, R. S. 1955. Conformity and character. *American Psychologist* 10, 191–198.

Culp, R. E., Cook, A. S. and Housley, P. C. 1983: A comparison of observed and reported adult-infant interactions: effects of perceived sex. *Sex Roles* 475–479.

Cunningham, J. A., Strassberg, D. S. and Haan, B. 1986: Effects of intimacy and sex role congruency on self-disclosure. *Journal of Social and Clinical Psychology* 4, 393–401.

Cunningham, M. R. 1979: Weather, mood and helping behaviour: quasi experiments with the sunshine samaritan. *Journal of Personality and Social Psychology* 37, 1947–1956.

Cunningham, M. R. 1986: Measuring the physical in physical attractiveness: quasi experiments on the sociobiology of female facial beauty. *Journal of Personality and Social Psychology* 50, 925–935.

Cunningham, M. R., Barbee, A. P. and Pilkingham, C. L. 1990: What do women want? Facial-metric assessments of multiple motives in the perception of male physical attractiveness. *Journal of Personality and Social Psychology* 59, 61–72.

Cutrona, C. C. and Russell, D. W. 1987: The provision of social relationships and adaptation to stress. In Jones, W. H. and Perlman, D. (eds) *Advances in personal relationships*. vol. 1, Greenwich, CT: JAI Press, pp. 69–108.

Dabbs, J. M. Jnr., Hopper, C. H., and Jurkovic, G. J. 1990: Testosterone and personality among college students and military veterans. *Personality and Individual Differences* 11, 1263–1269.

Dabbs, J. M. Jnr. and Morris, R. 1990: Testosterone, social class and antisocial behaviour in a sample of 4462 men. *Psychological Science* 1, 209–211.

Dabbs, J. M. Jnr., Ruback, R. B., Frady, R. L., Hopper, C. H. and Sgoutas, D. S. 1988: Saliva, testosterone and criminal violence amongst women. *Personality and Individual Differences* 9, 269–275.

Daly, M. and Wilson, M. 1988: *Homicide*. New York: Aldine de Gruyter.

Darley, J. M. and Batson, C. D. 1973: From Jerusalem to Jericho: a study of situational and dispositional variables in helping behaviour. *Journal of Personality and Social Psychology* 27, 100–108.

Darley, J. M. and Latané, B. 1968: Bystander intervention in emergencies: diffusion of responsibility. *Journal of Personality and Social Psychology* 8, 377–383.

Davis, J. H. 1973: Group decision and social interaction: a theory of social decision schemes. *Psychological Review* 80, 97–125.

Davis, K. 1949: *Human society*. New York: Macmillan.

Dawkins, R. 1989: *The selfish gene*. 2nd edn. Oxford: Oxford University Press.

Deaux, K. 1985: Sex and gender. *Annual Review of Psychology* 36, 49–81.

Defleur, M. A. and Westie, F. E. 1958: Verbal attitudes and overt acts: an experiment in the salience of attitudes. *American Sociological Review* 23, 667–673.

De Gilder, D. and Wilke, H. A. M. 1994: Expectation states theory and motivational determinants of social influence. *European Review of Social Psychology* 5, 243–269.

Delgado-Gaitan, C. 1994: Socialising young children in Mexican–American families: an intergenerational perspective. In Greenfield, P. M. and Cocking, R. M. (eds), *Cross cultural roots of minority child development*. Hillsdale, NJ: Lawrence Erlbaum Associates, pp. 41–54.

Denton, K. and Krebs, D. 1990 From the scene to the crome: the effect of alcohol and social context on moral judgement. *Journal of Personality and Social Psychology* 59, 242–248.

De Paulo, B. M. 1992: Non-verbal behaviour and self-presentation. *Psychological Bulletin* 111, 203–243.

De Paulo, B. M., Lanier, K. and Davis, T. 1983: Detecting deceit of the motivated liar. *Journal of Personality and Social Psychology* 45, 1096–1103.

Derlega, V. J., Metts, S., Petronio, S. and Margulis, S. 1993: *Self disclosure*. Newbury Park, CA: Sage.

Deutsch, H., Francince, M., LeBaron, D. and Fryer, M. 1987: What is in a smile? *Psychology of Women Quarterly* 11, 341–351.

Deutsch, M. 1949: An experimental study of the effects of cooperation and competition upon group processes. *Human Relations* 2, 199–231.

Deutsch, M. and Gerard, H. B. 1995: A study of normative and informational social influences upon individual judgement. *Journal of Abnormal and Social Psychology* 51, 629–636.

Devine, P. G. 1989: Stereotypes and prejudice: their automatic and controlled components. *Journal of Personality and Social Psychology* 56, 5–18.

Devine, P. G. and Ostrom, T. 1988: Dimensional versus information processing apparatus to social knowledge: The case of inconsistency management. In Bar-Tel, D. and Kruglanski, A. W. (eds), *The social psychology of knowledge*. Cambridge: Cambridge University Press, pp. 231–261.

De Vito, J. A. 1993: *Essentials of human communication*. New York: HarperCollins.

Diehl, M. and Stroebe, W. 1987: Productivity loss in brainstorming groups: towards the solution of a riddle. *Journal of Personality and Social Psychology* 53, 497–509.

Dillard, J. P., Hunter, J. E. and Burgoon, M. 1984: Sequential request persuasive strategies: meta analysis of the foot-in-the-door and door-in-the-face. *Human Communication Research* 10, 461–488.

Dillon, J. T. 1986: Questioning. In Hargie, O., Saunders, C. and Dickson, D. 1994: 3rd edn. *Social skills in interpersonal communication*. London: Routledge.

Dimatteo, M. R., Reiter, R. C. and Gambone, J. C. 1994: Enhancing medication adherence through communication and informed collaborative choice. *Health Communications* 6,4, 253–265.

Dindia, K. and Allen, M. (1992): Sex differences in self-disclosure; a meta analysis. *Psychological Bulletin* 112, 106–124.

Dion, K. L. and Dion, K. K. 1988: Romantic love: individual and cultural perspectives. In Sternberg, R. J. and Barnes, M. L. *The psychology of love*. New Haven, CT: Yale University Press, pp. 264–89.

Dion, K. L., Berscheid, E. and Walster, E. 1974: What is beautiful is good. *Journal of Personality and Social Psychology* 2, 285–290.

Dittes, J. E. 1959: Attractiveness of group as function of self-esteem and acceptance by group. *Journal of Abnormal and Social Psychology* 59, 77–82.

Dittes, J. E. and Kelley, H. H. 1956: Effects of different conditions of acceptance upon comformity to group norms. *Journal of Abnormal and Social Psychology* 53, 100–107.

Dix, T., Ruble, D. N., Grusec, J. E. and Nixon, S. 1986: Social cognition in parents: inferential and affective reactions to children of three age levels. *Child Development* 57, 879–894.

Dodd, D. K. 1985: Robbers in the classroom: a deindividuation exercise. *Teaching in Psychology* 12, 89–91.

Dodge, K. A. and Crick, N. R. 1990: Social information processing bases of aggressive behaviour in children. Special issue: Illustrating the value of basic research. *Personality and Social Psychology Bulletin* 16, 8–22.

Dodge, K. A. and Price, J. M. 1994: On the relation between social information processing and socially competent behaviour in early school-aged children. *Child Development* 65, 1385–1398.

Dollard, J., Doob, L. W., Miller, N. E., Mowrer, O. H. and Sears, R. R. 1939: *Frustration and aggression*. New Haven: Yale University Press.

Dovidio, J. F., Brigham, J. C., Johnson, B. T. and Gaertner, S. L. 1996: Stereotyping, prejudice and discrimination: another look. In Macrae, C. N., Stangar, C. and Hewstone, M. (eds), *Stereotypes and stereotyping*. New York: Guildford.

Dovidio, J. F., Elyson, S. L., Keating, C. F., Heltman, K. and Brown, C. E. *et al.* 1988:

The relationship of social power to visual displays of dominance between men and women. *Journal of Personality and Social Psychology* 54, 333–342.

Dovidio, J. F., Piliavin J. A., Gaertner, S. L., Schroeder, D. A. and Clark, R. D. 1991: The arousal cost reward model and the process of intervention. In Clark, M. S. (ed.) *Review of Personality and Social Psychology* 21: *prosocial behaviour.* Newbury Park, CA: Sage, pp. 86–116.

Downs, A. C. and Lyons, P. M. 1991: Natural observations of the links between attractiveness and initial legal judgements. *Personality and Social Psychology Bulletin* 17 541–547.

Driscoll, R., Davis, K. W. and Lipetz, M. E. 1972: Parental interference and romantic love. *Journal of Personality and Social Psychology* 24, 1–10.

Dubrovsky, V. J., Kiesler, S. and Sethna, B. N. 1991: The equalization phenomena: status effects in computer-mediated and face-to-face decision making groups. *Human Computer Interactions* 6, 119–146.

Duncan, B. L. 1976: Differential social perception and attribution of intergroup violence: testing the lower limits of stereotyping blacks. *Journal of Personality and Social Psychology* 34, 590–598.

Duncan, S. and Fiske, D. W. 1977: Face-to-face interaction research and theory. In Argyle, M. and Colman, A. 1995 (eds), *Social psychology.* Harlow: Longman.

Dunn, J. 1992: Siblings and development. *Current Directions in Psychological Science* 1,1, 6–9.

Dunn, J. F. and Plomin, R. 1990: *Separate lives: why siblings are so different.* New York: Basic Books.

Durkin, K. 1995: *Developmental social psychology: from infancy to old age.* Oxford: Blackwell.

Dutton, D. G. and Aaron, A. P. 1974: Some evidence for heightened sexual attraction under conditions of high anxiety. *Journal of Personality and Social Psychology* 30, 510–517.

Dweck, C. S. 1991: Self-theories and their goals: their role in motivation, personality and development. In Deinstbier, R. and Jacobs, J. E. (eds), *Nebraska Symposium on motivation.* Lincoln: University of Nebraska Press.

Eagly, A. 1995: The science and politics of comparing women and men. *American Psychologist* 50, 145–158.

Eagly, A. H., Ashmore, R. D., Makhijani, M. G. and Longo, L. C. 1991: What is beautiful is good but . . . a meta-analytic review of research on the physical attractiveness stereotype. *Psychology Bulletin* 110, 107–128.

Eagly, A. H. and Carli, L. 1981: Sex of researcher and sex-typed communications as determinants of sex differences and influenceability: a meta-analysis of social influence studies. *Psychological Bulletin* 90, 1–20.

Eagly, A. H. and Chaiken, S. 1993: *The psychology of attitudes.* San Diego, CA: Harcourt, Brace, Jovanovich.

Eagly, A. H. and Chrvala, C. 1986: Sex differences in conformity: status and gender role interpretations. *Psychology of Women Quarterly* 10, 203–220.

Eagly, A. H. and Johnson, B. T. 1990: Gender and leadership style: a meta-analysis. *Psychological Bulletin* 108, 233–256.

Eagly, A. H. and Karau, S. J. 1991: Gender and the emergence of leaders: a meta-analysis. *Journal of Personality and Social Psychology* 60, 685–710.

Eagly, A. H., Makhijani, M. G. and Klonsky, B. G. 1992: Gender and the evaluation of leaders: a meta-analysis. *Psychological Bulletin* 111, 3–22.

Eagly, A. H. and Mladinic, A. 1994: Are people prejudiced against women? Some answers from research on attitudes, gender stereotypes and judgements of competence. *European Review of Social Psychology* 5, 1–35.

Eagly, A. H. and Steffen, V. J. 1984: Gender stereotypes from the distribution of women and men into social roles. *Journal of Personality and Social Psychology* 46, 735–754.

Eagly, A. H. and Steffen, V. J. 1986: Gender and aggressive behaviour: a meta-analytic review of the social psychological literature. *Personality and Social Psychology Bulletin* 17, 306–315.

Eagly, A. H. and Wood, W. 1991: Explaining sex differences in social behaviour: a meta analytic perspective. *Personality and Social Psychology Bulletin* 17, 305–315.

Ebbesen, E. B., Kjos, G. L. and Konecni, V. J. 1976: Spatial ecology: its effect on the choice of friends and enemies. *Journal of Experimental Social Psychology* 12, 505–518.

Eden, D. 1990. Pygmalion without interpersonal contrast effects: whole groups gain from raising manager expectations. *Journal of Applied Psychology* 75, 394–398.

Ehrlich D., Guttman, I., Schonback, P. and Mills, J. 1957: Post-decision exposure to relevant information. *Journal of Abnormal and Social Psychology* 54, 98–102.

Eisenberg, N. 1979: Relationship of prosocial moral reasoning to altruism, political liberalism and intelligence. *Developmental Psychology* 15, 87–89.

Eisenberg, N., Fabes, R. A., Murphy, B., Karbon, M., Maszk, P., Smith, M., O'Boyle, C. and Suh, K. 1994: The relations of emotionality and regulation to dispositional and situational empathy-related responding. *Journal of Personality and Social Psychology* 66, 776–797.

Eisenberg-Berg, N. 1979: Relationship of prosocial moral reasoning to altruism, political liberalism and intelligence. *Developmental Psychology* 15, 87–89.

Ekman, P. 1982: *Emotion in the human face*. New York: Cambridge University Press.

Ekman, P. and Friesen, W. 1972: Hand movements. *Journal of Communication* 22, 353–374.

Ekman, P., Friesen, W., O'Sullivan, W. V., Chan, A., Diacoganni-Tarzartis, I., Heider, K., Krause, R., Le Compte, W. A., Pitcairn, T., Riccibitti, P. E., Scherer, K., Tomito, M. and Tzavaras, A. 1987: Universal and cultural differences in the judgements of facial expressions of emotion. *Journal of Personality and Social Psychology* 53, 712–717.

Elkin, A. P. 1961: *The aboriginal Australians*. London: Longman.

Elliot, A. J. and Devine, P. G. 1994: On the motivational nature of cognitive dissonance: dissonance as psychological discomfort. *Journal of Personality and Social Psychology* 67, 382–394.

Emler, N. and Hopkins, N. 1990: Reputation, social identity and the self. In Abrams, D. and Hogg, M. A. (eds), *Social identity theory: constructive and critical advances*. London: Harvester Wheatsheaf, 113–130.

Emler, N., Renwick, S. and Malone, B. 1983: The relationship between moral reasoning and political orientation. *Journal of Personality and Social Psychology* 45, 1073–80.

Endler, N. S. 1966: Conformity as a function of different reinforcement schedules. *Journal of Personality and Social Psychology* 4, 175–180.

Enright, R. D., Lapsley, D. K. and Levy, V. M. 1983: Moral education strategies. In Pressley, M. and Levin, J. R. (eds), *Cognitive strategy research: education application*. New York: Springer Verlag.

Erdley, C. A. and D'Agostino, P. R. 1989: Cognitive and affective components of automatic priming effects. *Journal of Personality and Social Psychology* 54, 741–747.

Erikson, E. H. 1968: *Identity: youth and crisis*. New York: W. W. Norton.

Eysenck, H. J. 1954: *The psychology of politics*. London: Routledge and Kegan Paul.

Eysenck, M. W. and Keane, M. T. 1995: *Cognitive psychology: a student's handbook*. Hove: Erlbaum.

Fazio, R. H. 1986: How do attitudes guide behaviour? In Sorrentino, R. M. and Higgins, E. T. (eds), *Handbook of motivation and cognition: foundations of social behaviour*. vol. 1. New York: Guilford Press.

Fazio, R. H. 1989: On the power and functionality of attitudes: the role of attitude accessibility. In Pratkanis, A., Breckler, S. J. and Greenwald, A. G. (eds), *Attitude structure and function*. Hillsdale, NJ: Erlbaum.

Feeney, J. A. and Noller, P. 1990: Attachment style as a predictor of adult romantic relationships. *Journal of Personality and Social Psychology* 58, 281–91.

Feeney, J. A., Noller, P. and Callan, V. J. 1994: Attachment style, communication and satisfaction in the early years of marriage. In Bartholemew, K. and Perlman, D. (eds), *Advances in personal relationships*. vol 5. London: Jessica Kingsley Publishers, pp. 269–308.

Feingold, A. 1988: Cognitive gender differences are disappearing. *American Psychologist* 43, 95–103.

Feingold, A. 1991: Sex differences in the effects of similarity and physical attractiveness on opposite sex attraction. *Basic and Applied Social Psychology* 12, 357–367.

Feingold, A. 1992: Good-looking people are not what we think. *Psychological Bulletin* 111, 304–341.

Feldman, R. S. and Rimé, B. (eds) 1991: *Fundamentals of non-verbal behaviour*. Cambridge: Cambridge University Press.

Felipe, N. J. and Sommer, R. 1966: Invasion of personal space. *Social Problems* 14, 206–214.

Feschback, N. 1980: The child as 'psychologist' and 'economist'. Two curricula. Paper presented at APA convention.

Festinger, L. 1954: A theory of social comparison processes. *Human Relations* 7, 117–140.

Festinger, L. 1957: *A theory of cognitive dissonance*. Stanford, CA: Stanford University Press.

Festinger, L. and Carlsmith, J. M. 1959: Cognitive consequences of forced compliance. *Journal of Abnormal and Social Psychology* 58, 203–210.

Festinger, L., Riecken, H. W., and Schachter, S. 1956: *When prophecy fails*. Minneapolis: University of Minnesota.

Festinger, L., Schachter, S. and Back, K. 1950: *Social pressures in informal groups: a study of human factors*. Stanford, CA: Stanford University Press.

Fiedler, F. E. 1971: Validation and extension of the contingency model of leadership effectiveness: a review of empirical findings. *Psychological Bulletin* 76, 128–148.

Fiedler, F. E. 1993: The leadership situation and the black box in contingency theories. In Chemers, M. M. and Ayman, R. (eds), *Leadership theory and research; perspectives and directions*. San Diego, CA: Academic Press

Fiedler, F. E. and Garcia, J. E. 1987: *Improving leadership effectiveness: cognitive resources and organisational performance*. New York: Wiley.

Fieldman, R. S. and Rime, B. *et al.* 1991: *Fundamentals of non-verbal behaviour*. Cambridge: Cambridge University Press.

Fincham, F. D. 1985: Attributions in close relationships. In Harvey, J. H. and Weary, G. (eds), *Attribution: basic issues and applications*. Orlando, FL: Academic Press.

Fincham, F. D. and Bradbury, T. N. 1993: Marital satisfaction, depression and attributions: a longitudinal analysis. *Journal of Personality and Social Psychology* 64, 442–452.

Fincham, F. D., Diener, C. I. and Hokada, A. 1987: Attributional style and learned helplessness; relationship to the use of causal schemata and depressive symptoms in children. *British Journal of Social Psychology* 26, 1–7.

Fincham, F. D., Hokada, A. and Sanders, R. 1989: Learned helplessness, test anxiety and academic achievement: a longitudinal analysis. *Child Development* 26, 138–145.

Fincham, F. D. and O'Leary, K. D. 1983: Causal inferences for spouse behaviour in maritally distressed and non-distressed couples. *Journal of Social and Clinical Psychology* 1, 42–57.

Fisch, H., Frey, S. and Hirsbruner, H. 1983: Analysing non-verbal behaviour in depression. *Journal of Abnormal Psychology* 92, 307–318.

Fishbein, M. and Ajzen, I. 1975: *Belief, attitude, intention and behaviour*. Reading, MA: Addison-Wesley.

Fishbein, M. and Ajzen, I. and Hindle, R. 1980: Predicting and understanding voting in American elections: effects of external variables. In Ajzen, I. and Fishbein, M. (eds), *Understanding attitudes and predicting human behaviour*. Englewood Cliffs, NJ: Prentice Hall.

Fisher, S. and Groce, S. 1990: Accounting practices in medical interviews. *Journal of Abnormal Psychology* 92, 307–318.

Fisher, S. G., Hunter, T. A. and Macrosson, W. D. K. 1998: The structure of Belbin's team roles. *Journal of Occupational and Organisational Psychology* 71, 283–288.

Fiske, A. P. 1991: The cultural relativity of selfish individualism: anthropological evidence that humans are inherently sociable. In Clark, M. S. (ed.) *Review of personality and social psychology: vol. 12 Prosocial behaviour*. Newbury Park, CA: Sage, pp. 176–214.

Fiske, S. T. 1980: Attention and weight in person perception: the impact of negative and extreme behaviour. *Journal of Personality and Social Psychology* 38, 889–906.

Fiske, S. T. and Neuberg, S. L. 1990: A continuum of impression formation, from category based to individualling processes: influences of information and motivation on attention and interpretation. In Zanna, M. (ed.), *Advances in experimental social psychology*. Vol. 23. San Diego: Academic Press, pp. 1–74.

Fiske, S. T. and Pavelchak, M. 1986: Category-based versus piecemeal affective responses: developments in schema triggered effect. In Sorrentino, R. M. and Higgins, E. T. (eds), *Handbook of motivation and cognitive foundations of social behaviour*. New York: Guilford, pp. 167–203.

Fiske, S. T. and Taylor, S, 1991: *Social cognition*. 2nd edn. New York: Random House.

Fletcher, G. J. O. and Fincham, F. D. 1991: Attribution processes in close relationships. In Fletcher, G. and Fincham, F. (eds), *Cognition in close relationships*. Hillsdale, NJ: Erlbaum, pp. 7–36.

Fletcher, G. J. O. and Ward, C. 1988: Attribution theory and processes: a cross-cultural perspective. In Bond, M. H. (ed.), *The cross-cultural challenge to social psychology*. Newbury Park, CA: Sage.

Foa, E. B. and Foa, U. G. 1980: Resource theory: interpersonal behaviour as exchange. In Gergen, K. J., Greeenberg, M. S. and Willis, R. H. (eds), *Social exchange: advances in theory and research*. New York: Plenum, pp. 77–101.

Ford, C. S. and Beach, F. A. 1951: *Patterns of sexual behaviour*. New York: Harper and Row.

Fösterling, F. 1988: *Attribution theory in clinical depression*. Chichester: Wiley.

Fox, S. 1980: Situational determinants in affiliation. *European Journal of Social Psychology* 10, 303–307.

Franco, F. M. and Maass, A. 1996: Implicit versus explicit strategies of out-group discrimination: the role of intentional control in biased language use and reward allocation. *Journal of Language and Social Psychology* 15, 335–359.

Fraser, C., Gouge, C. and Billig, M. 1971: Risky shifts, cautious shifts and group polarisation. *European Journal of Social Psychology* 1, 7–29.

Freedman, J. L. 1984: Effects of television violence on aggressiveness. *Psychological Bulletin* 92, 227–246.

Freedman, J. L and Fraser, S. C. 1966: Compliance without pressure: the foot-in-the-door technique. *Journal of Personality and Social Psychology* 7, 117–124.

French, J. R. P. and Raven, B. H. 1959: The bases of social power. In Cartwright, D. (ed.), *Studies in social power*. Ann Arbor, MI: Institute for Social Research.

Freud, S. 1905: *Fragment of an analysis of a case of hysteria (Dora)*. In Penguin Freud Library, vol. 8. Harmondsworth: Penguin.

Freud, S. 1930: *Civilisation and its discontents*. London: Hogarth Press.

Freud, S. 1932: *New introductory lectures on psychoanalysis*. Pelican Freud Library, Vol. 2, published 1973. Harmondsworth: Pelican.

Freud, A. and Dann, S. 1951: An experiment in group upbringing. *Psychoanalytical Studies of the Child* 6, 127–168.

Frey, D. and Rogner, O. 1987: The relevance of psychological factors in the convalescence of accident patients. In Semin, G. R. and Kralie, B. (eds), *Issues in contemporary German social psychology*. London: Sage.

Friend, R., Rafferty, Y. and Bramel, D. 1990: A puzzling misinterpretation of the Asch conformity study. *European Journal of Social Psychology* 20, 29–44.

Frisch, K. Von 1954: *The dancing bees*. London: Methuen.

Frost, D. E. and Stahelski, A. J. 1988: The systematic measurement of French and Raven's bases of social power in work groups. *Journal of Applied Social Psychology* 18, 375–389.

Fry, P. S. and Ghosh, R. 1980: Attributions of success and failure: comparison of cultural differences between Asian and Caucasian children. *Journal of Cross-Cultural Psychology* 11, 343–363.

Furstenberg, F. F. Jr. and Cherlin, A. J. 1991: *Divided families: what happens to children when parents part*. Cambridge, MA: Harvard University Press.

Gaertner, S. L. and Dovidio, J. F. 1977: The subtlety of white racism, arousal and helping behaviour. *Journal of Personality and Social Psychology* 35, 691–707.

Gaertner, S. L., Mann, J. Dovidio, J. F., Murrell, A. J. and Pomare, M. 1990: How does cooperation reduce inter-group bias? *Journal of Personality and Social Psychology* 59, 692–704.

Gaertner, S. L., Mann, J., Murrell, A. and Dovidio, J. F. 1989: Reducing intergroup bias: the benefits of recategorisation. *Journal of Personality and Social Psychology* 57, 239–249.

Gaertner, S. L., Rust, M., Dovidio, J. F., Backman, B. A. and Anastasio, P. A. 1993: The contact hypothesis: the role of a common ingroup identity on reducing intergroup bias. *Small Groups Research* 25(2), 244–249.

Gallagher, M. 1987: The microskills approach to counsellor training. In Hargie, O., Saunders, C. and Dickson, D. 3rd edn. *Social skills in interpersonal communication*. London: Routledge.

Gallois, C. 1993:The language and communication of emotion: interpersonal, intergroup or universal. *American Behavioural Scientist* 36, 309–338.

Garfinkel, H. 1964: Some studies of the routine grounds of everyday activities. *Social Problems*, 225–250.

Garland, H. A., Hardy, A. and Stephenson, L. 1975: Information search as affected by attribution type and response category. *Personality and Social Psychology Bulletin* 1, 612–615.

Garton, A. F. 1992: *Social interaction and the development of language and cognition*. Hove: Erlbaum.

Geen, R.G. 1991: Social motivation. *Annual Review of Psychology* 42, 377–391.

Geen, R. G. and Donnerstein, E. (eds) 1983: *Aggression: theoretical and empirical reviews*. New York: Academic Press.

Geen, R. G. and McCown, E. J. 1984: Effects of noise and attack on aggression and physiological arousal. *Motivation and Emotion* 8, 231–241.

Gerbner, G., Gross, L., Morgan, M. and Signorelli, N. 1986: Living with television: the dynamics of the cultivation process. In Bryant, J. and Zillman, D. (eds) *Perspectives on media effects*. Hillsdale, NJ: Erlbaum, pp. 17–40.

Gerrard, H. B. 1963: Emotional uncertainty and social comparison. *Journal of Abnormal and Social Psychology* 66, 6, 568–573.

Gilbert, D. T. 1989: Thinking lightly about others: automatic components of the social inference process. In Uleman, J. S. and Bargh, J. A. (eds), *Unintended thought*. New York: Guilford Press.

Gilbert, D. T. 1991: How mental systems believe. American Psychologist 46, 107–119.

Gilbert, D. T. 1995: Attribution and interpersonal perception. In Tesser, A. (ed.), *Advanced Social Psychology*. New York: McGraw-Hill.

Gilbert, D. T. and Jones, E. E. 1986: Perceiver-induced constraint: interpretations of self-generated reality. *Journal of Personality and Social Psychology* 50, 269–280.

Gilbert, D. T. and Malone, P. S. 1995: The correspondence bias. *Psychological Bulletin* 117, 21–38.

Gillen, K. and Muncer, S. J. 1995: Sex differences in the perceived causal structure of date rape. *Aggressive Behaviour* vol. 21, 2, 101–112.

Gilligan, C. 1982: *In a different voice: psychological theory and women's development*. Cambridge, MA: Harvard University Press.

Gilligan, C. and Wiggins, G. 1987: The origins of morality in early childhood relationships. In Kagan, J. and Lamb, S. (eds), *The emergence of morality*. Chicago: Chicago University Press.

Glaser, R., Rice, J., Sheridan, J., Fertel, R., Stout, J. C., Speicher, C., Pinsky, D., Kotur, M., Post, A., Beck, M. and Kiecolt-Glaser, J. 1987: Stress-related immune suppression: health implications. *Brain, Behaviour and Immunity* 1, 7–20.

Gleitman, L. R. and Wanner, E. 1982: Language acquisition: the state of the art. In Wanner, E. and Gleitman, L. R. (eds), *Language acquisition: the state of the art*. Cambridge: Cambridge University Press, pp. 3–48.

Gnepp, J. 1983: Children's social sensitivity: inferring emotions from conflicting cues. *Developmental Psychology* 19, 805–814.

Goffman, E. 1972: *Interaction ritual: essays in face-to face behaviour*. Harmondsworth: Penguin.

Goleman, D. 1990: Support groups may do more in cancer than relieve the mind. *The New York Times*, 18 October.

Gordon, R. A. 1993: The effect of strong versus weak evidence on the assessment of race stereotypical and non-stereotypical crimes. *Journal of Applied Social Psychology* 23, 734–749.

Gottman, J. M. and Levenson, R. L. 1988: The social psychophysiology of marriage. In Noller, P. and Fitzpatrick, M. A. (eds), *Perspectives on marital interaction*. Clevedon: Multilingual Matters, pp. 182–200.

Green, J. and Shellenberger, R. 1991: *The dynamics of health and wellness*. New York: Holt, Rinehart and Winston.

Greenbaum, P. and Rosenfeld, H. 1980: Varieties of touching in greetings: sequential structure and sex-related differences. *Journal of Non-Verbal Behaviour* 5, 13–25.

Greenberg, J., Williams, K. D. and O'Brien, M. K. 1986: Considering the harshest verdict first: biasing effects of mock-juror verdict. *Personality and Social Psychology Bulletin* 12, 41–50.

Greenburg, M. A. and Stone, A. 1992: Emotional disclosure about traumas and its relation to health: effects of previous disclosure and trauma severity. *Journal of Personality and Social Psychology* 63, 75–84.

Gregg, V., Gibbs, J. C. and Basinger, K. S. 1994: Patterns of developmental delay in moral judgement by male and female delinquents. *Merrill-Palmer Quarterly* 40, 538–553.

Griffit, W. B. and Veitch, R. 1971: Hot and crowded: influence of population density and temperature on interpersonal affective behaviour. *Journal of Personality and Social Psychology* 17, 92–98.

Gross, A. E. and Latané, J. G. 1974: Receiving help, reciprocation and interpersonal attraction. *Journal of Applied Social Psychology* 4, 210–223.

Grote, N. K. and Frieze, I. H. 1994: The measurement of friendship based love in intimate relationships. *Personal Relationships* 1, 275–300.

Grusec, J. E., Kuczynski, L., Rushton, J. P. and Simutis, Z. M. 1978: Modeling, direct instruction and attributions: effect on altruism. *Developmental Psychology* 14, 51–57.

Grusec, J. T. 1982: The socialisation of altruism. In Eisberg, N. (ed.) *The development of prosocial behaviour*. New York: Academic Press, pp. 65–90.

Guerin, D. and Gottfried, A. W. 1986: Infant temperament as a predictor of preschool behaviour problems. *Infant Behaviour and Development* 9, 152.

Guetzkow, N. and Simon, H. A. 1955: The impact of certain communication nets on organisation and performance in task-oriented groups. *Management Science* 1, 233–250.

Hall, E. T. 1996: *The hidden dimension*. Garden City, NY: Doubleday.

Hall, J. and Watson, W. H. 1970: Individual and group decision making. *Human Relations* 23, 299–317.

Hall, J. A. 1984. *Non-verbal sex differences. communication accuracy and expressive style*. Baltimore: Johns Hopkins University Press.

Hall, J. A. and Veccia, E. M. 1990: More 'touching' observations: new insights on men, women and interpersonal touch. *Journal of Personality and Social Psychology* 59, 1155–1162.

Hamblin, R. L. 1958; Leadership and crisis. *Sociometry* 21, 322–335.

Hamilton, D. L. and Gifford, R. K. 1976: Illusory correlation in interpersonal personal perception: a cognitive basis of stereotypic judgements. *Journal of Experimental Social Psychology* 12, 392–407.

Hamilton, D. L. and Sherman, J. W. 1989: Illusory correlations: implications for stereotype theory and research. In Bar-Tuls, D., Graumann, C. F., Kruglanski, A. W. and Stroebe, A. (eds) *Stereotyping and prejudice: changing conceptions*. New York: Springer.

Han, S. and Shavitt, S. 1993: Persuasion and culture: advertising appeals in individualistic and collective societies. Unpublished Ms. University of Illinois.

Hansen, J. E. and Schuldt, W. J. 1984: Marital self disclosure and marital satisfaction. *Journal of Marriage and the Family* 46, 923–926.

Hargie, O., Saunders, C. and Dickson, D. 1994: 3rd edn. *Social skills in interpersonal communication*. London: Routledge.

Harlow, H. F. 1959: Love in infant monkeys. *Scientific American*, 200 (6) 68–74.

Harré, R. 1979: *Social being: a theory for social psychology*. Oxford: Blackwell.

Harrigan, J. 1985. Listeners' body movements and speaking turns. *Communication Research* 12, 233–250.

Harrigan, J. A., Lucic, K. S., Kay, D. *et al.* 1991: Effect of expressor role and type of self-touching on observer's perceptions. *Journal of Applied Social Psychology* 21, 585–609.

Hartup, W. W. 1983: Peer relations. In Mussen, P. H. (ed.), *Handbook of child psychology.* vol 4. New York: Wiley.

Harvey, J. H., Town, J. P. and Yarkin, K. L. 1981: How fundamental is the fundamental attribution error? *Journal of Personality and Social Psychology* 40, 346–349.

Harvey, J. H., Wells, G. L. and Alvarez, M. D. 1978: Attribution in the context of conflict and separation in close relationships. In Harvey, J. H., Ickes, W. and Kidd, R. F. (eds), *New directions in attribution research.* vol 2. Hillsdale, NJ: Erlbaum, pp. 235–260.

Harvey, O. J. and Consalvi, C. 1960: Status and continuity to pressure in informal groups. *Journal of Abnormal and Social Psychology* 60, 182–187.

Hatfield, E. and Rapson, R. L. 1993: *Love, sex and intimacy: their psychology, biology and history.* New York: HarperCollins.

Hatfield, E. and Sprecher, S. 1986: *Mirror, mirror . . . the importance of looks in everyday life.* Albany, NY: State University of New York Press.

Hatfield, E., Sprecher, S., Pillemer, J. T., Greenberger, D. and Wexler, P. 1989: Gender differences in what is desired in the sexual relationship. *Journal of Psychology and Human Sexuality* 1, 39–52.

Hazan, C. and Shaver, P. 1990: Love and work: an attachment theoretical perspective. *Journal of Personality and Social Psychology* 59, 270–280.

Hearold, S. 1986: A synthesis of 1043 effects of television on social behaviour. In Comstock, G. (ed.) *Public communication and behaviour.* vol. 1. Orlando, FL: Academic Press, pp. 65–133.

Heider, F. 1944: Social perception and phenomenal causality. *Psychological Review* 40, 358–374.

Heider, F. 1946: Attitudes and cognitive organisation. *Journal of Psychology* 21, 107–112.

Heider, F. 1958: *The psychology of interpersonal relations.* New York: John Wiley and Sons.

Heilman, M. E., Block, C. J. and Lucas, J. A. 1992: Presumed incompetent? Stigmatization and affirmative action efforts. *Journal of Applied Psychology* 77, 536–544.

Heilman, M. E., Simon, M. C. and Repper, D. P. 1987: Intentionally favoured, unintentionally harmed? Impact of sex-based preferential selection as self-perceptions and self-evaluations. *Journal of Applied Psychology* 72, 62–68.

Helson, R. and Moane, G. 1987: Personality change in women from college to midlife. *Journal of Personality and Social Psychology* 53, 176–186.

Hemphill, J. K. 1950: Relations between the size of a group and the behaviour of 'superior leaders'. *Journal of Social Psychology* 32, 11–22.

Hendrick, S. S. and Hendrick, C. 1993: Lovers as friends. *Journal of Social and Personal Relationships* 10, 459–466.

Hess, E. H. 1965: Attitude and pupil size. *Scientific American* 212, 46–54.

Hetherington, E. M., Cox, M. and Cox, R. 1979: Play and social interaction in children following divorce. *Journal of Social Issues* 35, 26–49.

Hewstone, M. 1989: *Causal attribution: from cognitive processes to collective beliefs.* Oxford: Blackwell.

Hewstone, M. and Ward, C. 1985: Ethnocentrism and causal attribution in South-East Asia. *Journal of Personality and Social Psychology* 48, 614–623.

Hewstone, M., Stroebe, W. and Stephenson, G. (eds), 1996; *Introduction to social psychology.* Oxford: Blackwell.

Heymann, T. 1989: *On an average day.* New York: Fawcett Columbine.

Higgins, E. T. 1987: Self-discrepancy: a theory relating theory and affect. *Psychological Review* 94, 319–340.

Higgins, E. T. and Bargh, J. A. 1987: Social cognition and social perception. *Annual Review of Psychology* 38, 369–425.

Higgins, E. T., Bargh, J. A. Lombardi, W. 1985: The nature of priming effects on categorization. *Journal of Experimental Psychology: learning memory and cognition* 11, 59–69.

Higgins, E. T. and Bryant, S. L. 1982: Consensus information and the fundamental attribution error: the role of development and in-group versus out-group knowledge. *Journal of Personality and Social Psychology* 43, 35–47.

Hill, C.A. 1987: Affiliation motivation: people who need people but in different ways. *Journal of Personality and Social Psychology* 52, 1008–1018.

Hill, C. T., Rubin, Z. and Peplau, L. A. 1976: Breakups before marriage: the end of 103 affairs. *Journal of Social Issues* 32, 1, 147–168.

Hines, N. J. and Fry, D. P. 1994: Indirect models of aggression among women in Buenos Aires, Argentina. *Sex Roles* 30, 213–236.

Hirsh-Pasek, K. and Treiman, R. 1982: Doggerel: mothers in a new context. *Journal of Child Language* 9, 229–37.

Hockett, C. F. 1960: The origin of speech. *Scientific American* 203, 89–96.

Hoekstra, M. and Wilke, H. 1972: Wage recommendations in management groups; a cross-cultural study. *Nederlands Tijdschrift voor de Psychologie* 21, 266–272.

Hoffman, C., Lau, I. and Johnson, D. R. 1986. The linguistic relativity of person cognition: an English-Chinese comparison. *Journal of Personality and Social Psychology* 51, 1097–1105.

Hoffman, M. L. 1981: Is altruism part of human nature? *Journal of Personality and Social Psychology* 40, 121–137.

Hofstede, G. 1980: *Culture's consequences: international differences in work-related values*. Beverley Hills, CA:Sage.

Hogg, M., Turner, J. C. and Davidson, B. 1990: Polarised norms and social frames of reference: a test of the self-categorisation theory of group polarisation. *Basic and Applied Social Psychology* 11, 77–100.

Hogg, M. A. 1992: *The social psychology of group cohesiveness: from attraction to social identity*. London: Harvester Wheatsheaf.

Hogg, M. A. and Abrams, D. 1988: *Social identifications: a social psychology in intergroup relations and intergroup processes*. London: Routledge.

Hogg, M. A. and Mullen, B. A. 1998: Joining groups to reduce uncertainty: subjective uncertainty reduction and group identification. In Abrams, D. and Hogg, M. A. (eds), *Social identity and social cognition*. Oxford: Blackwell.

Hogg, M. A. and Turner, J. C. 1985: Interpersonal attraction, social identification and psychological group formation. *European Journal of Social Psychology* 15, 51–66.

Hogg, M. A. and Turner, J. C. 1987: Social identity and conformity: a theory of referent informational influence. In Doise, W. and Moscovici, S. (eds), *Current issues in European social psychology*. vol. 2. Cambridge: Cambridge University Press.

Hogg, M. A., Turner, J. C. and Davidson, B. 1990: Polarised norms and social frames of reference: a test of the self-categorisation theory of group polarisation. *Basic Applied Social Psychology* 11, 77–100.

Hogg, M. A. and Vaughan, G. M. 1995: *Social psychology: an introduction*. London: Prentice-Hall/Harvester.

Hollander, E. P. 1984: *Leaders, groups and influence*. New York: Oxford University Press.

Holtgraves, T. and Yang, J. 1990: Politeness as universal cross cultural perceptions of request strategies and inferences based on their use. *Journal of Personality and Social Psychology* 59, 719–729.

Hooff, J. van. 1967: The facial displays of the catarrhive monkeys and apes. In D. Morris (ed.), *Primate ethology*. London: Weidenfeld and Nicolson.

Hornstein, H. A. 1970: The influence of social models on helping. In McCauley, J. and Berkowitz, L. (eds) *Altruism and helping behaviour*. New York: Academic Press.

Horowitz, L. M., Rosenberg, S. E. and Bartholomew, K. 1993: Interpersonal problems, attachment styles and outcome in brief dynamic psychotherpay. *Journal of Consulting and Clinical Psychology* 61, 549–560.

House, J. S. 1981: *Work stress and social support*. Reading, MA: Addison-Wesley.

Houston, D. A. 1990: Empathy and the self: cognitive and emotional influences on the evaluation of negative affect in others. *Journal of Personality and Social Psychology* 59, 859–888.

Hovland, C. I., Janis, I. L. and Kelley, H. H. 1953: *Communication and persuasion*. New Haven, CO: Yale University Press.

Howard, L. 1990, Periscope. *Newsweek*, 9 July, p. 7.

Howitt, D., Billig, M. and Cramer, D. *et al*. 1989: *Social psychology: conflicts and continuities*. Milton Keynes: Open University Press.

Huesmann, L. R. and Eron, L. D. 1986: *Television and the aggressive child: a cross-national comparison*. Hillsdale, NJ: Erlbaum

Huesmann, L. R., Eron, L. D., Lefkowitz, M. M. and Walder, L. O. 1984: Stability of aggression over time and generations. *Developmental Psychology* 20, 1120–1134.

Huesmann, L. R., Eron, L. D. and Yarmel, P. W. 1987: Intellectual functioning and aggression. *Journal of Personality and Social Psychology* 52, 232–240.

Huff, C., Sproull, L. and Kiesler, S. 1989: Computer communication and organisational commitment: tracing the relationship in a city government. *Journal of Applied Social Psychology* 19, 1371–1391.

Hyman, H. H. and Sheatsley, P. B. 1954: The authoritarian personality: a methodological critique. In Christie, R. and Jahoda, M. (eds), *Studies in the scope of the authoritarian personality*. New York: Free Press.

Irish, J. T. and Hall, J. A. 1995: Interruption patterns in medical visits: the effects of role, status and gender. *Social Science Medicine*. 41, 6, 873–881.

Isen, A. M. 1970: Success, failure, attention and reaction to others: the warm glow of success. *Journal of Personality and Social Psychology* 15, 294–301.

Isen, A. M., Clark, M. and Schwartz, M. H. 1976: Duration of the effect of good mood on helping: 'Footprints in the sands of time'. *Journal of Personality and Social Psychology* 34, 385–393.

Isen, A. M. and Stalker, T. E. 1982: The effect of feeling state on evaluation of positive, neutral and negative stimuli when you 'accentuate the positive': do you eliminate the negative? *Social Psychology Quarterly* 45, 58–63.

Isenberg, D. J. 1986: Group polarisation: a critical review. *Journal of Personality and Social Psychology* 50, 1141–1151.

Islam, M. and Hewstone, M. 1993: Intergroup attributions and affective consequences of majority and minority groups. *Journal of Personality and Social Psychology* 65, 936–950.

Izard, C. E. 1994: Intimate and universal facial expressions: evidence from developmental and cross-cultural research. *Psychological Bulletin* 115, 288–299.

Jackson, L. A., Hunter, J. E., and Hodge, C. N. 1995: Physical attractiveness and intellectual competence: a meta-analytic review. *Social Psychology Quarterly*. Vol. 58, 108–122.

Jains, I. L. 1972: *Victims of groupthink*. 2nd edn. Boston: Houghton-Mifflin.

Jains, I. L. and Mann, L. 1977: *Decision making: a psychological analysis of conflict, choice and commitment*. New York: Free Press.

Janis, I. L. 1982: *Groupthink: psychological studies of policy decisions and fiascos.* Boston: Houghton-Mifflin.

Janis, I. L and Hovland, C. I. 1959: An overview of persuadability research. In Hovland, C. I. and Janis, I. L. (eds), *Personality and persuadability.* New Haven, Yale University Press.

Jellison, J. and Arkin, R. 1977: Social comparison of abilities: a self-presentation approach to decision making in groups. In Suls, J. M. and Miller, R. L. (eds), *Social comparison processes: theoretical and empirical perspectives.* Washington, DC: Hemisphere, pp. 35–57.

Johnson, D. W., Marauyama, G., Johnson, R., Nelson, D. and Skon, L. 1981: Effects of cooperative, competitive and individualistic goal structures on achievement: a meta-analysis. *Psychological Bulletin* 89, 47–62.

Johnson, R. D. and Downing, L. L. 1979: Deindividuation and valence of cues: effects on prosocial and antisocial behaviour. *Journal of Personality and Social Psychology* 37, 1532–1538.

Johnson, T. J., Feigenbaum, R. and Weibey, M. 1964: Some determinants and consequences of the teacher's perception of causality. *Journal of Educational Psychology* 55, 237–246.

Jones, B., Gray, A., Kavanagh, D., Moran, M., Norton, P. and Seldon, A. 1994: *Politics UK.* 2nd edn. Hemel Hempstead: Harvester Wheatsheaf.

Jones, E. E. 1990: *Interpersonal Perception.* New York: W.H. Freeman.

Jones, E. E. and Davis, K. E. 1965: From actions to dispositions: the attribution process in person perception. In Berkowitz, L. (ed.), *Advances in experimental social psychology.* Vol. 2, New York: Academic Press.

Jones, E. E. and Harris, V. A. 1967: The attribution of attitudes. *Journal of Experimental Social Psychology* 3, 1–24.

Jones, E. E. and McGillis, D. 1976: Correspondent inferences and the attribution cube: a comparative reappraisal. In Jarvey, J. H., Ickes, W. J. and Kidd, R. F. (eds), *New directions in attribution research.* Vol. 1, Hillsdale, NJ: Erlbaum.

Jones, E. E. and Nisbett, R. E. 1972: The actor and the observer: divergent perceptions of the causes of behaviour. In Jones, E. E., Kanouse, D. E., Kelley, H. H., Nisbett, R. E., Valins, S. and Weiner, B. (eds.), *Attribution: perceiving the causes of behaviour.* Morristown, NJ: General Learning Press.

Jones, S. E. and Yarborough, A. E. 1985: A naturalistic study of the meanings of touch. *Communication Monographs* 52, 19–56.

Joule, R. V. 1987: Tobacco deprivation: the foot-in-the-door technique versus the low ball technique. *Journal of Social Psychology* 17, 361–365.

Jussim, L., Eccles, J. and Madon, S. 1996: Social perception, social stereotypes, and teacher expectations: accuracy and the quest for the powerful self-fulfilling prophecy. *Advances in Experimental Social Psychology* 28, 281–388.

Kagan, J., Arcus, D., Snidman, N., Feng, W. Y., Hendler, J. and Greene, S. 1994: Reactivity in infants: a cross-national comparison. *Developmental Psychology* 30, 342–345.

Kahn, A., O'Leary, V. E., Krulewitz, J. E. and Lamm, H. 1980: Equity and equality: male and female means to a just end. *Basic and Applied Social Psychology* 1, 173–197.

Kalma, A. 1992: Gazing in triads: a powerful signal in floor appointment. *British Journal of Social Psychology* 31, 21–39.

Kandel, D. 1978: Homophily, selection and socialisation in adolescent friendships. *American Journal of Sociology* 84, 427–36.

Kandel, D., Kessler, R. and Margulies, R. 1978: Antecedents of adolescent initiation into stages of drug use. *Journal of Youth and Adolescence* 7, 13–40.

Kaplan, M. F. and Miller, C. E. 1987: Group decision making and normative versus informational influence; effects of type of issue and assigned decision rule. *Journal of Personality and Social Psychology* 53, 306–313.

Karau, S. J. and Williams, K. D. 1993: Social loafing: a meta-analytic review and theoretical integration. *Journal of Personality and Social Psychology* 65, 681–706.

Karen, R. 1994: *Becoming attached*. New York: Warner Books.

Kassin, S. M. and Pryor, J. B. 1985: The development of attribution processes. In Pryor, J. B. and Day, J. D. (eds), *The development of social cognition*. New York: Springer-Verlag.

Kastenbaum, R. 1965: Wine and fellowship in ageing: an exploratory action program. *Journal of Human Relations* 13, 266–275.

Kastenbaum, R., Kastenbaum, B. K. and Morris, J. 1989: *Strengths and preferences of the terminally ill: data from the National Hospice Demonstration Study*.

Katz, D. 1960: The functional approach to the measurement of attitudes. *Public Opinion Quarterly* 24, 163–204.

Katzev, A. R., Warner, R. L. and Acock, A. 1994: Girls or boys? Relationship of child gender to marital instability. *Journal of Marriage and the Family* 56, 89–100.

Kaufman, I. C. and Rosenblum, L. A. 1969: Effects of separation from mother on the emotional behaviour of infant monkeys. *Annual of the New York Academy of Science* 158, 681–95.

Kaye, K. 1982: *The mental and social life of babies*. Chicago: Chicago University Press.

Keller, L. M., Bouchard, T. J., Aarvey, R. D., Segal, N. L. and Davis, R. V. 1992: Work values: genetics and environmental influences. *Journal of Applied Psychology* 77, 79–88.

Kelley, H. H. 1950: The warm-cold variable in first impressions of persons. *Journal of Personality* 18, 431–439.

Kelley, H. H. 1967: Attribution theory in social psychology. *Nebraska Symposium on motivation* 14,192–241.

Kelley, H. H. 1972: Causal schemata and the attribution process. In Jones, E. E. *et al.* (eds), *Attribution: perceiving the causes of behaviour*. Morristown, NJ: General Learning Press.

Kelley, H. H. 1973: The processes of causal attribution. *American Psychologist* 28, 107–128.

Kelley, H. H., Berscheid, E., Christensen, A., Harvey, J. H., Huston, T. L., Levinger, G., McClintock, E., Peplau, L. A. and Peterson, D. R. (eds), 1983: *Close relationships*. San Francisco: Freeman.

Kelman, H. C. 1958: Compliance, identification and internalization: three processes of attitude change. *Journal of Conflict Resolution* 2, 51–60.

Kelman, H. C. 1967: Human use of human subjects: the problem of deception in social psychology. *Psychological Bulletin* 67, 1–11.

Kendon, A. 1967: Some functions of gaze direction in social interaction. *Acta Psychologica* 28, 1, 1–47.

Kerr, N. L. 1982: The jury trial. In Konecni, V. J. and Ebbeson, E. B. (eds*)*, *The criminal justice system: a social-psychological analysis*. San Francisco: Freeman.

Kiesler, S. and Sproull, L. 1992: Group decision making and communication technology. *Organisational Behaviour and Human Decision Processes* 52, 96–123.

Killian, M. 1952: The significance of multiple group membership in disaster. *American Journal of Sociology* 57, 309–313.

Kilman, W. and Mann, L. Level of destructive obedience as a function of transmitter and executant roles in the Milgram obedience paradigm. *Journal of Personality and Social Psychology* 29, 696–702.

Kirchler, E. and Davis, J. H. 1986: The influence of member status differences and task type on group consensus and member position change. *Journal of Personality and Social Psychology* 51, 83–91.

Kitayama, A., Markus, H. R. and Matsumoto, H. 1995: Culture, self and emotion: a cultural perspective on 'self-conscious' emotions. In Tangrey, J. P. and Fisher, K. W. (eds), *Self-conscious emotions: the psychology of shame, guilt, embarrassment and pride*. New York: Guilford Press.

Klaus, M. H. and Kennell, J. H. 1976: *Maternal infant bonding: the effect of early separation or loss on family bonding*. St Louis: Mosby.

Kleinke, C. L., Meeker, F. B. and Staneski, R. A. 1986: Preference for opening lines: comparing ratings for men and women. *Sex Roles* 15, 585–600.

Klentz, B., Beaman, B., Mapelli, S. D. and Ullrich, J. R. 1987: Perceived physical attractiveness of supporters and non-supporters of the women's movement: an attitude similarity mediated error (ASME). *Personality and Social Psychology Bulletin* 13, 513–523.

Knapp, M. L., Cody, M. J. and Reardon, K. Non-verbal signals. In Knapp, M. L. and Miller, G. R. 1994. 2nd edn. *Handbook of interpersonal communication*. London: Sage Publications.

Knapp, M. L. and Hall, J. A. 1992: *Non-verbal communication in human interaction*. 3rd edn. Fort Worth: Harcourt Brace Jovanovich.

Knight, G. P., Johnson, L. G., Carlo, G. and Eisenberg, N. 1994: A multiplicative model of the dispositional antecedents of a prosocial behaviour: predicting more of the people more of the time. *Journal of Personality and Social Psychology* 66, 178–183.

Kobak, R. R. and Hazan, C. 1991: Attachment in marriage: effects of security and accuracy of working models. *Journal of Personality and Social Psychology* 38, 751–763.

Kogan, N. and Wallach, M. A. 1967: The risky shift phenomenon in small decision making groups: a test of the information exchange hypothesis. *Journal of Experimental Social Psychology* 3, 75–85.

Kohlberg, L. 1976: Moral stages and moralisation: a cognitive developmental approach. In Lickona, T. (ed.), *Moral development and behaviour*. New York: Holt, Rinehart and Winston.

Krantz, S. E. and Rude, S. 1984: Depressive attributions: selection of difference causes or assignment of different meanings? *Journal of Personality and Social Psychology* 47, 103–203.

Kravitz, D. A. and Martin, B. 1986: Ringelmann rediscovered: the original article. *Journal of Personality and Social Psychology* 50, 936–941.

Krebs, D. L. and Miller, D. T. 1985: Altruism and aggression. In Lindzey, G. and Aronson, E. (eds) *Handbook of social psychology*. 3rd edn. vol. 2. New York: Random House, pp. 1–71.

Krebs, R. L. 1967: Some relations between moral judgement, attention and resistance to temptation. Unpublished doctoral dissertation, University of Chicago, Chicago.

Krosnick, J. A., Betz. A. L., Jussim, L. J. and Lynn, A. R. 1992: Subliminal conditioning of attitudes. *Personality and Social Psychology Bulletin* 18, 152–162.

Kulik, J. A. 1983: Confirmatory attribution and the perpetuation of social beliefs. *Journal of Personality and Social Psychology* 44, 1171–1181.

Kulik, J. A. and Mahler, H. I. M. 1989: Stress and affiliation in a hospital setting: preoperative room-mate preferences. *Personality and Social Psychology Bulletin* 15, 183–193.

Kulik, J. M., Mahler, H. I. M. and Earnest, A. 1994: Social comparison and affiliation under threat: going beyond the affiliate choice paradigm. *Journal of Personality and Social Psychology* 66, 301–309.

Kulka, R. A. and Kessler, J. B. 1978: Is justice really blind? The influence of litigant's physical attractiveness on juridical judgement. Journal of Applied Social Psychology 8, 366–381.

Kunda, Z. and Thagard, P. 1996. Forming impression from stereotypes, traits and behaviours: a parallel-constraint-satisfaction theory. *Psychological Review* 103, 284–308.

Lamb, M. and Sternberg, K. M. 1990: Do we really know how daycare affects children? *Journal of Applied and Developmental Psychology* 11, 351–379.

Landy, D. and Sigall, H. 1974: Beauty is talent: task evaluation as a function of the performer's physical attractiveness. *Journal of Personality and Social Psychology* 29, 299–304.

La Piere, R. T. 1934: Attitudes versus actions. *Social Forces* 13, 230–237.

Laplace, A. C., Chermack, S. T. and Taylor, S. P. 1994: Effects of alcohol and drinking experience on human physical aggression. *Personality and Social Psychology Bulletin* 20, 439–444.

Larsen, K. and Smith, C. K. 1981: Assessment of non-verbal communication in the patient–physician interview. *Journal of Family Practice* 12, 481–488.

Latané, B. and Darley, J. M. 1970: *The unresponsive bystander: why doesn't he help?* New York: Appleton-Century-Crofts.

Latané, B., Nida, S. A. and Wilson, D. W. 1981: The effects of group size on helping behaviour. In Rushton, J. P. and Sorrentino, R. M. (eds) *Altruism and helping behaviour.* Hillsdale, NJ: Erlbaum, pp. 287–313.

Latané, B., Williams, K. and Harkins, S. 1979: Many hands make light work: the causes and consequences of social loafing. *Journal of Personality and Social Psychology* 37, 822–832.

Law, D. J., Pellegrino J. W. and Hunt, E. B. 1993: Comparing the tortoise and the hare: gender differences and experience in dynamic spatial reasoning tasks. *Psychological Science* 4, 35–40.

Leavitt, H. J. 1951: Some effects of certain patterns on group performance. *Journal of Abnormal and Social Psychology* 46, 38–50.

Le Bon, G. 1908: *The crowd: a study of the popular mind.* London: Unwin.

Leibert, R. M. and Sprafkin, J. 1988: The early window effects on television and youth. 3rd edn. New York: Pergamon Press.

Lepowsky, M. 1994: Women, men and aggression in an egalitarian society. *Sex Roles* 30, 199–211.

Lerner, M. J. 1980: *The belief in a just world: a fundamental delusion.* New York: Plenum Press.

Leventhal, H. 1970: Findings and theory in the study of fear communications. In Berkowitz, L. (ed.), *Advances in experimental social psychology.* vol. 5. New York: Academic Press.

Levinger, G. 1980: Toward the analysis of close relationships. *Journal of Experimental Social Psychology* 16, 510–544.

Levinson, D. J., Darrow, C. N., Klein, E. B., Levinson, M. H. and McKee, B. 1978: *The seasons of a man's life.* New York: Knopf.

Levy, M. B. and David, K. E. 1988: Love styles and attachment styles compared: their relation to each other and to various relationship characteristics. *Journal of Social and Personal Relationships* 5, 429–471.

Lewin, K., Lippett, R. and White, P. K. 1939: Patterns of aggressive behaviour in experimentally created 'social climates'. *Journal of Social Psychology* 10, 271–299.

Ley, P. 1988: *Communicating with patients: improving communication, satisfaction and compliance.* London: Croom Helm.

Liberman, A. and Chaiken, S. 1992: Defensive processing of personally relevant health messages. *Personality and Social Psychology Bulletin* 18, 669–679.

Liebert, R. M. and Sprafkin, J. 1988: *The early window: effects of television on children and youth.* 3rd edn. New York: Pergamon Press.

Liebrand, D., Messick, D. and Wilke, H. (eds) 1992: *A social psychological approach to social dilemmas.* New York: Pergamon Press.

Lightdale, J. R. and Prentice, D. A. 1994: Rethinking sex differences in aggression: aggressive behaviour in the absence of social roles. *Personality and Social Psychology Bulletin* 20, 34–44.

Lightfoot, C. 1997: *The culture of adolescent risk taking.* Guilford: New York.

Likert, R. 1932: A technique for the measurement of attitudes. *Archives of Psychology* 22, 40.

Linssen, H. and Hagendoorn, L. 1994. Social and geographical factors in the explanation of the content of European nationality stereotypes. *British Journal of Social Psychology* 33, 165–182.

Linville, P. W. 1985: Self-complexity and affective extremity: don't put all your egs in one cognitive basket. *Social Cognition* 3, 94–120.

Linville, P. W.. 1987. Self complexity as a cognitive buffer against stress-related depression and illness. *Journal of Personality and Social Psychology* 52, 663–676.

Linville, P. W., Fischer, G. T. W. and Salovey, P. 1989: Perceived distributions of the characteristics of in-group and out-group members: empirical evidence and a computer simulation. *Journal of Personality and Social Psychology* 57, 165–188.

Locke, D. and Pennington, D. 1982: Reasons and other causes: their role in attribution processes. *Journal of Personality and Social Psychology* 42, 212–223.

Locke, K. D. and Horowitz, L. M. 1990: Satisfaction in interpersonal interactions as a function of similarity in level of dysphoria. *Journal of Personality and Social Psychology* 58, 823–831.

London, P. 1970: The rescuers: motivational hypotheses about Christians who saved Jews from the Nazis. In McCauley, J. R. and Berkowitz, L. (eds), *Altruism and helping behaviour.* New York: Academic Press, pp. 241–250.

Lord, C. G. 1997: *Social psychology.* Fort Worth: Harcourt Brace College Publishers.

Lord, R.G., de Vader, C. L. and Alliger, G. M. 1986: A meta-analysis of the relation between personality traits and leadership perceptions. *Journal of Applied Psychology* 71, 402–410.

Lore, R. K. and Schultz L. A. 1993: Control of human aggression: a comparative perspective. *American Psychologist* 48, 16–25.

Lorenz, K. 1966: *On aggression.* New York: Harcourt, Brace and World.

Losch, M. E. and Cacioppo J. T. 1990: Cognitive dissonance may enhance sympathetic tonus, but attitudes are changed to reduce negative effect rather than arousal. *Journal of Experimental Social Psychology* 26, 289–304.

Lott, A. J. and Lott, B. E. 1972: The power of liking: consequences of interpersonal attitudes derived from a liberalised view of secondary reinforcement. In Berkowitz, L. (ed.), *Advances in experimental social psychology.* vol. 6. New York: Academic Press, pp. 109–148.

Lovdal, L. T. 1989: Sex role messages in television commercials: an update. *Sex Roles* 21, 715–724.

Luchins, A. S. 1957: Primacy and recency in impression formation. In C. Hovland (ed.), *The order of presentation in persuasion.* New Haven, CO: Yale University Press.

Lynn M. and Mynier, K. 1993: Effect of server-posture on restaurant tipping. *Journal of Applied Social Psychology* 23, 678–685.

Maass, A. and Clark, R. D. 1983: Internalisation versus compliance: differential processes underlying minority influence and conformity. *European Journal of Social Psychology* 13, 197–215.

Maccoby, N., Farquhar, J. W., Wood, P. D. R., and Alexander, J. K. 1977: Reducing the risk of cardiovascular disease: effects of a community-based campaign on knowledge and behaviour. *Journal of Community Health* 3, 100–114.

Mackie, D. M. and Hamilton, D. L. (eds), 1993: *Affect, cognition and stereotyping: interactive processes in group perception*. San Diego, CA: Academic Press.

Mackintosh, N. J. (ed.) 1995: *Cyril Burt: fraud or framed?* Oxford: Oxford University Press.

Macrea, C. N., Milne, A. B. and Bodenhausen, G. V. 1994: Stereotypes as energy-saving devices: a peek inside the cognitive toolbox. *Journal of Personality and Social Psychology* 66, 37–47.

Madon, S., Jussim, L. and Eccles, J. 1997: In search of the powerful self-fulfilling prophecy. *Journal of Personality and Social Psychology* 72, 4, 791–809.

Maio, G. R., Esses, V. M. and Bell, D. W. 1994: The formation of attitudes towards new immigrant groups. *Journal of Applied Social Psychology* 24, 1762–1776.

Major, B. and Adams, J. B. 1983: Role of gender, interpersonal orientation, and self-presentation in distributive justice behaviour. *Journal of Personality and Social Psychology* 45, 598–608.

Mann, R. D. 1959: A review of the relationships between personality and performance in small groups. *Psychological Bulletin* 56, 241–270.

Mantell, D. M. 1971: The potential for violence in Germany. *Journal of Social Issues* 27, 101–112.

Marks, G. and Miller, N. 1982: Target attractiveness as a mediator of assumed attitude similarity. *Personality and Social Psychology Bulletin* 8, 728–735.

Marks, G. and Miller, N. 1987: Ten years of research on the false consensus effect: an empirical and theoretical review. *Psychological Bulletin* 102, 72–90.

Markus, H. 1977: Self schemata and processing information about self. *Journal of Personality and Social Psychology* 35, 63–78.

Markus, H., Hamill, R. and Sentis, K. 1987: Thinking fat: self schemas for body weight and the processing of weight relevant information. *Journal of Applied Social Psychology* 17, 50–71.

Markus, H. and Nurius, P. 1986: Possible selves. *American Psychologist* 41, 954–969.

Marques, J. M. 1988: The black sheep effect: judgmental extremity towards ingroup members, in inter- and intra-group situations. *European Journal of Social Psychology* 18, 28–72.

Marques, J. M., Yzerbyt, V. Y. and Rijsman, J. B. 1988: Context effects on intergroup discrimination: ingroup bias as a function of experimenters' provenance. *British Journal of Social Psychology* 27, 301–318.

Martin, R. 1988: In-group and Out-group minorities: differential impact upon public and private response. *European Journal of Social Psychology* 18, 39–52.

Matsumoto, D. 1990: Cultural similarities and differences in display rules. *Motivation and Emotion* 14, 195–214.

Matthews, K. A. 1982: Psychological perspectives on the Type A behaviour pattern. *Psychological Bulletin* 91, 293–323.

McArthur, L. Z. 1972: The how and why of what: some determinants and consequences of causal attribution. *Journal of Personality and Social Psychology* 22, 171–193.

McClelland, D. C. 1985: *Human motivation*. Glenview, IL: Scott, Foresman.

McConnell, A. R., Sherman, S. J. and Hamilton, D. L. 1994: Illusory correlation in the perception of groups: an extension of the distinctiveness-based account. *Journal of Personality and Social Psychology* 67, 414–429.

McCrae, R. R. and Costa, P. T. 1988: Psychological resilience among widowed men and women: a 10 year follow up of a national sample. *Journal of Social Issues* 44,3, 129–142.

McDougall, W. 1908: *An introduction to social psychology*. London: Methuen.

McGarty, G. and Penny, R. E. C. 1988: Categorisation, accentuation and social judgement. *British Journal of Social Psychology* 27, 147–157.

McGrath, J.E. 1984: *Groups: interaction and performance*. Englewood Cliffs, NJ: Prentice-Hall.

McGuire, W. J. 1969: The nature of attitudes and attitude change. In Lindzey, G. and Aronson, E. (eds), *Handbook of social psychology*. Vol. 3. Reading, MA: Addison-Wesley.

McGuire, W. J. 1985: Attitudes and attitude change. In Lindzey, G. and Aronson, E. (eds), *Handbook of social psychology*, 3rd edn. New York: Random House.

McLeod, J. D. and Eckberg, D. A. 1993: Concordance for depressive disorders and marital quality. *Journal of Marriage and the Family* 55, 733–746.

Mednick, S. A. and Kandel, E. S. 1988: Congenital determinants of violence. *Bulletin of the American Academy of Psychiatry and the Law* 16, 101–109.

Meeus, W. and Raaijmakers, Q. 1986: Adminstrative obedience as a social phenomenon. In Doise, W. and Moscovici, S. (eds), *Current issues in European social psychology*, vol. 2. Cambridge: Cambridge University Press.

Mehrabian A. 1972: Non-verbal communication. In Cole, J. (ed.), *Nebraska symposium on motivation*. 19, 107–162.

Merton, R. 1948: The self-fulfilling prophecy. *Antioch Review* 8, 193–210.

Messer, D. J. 1983: The redundancy between adult speech and nonverbal interaction: a contribution to acquisition? In Golinkoff, R. M. (ed.), *The transition from prelinguistic linguistic communication*. Hillsdale, NJ: Erlbaum.

Messick, D. M. and Brewer, M. B. 1982: Solving social dilemmas. In Wheeler, L. and Shaver, P. (eds), *Review of personality and social psychology*. vol. 4. Beverly Hills, CA: Sage.

Messick, D. M., Wilke, H., Brewer, M. B., Kramer, R. M., Zempe, P. E. and Lui, L. 1983: Individual adaptations and structural changes as solutions to social dilemmas. *Journal of Personality and Social Psychology* 44, 294–309.

Milgram, S. 1963: Behavioural study of obedience. *Journal of Abnormal and Social Psychology* 67, 371–378.

Milgram, S. 1974: *Obedience to authority*. London: Tavistock.

Milgram, S. 1992: *The individual in a social world: essays and experiment.s* 2nd edn. New York: McGraw-Hill.

Miller, D. T. 1977: Altruism and the threat to a belief in a just world. *Journal of Experimental Social Psychology* 13, 113–124.

Miller, D. T. and Ross, M. 1975: Self-serving biases in the attribution of causality: fact or fiction? *Psychological Bulletin* 82, 213–215.

Miller, G. R. and Stiff, J. B. 1993: *Receptive communication*. London: Sage Publications.

Miller, J. G. 1984: Culture and the development of everyday social explanation. *Journal of Personality and Social Psychology* 46, 961–978.

Miller, J. G., Bersoff, D. M. and Harwood, R. L. 1990: Perceptions of social responsibility in India and the United States: moral imperatives or personal decisions? *Journal of Personality and Social Psychology* 58, 33–47.

Miller, N. E. and Bugelski, R. 1948: Minor studies in aggression: the influence of frustrations imposed by the ingroup on attitudes towards outgroups. *Journal of Psychology* 25, 437–442.

Minard, R. D. 1952: Race relations in the Pacohontas coal field. *Journal of Social Issues* 8, 29–44.

Mixon, D. 1972: Instead of deception. *Journal for the Theory of Social Behaviour* 2, 145–178.

Mioghaddam, F. M., Taylor, D. M. and Wright, S. C. 1993: *Social psychology in cross-cultural perspective*. New York: WH Freeman and Co.

Miranda, F. S. B., Caballero, R. B., Gomez, M. N. G. and Zamorano, M. A. M. 1981: Obediencia a la autoridad. *Psizuis Z*, 212–221.

Montemayor, R. 1983: Parents and adolescents in conflict: all families some of the time and some families most of the time. *Journal of Early Adolescence* 3, 83–103.

Moreland, R. L., Argote, L. and Krishnan, R. 1996: Socially shared cognition at work: transactive memory and group performance. In Nye, J. L. and Bower, A. M. (eds), *What's social about social cognition?* Thousand Oaks, CA: Sage.

Moreland, R. L. and Beach, S. R. 1992: Exposure effects in the classroom: the development of affinity among students. *Journal of Experimental Social Psychology* 28, 255–276.

Morris, D., Collett, P., Marsh, P. *et al.* 1979: *Gestures: their origins and distribution*. London: Cape.

Morris, M. W. and Peng, K. P. 1994: Culture and cause: American and Chinese attributions for social physical events. *Journal of Personality and Social Psychology* 67, 949–971.

Morris, W. N. and Miller, R. S. 1975: The effects of consensus-breaking and consensus-preempting partners in reduction of conformity. *Journal of Experimental Social Psychology* 11, 215–223.

Morrow, N. C., Hargie, O., Donnelly, H. *et al.* 1994. 'Why do you ask'? A study of questioning behaviour in pharmacist-client consultations. In Hargie, O., Saunders, C. and Dickson, D. 3rd edn. *Social skills in interpersonal communication*. London: Routledge.

Moscovici, S. 1976: *Social influence and social change*. European Monographs in Social Psychology. vol. 10. London: Academic Press.

Moscovici, S. 1980: Toward a theory of conversion behaviour. In Berkowitz, L. (ed.), *Advances in experimental social psychology*. vol. 13. New York: Academic Press.

Moscovici, S. 1985: Social influence and conformity. In Lindzey, G. and Aronson, E. (eds), *Handbook of social psychology*. New York: Random House.

Moscovici, S. and Faucheux, C. 1972: Social influence, conformity bias and the study of active minorities. In Berkowitz, L. (ed.) *Advances in experimental social psychology*. vol. 6. London: Academic Press.

Moscovici, S, Lage, E. and Naffrechoux, M. 1969: Influence of a consistent minority on the response of a majority in a colour perception task. *Sociometry* 32, 365–379Moscovici, S.. and Nemeth, C. 1974: Social influence: minority influence. In C. Nemeth (ed.), *Social psychology: classic and contemporary integrations*. Chicago: Rand McNally.

Moscovici, S. and Personnaz, B. 1986: Studies on latent influence by the spectrometer method: the impact of psychologisation in the case of conversion by a minority or a majority. *European Journal of Social Psychology* 16, 345–360.

Moscovici, S. and Zavalloni, M. 1969: The group as a polarizer of attitudes. *Journal of Personality and Social Psychology* 12, 125–135.

Muczyk, J. P. and Riemann, B. C. 1987: The case for directive leadership. *Academy of Management Review* 12, 647–687.

Mueller, E. and Lucas, T. 1975: A developmental analysis of peer interaction among toddlers. In Lewis, M. and Rosenblum, L. A. (eds), *Friendship and peer relations*. New York: Wiley Interscience.

Mugny, G., Kaiser, C. *et al.* 1984: Inter-group relations, identification and social influence. *British Journal of Social Psychology* 23, 317–322.

Mugny, G. and Pérez, J. A. 1991: *The social psychology of minority influence*. Cambridge: Cambridge University Press.

Mullen, B. 1986: Atrocity as a function of lynch mob composition: a self-attention perspective. *Personality and Social Psychology Bulletin* 12, 187–197.

Mullen, B. 1991: Group composition, salience and cognitive representations: the phemenology of being in a group. *Journal of Experimental Social Psychology* 27, 297–323.

Mullen, B., Salas, E. and Driskell, J. E. 1989: Salience motivation, and artifact as contributions to the relation between participation rate and leadership. *Journal of Experimental Social Psychology* 25, 545–549.

Murstein, B. L., Merighi, J. R. and Vyse, S. A. 1991: Love styles in the United States and France: a cross-cultural comparison. *Journal of Social and Clinical Psychology* 10, 37–46.

Mydans, D. G. 1992: *The pursuit of happiness*. New York: Avon Books.

Myers, D. G. 1982: Polarising effects of social interaction. In Braudstatter, H., Davis, J. H. and Stocker-Kreichgauer, G. (eds), *Group decision making*. New York: Academic Press.

Nemeth, C., Mayseless, O. *et al.* 1990: Exposure to dissent and recall information. *Journal of Personality and Social Psychology* 58, 429–437.

Nemeth, C. and Wachtler J. 1973: Consistency and modification of judgement. *Journal of European Social Psychology* 9, 65–79.

Nemeth, C. and Kwan, J. 1987: Minority influence, divergent thinking and the detection of correct solutions. *Journal of Applied Social Psychology* 17, 788–789.

Nettles, E. J. and Loevinger, J. 1983: Sex role expectations and ego level in relation to problem marriages. *Journal of Personality and Social Psychology* 45, 676–687.

Neugarten, B. L. 1977: Personality and ageing. In Birren, J. E. and Schaie, K. W. (eds), *Handbook of the psychology of ageing*. New York: Van Nostrand Reinhold.

Neugarten, B. L., Havighurst, D. J. and Tobin, S. S. 1968: Personalty and patterns of ageing. In Neugarten, B. L. (ed.), *Middle age and ageing*. Chicago: University of Chicago Press.

Newcomb, T. M. 1950: *Social psychology*. New York, Dryden.

Newcomb, T. M 1961: *The acquaintance process*. New York: Holt, Rinehart and Winston.

Nisbett, R. E., Caputo C., Legant, P. and Marecek, J. 1973: Behaviour as seen by the actor and the observer. *Journal of Personality and Social Psychology* 27, 154–164.

Nolen-Hoeksema, S., Girgus, J. S. and Seligman, M. E. P. 1992: Predictions and consequences of childhood depressive symptoms: five year longitudinal study. *Journal of Abnormal Psychology* 101, 405–422.

Ohbuchi, K., Kameda, M. and Agarie, N. 1989: Apology as aggression control: its role in mediating appraisal of and response to harm. *Journal of Personality and Social Psychology* 56, 219–227.

Oliner, S. P. and Oliner, P. M. 1988: *The altruistic personality: rescuers of Jews in Nazi Europe*. New York: Free Press.

Olson, J. M. and Zanna, M. P. 1993: Attitudes and attitude change. *Annual Review of Psychology* 44, 117–154.

Ong, L. M. L., Dehaes, J., Hoos, A. M. and Lammes, F. B. 1995: Doctor-patient communication: a review of the literature. *Social Science and Medicine* 40, 7, 903–918.

Oppenheim, A. N. 1992: *Questionnaire design, interviewing and attitude measurement*. 2nd edn. London: Pinter.

Orlofsky, J. C., Marcia, J. E. and Lesser, I. M. 1973: Ego identity status and the intimacy versus isolation crisis of young adulthood. *Journal of Personality and Social Psychology* 2, 211–19.

Orne, M. T. 1962: On the social psychology of the psychology experiment: with particular reference to demand characteristics and their implications. *American Psychologist* 17, 776–783.

Osborn, A. F. 1957: *Applied imagination*. New York: Scribners.

Osgood, C. E., Suci, G. J. and Tannenbaum, P. H. 1957: *The measurement of meaning*. Urbana: University of Illinois Press.

Oskamp, S. 1977: *Attitudes and opinions*. Englewood Cliffs, NJ: Prentice-Hall.

Oskamp, S. (ed.) 1988: Actions towards U.S. and Russian actions: a double standard. *Psychological Reports* 16, 43–46.

Owens, G. and Ford, J. G. 1978: Further consideration of the 'What is beautiful is good' finding. *Social Psychology* 41, 73–75.

Oyama, S. 1991: Bodies and minds: dualism in evolutionary theory. *Journal of Social Issues* 47,3, 27–42.

Ozer, E. M. 1998: America's adolescents: are they healthy? Paper presented at the 106th APA Conference, San Francisco.

Pallak, S. R. 1983: Salience of a communicator's physical attractiveness and persuasion: a heuristic versus systematic processing interpretation. *Social Cognition,* 2, 156–168.

Papini, D., Farmer, F., Clark, S. *et al.* (1990): Early adolescent age and gender differences in patterns of emotional self-disclosure to parents and friends. *Adolescence* 25, 959–976.

Parke, R. D., Berkowitz, L., Leyens, J. P., West, S. G. and Sebastian, R. J 1977: Some effects of violent and nonviolent movies on the behaviour of juvenile delinquents. In Berkowitz, L. (ed.) *Advances in experimental social psychology.* vol. 10. New York: Academic Press, pp. 135–172.

Parker, J. G. and Asher, S. R. 1987: Peer relations and later adjustments: are low accepted children 'at risk'? *Psychological Bulletin* 102, 358–389.

Parten, M. B. 1971: Social play among school age children. In Herron, R. E. and Sutton-Smith, B. (eds), *Child's play.* New York: Wiley. Reprinted from Journal of Abnormal and Social Psychology 28 (1933), 136–147.

Patterson, M. L. 1987: Presentational and effect management functions of non-verbal involvement. *Journal of Non-verbal Behaviour* 11, 110–122.

Patterson, M. L. 1990: Functions of non-verbal behaviour in social interaction. In Giles, H. and Robinson, W. P. (eds), *Handbook of language and social psychology.* Chichester: Wiley.

Paulhas, D. 1983: Sphere-specific measures of perceived control. *Journal of Personality and Social Psychology* 44,1253–1265.

Paulus, P. B. 1988: *Prison crowding: a psychological perspective.* New York: Springer Verlag.

Paulus, P. B. (ed.), 1989: *Psychology of group influence.* Hillsdale, NJ: Erlbaum.

Pavelchak, M. A. 1989: Piecemeal and category-based evaluation: an ideographic analysis. *Journal of Personality and Social Psychology* 56, 354–363.

Peabody, D. 1985: *National characteristics.* New York: Cambridge University Press.

Pennebaker, J. W. 1990: *Opening up.* New York: Morrow.

Pennington, D. C. 1981: The Yorkshire Ripper police enquiry: hindsight and social cognition. *British Journal of Social Psychology* 12, 318–333.

Perlman, D. 1990: Heart risk lowered in community experiment. *San Francisco Chronicle*, 18 July, p. 1.

Pessin, J. 1933: The comparative effects of social and mechanical stimulation on memorising. *American Journal of Psychology* 45, 263–270.

Peterson, A. C. 1987: Those gangly years. *Psychology Today*, 28–34.

Pettigrew, T. 1959: Regional differences in anti-negro practice. *Journal of Abnormal and Social Psychology* 59, 28–56.

Pettigrew, T. F. 1979: The ultimate attribution error: extending Allport's cognitive analysis of prejudice. *Personality and Social Psychology Bulletin* 5, 461–476.

Petty, R. E. and Cacioppo, J. T. 1984: The effects of involvement on responses to argument quantity and quality: central and peripheral routes to persuasion. *Journal of Personality and Social Psychology* 46, 69–81.

Petty, R. E. and Cacioppo, J. T. 1986: *Communication and persuasion: central and peripheral routes to attitude change.* New York: Springer-Verlag.

Petty, R. E. and Cacioppo, J. T. 1990: Involvement and persuasion: tradition versus integration. *Psychological Bulletin* 107, 367–374.

Petty, R. E. and Cacioppo, J. T., Strathman, A. J. and Preister, J. R. 1994: To think or not to think: exploring two routes to persuasion. In Shavitt, S. and Brock, T. C. (eds), *Persuasion.* Boston: Allyn and Baum.

Pfeifer, J. E. and Ogloff, J. R. P. 1991: Ambiguity and guilt determinations: a modern racism perspective. *Journal of Applied Social Psychology* 21, 1713–1725.

Phillips, D. P. 1986: Natural experiments on the effects of mass media violence on fatal aggression: strengths and weaknesses of a new approach. In Berkowitz, L. (ed.) *Advances in experimental social psychology.* vol. 19. New York: Academic Press, pp. 207–250.

Piaget, J. 1952: *The origins of intelligence in children.* New York: International Universities Press.

Piliavin, J. A., Dovidio, J. F., Gaertner, S. L. and Clark, R. D. 1981: *Emergency intervention.* New York: Academic Press.

Platz, S. J. and Hosch, H. M. 1988: Cross racial/ethnic eyewitness identification: a field study. *Journal of Applied Social Psychology* 18, 972–984.

Posner, R. 1989: 'What is culture? Toward a semniotic explication of anthropological concepts. In Miell, D. and Dallos, R. 1996 (eds), *Social interactions and personal relationships.* London: Sage.

Potter, J. and Wetherell, M. 1987: *Discourse and social psychology: beyond attitudes and behaviour.* London: Sage.

Powell, M. C. and Fazio, R. M. 1984: Attitude accessibility as a function of repeated attitudinal expression. *Personality and Social Psychology Bulletin* 10, 139–148.

Price, J. M. and Dodge, K. A. 1989: Reactive and proactive aggression in childhood: relations to peer status and social context dimensions. *Journal of Abnormal Child Psychology* 17, 455–71.

Prins, K. S., Buunk, B. P. and Van Yperen, N. W. 1993: Equity, normative disapproval and extramarital relationships. *Journal of Social and Personal Relationships* 10, 39–53.

Radley, A. 1996: Relationships in detail: the study of social interaction. In Miell, D. and Dallos, R. (eds) *Social interaction and personal relationships.* London: Sage.

Raven, B. H. 1993: The bases of power: origins and recent developments. *Journal of Social Issues* 49, 227–251.

Reddy, V., Dale, H., Murray, L. and Trevarthen, C. 1997: Communication in infancy: mutual regulation of affect and attention. In Bremner, G., Slater, A. and

Butterworth, G. (eds), *Infant development, recent advances*. Sussex: Psychology Press, Taylor and Francis.

Reeder, G. D., Fletcher, G. J. and Furman, K. 1989: The role of observers' expectations in attitude attribution. *Journal of Experimental Social Psychology* 25,168–188.

Regan, D. T., Williams, M. and Sparling, S. 1972: Voluntary expiation of guilt: a field experiment. *Journal of Personality and Social Psychology* 24, 42–45.

Remland, M. S., Jones, T. S., and Brinkman, H. 1995: Interpersonal distance, body orientation and touch: effects of culture, gender and age. *Journal of Social Psychology* 135, 3, 281–297.

Rhodewalt, F. and Davison, J. 1983: Reactance and the coronary-prone behaviour pattern: the role of self-attribution in response to reduced behavioural freedom. *Journal of Personality and Social Psychology* 44, 220–228.

Riggio, R. E. 1993: Social interaction skills and non-verbal behaviour. *Journal of Language and Social Psychology* 14, 3, 289–311.

Ringelmann, M. 1913: Recherches sur les moteurs animés: travail de l'homme. *Annales de l'Institut National Agronomique*. 12, 1–40.

Robbins, S. P. 1998: *Organisational behaviour*. Englewood Cliffs, NJ: Prentice-Hall.

Robertson, J. and Robertson, J. 1971: Young children in brief separation: a fresh look. *Psychoanalytic Study of the Child* 26, 264–315.

Rodin, J. and Langer, E. J. 1977: Long-term effects of a control relevant intervention with the institutionalised aged. *Journal of Personality and Social Psychology* 35, 879–902.

Rodin, M. J. 1987: Who is memorable to whom? A study of cognitive disregard. *Social Cognition* 5, 144–165.

Roethlisberger F. J. and Dickson, J. 1939: *Management and the worker*. Cambridge, MA: Harvard University Press.

Rofé Y. 1984: Stress and affiliation: a utility theory. *Psychological Review* 91, 235–250.

Rokeach, M. 1960: *The open and closed mind*. New York: Basic Books.

Rokeach, M. 1968: *Beliefs, attitudes and values*. San Francisco: Jossey-Bass.

Rokeach, M., Smith, P. W., and Evans, R. I. 1960: Two kinds of prejudice or one? In Rokeach, M. (ed.), *The open and closed mind*. New York: Basic Books.

Roker, D., Player, K. and Coleman, J. 1998: Exploring adolescent altruism: British young people's involvement in voluntary work and campaigning. In Yates, M. and Youniss, J. (eds) *Community service and civic engagement in youth: international perspectives*. Cambridge: Cambridge University Press.

Rook, K. S. 1987: Reciprocity of social exchange and social satisfaction among older women. *Journal of Personality and Social Psychology* 52, 145–154.

Rosch, E. and Mervis, C. 1975: Family resemblances: studies in the internal structure of categories. *Cognitive Psychology* 7, 573–605.

Rose, S. and Frieze, H. 1993: Young singles' contemporary dating scripts. *Sex Roles*, 28, 499–509.

Rosenbaum, M. E. 1986: The repulsion hypothesis: on the non-development of relationships. *Journal of Personality and Social Psychology* 51, 1156–1166.

Rosenberg, E. L. and Ekman, P. 1994: Coherence between expressive and experiential systems in emotion. *Cognition and Emotion* 8, 201–229.

Rosenberg, S., Nelson, C. et al. 1968: A multidivisional approach to the structure of personality impressions. *Journal of Personality and Social Psychology* 9, 283–294.

Rosenthal, R 1969: Interpersonal expectations: effects of experimenter's hypothesis. In Rosenthal, R. and Rosnow, L. (eds), *Artifacts in behavioural research*. New York: Academic Press.

Rosenthal, R. 1985: From unconscious experimental bias to teacher expectancy effects. In Dusek, J. B., Hall, V. C. and Meyer, W. J. (eds), *Teacher expectancies*. Hillsdale, NJ: Erlbaum, pp. 37–65.

Rosenthal, R. 1991: Meta-analysis: a review. *Psychosomatic medicine*. 53, 247–271.

Rosenthal, R and Fode, K. L. 1963: The effect of experimenter bias on the performance of the albino rat. *Behavioural Science* 8, 183–189.

Rosenthal, R. and Jacobson, L. F. 1968: *Pygmalion in the classroom*. New York: Holt, Rinehard and Wilson.

Rosnow, R. L. 1981: *Paradigms in transition: the methodology of social enquiry*. Oxford: Open University Press.

Ross, L. 1977: The intuitive psychologist and his shortcomings. In L. Berkowitz (ed.), *Advances in experimental social psychology*. vol. 10. New York: Academic Press.

Ross, L., Bierbrauer, G. and Polly, S. 1974: Attribution of education outcomes by professional and non-professional instructors. *Journal of Experimental Social Psychology* 29, 609–618.

Ross, L. D., Amabile, T. M. and Steinmetz, J. L. 1977: Social roles, social control and biases in social-perception processes. *Journal of Personality and Social Psychology* 35, 485–494.

Ross, L. D., Greene, D. and House, P. 1977: The false consensus effect: an egocentric bias in social perception and attribution processes. *Journal of Experimental Social Psychology* 13, 279–301.

Roter, D. L. and Hall, J. A. 1992: *Doctors talking with patients, patients talking with doctors*. Westport, CT: Auburn House.

Rotter, J. B. 1966: Generalised expectancies for internal versus external control of reinforcements. *Psychological Monographs* 80.

Ruback, R. B. and Weiner, N. A. (eds) 1995: *Interpersonal violent behaviours: social and cultural aspects*. New York: Springer Publishing.

Rubin, J. Z. 1973: *Liking and loving*. New York: Holt, Rinehart and Winston.

Rubin, J. Z., Hill, C. T., Peplau, L. A. and Dunkel-Schetter, C. 1980: Self disclosure in dating couples: sex roles and the ethic of openness. *Journal of Marriage and the Family* 42, 305–317.

Rubin, J. Z., Provenzano, F. J. and Luria, Z. 1974: The eye of the beholder: parent's views on sex of newborns. *American Journal of Orthopsychiatry* 44, 512–19.

Rugs, D. and Kaplan, M. F. 1993: Effectiveness of informational and normative influences in group decision making depends on the group interactive goal. *British Journal of Social Psychology* 32, 147–158.

Rushton J. P. 1980: *Altruism, socialisation and society*. Englewood Cliffs, NJ: Prentice-Hall.

Rushton J. P. 1981: The altruistic personality. In Rushton, J. P. and Sorrentino, R. M. (eds) *Altruism and helping behaviour: social personality and developmental perspectives*. Hillsdale, NJ: Erlbaum, pp. 251–266.

Rushton, J. P. and Teachman, G. 1978: The effects of positive reinforcements, attributions and punishment on model induced altruism in children. *Personality and Social Psychology Bulletin* 4, 322–25.

Rutkowski, G. K., Gruder, C. L. and Romer, D. 1983: Group cohesiveness, social norms and bystander intervention. *Journal of Personality and Social Psychology* 44, 545–52.

Rutter, D. R. 1984: *Looking and seeing: the role of visual communication in social interaction*. New York: Wiley and Sons.

Rutter, D. R. and Robinson, B. 1981: An experimental analysis of teaching: theoretical and practical implications for social psychology. *Progress in applied social psychology*. Chichester: Wiley.

Rutter, M. 1981: *Maternal deprivation reassessed*. 2nd edn.Harmondsworth: Penguin.

Ruvolo, A. and Markus, H. 1992: Possible selves and performance: the power of self-relevant imagery. *Social Cognition* 9, 95–124.

Sadalla, E. K., Kenricke, D. T. and Bershure, B. 1987: Dominance and heterosexual attraction. *Journal of Personality and Social Psychology* 52, 730–738.

Sagi, A. and Hoffman, M. 1976: Empathetic distress in the newborn. *Developmental Psychology* 12, 175–176.

Sanders, G. S. and Baron, R. S. 1977: Is social comparison relevant for producing choice shifts? *Journal of Experimental Social Psychology* 13, 303–314.

Sandford, N. 1956: The approach of the authoritarian personality. In McCary, J. L. (ed.), *Journal of personality*. New York: Grove Press.

Sarnoff, I. and Zimbardo, P. 1961: Anxiety, fear and social affiliation. *Journal of Abnormal and Social Psychology* 62, 356–363.

Savin-Williams, R. C. and Demo, D. H. 1984: Developmental change and stability in adolescent self-concept. *Developmental Psychology* 20, 1100–1110.

Schachter, S. 1951: Deviation, rejection and communication. *Journal of Abnormal Social Psychology* 46, 190–207.

Schachter, S. 1959: *The psychology of affiliation: experimental studies on the source of gregariousness*. Stanford, CA: Stanford University Press.

Schaffer H. R. and Emerson, P. E. 1964: The development of social attachments in infancy. *Monographs of the Society for Research on Child Development*, No. 29.

Scher, S. and Cooper, J. 1989: Motivational basis of dissonance: the singular role of behavioural consequences. *Journal of Personality and Social Psychology* 56, 899–906.

Schieffelin, B. B. 1990: *The give and take of everyday life: language socialisation of Kaluli children*. Cambridge: Cambridge University Press.

Schimmack, U. 1996: Cultural influences on the recognition of emotion by facial expressions: individualistic or Caucasian cultures? *Journal of Cross-Cultural Psychology* 27, 1, 37–50.

Schlossberg, N. K. 1987: Taking the mystery out of change. *Psychology Today*, 74–75.

Schneider-Rosen, K., Braunwald, K. G., Carlson, V. and Cicchetti, D, 1985: Current perspectives in attachment theory: illustration from the study of maltreated infants. In Bretherton, L. and Waters, E. (eds), *Growing points of attachment theory and research*. Monographs of the Society for Research in Child Development, 50 (1–2, Serial No. 209).

Schullo, S. A. and Alperson, B. L. 1984: Interpersonal phenomenology as a function of sexual orientation, sex, sentiment, and trait categories in long term dynamic relationships. *Journal of Personality and Social Psychology* 47, 983–1002.

Schultz, W. C. 1958: The interpersonal underworld. *Harvard Business Review* 36, 123–135.

Schurz, G. 1985: Experimentelle? berprüfung Zusammenhangs zwischen Persönlichkeits merkmalen und der Bereitschaft zum destruktiven Gehorsam gegenüber Autoritaten. *Zeitschrift für Experimentelle und Angewandte Psychologie* 32, 160–177.

Schwartz, S. H. 1975: The justice need and the activation of humanitarian norms. *Journal of Social Issues* 31, 111–136.

Schwartz, S. H. and Gottlieb, A. 1980: Bystander anonymity and reaction to emergencies. *Journal of Personality and Social Psychology* 39, 418–430.

Schwartzer, R. and Leppin, A. 1989: Social support and health: a meta analysis. *Psychology and Health* 3, 1–15.

Schwartz, N. and Clore, G. L. 1983: Mood, misattribution and judgements of well being: informative and directive functions of affective states. *Journal of Personality and Social Psychology* 45, 513–523.

Schwarz, N. and Clore, G. L. 1988: How do I feel about it? Informative functions of affective states. In Fielder, K. and Forgas, J. (eds), *Affect, cognition and social behaviour*. Toronto: Hogrefe.

Secord, P. F. and Backman, C. W. 1974: *Social psychology*. 2nd edn. Tokyo: McGraw-Hill.

Seeman, M., Seeman, T. and Sayles, M. 1985: Social networks and health status. *Social Psychology Quarterly* 48, 237–248.

Segal, M. W. 1974: Alphabet and attraction: an unobtrusive measure of the effect of propinquity in a field setting. *Journal of Personality and Social Psychology* 30, 654–57.

Seligman, M. E. P. 1975: *Helplessness*. San Francisco: Freeman.

Seligman, M. E. P., Abramson L. Y., Semmel, A. R. and Von Baeyer, C. 1979: Depressive attributional style. *Journal of Abnormal Psychology* 88, 242–247.

Shanab, M. E. and Yahga, K. A. 1978: A cross-cultural study of obedience. *Bulletin of the Psychonomic Society* 11, 267–269.

Sharpe, D., Adair, J. G. and Roese, N. J. 1992: Twenty years of deception research: a decline in subjects' trust. *Personality and Social Psychology Bulletin* 18, 585–590.

Shaver, P. and Klinnert, M. 1982: Schachter's theories of affiliation and emotion: implications for developmental research. In Wheeler, L. (ed.), *Review of personality and social psychology*. vol. 3. Beverly Hills, CA: Sage, pp. 27–72.

Shaw, M. E. 1981: *Group dynamics: the social psychology of small group behaviour*. 3rd edn. New York: McGraw-Hill.

Sheehan, P. W. 1983: Age trends and the correlates of children's television viewing. *Australian Journal of Psychology* 35, 417–431.

Sherif, M. 1936: The psychology of social norms. New York: Harper and Row.

Sherif, M. 1966: *Group conflict and cooperation: their social psychology*. London: Routledge and Kegan Paul.

Sherman, L. W. and Berk, R. A. 1984: The specific deterrent effects of arrest for domestic assault. *American Sociological Review* 49, 261–272.

Sherman, S. J. 1980: On the self-erasing nature of errors of prediction. *Journal of Personality and Social Psychology* 39, 211–221.

Shipley, R. H. 1981: Maintenance of smoking cessation: effect of follow-up letters, smoking motivation, muscle tension and locus of control. *Journal of Consulting and Clinical Psychology* 49, 982–984.

Shotland, R. L. and Straw, M. K. 1976: Bystander response to an assault: when a man attacks a woman. *Journal of Personality and Social Psychology* 34, 990–999.

Shweder, R. A., Much, N. C., Mahapatra, M. and Park, L. 1994: The 'big three' of morality (autonomy, community and divinity), and the 'big three' explanations of suffering, as well. In Brandt, A. and Rozin, P. (eds), *Morality and Health*. Stanford, CA: Stanford University Press.

Siegal, J. 1950: Effects of objective evidence of expertness, non-verbal behaviour and subject sex on client-perceived expertness. *Journal of Counselling Psychology* 27, 117–121.

Simon, L., Greenberg, J. and Brehm, J. 1995: Trivialization: the forgotten mode of dissonance reduction. *Journal of Personality and Social Psychology* 68, 247–260.

Simpson, J. A. 1990: Influence of attachment styles on romantic relationships: factors involved in relationship stability and emotional distress. *Journal of Personality and Social Psychology* 53, 683–692.

Simpson, J. A., Rholes, W. S. and Nelligan, J. S. 1992: Support seeking and support giving within couples in an anxiety-provoking situation: the role of attachment styles. *Journal of Personality and Social Psychology* 62, 434–446.

Singer, J. L. and Singer, D. G. 1981: *Television, imagination and aggression: a study of preschoolers*. Hillsdale, NJ: Erlbaum.

Singh, D. 1993: Adaptive significance of female physical attractiveness: role of waist to hip ratio. *Journal of Personality and Social Psychology* 65, 293–307.

Sistrunk, F. and McDavid, J. W. 1971: Sex variable in conformity behaviour. *Journal of Personality and Social Psychology* 17, 200–207.

Skrowronski, N. J. and Carlston, D. E. 1989: Negativity and extremity biases in impression formation: a review of explanations. *Psychological Bulletin* 105, 131–142.

Slater, P. E. 1958: Contrasting correlates of group size. *Sociometry* 21, 129–139.

Smith, E. R. and Mackie, D. M. 1995: *Social psychology*. New York: Worth Publishers.

Smith, H. J., Archer, D. and Costanzo, M. 1991: Just a hunch: accuracy and awareness in person perception. *Journal of Non-Verbal Behaviour* 15, 3–18.

Smith, M. B., Bruner, J. S. and White, R. W. 1956: *Opinions and personality*. New York: John Wiley and Sons.

Smith, P. B. and Harris Bond, M. 1993: *Social psychology across cultures: analysis and perspective*. London: Harvester-Wheatsheaf.

Smith, R. E., Vanderbil, T. K. and Callen, M. B. 1973: Social comparison and bystander intervention in emergencies. *Journal of Applied Social Psychology* 3, 186–196.

Smolowe, J. 1993: Intermarried . . . with children. *Time* (Fall special issue), pp. 54–59.

Snarey, J. 1987: A question of morality. *Psychological Bulletin* 97, 202–232.

Smow, C. E. 1986: Conversations with children. In Fletcher, P. and Garman, M. (eds), *Language acquisition*. 2nd edn. Cambridge: Cambridge University Press, pp. 69–89.

Snyder, M. 1979: Self-monitoring processes. In Berkowitz, L. (ed.), *Advances in experimental social psychology*. vol. 12. New York: Academic Press.

Snyder M. and De Bono, K. G. 1985: Appeals to image and claims about quality: understanding the psychology of advertising. *Journal of Personality and Social Psychology* 49, 586–597.

Snyder, M., Tanke, E. D. and Berscheid, E. 1977: Social perception and interpersonal behaviour: on the self-fulfilling nature of social stereotypes. *Journal of Personality and Social Psychology* 35, 656–666.

Sommer, R. 1969: *Personal space*. Englewood Cliffs. NJ: Prentice-Hall.

Sommer, R., Wynes, M. and Brinkley, G. 1992: Social facilitation effects in shopping behaviour. *Environment and Behaviour* 24, 285–297.

Sorrentino, R. M. and Field, N. 1986: Emergent leadership over time: the functional value of positive motivation. *Journal of Personality and Social Psychology* 50, 1091–1099.

Spitz, R. A. 1945: Hospitalism: an inquiry into the genesis of psychiatric conditions in early childhood. In Freud, A., Hartman, H. and Kris, E. (eds), *The psychoanalytic study of the child*. vol. 1. New York: International University Press, pp. 53–74.

Spivey, C. V. and Prentice-Dunn, S. 1990: Assessing the directionality of deindividuated behaviour: effects of deindividuation, modeling and private self consciousness on aggressive and prosocial responses. *Basic and Applied Social Psychology* 11, 387–403.

Staats, A. W., Staats, C. K. and Crawford, H. L. 1962: First order conditioning of meaning and the parallel conditioning of G.S.R. *Journal of General Psychology* 67, 159–167.

Stainton Rogers, R. S., Stenner, P., Gleeson, K., and Stainton Rogers, W. 1995: *Social psychology: a critical agenda*. Cambridge: Polity Press.

Stakelski, A. J., Frost, D. E. and Patch, M. E. 1989: The use of socially dependent bases of power: French and Raven's theory applied to work group leadership. *Journal of Applied Social Psychology* 19, 283–297.

Stang, D. J. 1973: Effects of interaction rate on ratings of leadership and liking. *Journal of Personality and Social Psychology* 27, 405–408.

Stangor, C. and Lange, J. E. 1994: Mental representations of social groups: advances in understanding stereotypes and stereotyping. *Advances is Experimental Social Psychology* 26, 357–416.

Stangor, C. and Ruble, D. N. 1989: Strength of expectancies and memory for social information: what we remember depends on how much we know. *Journal of Experimental Social Psychology* 25, 18–35.

Stark, P. A. and Traxler, A. J. 1974: An empirical validation of Erikson's theory of identity crisis in late adolescence. *Journal of Psychology* 86, 25–33.

Stasser, G., Taylor, L. A. and Hanna, C. 1989: Information sampling in structured and unstructured discussions of three- and six-person groups. *Journal of Personality and Social Psychology* 57, 67–78.

Steel, L. 1991: Interpersonal correlates of trust and self-disclosure. *Psychological Reports* 68, 1319–1320.

Steele, C. M. and Josephs, R. A. 1990: Alcohol myopia: its prized and dangerous effects. *American Psychologist* 45, 921–933.

Steinberg, L. 1989: Pubertal maturation and parent-adolescent distance: an evolutionary perspective. In Adams, G. R., Motemayor, R. and Gullotta, T. P. (eds), *Biology of adolescent behaviour and development*. Newbury Park, CA: Sage, pp. 71–97.

Steinberg, L. 1990: Autonomy, conflict and harmony in the family relationship. In Feldman, S. S. and Elliott, G. R. (eds), *At the threshold: the developing adolescent*. Cambridge, MA: Harvard University Press, pp. 255–276.

Steiner, I. D. 1972: *Group processes and group productivity*. New York: Academic Press.

Steiner, I. D. 1976: Task performing groups. In Thibaut, J. W. and Spencer, J. T. (eds), *Contemporary topics in social psychology*. Morristown, NJ: General Learning Press.

Stern, P.C. 1992: Psychological dimensions of global environmental change. *Annual Review of Psychology* 43, 269–302.

Sternberg, R. J. 1986: A triangular theory of love. *Psychological Review* 93, 119–135.

Stiff, J. B., Miller, G. R., Sleight, C., Montageau, P. A., Garlick, R. and Rogan, R. 1989: Explanations for visual cue primacy in judgements of honesty and deceit. *Journal of Personality and Social Psychology* 56, 555–564.

Stoner, J. A. F. 1961: *A comparison of individual and group decisions involving risk*. Cambridge, MA: Massachusetts Institute of Technology.

Storms, M. D. 1973: Videotape and the attribution process: reversing actors' and observers' points of view. *Journal of Personality and Social Psychology* 27, 165–175.

Strack, F. and Schwartz, N. 1992: Communication influences in standardised question situations: the cause of implicit collaboration. In Semin, G. and Fielder, K. (eds), *Self-disclosure in the therapeutic relationship*. New York: Plenum Press.

Straus, M. A. and Sweet, S. 1992: Verbal/symbolic aggression in couples: incidence rates and relationships to personal characteristics. *Journal of Marriage and the Family* 54, 346–357.

Strickland, B. R. 1974: Internal-external expectancies and cardiovascular functioning.

In Perlmuter, L.C. and Monty, A. (eds), *Choice and perceived control.* Hillsdale, NJ: Erlbaum.

Strodbeck, F. L. 1957: Social studies in jury deliberations. *American Sociology Review* 22, 713–719.

Stroebe, W., Insko, C. A., Thompson, V. D. and Layton, B. D. 1971: Effects of physical attractiveness, attitude similarity and sex on various aspects of interpersonal attraction. *Journal of Personality and Social Psychology* 18, 79–91.

Stroebe, W. and Stroebe, M. S. 1986: Beyond marriage: the impact of partner loss on health. In Gilmour, R. and Duck, S. (eds), *The emerging field of personal relationships.* Hillsdale, NJ: Erlbaum, pp. 203–224.

Stroessner, S. J., Hamilton, D. L. and Mackie, D. M. 1992: Affect and stereotyping: the effect of induced mood on distinctiveness-based illusory correlation. *Journal of Personality and Social Psychology* 62, 564–576.

Summers, R. J. 1991: The influence of affirmative action on perceptions of beneficiary's qualifications. *Journal of Applied Social Psychology* 21, 1265–1276.

Surin K., Aikin, K. J., Hall, W. S. and Hunter, B. A. 1995: Sexism and racism: old-fashioned and modern prejudices. *Journal of Personality and Social Psychology* 68, 199–214.

Sura, C. A. and Longstreth, M. 1990: Similarity of outcomes, interdependence and conflict in dating relationships. *Journal of Personality and Social Psychology* 59, 501–516.

Sweeney, P. D., Anderson, K. and Bailey, S. 1986: Attributional style in depression: a meta-analytic review. *Journal of Personality and Social Psychology* 50, 974–991.

Tajfel, H. 1970: Experiments in intergroup discrimination. *Scientific American* 223, 96–102.

Tajfel, H. 1978a: *Differentiation between social groups: studies in the social psychology of intergroup relations.* New York: Academic Press.

Tajfel, H. 1978b: Intergroup behaviour: group perspectives. In Tajfel, H. and Fraser, C. (eds), *Introducing social psychology.* Harmondsworth: Penguin.

Tajfel, H and Billig, M. 1974: Familiarity and categorization in intergroup behaviour. *European Journal of Social Psychology* 1, 149–177.

Tajfel, H. and Turner, J. C. 1986: The social identity theory of intergroup behaviour. In Worschel, S. and Austin, W. G. (eds), *Psychology of intergroup relations.* 2nd edn. Monterey, CA: Brooks/Cole.

Tajfel, H. and Wilkes, A. L. 1963: Classification and quantitative judgement. *British Journal of Psychology* 54, 101–114.

Tambs, K. and Moum, T. 1992: No large convergence during marriage for health, lifestyle and personality in a large sample of Norwegian spouses. *Journal of Marriage and the Family* 59, 957–971.

Tardy, C. H. 1988: Self-disclosure: objectives and methods of measurement. In Tardy, C. H. (ed.), *A handbook for the study of human communication.* New Jersey: Ablex.

Taylor, S. E. 1995: *Health psychology.* New York: McGraw-Hill.

Taylor, S. E. and Fiske, S. T. 1981: Getting inside the head: methodologies for process analysis in attribution and social cognition. In Harvey, J. H., Ickes, W. J. and Kidd, R. F. (eds), *New directions in attribution research.* vol. 3. Hillsdale, NJ: Erlbaum, pp. 459–524.

Taylor, S. P. and Sears, J. D. 1988: The effects of alcohol and persuasive social pressure on human physical aggression. *Aggressive Behaviour* 14, 237–243.

Terry, D. 1993: Fear and ghosts: the world of Marcus, 19. *The New York Times*, 11 April, p. 16.

Tesser, A. and Shaffer, D. R. 1990: Attitudes and attitude change. *Annual Review of Psychology* 41, 479–523.

Tetlock, P. E. and Manstead, A. S. R. 1985: Impression management versus intrapsychic explanations of social psychology: a useful dichotomy? *Psychological Review* 92, 59–77.

Tetlock, P. E., Peterson, R. S., McGuire, C., Chang, S. and Feld, P. 1992: Assessing political group dynamics: a test of the groupthink model. *Journal of Personality and Social Psychology* 63, 403–425.

Thibaut, J. W. and Kelley, H. H. 1959: *The social psychology of groups*. New York: Wiley.

Thoits, P. A. 1986: Social support as coping assistance. *Journal of Consulting and Clinical Psychology* 54, 416–423.

Thomas, A. and Chess, S. 1977: *Temperament and development*. New York: Brunner/Mazel.

Thomas, A., Chess S. and Birch, H. 1970: The origin of personality. *Scientific American* August, 11–13.

Tizard, B. and Hodges, J. 1978: The effect of early institutional rearing on the development of eight year old children. *Journal of Child Psychology and Psychiatry* 19, 99–118.

Tizard, B. and Joseph, A. 1970: Cognitive development of young children in residential care: a study of children aged 24 months. *Child Development* 11, 177–186.

Tizard, B. and Rees, J. 1974: A comparison of the effects of adoption, restoration to the natural mother and continued institutionalisation on the cognitive development of four year old children. *Child Development* 45, 92–9.

Tolstedt, B. E. and Stokes, J. P. 1984: Self-disclosure, intimacy and the depenetration process. *Journal of Personality and Social Psychology* 46, 84–90.

Travis, L. E. 1925: The effect of a small audience upon eye-hand coordination. *Journal of Abnormal and Social Psychology* 20, 142–146.

Triandis, H. C. 1994: *Culture and social behaviour*. New York: McGraw-Hill.

Triandis, H. C., Bomtempo, R., Villareal, M. J., Asai, M. and Lucca, N. 1988: Individualism and collectivism: cross cultural perspectives on self-ingroup relationships. *Journal of Personality and Social Psychology* 54, 323–338.

Triplett, N. 1898: The dynamogenic factors in pacemaking and competition. *American Journal of Psychology* 9, 507–533.

Trolier, T. K. and Hamilton, D. L. 1986. Variables influencing judgements of correlational relations. *Journal of Personality and Social Psychology* 50, 879–888.

Tronick, E. Z. 1989: Emotions and emotional communication in infants. *American Psychologist* 44, 112–119.

Turner, J. C. 1978: Social categorization and social discrimination in the minimal group paradigm. In Tajfel, H. (ed.), *Differentiation between social groups*. New York: Academic Press.

Turner, J. C. 1982: Towards a cognitive redefinition of the social group. In Tajfel, H. (ed.), *Social identity and intergroup relations*. Cambridge: Cambridge University Press.

Turner, J. C. 1985: Social categorization and the self-concept: a social-cognitive theory of group behaviour. In Lawler, E. J. (ed.), *Advances in group processes: theory and research*. vol. 2. Greenwich, CT: JAI Press.

Turner, J. C., Hogg, M. A., Oakes, P. J., Reicher, S. D. and Wetherell, M. S. 1987: *Rediscovering the social group: a self-categorization theory*. Oxford: Blackwell.

Turner, M. E., Pratkanis, A. R., Probusco, P. and Leve, C. 1992: Threat, cohesion and group effectiveness: testing a social identity maintenance perspective on groupthink. *Journal of Personality and Social Psychology* 63, 781–796.

Tushman, M. L. 1978: Technical communication in research and development laboratories: the impact of project work characteristics. *Academy of Management Journal* 21, 624–645.

Tversky, A. and Kahneman, D. 1973: Availability: a heuristic for judging frequency and probability. *Cognitive Psychology* 5, 207–232.

Tversky, A. and Kahneman, D. 1982: Judgement under uncertainty: heuristics and biases. In Kahneman, D., Slovic, P. and Tversky, A. (eds), *Judgement under uncertainty*. Cambridge:Cambridge University Press, pp. 3–20.

Vaillant, G. E. 1977: *Adaptation to life: how the best and brightest come of age.* Boston: Little Brown.

Van Avermaet, E. 1996: Social influence in small groups. In Hewstone, M., Stroebe, W. and Stephenson, G. (eds), *Introduction to social psychology*. Oxford: Blackwell.

Van Den Boom, D. C. 1994: The influence of temperament and mothering on attachment and exploration: an experimental manipulation of sensitive responsiveness among lower class mothers with irritable infants. *Child Development* 65, 1457–1477.

Voland, E. 1993: *Grundriss der Soziobiologie.* Stuttgart: Fischer.

Von Ehrenfels, V. R. 1961: A trend in the development of national units. *Tamil Culture* 9, 1–12.

Wallbott, H. G. and Scherer, K. R. 1986: Cues and channels in emotion recognition. *Journal of Personality and Social Psychology* 51, 690–699.

Waller, N. G., Kojetin, B. A., Bouchard, T. J., Lykken, D. T. and Tellegen, A. 1990: Genetic and environmental influences on religious interests, attitudes and values: A study of twins reared apart and together. *Psychological Science* 1, 138–142.

Wallston, B. S. and Wallston, K. A. 1978: Locus of control and health: a review of the literature. *Health Education Monographs* 6, 107–111.

Walster, E., Aronson, E. and Abrahams, D. 1966a: On increasing the persuasiveness of a low prestige communicator. *Journal of Experimental Social Psychology* 2, 235–242.

Walster, E., Aronson, V., Abrahams, D. and Rottman, L. 1966b: The importance of physical attractiveness in dating behaviour. *Journal of Personality and Social Psychology* 4, 508–516.

Walster, E., Walster, G. W. and Berscheid, E. 1977: *Equity: theory and research.* Boston: Allyn and Bacon.

Ward, M. J. and Carlson, E. A. 1995: Associations among adult attachment representation, maternal sensitivity and infant mother attachment in a sample of adolescent mothers. *Child Development* 66, 69–79.

Warren, B. L. 1966: A multiple variable approach to the assertive mating phenomenon. *Eugenics Quarterly* 13, 285–298.

Warren, P. E. and Walker, I. 1991: Empathy, effectiveness and donations to charity: social psychology's contribution. *British Journal of Social Psychology* 30, 325–337.

Waterman, A. S. 1982: Identity development from adolescence to adulthood: an extension of theory and a review of research. *Developmental Psychology* 18, 341–358.

Waterman, A. S. and Waterman, C. K. 1971: A longitudinal study of changes in ego identity during the freshman year at college. *Developmental Psychology* 5, 167–73.

Watson, J. B. 1913: Psychology as a behaviourist views it. *Psychological Review* 20, 158–177.

Watson, M. W. 1981: The development of social roles: a sequence of social cognitive development. *New Directions for Child Development* 12, 33–41.

Weatherley, D. 1961: Anti-Semitism and the expression of fantasy aggression. *Journal of Abnormal and Social Psychology* 62, 454–457.

Wegner, D. M. and Schaffer, D. 1978: The concentration of responsibility: an objective self-awareness analysis of group size effects in helping situations. *Journal of Personality and Social Psychology* 36, 147–55.

Weiner, B. 1979: A theory of motivation for some classroom experiences. *Journal of Educational Psychology* 71, 3–25.

Weiner, B. 1985: Spontaneous causal thinking. *Psychological Bulletin* 97, 74–84.

Weiner, B. 1986: *An attribution theory of motivation and emotion*. New York: Springer-Verlag.

Weiner, B. 1995: *Judgements of responsibility*. New York: Guilford.

Weiner, M., Derea, S., Rubinow, S. and Geller, J. 1972: Non-verbal behaviour and non-verbal communication. *Psychological Review* 79, 185–214.

Weisenthal, D. L., Endler, N. S. *et al*. 1976: Reversibility of relative competence as a determinant of conformity across different perceptual tasks. *Representative Research in Social Psychology* 7, 35–43.

Weiss, R. S. 1975: *Marital separation*. New York: Basic Books.

Wetherell, M. S. 1987: Social identity and group polarization. In Turner, J. C. *et al.* (eds), *Rediscovering the social group*. Oxford: Blackwell.

Wetzel, C. G. and Insko, C. A. 1982: The similarity-attraction relationship: is there an ideal one? *Journal of Experimental Social Psychology* 18, 253–276.

Wetzel, C. G. and Walton, M. D. 1985: Developing biased judgements: the false consensus effect. *Journal of Personality and Social Psychology* 49, 1352–1359.

Weyant, J. 1978: The effect of mood states, costs and benefits on helping. *Journal of Personality and Social Psychology* 36, 1169–76.

Wheeler, L. 1974: Social comparison and selective affiliation. In Huston, T. (ed.), *Foundations of interpersonal attraction*. New York: Academic Press, pp.309–329.

Whitbourne, S. K., Zuschlag, M. K., Elliott, L. B. and Waterman, A. D. 1992: Psychosocial development in adulthood: a 22-year sequential study. *Journal of Personality and Social Psychology* 63, 260–271.

White, G. L., Fishbein, S. and Rutstein, J. 1981: Passionate love: the misattribution of arousal. *Journal of Personality and Social Psychology* 41, 56–62.

Wicklund, R. A. and Brehm, J. W. 1976: *Perspectives in cognitive dissonance*. Hillsdale, NJ: Erlbaum.

Widmeyer, W. N., Brawley, L. R. and Carron, A. V. 1985: *The measurement of cohesion in sports teams: the group environment questionnaire*. London, Ontario: Sports Dynamics.

Widmeyer, W. N. and Loy, J. W. 1988: When you're hot, you're hot! Warm-cold effects in first impressions of persons in teaching effectiveness. *Journal of Educational Psychology* 80, 118–121.

Wilder, D. A. and Shapiro, P. 1991: Facilitation of outgroup stereotypes by enhanced group identity. *Journal of Experimental Social Psychology* 27, 431–452.

Wilke, H. A. M. and Meertens, R. W. 1994: *Group performance*. London: Routledge.

Williams, K. J., Suls, J., Alliger, G. M., Learner, S. M. and Wan, C. K. 1991: Multiple role juggling and daily mood states in working mothers: an experience sampling method. *Journal of Applied Psychology* 76, 633–638.

Wills, T. A. 1991: Social support and interpersonal relations. In Clark, M. S. (ed.), *Prosocial behaviour*. Beverly Hills, CA: Sage, pp. 265–289.

Wilson, E. O. 1975: *Sociology*. Cambridge, MA: Harvard University Press.

Witelson, S. E. 1994: Sex differences in numerical density of neurons in human auditory association cortex. Paper presented at the annual meeting of the Society for Neuroscience, Miami.

Wolff, P. H. 1969: The natural history of crying and other vocalisations in infancy. In Foss, B. M. (ed.), *Determinants of infant behaviour*. London: Methuen.

Wyer, R. S. Jr. and Srull, T. K. 1994: *Handbook of social cognition*. 2nd edn. New York: Erlbaum.

Yeschke, C. 1987: *Interviewing: an introduction to interrogation*. Illinois: Thomas.

Yoshikawa, H. 1994: Prevention as cumulative protection: effects of early family support and education on chronic delinquency and its risks. *Psychological Bulletin* 115, 28–54.

Zahn, G. L. 1991: Face-to-face communication in an office setting: the effects of position, proximity and exposure. *Communication Research* 18, 737–754.

Zajonc, R. B. 1965: Social facilitation. *Science* 149, 269–274.

Zajonc, R. B. 1968: Attitudinal effects of mere exposure. *Journal of Personality and Social Psychology* 9, 1–27.

Zajonc, R. B., Adelmann, P. K., Murphy, S. T. and Niedenthal, P. M. 1987: Convergence in physical appearance of spouses. *Motivation and Emotion* 11, 335–346.

Zillman, D. 1978: Attribution and misattribution of excitatory reactions. In Harvey, J. H., Ickes, W. and Kidd, R. F. (eds), *New directions in attribution research*. vol. 2. Hillsdale, NJ : Erlbaum, pp. 335–368.

Zillman, D. 1979: *Hostility and aggression*. Hillsdale, NJ: Erlbaum.

Zillman, D. 1983: Arousal and aggression. Geen, R. G. and Donnerstein, E. I. (eds) *Aggression: theoretical and empirical reviews. vol. 1: theoretical and methodological issues*. New York: Academic Press, pp.75–101.

Zillman, D. 1984: *Connections between sex and aggression*. Hillsdale, NJ: Erlbaum.

Zillman, D., Baron, R. and Tamborini, R. 1981: Social costs of smoking: effects of tobacco smoke on hostile behaviour. *Journal of Applied Social Psychology* 11, 548–561.

Zimbardo, P. G. 1969: The human choice: individuation, reason and order versus deindividuation, impulse and chaos. In Arnold, W. J. and Levine, D. (eds), *Nebraska symposium in motivation*. Lincoln: University of Nebraska Press.

Zimbardo, P. G., Banks, W. C., Haney, C. and Jaffe, D. 1973: The mind is a formidable jailer: a Pirandellian prison. *The New York Times Magazine*, 8 April, 38–60.

Zimmerman, D. M. and West, C. 1975: Sex roles, interruptions and silences in conversation. In Thorne, B. and Henley, N. (eds), *Language and sex*. Mass.: Rowly.

Zuckerman, M. 1979a: Attribution of success and failure revisited, or: the motivational bias is alive and well in attribution theory. *Journal of Personality* 47, 245–287.

Zuckerman, M. 1979b: *Sensation seeking: beyond the optimal level of arousal*. Hillsdale, NJ: Erlbaum.

Index